Strategic Management of Innovation Networks

Suitable tor a one- or two-semester course for undergraduate and graduate students, this interdisciplinary textbook explains the diverse aspects of innovation and social networks, which occupy a central place in business and policy agendas. Its unified approach presents networks as nested systems that can span organisations, industries, regions and markets, giving students a holistic perspective and reducing the amount of effort required to learn the theoretical framework for each layer. With engaging real-world examples, the text also provides a practical guide on how to manage networks to increase innovation performance. Topics covered include forming teams to foster creativity, selecting partners and leveraging partnerships for learning, managing organisational change, and sponsoring technologies in communities. Students will learn the metrics used in social network analysis and how they are interpreted and applied. Suggested reading lists and online resources offer opportunities for further review and practice.

Müge Özman is Professor of Management at Institut Mines-Télécom, Télécom École de Management, Paris. She has held academic positions in Maastricht University and Middle East Technical University, and has been a visiting professor in University of Strasbourg and Aix-Marseille University. She has worked on major projects on innovation funded by the European Union and Agence National de la Recherche (ANR)

T0331980

Strategic Management of Innovation Networks

Müge Özman

Institut Mines-Télécom, Télécom École de Management France

CAMBRIDGE
UNIVERSITY PRESS

University Printing House, Cambridge CB2 8BS, United Kingdom

One Liberty Plaza, 20th Floor, New York, NY 10006, USA

477 Williamstown Road, Port Melbourne, VIC 3207, Australia

4843/24, 2nd Floor, Ansari Road, Daryaganj, Delhi - 110002, India

79 Anson Road, #06-04/06, Singapore 079906

Cambridge University Press is part of the University of Cambridge.

It furthers the University's mission by disseminating knowledge in the pursuit of
education, learning, and research at the highest international levels of excellence.

www.cambridge.org
Information on this title: www.cambridge.org/9781107071346
10.1017/9781107775534

© Müge Özman 2017

First published 2017

Printed in the United Kingdom by Clays, St Ives plc in 2017

A catalogue record for this publication is available from the British Library.

Library of Congress Cataloging in Publication Data
Names: Özman, Müge, author.
Title: Strategic Management of Innovation Networks Affiliation / Müge Özman,
Institut Mines-Telecom, Télécom École de Management France.
Description: Cambridge, United Kingdom ; New York, NY, USA : Cambridge
University Press, 2017. | Includes bibliographical references and index.
Identifiers: LCCN 2016035037| ISBN 9781107071346 (Hardback) | ISBN 9781107416796 (Paperback)
Subjects: LCSH: Cooperative industrial research. | Research, Industrial–Management. | Personnel
management. | Creative ability in business. | Strategic planning. | BISAC: BUSINESS &
ECONOMICS / Entrepreneurship.
Classification: LCC T175.5 .O96 2017 | DDC 658/.046–dc23 LC record available at
https://lccn.loc.gov/2016035037

ISBN 978-1-107-07134-6 Hardback
ISBN 978-1-107-41679-6 Paperback

To the memory of my beloved father, Prof. Dr. Aydoḡan Özman.

Contents

List of Figures

List of Tables

List of Boxes

Preface

The cover illustration of this book shows a detail from a piece of indigenous Australian art. Traditionally, Aboriginal artists used a variety of symbols in their paintings, many of which represent natural features, like water flows, hills or rock holes. These paintings were sometimes used as maps, giving travellers information about the landscape. In a way, networks in the modern economy are similar to these works of art, in the sense that they show the distribution of resources and power, the organisation of work or the flow of knowledge between actors. Networks give a bird's-eye view of different industrial or organisational landscapes.

Networks are important to innovation because innovation is a social and collective process that involves a wide range of actors and the interactions between them. This importance is reflected in the contemporary literature on networks and innovation, where research crosses disciplinary boundaries, bringing insights from sociology, economics, management, organisation theory, physics, geography and psychology. This makes for a rich variety of inputs but it also represents a challenge in finding a common language to bridge them. The aim of this book is to provide that bridge and to improve our understanding of how networks function inside and outside organisations, their implications for different aspects of the innovation process, and how they form and evolve. This book has a wide, cross-disciplinary scope supported by suggestions for further reading for those who want to explore any of the topics more extensively.

While the literature on innovation networks has grown steadily over the last three decades, the implications of this research for managing innovation have been less visible. This is surprising, given the many ways in which a good understanding of networks can help manage innovation, for example by fostering creativity, leveraging partnerships for learning, selecting partners, managing organisational change, sponsoring technologies or novelties in the market, and managing supplier relations.

The management of innovation networks benefits an organisation in two ways. First, it enables informed interventions in networks – like partner selection and team formation – that help an organisation obtain a strategically privileged position in accessing critical resources and capabilities for innovation. Second, and more indirectly, understanding the networks within and surrounding organisations helps to improve the effectiveness of many aspects of innovation management. For example, understanding the distribution of knowledge inside a firm can be highly relevant; social network analysis techniques can be used to map the nature of the knowledge base.

This book has been written for graduate or advanced undergraduate students, practitioners and researchers in the fields of social networks and innovation. It is a practical, action-oriented guide to managing the innovation process through a network perspective, based on important theoretical results. It provides a comprehensive view of networks and demonstrates how the concepts and techniques of the social network perspective work in practice. It also reviews new insights in emerging fields, explores major debates and provides succinct but comprehensive coverage of diverse topics in the field.

In this book I take an evolutionary approach to two sides of the innovation process: search and selection. Search activities are related to generating innovation, while selection processes are related to promoting and diffusing novelties. During search, networks help to recognise opportunities, create, learn, explore and ultimately generate innovations in a system. With selection, networks affect the way people influence others and are influenced by them, choose between alternatives or provide insights in sponsoring novel projects.

The first part of the book is introductory, with each chapter dedicated to one aspect of an innovation network. Chapter 1 explains the meaning of innovation networks and introduces the innovation network box, which is composed of three dimensions: the purpose of network management, the type of networks that fit the purpose and what social network metrics to apply (Figure 0.1). Chapter 2 explores the nature of innovation and why a network approach is relevant to understanding and managing it. The search and selection processes are explained in detail in this chapter. In Chapter 3 I introduce networks as nested systems, composed of teams, departments, business units, firms and industries, in increasing order of aggregation. I also distinguish between different network levels, for example, inter-organisational, intra-organisational and market. Chapter 4 looks at the types of data and social network analysis techniques used to analyse innovation

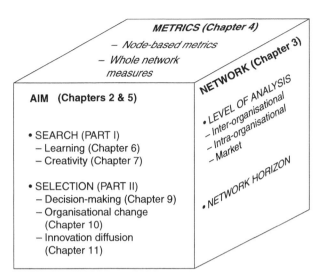

Figure 0.1   Innovation Network Box and the Planning of the Book

networks for different purposes and explores major debates in social network theories. In Chapter 5 I investigate the scope, aims and benefits of network management and introduce a practical guide for managing innovation networks, including critical parameters.

Part II explores the role of networks in search activities. In Chapter 6, I explain how the exploration and exploitation dimensions of organisational learning are related to alliances, alliance portfolios and networks. Chapter 7 focuses on creativity and networks. I look at creativity as both an individual attribute and a social process in which the functioning of teams, and the structure of the broader network, are significant. Chapter 8 examines the role of modularity, an important aspect of new product development that has implications for the effective management of relations between teams and between firms. In this chapter, I also look at the role of networks in user innovation.

Part III explores the role of networks in selection. In Chapter 9 I examine how networks act as signals when selecting among different innovation projects (venture capital decisions or building coalition and obtaining support and resources in intrapreneurial activities). In this chapter, I also review cognitive biases that may be rooted in networks and influence managerial decision-making. Chapter 10 focuses on how the social network approach helps in change management. What does the structure of an organisation's informal networks reveal about possible resistance to change? What will post-change networks look like? Who are the most likely influentials who will help build coalition? Chapter 11 explores the classic literature on social networks and diffusion and more recent approaches. How do ideas and innovations spread on online social media? Who are the influential people, and how do we find them? What does the structure of social network platforms reveal about the patterns of influence and diffusion between people?

The fourth and final part of the book explores the hinterland of network evolution. Chapter 12 is concerned with the antecedents of tie formation and dissolution within inter-personal and inter-organisational networks. I explore mechanisms like the role of individual attributes (experience, knowledge, personality), dyadic attributes (similarity, proximity, etc.) and past networks. Building on the insights developed in Chapter 12, Chapter 13 explores network evolution. Some structural regularities in real-world networks are explained, as well as the factors that drive their emergence and evolution, including important events, firms' strategies, institutional, technological and market-related factors and the interrelations between them.

Finally it is important to mention that the network approach in innovation is a relatively young field, yet it is growing fast. While in just one or two decades much work has been done in terms of research, there is still much to be done in the future, not only in terms of research, but also to translate theoretical findings into action-oriented guides. I hope that this book serves as a useful source in this sense.

Acknowledgements

I have had useful feedback from and the support of many colleagues and friends in writing this book. In particular, I thank my colleagues in Télécom Ecole de Management, and in particular Madeleine Besson and the KIND Research group for their support, as well as useful discussions in seminars. In addition I would like to mention UNU-MERIT (United Nations University-Maastricht Economic Research Institute on Innovation and Technology) where I started my studies on innovation and networks. Their deep expertise in innovation, together with a very collaborative and friendly environment, was an important beginning for me, which motivated me in my later research as well. I consider myself very lucky to have had the chance to work with Robin Cowan, who was very influential in my interest in networks, as well as Patrick Llerena, from the University of Strasbourg (BETA), with whom our joint research projects were always a source of motivation. Teoman Pamukçu, Erkan Erdil, Semih Akçomak from TEKPOL in Middle East Technical University (Ankara), as well as Bulat Sanditov, Altay Özaygen, and Cédric Gossart from Télécom Ecole de Management were especially helpful in providing corrections and help in the text. My conversations with John Bessant, Martin Kilduff, Pascal Le Masson and Geert Duysters about this book encouraged me to a large extent in this project and gave new ideas. In addition, the case studies conducted in the context of the project Better Business Models (BBM) funded by the Agence National de la Recherche (ANR), and our project meetings were very useful in gaining new insights about many practical aspects of network management by firms. I also warmly thank this book's Commissioning Editor Paula Parish, as well as Stephen Acerra and Dominic Stock at Cambridge University Press, for their interest in this project, useful feedbacks and support, and Sally Simmons from Cambridge Editorial for her assistance with the editorial process. Last, but not least, there is my family. I am grateful to my mother Dalga Özman and my sister Aylin Özman for being always there for me and for their endless support and love. I thank my partner Cédric and my son Léo Ege for maintaining a cheerful and motivating environment around me during the process of writing this book.

PART I

Opening the Black Box of Innovation Networks

1 Introduction

The relation between what we see and what we know is never settled. Each evening we see the sun set. We know that the earth is turning away from it. Yet the knowledge, the explanation, never quite fits the sight.

John Berger, *Ways of Seeing*

In this chapter we define the network perspective, and its role in understanding and managing innovation. We distinguish between the different ways in which the term network is understood in different contexts. We clarify the scope of social network theory and social network analysis, as well as the meaning of social networks, business networks, and knowledge networks. We describe an innovation network with the help of three dimensions that characterise it: the innovation stage (why do we carry out network analysis?), level of analysis (which networks do we analyse?), and social network metrics (which social network metrics should we use?). We distinguish between two kinds of managerial activities in which a network perspective is useful: direct network interventions and situation analysis.

At first glance, there is little in common between the Seven Bridges of Königsberg and the New York Training School for Girls. Yet they mark the beginnings of a particular way of seeing what is around us, which is today referred to as the network perspective. In 1736 Leonhard Euler found a mathematical solution to the problem of devising the most efficient way of negotiating the city of Königsberg on foot: the Seven Bridges of Königsberg is often quoted as the first study in graph theory.[1] Graph theory refers to the application of mathematical concepts and theories to a system that is composed of nodes and edges. Euler saw areas of land and bridges as a network of four nodes and seven links respectively (Figure 1.1). Two hundred years later, in a very different

---

[1] Euler's problem was that all the bridges could be crossed once only but all the pieces of land had to be visited. Euler showed that, for such a path to exist, the number of nodes with an odd number of ties must be either zero or two.

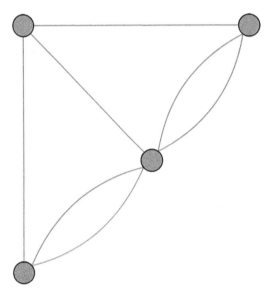

Figure 1.1   The Seven Bridges of Königsberg Represented as a Network
Note: Nodes are areas of land, and edges are the bridges between them.

context, a leading sociologist, Jacob Moreno, conceived a similar network for the New York Training School for Girls, which had a problem with runaway students. Moreno saw the girls as nodes and explained their runaway patterns by examining influence between them (Figure 1.2). His experimental work on this case is considered the leading study in sociometry today.[2]

These two contributions in strikingly different contexts reveal just how broad a range of phenomena can be regarded as networks. We are witnessing this vividly in our contemporary world where there seem to be networks everywhere: in scientific research, the popular media and in business. Aside from the interest in online communities like Twitter and Facebook, we have learned about organised crime networks in Sicily, social networks of characters in Homer's *Odyssey* and even the networks of common flavour compounds across ingredients in different parts of the world.[3]

---

[2] Moreno published his research in his book *Who Shall Survive* (1934). Also see the *New York Times* article, 'Emotions Mapped by New Geography: Charts Seem to Portray the Psychological Currents of Human Relationships' on 3 April 1934. For the history of social network analysis, see Freeman (2004). Cartwright and Harary's (1956) article about linking mathematical graph theory and sociology is now considered a classic.

[3] For the network of flavours, see Ahn et al. (2011); 'Social networks of Homer's Odyssey' is found in Miranda, Baptista and Pinto (2013); for the network study of businesses involved in organised crime in Sicily, see Gurciullo (2014).

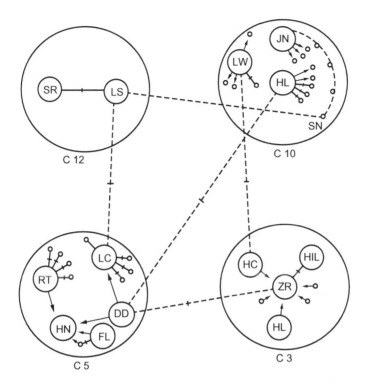

Figure 1.2   Possible Influence Patterns between Fourteen Individuals in Four Cottages are Shown as a Network
Source: Moreno (1934)

A network perspective is particularly valuable when applied to innovation, since innovation is mainly about the flow of knowledge and resources between a variety of actors. I use the term *flow of knowledge* in the general sense: it covers scientific or technical knowledge shared between inventors, experience using a technology shared among peers, 'who knows what' in an organisation or industrial district. A network perspective is an opportunity to take a bird's-eye view of knowledge flows between people, technologies and organisations.

The complex relations that drive the creation and diffusion of innovations can be better understood by taking a network perspective. Innovation is a multi-faceted activity encompassing creativity, learning, the diffusion of ideas and practices and social influence. There are significant interactions between a wide range of actors in all these diverse areas.

Partnerships between firms, collaboration among scientists, an integrated civil society and increased opportunities for users to participate in innovation are all developments that have been seen in recent years. Innovation has

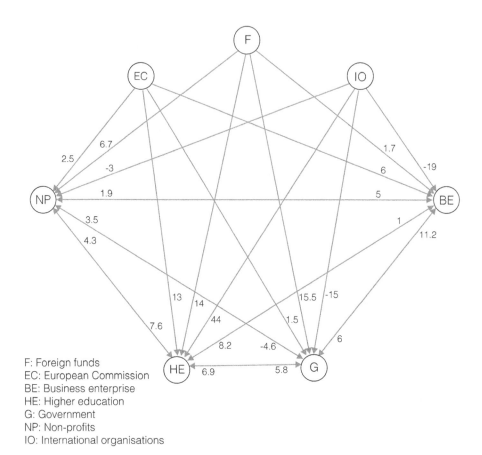

F: Foreign funds
EC: European Commission
BE: Business enterprise
HE: Higher education
G: Government
NP: Non-profits
IO: International organisations

Figure 1.3   Average Annual Growth in the Flow of R&D Funds between Sectors in the Period 2000–12

become increasingly receptive to all sorts of collaboration: with suppliers, customers, competitors, universities and research labs. Through networks, innovators access complementary resources, inform themselves about others' roles and identity and achieve timeliness in accomplishing their goals by combining resources. The resources, knowledge and capabilities of different stakeholders are increasingly integrated and shared through networks. The network in Figure 1.3 shows the average annual growth in the flow of R&D funds between sectors in the period 2000–12. The increasingly collective nature of the R&D is evident in the growth of funding among nearly all stakeholders.

With these developments in mind, using a lens through which we can see the interdependences between technologies, people and organisations, and how they change over time is increasingly relevant for better innovation performance. In an increasingly interconnected world what managers and entrepreneurs need is less about what to do, and more about how to see. But what do we mean by a network perspective?

1.1 The Network Perspective

In the most common use of the term, a network links an actor (which can be an individual, a group or a firm) with other actors in a certain context. Some network positions confer advantages while others actively prevent people from accessing opportunities. This is nothing new; as long ago as the seventeenth century, Shakespeare was writing in *Othello*, 'Preferment goes by letter and affection,/And not by old gradation'.[4]

Social network theory deals with how social structure constrains and enables the behaviour and performance of actors, as well as the behavioural and social psychological factors that influence the formation and dissolution of ties between them.[5] Social networks are made up of ties that signify affection (or the lack of it) between human beings. The field of social networks is a sub-field of sociology and social psychology is a proximate field.[6]

Social network analysis (SNA) was originally developed in the field of sociology and draws upon graph theory, offering a range of mathematical tools to analyse the structure of networks. SNA can be used to analyse any kind of network as long as relations are mapped in the form of nodes and edges. For example, a network whose nodes are patents and whose links are citations can be analysed with SNA, although a patent network is not a social network.

The four core concepts of the network research programme highlighted by Kilduff, Tsai and Hanke (2006) can be used to clarify the meaning of a network perspective. These are:

- **Primacy of relations:** the social network research programme takes relations as the main force behind change and economic action. This is

---

[4] *Othello*, Act I, Scene I.

[5] For a collection of early articles, see Leinhardt (1977) and Holland and Leinhardt (1979). See Barnes (1979) for a discussion of social network theory and methodology. Also see Cross, Parker and Sasson (2003) for a collection of more recent and classic articles (especially from the 1980s and 1990s).

[6] See Kilduff and Tsai (2003) for organisational social networks, in which they explore theories imported from the social psychology and 'home-grown' theories within the social network discipline. An exploration of the most recent issues in organisational social research can be found in Brass et al. (2014).

different from the individualistic and atomistic approaches in mainstream economic theories, where the subject of analysis is the individual (Borgatti and Foster, 2003).

- **Ubiquity of embeddedness:** economic action is embedded in inter-personal relationships (Granovetter, 1985).
- **Social utility of network connections:** network relations confer opportunities and constraints on actors.
- **Structural patterning of social life:** the apparent complexity of social life can be explained in terms of the architecture of relationships, represented by networks. In this sense, a group is not a social network as it connotes the whole rather than showing who is connected to whom.

The network perspective used in this book is both narrower and broader than the scope expressed in these four points. It is narrower, because the focus of the book is on innovation; broader, because it is not only on social networks that connote affection or the lack of it. This book examines a wide range of other networks that are important to understanding innovation. To Kilduff, Tsai and Hanke's (2006) four core concepts, this book adds:

- **Focus on innovation:** innovation includes search processes, where a knowledge base expands and becomes more diverse and new opportunities are recognised and turned into products, and selection processes through which novelties diffuse and are accepted or rejected in the market or among users. Networks play an important role in both search and selection.
- **Not confined to a particular sector:** we tend to think of private enterprise as the main sector that produces innovations. While this is accurate according to the formal R&D data, many other sectors generate innovations. Non-governmental organisations (NGOs), governments, public research labs and users also innovate.[7] This is happening more and more, as the impact of communities, crowds and participatory open source projects demonstrates.
- **All types of network that are relevant to innovation:** social network metrics can be applied to all networks, regardless of how we define a node. For example, centralisation of a network, which measures the extent to which a network has a dense core and a sparse periphery, can be calculated for an inter-personal, patent or strategic alliance network. However, the implications of centralisation depend on the context of investigation and

---

[7] The earliest investigation of user innovation, now a classic, is by Von Hippel (1978).

node type, whether this concerns innovation diffusion, finding a creative solution to a problem or indeed something else entirely.

- **Governance:** different governance mechanisms can be viewed as networks. This book is not concerned with 'orchestrated' networks formed on the initiative of an authority.[8] Rather, it focuses on self-organising networks, which are governed by the independent and autonomous decisions of a wide range of actors and form from the bottom up.

1.2 The Changing Meaning of Networks and Innovation

Words often acquire new interpretations that reflect their economic, technological or institutional context. This is the case with 'innovation' and 'network'. Since the beginning of the twentieth century innovation has been understood to be a major driver of economic growth in many economies. This understanding was accompanied by dissatisfaction with the way it was viewed in mainstream economics theory, where it was considered a 'black box' (Rosenberg, 1983). While mainstream economists left this black box to be studied by other technical disciplines, evolutionary economics gave innovation a central role, contributing significantly to our understanding of its sources and its effects in the economy (Nelson and Winter, 1982). For a long time, positive efficiency effects of innovation were studied as a major criterion in defining economic performance. However, this pro-innovation perspective has been slowly changing over recent years, giving rise to discourses that emphasise the quality of innovation in terms of its impact on welfare, equality and the environment. This is evident in new terms like 'pro-poor approaches' and 'social', 'frugal', 'eco' and 'inclusive' innovation. Leaving aside the conceptual ambiguities of the everyday use of the word, and taking innovation as *diffused novelty in a certain context*, one of the persistent aspects of innovation is that relations between people, ideas, knowledge and artefacts are an essential part of it. This is particularly the case today, when better innovation requires diverse stakeholders, from sometimes distant societies, who interact through networks.

Interpretation of the word network has also changed over time. Scientific progress, inventions and innovation have *always* been driven by relations

---

[8] This specific governance mechanism, where the network is coordinated by a central actor, is referred to as 'orchestration' in the literature (see Dhanaraj and Parkhe, 2006).

between people.[9] Yet in the course of just a few decades, the term 'network' started to take a central position in the agendas of business, policy, academia and the population at large. There are some explanations for the relatively recent popularity of networks that particularly stand out. The first reflects a change in the scientific paradigm, with an increasing interest in open systems in many fields of science during the last fifty years. Open systems emphasise interrelations between parts of a system, rather than focusing on the individual elements that constitute them (Scott and Davis, 2007). The second is the development during the second half of the twentieth century of sophisticated computational tools that allow these interrelations to be analysed. A third reason is appealingly expressed by Ronald Burt, and applies to a specific use of the term: 'One of the opening acts of the 21st century was venture capital discovering social networks' (Burt, 2005: 1). In other words, social networks and the analysis of them are no longer confined to the realms of research and policy; with the rising popularity of online websites, they have become the means of communication for the masses.

Like innovation, the development of network research has also been accompanied by an increasingly 'pro-network' approach in business and policy debates. Today, networks are seen as the remedy for many problems, and collaboration is largely perceived to be a *sine qua non* of innovation. Throughout this book we will uncover the cases in which this is so, but also highlight that the effect of collaboration on innovation depends on a myriad of factors that should also be taken into account.

1.3   What is an Innovation Network?

It is not easy to define an innovation network. This is because innovation is not just the result of systematic efforts to innovate; it is also the result of serendipitous events that occur in daily life (see Box 1.1) and spark an unexpected idea that may produce a radical turnaround. If innovation were only the result of systematic efforts, an innovation network would include only activities *aimed* at innovation, and R&D departments would be the main network actors. However, the fact that there is always scope for learning and novelty creation during, or as a result of, human interactions broadens the conceptualisation of an innovation network significantly. Human interactions can ignite ideas, novelties and ultimately innovations.

---

[9] See Moon (2014) on the history of inventions and social networks.

Box 1.1 'Engineering serendipity'[1] by Creating Network Opportunities

The word 'serendipity' was first coined in 1754 by the novelist Horace Walpole, who used it to mean a pleasant surprise, referring to the Persian fairy tale of Serendip. The role of serendipity in invention is well documented; consider, for example, the 3M Post-it® note, which was invented accidentally by Spencer Silver while he was trying to come up with a super-strong glue – or potato chips, invented when Chef George Crum cut potatoes exaggeratedly thinly and over-fried them to satisfy a customer's insistent demand for crispy French fries. The role of networks in serendipitous innovations is increasingly recognised, and spaces designed to facilitate chance meetings and leverage cross-synergies in an office environment are becoming the norm in innovative enterprises. In other words, serendipity – accidental innovation – is increasingly 'engineered' through network management and the design of spaces. In 2007, Bettencourt, Lobob and Strumsky (2007) revealed a scaling effect in cities. Using an extensive dataset that covered US, European and Chinese cities, they found that the scale parameter of innovation as a function of population was greater than unity, meaning that, as cities grow, there is an increasing returns effect, whereby innovative ideas grow more rapidly than the city itself. The design of Google's new campus also reflects this. The main criterion was to facilitate 'casual collisions of the workforce', so that no employee in the 1.1 million square foot complex would be more than 2.5 minutes' walk from any other (Goldberger, 2013). 'Some of the best decisions and insights come from hallway and cafeteria discussions', according to a Yahoo Inc. internal memo sent to employees by CEO Marissa Meyer in February 2013, when she asked all employees to be physically present in the company's offices instead of working from home (Swisher, 2013).

[1] *Lindsay* (2013).

Max Gunther, in his book *The Luck Factor* (1977), observed the spider-web-like relations surrounding 'lucky' people that give them the capability to combine bits and pieces of knowledge and opportunities. Diverse networks increase possibilities for novelty, because they expand the space in which elements can be put together in different configurations. Any kind of network can be a potential innovation network, if it ignites creative ideas, introduces or diffuses a novelty. Fortunately, at this point social network theories become helpful in enabling us to understand which types of network are more likely to be innovative, and which are not. In other words, although we cannot a priori identify an innovation network, through social network theories we can distinguish between those that are more likely to create novelties and those that are not.

Given these difficulties in defining an innovation network, we should at least clarify some terms that are frequently used, including social, knowledge, business and innovation networks. Social networks involve relations that

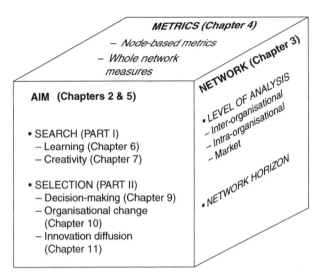

Figure 1.4   Three Dimensions of Innovation Network

connote affection between human beings, like friendship, advice, and trust (or the opposite). Knowledge networks emphasise the flow of knowledge between nodes of a network; for example, a patent citation network is a knowledge network. But note that two inventors who are friends can also cite each other, so knowledge and social networks can coincide, and often do. A business network emphasises commercial relations between firms – for example, between suppliers and customers – and its links can be events like sales, purchases or deliveries. In an innovation network relations imply conceiving and creating a novelty and disseminating it to a wider audience. Therefore, differently from social, knowledge and business networks, which are defined according to nodes and links, the definition of an innovation network is based on the ex post *implications* of the network. All these networks are interwoven, yet analysts focus on what is relevant for the immediate purpose at hand.

In this book we will examine an innovation network based on three dimensions: first, why we carry out network analysis; second, what type of network is concerned; and third, what SNA metrics we should use to analyse the network. These three dimensions are illustrated in Figure 1.4.

- **Aim:** innovation network analysis can be carried out for a variety of purposes. I distinguish two broad categories. The first is *search*, which involves all activities concerned with the conception and creation of innovations at first hand. New ideas are conceived, new projects are created, solutions to problems are generated, new opportunities are recognised and the knowledge space expands as learning occurs. As innovations are generated, markets and institutions narrow down variety through *selection*. If search expands the space of possibilities, selection narrows it down, as innovations diffuse throughout an organisation or the economy. There are many examples of selection, including selecting investment projects in a firm, selecting an entrepreneur for financing, selecting which different products or technologies to purchase, or selecting which management models to follow.

- **Network:** the kind of network analysed should be decided on the basis of the reasons for undertaking network analysis. Networks can be analysed at various *levels*, intra-organisational, inter-organisational and the market. At each of these levels, different *units* can be taken as nodes, for example people, teams, firms, artefacts, subjects and so on. Defining the level and unit of analysis depends on our purpose. It is also necessary to decide whether to *zoom in* or *zoom out* of networks. In other words, should we make a deep analysis of a close-up network, or an aggregate analysis of the wider network? This decision is the *network horizon*.

- **Metrics:** which SNA metrics should be used to analyse the networks? Metrics refer to the measures and concepts used to measure the structural characteristics of a social network. They can be node-based, like centrality, which shows the prominence of an actor in a network, and network-based, like centralisation of the overall network. An important aspect of innovation network management is to assess which metrics have what implications in a given context. For example, what does centrality imply for diffusion of a product? What does the density of a firm's alliance network imply for its innovation performance? How might the centrality (or influence) of actors change as a result of implementing a new technology in an organisation? How will organisational change re-shape informal networks?

1.4 The Structure-agency Debate and Network Management

Social network research has been criticised for a number of reasons, including its structuralist agenda.[10] According to these criticisms, a network approach is

---

[10] For the structure-agency issue in network research see Emirbayer and Goodwin (1994). The authors stress that network research is predominantly structuralist in its approach, emphasising the impact of network structure on behaviour and performance and leaving little space for individual action, intention and agency. Over the last few years the question of network emergence, evolution and formation, as well as the role of individual attributes in tie formation, has attracted increasing attention.

largely about how structure constrains and/or enables actors' actions rather than emphasising how their individual and intentional actions change their networks. Many innovation studies use regression models to estimate the impact of network structure on a measure of innovative performance. For example, they have found that centrality in an industry network facilitates access to resources and increases innovative performance. The structuralist criticism is legitimate because assuming this kind of causality undermines attempts to understand the process through which an actor becomes central in the first place. In addition, in its purest form, the structuralist perspective assumes that individual attributes have no significance in how actors come to occupy certain network positions. Consequently, during recent years more studies have been carried out on the relation between individual attributes, tie formation patterns and the ways networks form and evolve. The criticism is also relevant because most social network research is not explicit about the managerial implications of its results (Borgatti, Brass and Halgin, 2014).[11] The aim of this book is to fill this gap in innovation management.

1.4.1   Direct Network Interventions

First, network management includes direct interventions in a network, which means forming or breaking ties to increase innovation performance. Examples of network interventions include scanning potential alliance partners or stakeholders that best complement the capabilities of an organisation, or forming project teams. At a broader level, network interventions are represented by inducement mechanisms, for example, government funds to foster cooperation between different stakeholders. Some network interventions are more coercive than others. Management often has the power to intervene in formal networks through the allocation of employees to projects, by organising interdepartmental meetings and interactions, or by coordinating workflows and exchanges between people. However, such coercive power is generally absent at the inter-organisational level. Many organisations select partners autonomously and the consent of both sides is required. While these can make network

We now have a better understanding of network emergence and evolution; however, it is important to note that explaining network evolution is different from explaining actors' intentions in guiding the evolution of networks. On network evolution and strategy, see, for example, Baum and Rowley (2008). Also see Borgatti, Brass and Halgin (2014) for a discussion of these and other criticisms, their pertinence and directions for future research.

[11] See Baker (2000) for personal network management; Cross and Parker (2004) for intra-organisational network management;, Johnson (2009) for management of knowledge networks.

interventions more difficult in practice, developing network management capabilities can significantly reduce the risks and uncertainties involved. Organisations can increase the effectiveness of their partner search and collaborations by developing their network management capabilities.

1.4.2   Situation Analysis

Second, network management includes carrying out network analysis to have a better understanding of the current situation in different contexts.

Change Management. A good understanding of how informal social networks function within an organisation can significantly increase the chances of implementing a change project. Informal ties are not revealed by formal organisation charts yet they can be very important for finding out 'how work really gets done' (Cross and Parker, 2004). For example, Cascioro and Lobo (2005) examine whether competence or likeability is a more likely factor in getting a job done in organisations. People prefer 'loveable stars', that is, people who are both smart and likeable. But surprisingly, when it comes to making a choice between a 'competent jerk' and a 'loveable fool', people go for the latter, even at the expense of losing the competences of the former. Cascioro and Lobo stress the importance of identifying loveable fools, and positioning them strategically in an organisation. A network perspective is also useful in organising workspaces to foster chance meetings of employees where creativity is a critical component of success. Box 1.1 explains how this kind of serendipity can be engineered in an organisation, taking examples from Google and Yahoo.

Knowledge Management. The words of former HP CEO, Lew Platt – 'If only HP knew what HP knows' – are frequently quoted in the field of knowledge management. Through network analysis can help detect boundary spanners, the people who play a key role in the knowledge flows in and out of an organisation. Network analysis also shows where knowledge resides in an organisation and how it is distributed, concentrated, shared and integrated. Opening communication channels to ensure the transfer of best practices and foster cross-domain synergies can significantly increase the innovative potential of organisations – and to do this a very good understanding of current networks is required.

Decision-making. Network perspective is also important in decision-making processes. Behavioural theories suggest that cognitive biases are common in strategic decision-making (Tversky and Kahneman, 1974) and that managers can receive skewed feedback from their teams. Network analysis helps people see whether their network might cause or augment such biases.

Industry Analysis. A network perspective is also useful for understanding the competitive positioning of a firm in the industry landscape. This is rather like driving on a highway, when the driver knows where she is going and the junctions that lie immediately ahead but has no sense of the other roads and crossings for twenty kilometres around. In other words, her cognitive representation of her position in the landscape is restricted and imprecise. The organisations that occupy an industry landscape are similarly myopic. A network approach provides a sort of GPS that shows actors where they are or should be positioned in this landscape, and can also guide them about which roads to take and which to avoid. Networks also help positioning vis-à-vis other actors in the system. This has important implications. Many studies show that knowledge is highly *localised*. Organisations often *search* for new knowledge in the vicinity of their existing competences. In other words, their search for new knowledge is strongly bounded by what they already know. But innovation requires a broadening of perspectives, thinking outside the box and searching in unfamiliar terrains. Distant opportunities can be seen better with the help of network analysis.

Discussion Questions

1. What is meant by network perspective? Can you think of different kinds of relations that can be represented as networks? In your example:
   a. How do you define the nodes and links?
   b. What can be the uses of taking a network perspective?

2. What is the difference between a social network and a knowledge network? Give an example of a social network that is also a knowledge network.

3. What are the different ways in which network analysis is used in innovation management? Can you find an example, from your own organisation, in which the following will be useful:
   a. Direct network intervention
   b. Situational analysis?

   In which way will network management be useful in your examples?

2 Two Sides of Innovation: Search and Selection

Invention, it must be humbly admitted, does not consist in creating out of void, but out of chaos...

Mary Shelley, Introduction to *Frankenstein*

This chapter explores the nature of innovation by focusing on five characteristics that are common to a number of different contexts: clustering; uncertainty; path dependence; collaboration; and recombination. We show how a relational approach leads to a better understanding of innovation processes. A historical overview of different innovation models is provided, and the implications of these historical models for relations between different actors are discussed. We explore alternative relational approaches, and highlight their strengths and weaknesses. Finally, we explore the search and selection processes in more detail, and show how networks feature in each of these.

Why are interactions between diverse actors such an important part of innovation? Consider the following news headlines:

BlaBlaCar, the new twinkling star of the 'sharing economy', boasts 8m members in 12 European countries. In Russia, the latest addition, it has signed up 250,000 within a few months. Weekend trips out of Moscow, says Mr Brusson, have been popular.[1] (*The Economist*, 5 July 2014)

Accenture to acquire Agilex to enhance digital capabilities in analytics, cloud and mobility for federal agencies. (Accenture.com, 9 February 2015)

Cosmo Pharmaceuticals file lawsuit against Actavis for patent infringement of Uceris patents. (Reuters, 25 February 2015)

The complexity of digital media is forcing formerly warring departments at publishers to call truces and work together. The *New York Times* and *Washington Post* now have 'ad innovations units' that look to the newsroom for inspiration for new ad products. (digiday.com, 17 April 2014)

---

[1] The article quotes Nicolas Brusson, the co-founder and Chief Operating Officer (COO) of BlaBlaCar.

IBM positions itself as large broker of health data. IBM partners with Apple, Johnson & Johnson, Medtronic to form Watson Health data venture. (*Wall Street Journal*, 15 April 2015)

How Georgia became the biggest electric vehicle market in the US? 'That's part of building sustainable businesses,' Francis says. 'The pressure of leaders in business . . . makes people think: If they're doing it and I'm not, should I consider it?' (*Guardian Sustainable Business*, 8 January 2015)[2]

Biomimicry continues to evolve: fly inspires tiny microphone. (*Forbes*, 30 July 2014)

Why do people put solar on their roofs? Because other people put solar on their roofs. (washingtonpost.com/wonkblog, 23 October 2014)

PepsiCo, Unilever, Heineken, M&S and Tesco worked with academics and sustainability specialists to produce Cool Farm Tool: an online greenhouse gas calculator that helps farmers work out the impact of various operations on environment and productivity. (*Guardian Sustainable Business*, 15 May 2014)

A common theme in these news stories is the interaction between ideas, people or organisations. Some of these interactions reflect discord between actors, for example, Cosmo Pharmaceuticals. Others are about peer influence on the adoption of technology, as in the stories about solar panels and electric vehicles in Georgia. One is a story about combining unrelated notions (flies and electronics). Other stories describe business models based on new forms of exchange between people (BlaBlaCar in Europe and internal reorganisation in the publishing industry as a response to media digitalisation). There are also stories about firms joining forces to enhance capabilities (Coolfarmtool and Accenture's acquisition of Acquis). What is it about innovation that makes interactions so important?

Some of these news stories indicate searching for, generating or appropriating value from innovations, like the new 'ad innovation unit' in the *New York Times*. Others reflect an ongoing selection process, where technology is chosen by users in a particular geographical area or market (e.g. solar panels). These point to two important innovation processes: search and selection. What are search and selection mechanisms and why is a network approach appropriate for managing them?

---

[2] This article explores the reasons behind the rapid growth of electric vehicles in Georgia, Atlanta. Collaboration between stakeholders is mentioned as one of the important factors. The article quotes Don Francis, executive director of Clean Cities-Georgia, a partnership formed between various stakeholders from private companies, government, NGOs and laboratories.

Innovation is a collective and social activity that involves interactions between diverse actors. There are many different schools of thought about the interdependence of diverse stakeholders, why they collaborate, are influenced, share or collide in markets. This chapter deals with these approaches and theoretical streams and explores what gives interactions their central role in innovation. It takes a detailed look at search and selection processes and the role networks play in them.

2.1   Growing Role of Interactions in Innovation Studies: 1950 Onwards

Over the last forty years, innovation studies has grown rapidly to become a new scientific field (Fagerberg and Verspagen, 2009). Research has focused on the sources of invention and innovation, the appropriability of innovation by different stakeholders, inter-sectoral and international differences in innovation capabilities, the role of idiosyncratic competences of organisations in the innovation process, and the internal processes that drive or impede innovation within organisations. The theoretical roots of this discipline are interdisciplinary, drawing on sociology, evolutionary economics, management, geography and organisation theory. Schumpeter's views have been particularly influential on the development of the field (see Box 2.1).[3]

A glance at the history of innovation management models since the 1950s reveals the increasing role attributed to interdependencies and interactions in the innovation process. Here it is useful to consider Marinova and Phillimore's (2003) six models of innovation.

- **Black box models:** during the 1950s, the black box model of innovation recognised technological progress as the main factor behind economic growth, following Solow's (1957) analysis of total factor productivity in the US between 1909 and 1949, where he found that 90 per cent of per capita output could be attributed to technological change. Models in this tradition are called black box because their emphasis is on inputs and outputs, treating the *process* of transformation (that is, innovation) as a black box, without exploring it.

---

[3] See Nelson and Winter (1982) and Dosi and Nelson (1994) for the fundamentals of evolutionary economics. For the evolution of the field of innovation studies see Fagerberg (2004); for a bibliometric network analysis of the field, see Fagerberg and Verspagen (2009) and Fagerberg, Fosaasa and Sappraserta (2012).

Box 2.1 Innovation Studies and Evolutionary Economics

The evolutionary theory of technological change and innovation is rooted in Schumpeterian economic theory. Schumpeter's Mark I and Mark II regimes influenced the way in which the relationship between market structure and innovation was understood in early innovation studies. Schumpeter's early work stressed the role of entrepreneurship, creative destruction and flexible small firms as the main driver of innovation (Mark I). In his later work, he discussed the importance of large, vertically integrated corporations and R&D labs as key sources of innovation (Mark II). Schumpeterian insights were important in forming the backbone of an evolutionary economic theory that put entrepreneurship and innovation at the centre of economic change. Since the publication of Nelson and Winter's *An Evolutionary Theory of Economic Change* (1982), problems with the way mainstream theories treat innovation have been better understood, especially in relation to unrealistic and restrictive assumptions and the emphasis on equilibrium. Today, evolutionary concepts are largely infused into innovation studies. According to Dosi and Marengo (2007), evolutionary economics:

- supports a process view of economic and social systems (why something exists);
- is based on micro-founded theories (what agents do and why they do it);
- assumes an imperfect understanding of the world by agents (who are boundedly rational);
- maintains that bounded rationality, routines (habits) and path-dependent learning processes entail largely heterogeneous agents;
- allows for the possibility of novelty and innovation in its theoretical framework (rather than taking innovation as exogenous to the system);
- takes heterogeneities in the population as a source of variety and at the same time reveals the market-level selection mechanisms at work, in explaining differential firm growth and performance;
- regards patterns in which micro-level interactions result in certain aggregate outcomes as 'emergent';
- focuses on the co-evolution of higher-level institutions, norms, organisational conduct and micro-level processes, rather than taking the micro and the macro as separate constructs.

- **Linear models:** during the 1960s and 1970s, researchers began to focus on the specific processes that give rise to innovation. At first, so-called linear models of innovation put scientific developments at the heart of the innovation process. Scientific progress determines the direction of technological change, by giving rise to inventions, which are followed by development, manufacturing and marketing activities, and ultimately diffusion in the economy. Subsequent innovation models extended these *technology push* models to incorporate the role of user needs; these are referred to as demand-pull models. These approaches took the direction of technical change from the market towards R&D, emphasising the needs of the market as the main driver of innovative efforts by private firms (necessity is the mother of invention). In addition, demand-pull models incorporated the role of users, who can have an important role in the innovation process (Von Hippel, 1976), rather than pure scientists.

- **Interactive models:** linear models of innovation were criticised (Mowery and Rosenberg, 1979) because they did not take into account the feedback loops between different phases of the innovation process. Referred to as interactive models by Marinova and Phillimore (2003),[4] later approaches recognised the importance of links between different parts of the innovation process, in particular marketing, manufacturing and design. These models prioritised neither science and technology nor the market as the main driver of innovation; rather they highlighted the mutual interaction between different stages, maintaining that innovation can occur at any point in marketing, design, production and distribution processes, as a result of a feedback mechanism between the different stages.
- **System models:** these models emphasise interdependencies among a broader range of actors. In the 1970s, globalisation gained momentum, as did the importance of manufacturing processes, where the use of generic technologies diffused. Two oil crises revealed the importance of cost savings. Firm boundaries grew blurred, as firms became increasingly dependent on each other to develop innovations. One of the hallmarks of this period is national systems of innovation approach (Lundvall, 1992). This approach emphasises the role of institutions working collectively and individually in developing and diffusing new technologies. These institutions differ in size, level of economic development and level of concern about specific policy problems across different countries (Marinova and Phillimore, 2003).
- **Evolutionary models:** during the same period, evolutionary models grew out of increasing dissatisfaction with the mechanical view and equilibrium-based approaches of neoclassical economics, which failed to take into account the complex and rapidly evolving nature of technological change. Underlying the evolutionary perspective is the premise that a biological metaphor, combined with insights from organisation theory, is more suitable to understanding innovation and technological change (see Box 2.1).
- **Economic geography:** another group of models combines insights from economic geography and sociology and focuses on the role of regional clusters in innovation.[5] In these models innovation is seen in relation to a concept of space (geographical, organisational, etc.), where the clustering of innovation activities and localised knowledge are essential features.

---

[4] Marinova and Phillimore's (2003) models are an extension of Rothwell's (1994) five generations of innovation.

[5] The innovative milieus models (Camagni, 1991).

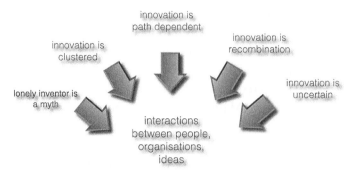

Figure 2.1   The Five Persistent Characteristics of Innovation

A closer look at these models reveals that each of them indicates different networks, summarised in Table 2.1.

The growing role of interactions in innovation models is also attributable to the increasing complexity and interdependence of products and knowledge bases, which have made it more and more difficult for firms to be self-sufficient. This can be explained by a general trend towards systemic analysis in the sciences in the second half of the twentieth century. It was in this period that the network approach gained momentum, with its focus on the relations between elements of a system. Interaction-based perspectives were largely a reaction to the individualistic approaches that characterised the social sciences in the 1950s. James Coleman, a leading sociologist, notes that before this time there were no tools for analysing interactions, a serious impediment that resulted in 'extraordinarily elaborated methods' for analysing the behaviour of individual entities, rather than systems (Coleman, 1986: 1316). Unlike approaches that focus on individual attributes and capabilities, an interactions-based approach underlines the systemic interdependences between elements of a system. Box 2.2. summarises these approaches in innovation and science and technology studies.

What is it in the nature of innovation that makes relations between elements so important? Five persistent characteristics of innovation, valid across many different contexts, are illustrated in Figure 2.1.

2.2   The Myth of the Lonely Inventor: Knowledge Flow between People

Traditionally, innovation was associated with the image of a genius inventor working alone in a laboratory. Today we know that this image is largely a myth. Innovation is not an isolated process attributable to a solitary inventor.

Box 2.2 Interaction-based Approaches in Science, Technology and Innovation Studies

Actor Network Theory (ANT)

ANT[1] was developed by Michel Callon, Bruno Latour and Johnson Law. It does not have a structural perspective on networks as SNA does. Instead, the word 'network' is used to reflect the 'foci' through which meanings and interpretations are formed and shaped as artefacts and humans and technologies interact. For example, Callon defines a techno-economic network as being composed of three realms in continuous interaction: a scientific pole, a technical pole and the market (Callon, 1991). Neither economics nor sociology can by themselves account for these interactions, as sociology focuses on relationships and economics on intermediaries. These cannot be separated, as they define and shape each other. ANT favours ethnographic field methods; an important advantage of the approach is its attention to the formation of conflict and rivalry in networks (Smith-Doerr and Powell, 2005).

Models Exported from Positive Sciences

These approaches draw analogies between biology and physics and social systems; models imported from physics and biology are used to model interactions in the economic and social spheres.[2] Some commonly used modelling frames include genetic algorithms and statistical mechanics. Genetic algorithms permit the generation of modelling variety and selection processes in innovation, by coding technologies (or other entities) as strings. The degree of adaptation of an individual string to the external environment is evaluated using a fitness function. Approaches that rely on statistical mechanics draw an analogy between atoms and social actors, and are used to model social influence in the diffusion of innovations (for example, the Ising model). While such analogies have been used to model learning and innovation, they have also been criticised for a number of reasons, particularly when they are not well suited to economic phenomena (Gallegati et al., 2006).

Open Innovation

Chesbrough's (2003) open innovation model has received increasing attention. Its main line of argument is that instead of insisting on a closed and competitive management philosophy, firms should embrace an approach that emphasises open innovation, sharing and collaborating with diverse stakeholders, including other firms and producers and users of complementary goods.

Markets as a Network Approach (IMP)

Unlike these approaches, IMP is explicitly concerned with networks. It was introduced by Hakansson et al. (2009) and has gained momentum, especially in Europe. The proximate field of relationship marketing focuses on business networks of buyers and sellers and is methodologically based on case studies. An important advantage of case studies is that they permit an analysis of tie content. A disadvantage of this approach is that it focuses on the connections around a particular organisation, with less emphasis on the structure of overall networks. In addition, it is not specifically knowledge- or innovation-oriented.

> **Box 2.2** (cont.)
>
> ### Economic Geography and Regions
> In their bibliometric network analysis, Fagerberg and Verspagen (2009) found that geography and policy formed one of the main branches of innovation studies. In general, this field is concerned with the spatial clustering of innovation, its causes, consequences and the development of policies designed to increase the innovative performance of geographical clusters. In this approach, learning is localised and institutions have a central role in shaping regional innovation performance. Two influential research streams in this area have been national systems of innovation (Lundvall, 1992) and sectoral systems of innovation (Malerba, 2002). A structural network approach is also commonly used in this field, mainly to model spatial knowledge flows between actors.
>
> [1] On actor network theory, see Latour (2005).
> [2] On interactions based models, see for example Arthur, Durlauf and Lane (1997) and Brock and Durlauf (2000).

Table 2.1 Six Models of Innovation and Networks

Innovation model	Explanation	Network implications
Black box	Focuses only on inputs and outputs; the process of innovation is a black box	Black box
Linear models	Push (technology) and pull (demand) models, which take innovation as largely unidirectional	Networks of scientists and inventors; networks with users
Interactive models	Innovation based on the mutual dependence between different functions (e.g. design, marketing, manufacturing, R&D)	Intra-organisational networks and ties that connect different functions generating innovation
Systems models	Innovation as the process of development and diffusion of technologies within a framework that shapes and is shaped by a set of institutions	Macro-level networks, including policy-makers, scientists, regions, organisations
Evolutionary models	Innovation as a dynamic, collective process, in which variety is generated and selection processes are at work	Inter-organisational and intra-organisational networks
Innovative milieus	Emphasises the localised nature of innovation and the importance of regional clusters	Networks in regional clusters

Instead, it connotes interactions between a variety of actors, and one of the essential aspects of innovation is the way these actors learn from each other within communities, teams and other organisational contexts. Learning from others is a way to complement our own knowledge. Through a variety of

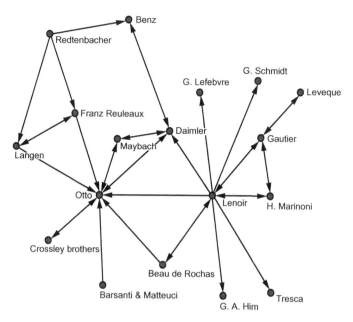

Figure 2.2   Network between Inventors of Internal Combustion Engine

interactions, which can be represented as networks, inventors enhance their creativity side, scientific knowledge and knowledge of market needs. Singh and Fleming (2010) analysed nearly 500,000 patents and found that patents granted to inventors working in teams or with organisational affiliations are significantly more likely to generate breakthroughs than single inventors.[6] Moreover, working in a team not only increases the chances of break-throughs but also reduces the likelihood of particularly poor outcomes (Singh and Fleming, 2010). Similarly, Uzzi, Mukherjee, Stringer and Jones (2013) found that highly cited scientific papers are 40 per cent more likely to have multiple than sole authors.

Collaboration between inventors or scientists is not a recent phenomenon. Figure 2.2 shows a partial network showing the influence between inventors involved in the development of the internal combustion engine, based on the historical analysis made by Moon (2014). The network shows two central inventors. One is the Belgian Jean Joseph Etienne Lenoir and the other Nikolaus Agustus Otto, a German.

---

[6] The authors find that team-based patents are 28% more likely than patents from single inventors to be in the 95th percentile of citations (p. 49), and that sole inventors are more likely than teams to produce particularly poor outcomes.

Hargadon's (2003) much cited study of Thomas Edison's laboratory at Menlo Park also demonstrates the networked nature of invention. Although most people consider Edison the inventor of the electric lightbulb, innovation at Menlo Park was nurtured by an environment in which intensive knowledge exchanges took place between engineers.

The knowledge of diverse actors is important in innovation, not only that of inventors. In addition to networks of inventors, which are characterised by the flow of technical knowledge, innovation networks contain networks of financial sources (like venture capitalists), marketing and sales teams, manufacturing firms and other actors who contribute to commercialising and popularising inventions. Knowledge flow is not only confined to producers of innovation; it extends to the users who share their experiences of innovative products with others.

2.3   Innovation is Clustered

Innovation is clustered locally, industrially and historically (Fagerberg, 2004). The notion of clustering of innovative activity finds its roots in the work of Joseph Schumpeter, who showed the possible relation between clusters, business cycles and long waves in the economy.[7] A famous example of local clustering of innovation is the much studied Silicon Valley. In a famous study, Saxenian (1994) showed how dense communication networks between people were accompanied by rapid technological change in the region. This pattern of open exchange and communications was very different from the way another centre of high-technology innovation, Route 128, operated. The Route 128 firms were more closed than their counterparts on the West Coast. Similar geographical clusters can be observed in many other parts of the world. For example, the northern Italian district of Emilia-Romagna has clusters of economic activities ranging from automobiles to footwear. Baden-Württemberg and Jena in Germany, Sophia Antipolis in France and the Suzhou Industrial Park in China are all well known and studied.

Innovation is not only locally clustered, it is also clustered industrially and historically. Knowledge is cumulative and builds upon itself. In many technologies this cumulative process is not linear; there are periods in which knowledge accumulates at faster rates. Moon (2014) shows how the nonlinear accumulation of knowledge is accompanied by the exponential

---

[7] On Schumpeterian business cycles see Freeman (1990) and Freeman and Perez (1988).

Box 2.3 Clustering in Time and Space: the Case of Computers

Developments in the computer industry illustrate how innovations cluster in time and space, as well as the role of recombination. The origins of the computer industry can be traced back to the R&D activities of a few large companies, such as IBM and Xerox Parc, between the 1940s and 1970s; these helped to establish the field of computer science. During the 1970s and 1980s, a close-knit network of physicists, computer scientists and talented recent graduates of leading universities played a major role in the development of computers. Their knowledge domains were diverse, and included neuroscience, electronics, psychology, programming, design, human-computer interactions, pattern recognition, hardware manufacturing and physics. Silicon Valley was especially dynamic in rapidly generating inventions, forming a social and technological focus through which specialists were continuously interacting, learning from each other, creating and sharing new knowledge and contributing to the building of many electronic products. There was a strong clustering of technological competences and innovative activities in this new industry.

One limitation of computers in the 1970s was that they were too big to be portable. As explained by Moggridge (2007), the 'Grid Compass' was an early portable computer. Significant problems, including memory size, modems and screens, were eventually solved by engineers from various companies, including Intel, which supplied the bubble memory, Racal Vadic, which designed the modem, and Sharp Electronics, which designed the electroluminescent screen. Portability became a new design feature, requiring specialised knowledge of how the components, now much smaller in size, worked together. Soon portability became the core competence of some firms, which developed personal digital assistants (PDAs) and tablet computers.

---

growth of inventor networks in different technologies. Figure 2.3 shows major developments in the aviation industry. Inventions are particularly concentrated after the 1880s and until 1900. The early development of the computer industry (see Box 2.3) illustrates a similar nonlinear knowledge accumulation. These are just two examples that show how innovation is clustered in certain periods, industries and regions.

2.4 Innovation is Path-dependent

Path-dependence is a process whereby historical accidents or random events can result in a few technologies becoming dominant in a market (Arthur, 1989; David, 1985). What is more, the 'winning' technology is not necessarily the most efficient one. Historically insignificant events can drive market share in such a way that an inefficient technology can be selected by the

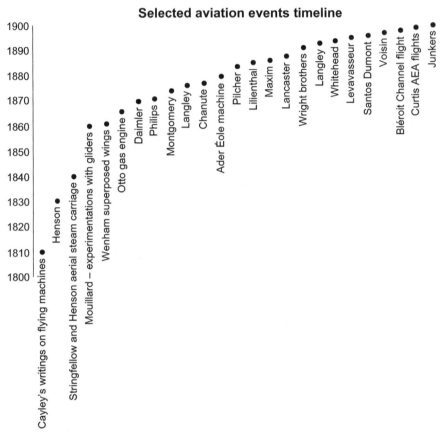

Figure 2.3   The Temporal Clustering of Innovations in Aviation
Note: Adopted from Moon (2014).

market, where improvements to the technology are rewarded and attempts to revert to the old version incur increasing costs. In other words, self-reinforcing mechanisms drive market competition.

Networks play an important role in self-reinforcement processes. In some cases the number of adopters in a local network (friends, peers, colleagues) can influence an individual's selection of a technology. Mobile phone subscriptions or online social networking sites provide good examples of this. In addition, the higher the number of adopters, the more investments are made in the infrastructure that supports a technology, which contributes further to its growth.

In addition to these externalities, networks provide another explanation for path-dependence: social learning. There is often uncertainty about technologies when they are first introduced in a market. Research shows that social networks are especially important in diffusing early adopters' experiences of new technologies. These user networks can mitigate the negative impact of uncertainty in technology adoption.

As self-reinforcement can lead relatively inefficient technologies to dominate in markets, researchers have begun to question how paths can be created using various intervention policies and strategies in order to direct the evolution of technologies along sustainable paths, sometimes through network interventions (Garud and Karnoe, 2001).

2.5   Recombination is Central in Innovation

The history of technological change is full of examples of innovations that are the result of recombining previously existing but disparate elements in novel ways.[8] At the micro-level, recombination is a cognitive activity based on analogous thinking, that is, the application of knowledge in one area to other, possibly unrelated areas. For example, it is used in strategy-making (Gavetti and Rivkin, 2005), product innovations (Gassman and Zeschky, 2008), problem-solving and creativity. One of the building blocks of recombination is variety. Termed 'recombinant growth' by Weitzman (1998), the probability of innovation is higher when there is more variety in a system that can potentially be recombined. Recombination can happen accidentally or can be incentivised through systematic analogous thinking. Box 2.4 gives some examples of recombination.

2.6   Innovation is Uncertain

Uncertainty is a pervasive characteristic of the innovation process. First, the R&D process itself is uncertain. Basic and applied research often requires large investments of time and money and the likelihood of success is largely unknown in advance. This uncertainty is especially prevalent in science-based industries like biotechnology, pharmaceuticals or nanotechnology. Another source of uncertainty is the lack of prior knowledge about possible future uses of a technology (Rosenberg, 1996). There are many innovations for which alternative areas of use become apparent as other related

---

[8] See, for example, Basalla (1988) and Arthur (2009).

Box 2.4 Recombination in Practice: Examples

Recombination is the association of previously unconnected elements. Analogous thinking is an essential part of recombination; it refers to the process by which an element originally designed for a particular purpose is used to solve a problem in another context, through an association of the two contexts. In the new context, various elements can be recombined to create a new feature. Here are some examples of recombination and analogous thinking.

- Gutenberg's printing press – an early example. As all of its elements, including moving type and even the press itself, already existed, the press can be seen as a product of bricolage, rather than a technology designed from scratch. Movable type was invented by a Chinese blacksmith and presses were widely used to press grapes for winemaking during the mid-1400s in Germany.
- Punch cards were used in the weaving industry from the 1700s onwards. They were significantly improved by Joseph Marie Jacquard in 1801, in an invention known as the Jacquard loom. In the twentieth century, they were widely used first in the data processing industry and then in computers.
- Schilling (2012) explains that before the end of the 1990s, doctors found it difficult to diagnose intestinal disorders because there was no equipment to allow them to see inside the intestines. The technical expertise came from an engineer working for the Israeli Army, where mini cameras were used inside missiles. This technician later joined forces with a team of scientists from the UK and a medical equipment company. The first swallowable camera pills were introduced to the market in April 2000.
- Reebok pump shoes were developed by a very diverse team that came up with the idea of using intravenous bag technologies in an air bladder (Hargadon, 2003).
- Nike Inc. and the computer giant Apple collaborated on a joint research project aimed at designing smart jogging shoes. These smart shoes enabled wearers to record their running performance on their iPods, through sensors in their shoes. Through this joint research project, both companies gained knowledge of a field completely different from their own and benefited from mutual network effects.

Further Reading

Johnson, S. (2010). *Where Good Ideas Come From: The Natural History of Innovation*, New York, NY: Riverhead Books.

technologies develop in time. As Nathan Rosenberg (1996) points out, most of the time technologies are developed to solve very specific and narrowly defined problems. But once a solution is found to a specific problem, alternative uses for it can be discovered, often by someone other than the original inventor. A historically significant example is the steam engine, which was originally invented in the eighteenth century to pump water out of flooded mines. Later on the steam engine became a general source of power in a variety of industries, ranging from textiles to transportation.

There is also significant market uncertainty, because often it is not possible to predict how markets will respond to an innovation. Arthur (1996) uses a gambling metaphor to describe the sources of uncertainty:

[P]art of the game is to choose which games to play, as well as playing them with skill. We can imagine the top figures in high tech – the Gateses and Gerstners and Groves of their industries – as milling in a large casino. Over at this table, a game is starting called multimedia. Over at that one, a game called Web services. In the corner is electronic banking. There are many such tables. You sit at one. How much to play? you ask. Three billion, the croupier replies. Who'll be playing? We won't know until they show up. What are the rules? Those'll emerge as the game unfolds. What are my odds of winning? We can't say. Do you still want to play? (Arthur, 1996: 104)

One way innovators deal with uncertainty is to communicate and collaborate with others, in order to follow market developments and trends, share the risks of R&D and make use of others' complementary resources.

2.7 Search and Networks

Innovation has two sides: the creation of a novelty and the diffusion of it. These two sides are neither consecutive nor orderly. Rather they are embedded within each other and can happen simultaneously. But in terms of the role of networks, they are distinct. In the creation of a novelty, actors use networks to search external knowledge and resources that can be combined with theirs, and to recognise new opportunities. In search activities, networks can help increase variety and multiply possibilities of recombination.

Experimenting with the unknown, acquisition of new knowledge, learning-by-doing and trial and error constitute search processes in innovation. The most straightforward formal search activity is R&D. In addition to R&D, search can also be embedded in the routine activities of firms, like marketing, sales, design and manufacturing. Moreover, inspirations, or random accidents that provoke a spark, are also search activities. Search sometimes takes place through interactions with suppliers, users, competitors, professional and trade associations, commercial and public research labs and universities. In search, the role of networks is prevalent in two processes: learning and creativity.

2.7.1   Learning

Search activities are accompanied by individual and organisational learning. Learning is task-related but organisations also learn *how to learn*. Learning often takes place in familiar areas by deepening existing competences but it also takes place in unfamiliar or distant fields, as firms search for new opportunities. Inter-organisational ties are used to acquire new knowledge and access resources elsewhere in the industry. At the same time, intra-organisational networks enable the sharing and diffusion of externally acquired knowledge that has been internalised in processes by all units in the organisation.

2.7.2   Creativity

An important part of search is the initial sparks that have the potential to be developed into products, services or new business models. Networks play an important role in the conception of novel ideas. In particular, the composition of teams, different types of intermediaries that connect actors, intra-organisational friendship networks or the organisation of workspaces can influence the generation of novel ideas. Informal networks within an organisation can have a significant effect on the extent to which people are motivated to express ideas openly and resolve conflicts, vital when creative ideas are being put into practice.

2.8   Selection and Networks

Selection processes are related to how actors accept or reject a novelty. Their choices not only depend on their idiosyncratic tastes and preferences, but also on how they are influenced by each other through their networks. Networks play an important role in selection through the diffusion of information by word-of-mouth and the way actors influence one another. A product, service, procedure, new organising principle or reorganisation is novel only to the extent that it is perceived as such by the population exposed to it. Therefore the social structure to which an innovation is introduced is critical to the way it is perceived and adopted. Social networks have an important part in the spread of ideas, practices and products. Whichever way diffusion is taken, it shows a selection mechanism at work. Whether selection is made by potential users in the market, firms in an industry, different stakeholders, the members of an organisation or a community, the acceptance (or not) of novelty signals selective pressures. Selection processes almost always imply the prioritisation of something over alternatives. Whereas search activities increase the space for these alternatives, selection narrows it. In selection, the role of networks is prevalent in signalling quality of actors, in managing change, and in diffusion of innovations.

2.8.1   Signalling

Innovation depends on how management (or other decision-makers) receive information and make sense of the environment by processing it. This determines how managers think the organisation can survive and prosper, including where and how to search, which markets to enter, which fields of activities to invest in and which strategic alliance partners to select. Networks filter information and shape the way that managers form mental models of the environment. Similar decisions are made by entrepreneurs in selecting sources of funding and by venture capital firms in selecting the ventures in which to invest. In decisions that involve a target actor the networks surrounding the target yield signals about its inherent qualities when such information may not be readily available in the market.

2.8.2   Organisational Change

These selective processes are not only confined to markets; they are also at work inside organisations, particularly during major change initiatives. The introduction of a new technology, implementation of a new management system or a major reorganisation are examples of major change projects. Although change inside an organisation is more coercive than selection decisions made by independent entities in the market, the impact of social influence is similar. People are influenced by the opinions of others in their reference group and they seek information from their co-workers when faced with uncertainty. The diffusion of certain practices, processes or technologies between organisations also signals a selection mechanism at work, albeit at a more macro-level. For example, more organisations are adopting management systems to increase the coordination and control of the environmental impact of their operations. In this case selection operates through conformity and the influence of other organisations in a particular field (DiMaggio and Powell, 1983).

2.8.3   Innovation Diffusion

Various aspects of the diffusion process are strongly related to the networks operating between potential users in the market.

- **Network effects:** some products or services yield higher utility when more people adopt them. For example, social networking platforms like Facebook, or some online network-based games, illustrate how the number of existing participants determines the extent of further participation. Such products or services rely on users' tendency to adopt a similar product as their peers. In other words, increasing returns drive systems towards standardisation or at the very least reduction of variety in the system.
- **Learning effects:** strength of selection also depends on increasing returns through learning. Users accumulate knowledge and experience in using a certain technology, which increases the time and energy required to learn new or alternative technologies. A famous example is the QWERTY keyboard; David (1985) showed that the knowledge accumulated around this standard layout resulted in its ultimate gain against the more efficient Dvorak Simplified Keyboard (DSK). In these cases, as users learn more about one particular system, the switching costs of shifting to other systems increase, reducing variety in the market.
- **Trends:** word-of-mouth can speed up the diffusion of a novelty even when there are no physical or learning-oriented network effects. Trends and fads that spread quickly in the market illustrate this. For example, Gladwell (2000) takes the case of Hush Puppies shoes. Sales had fallen so low by 1994 that the US manufacturer was considering phasing out the brand; then sales suddenly exploded and the shoes became fashion items in the space of just a few months. Gladwell explains that the turn-round happened through word-of-mouth in the market, initiated by a handful of young people in New York City and taken up by high-end designers.
- **Social influence:** the behaviour and ideas of peers influences the choices made by members of a reference group. This can be due to a cohesion effect, whereby an individual is increasingly exposed to a particular novelty and sympathises with it, out of concern to conform to peer behaviour, or because of social comparison. People mimic the choices made by others whom they perceive to share their social status.

The role of networks in search and selection processes is summarized in Figure 2.4.

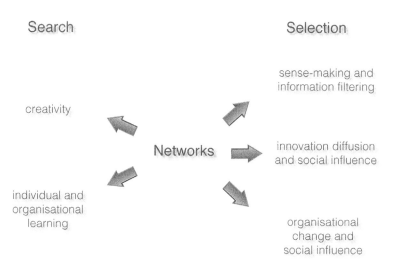

Figure 2.4   The Role of Networks in Search and Selection Processes

Discussion Questions

1. Explain what is meant by search process in innovation. Give an example of a search activity from an organisation that you know. How can network perspective be useful in this example?

2. Explain what is meant by selection process in innovation. Give an example of selection of an innovation in a market, an industry or a community. How can network perspective be useful in selection process?

3. Explain the difference between market and technological uncertainties. How do networks help in reducing uncertainty? Can networks also augment uncertainty? Can you find examples for the latter case?

4. What are the different interactions-based approaches in economics and management?

3   Network as a Nested System

The goal of science is to make the wonderful and the complex understandable and simple, but not less wonderful.

Herbert Simon

In this chapter we introduce networks as nested systems, where teams, departments, organisations and entire industries may be analysed as networks. We clarify level of analysis, unit of analysis and the network horizon. Three levels of analysis in innovation networks are described: intra-organisational; inter-organisational and the market. The notion of network horizon is introduced. We explore examples of innovation networks across different levels, units and horizons. Finally a number of theoretical frameworks are introduced that help the reader to understand intra- and inter-organisational networks.

The Bibliothèque Nationale de France (BNF) in Paris is the largest documentation centre in France and contains an estimated 14 million resources, including print material, manuscripts, photographs, maps, coins, medals and multimedia documents. The BNF is organised into fourteen departments across five sites and has 2,400 employees (as of 2013).[1] One of these sites is the Bibliothèque de l'Arsenal, which is devoted to sixteenth- to nineteenth-century French arts, literature and historical documents. The thirteen remaining departments are specialised in widely differing fields. One of the strengths of the BNF is its openness to external collaboration, and it is involved in many networks at national, European and international levels. Examples include participating in joint electronic databases with other libraries in France and abroad, carrying out research alliances that require close coordination and working with partners on a regular basis. One of its projects is the development of Gallica, its electronic library system. Gallica is the result of collaboration between many institutions, including the

---

[1] Information about the BNF can be found in the Annual Report 2013, accessible at webapp.bnf.fr/rapport/pdf/rapport_2013.pdf, accessed 22 July 2106.

Ministry of Culture, Centre National du Livre (National Book Centre), Syndicat national de l'édition (Publishers Association), private firms and other electronic resource distributors. Inside France, the BNF is part of a national network of libraries and participates in research programmes and committees, provides expertise in document restoration and preservation, and is involved in the organisation of promotional and digitisation activities.

BNF is a nested network; it is a single node in an inter-organisational network in France and abroad. But BNF is also an inter-organisational network in itself. At this second level of the nested network, the nodes are each of its fourteen departments of which the Bibliothèque de l'Arsenal is one. Further down in this nested network, the Bibliothèque de l'Arsenal and the other thirteen departments can also be seen as individual networks. At this third level, each library is a network of individual departments or teams – human resources, public services, project teams, electronic support and so on. Furthermore, each of these departments is composed of people who belong to informal networks, cutting across departmental and organisational boundaries.

The BNF is not an exception. All organisations can be seen as nested networks and social network analysis can be performed at inter-organisational, intra-organisational or market levels. One of the capabilities in network management is to understand what level of analysis has what implications in different innovation processes. This chapter explores how networks at each level of analysis are related to different aspects of the innovation process. It also introduces the notion of network horizon, which is related to the question of how far to extend consideration of a network, depending on a specific aim.

3.1 Hierarchical Nesting of Networks

It is useful to think of innovation networks in terms of level and unit of analysis, and network horizon.

- **Level of analysis:** refers to the distinction between inter-organisational, intra-organisational and market levels. Inter-organisational networks include ties that are external to organisations and intra-organisational networks consist only of ties that are internal to an organisation. The choice of where the boundaries of an organisation are drawn depends on the analyst. The market level includes networks of users.
- **Unit of analysis:** refers to how a node is defined in a network, which can be an individual, team, organisation, concept or artefact. Concepts can be

knowledge fields, technology domains or keywords; common artefacts used are patents, products and publications.
- **Network horizon:** refers to the question of how far to look in a network. This can be the dyad level, which includes a pair of nodes; the egocentric level, which takes a focal node (ego) and the nodes that ego has ties with (alters), and the ties between those alters; or the broader network level, which encompasses a wider range of actors in a given industry, technology or organisation.

While unit of analysis is concerned with how nodes are defined, level of analysis refers to whether the network is built to analyse the patterns of relations that are internal or external to an organisation or market. Figure 3.1 illustrates these with a hypothetical nested network. The nodes and solid edges show individuals and the ties between them, which can be friendship, advice, co-working and so on. Organisational boundaries are shown as

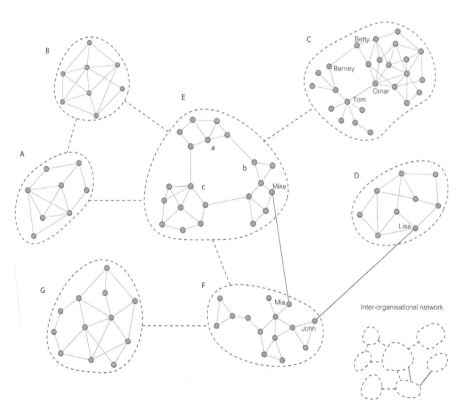

Figure 3.1   Networks as Nested Systems: Distinguishing between the Intra-organisational and Inter-organisational Levels

dotted borders that surround nodes. There are a total of seven organisations, A–G. Dotted edges between organisations show inter-organisational ties. Each organisation is shown as a cluster of people who have more ties between themselves internally than ties with others external to the organisation. In one of the organisations, E, three departments are shown: a, b and c.

The smaller figure at the lower right of Figure 3.1 shows the same network, taking *organisations* as unit of analysis and *inter-organisational* as level of analysis. The position of organisations in a strategic alliance network determines their access to external resources and capabilities, which can be critical in innovation. An example of an inter-organisational network with *inventor* as unit of analysis is a network showing co-inventions between different organisations. For example, in the network in Figure 3.1 assume Mike and Mia have co-published a patent, as have Lisa and John. Including all inventor collaborations that take place across different firms would yield an inter-organisational network with *individual* as the unit of analysis.

Of course real-world networks are often more complex than the one shown in Figure 3.1 and there are also many ways in which networks can be constructed. To clarify many different possibilities, Table 3.1 summarises possible units and levels of analysis, as well as tie and node definitions that are commonly used in the analysis of innovation networks.

3.2   The Network Horizon: How Far to Look

The network horizon is rather like 'zooming in' on and 'zooming out' of networks. Network horizon refers to how far to look in a network, beyond immediately adjacent nodes. The network horizon can be taken as a continuum, ranging from the shortsighted consideration of the most proximate nodes and ties, to overseeing the architecture of relations that lie further ahead. When we take a broader perspective of the network, the emphasis shifts from nearest (or adjacent) partners to the network as a whole.

It is useful to think of networks in terms of horizon because sometimes it is necessary to zoom out to see the big picture, and at other times it is necessary to zoom in on the qualitative aspects of a few individual ties. For example, deep resource commitment to a single alliance might risk ignoring possible synergies with different alliances. Failing to oversee the whole network of different departments within a firm might prevent the cross-fertilisation of ideas and transfer of relevant know-how across units and reinforce departmental silos. Sometimes zooming out can show where knowledge is

Table 3.1 Levels and Units of Analysis (Examples)

		Unit of Analysis		
		Individual	Group	Concepts, Artefacts, Products
	Nodes can be:	• inventors • employees • board members • managers • potential or current consumers	• organisations • departments • Strategic business units (SBUs) • teams	• knowledge fields • technologies • patents • keywords • competences • publications
Market	*Links can be:*	• influence	• influence or imitation between complementors, communities	• interdependence between products
Level of Analysis Inter-organisational	*Links can be:*	• co-patenting • inventor mobility • board interlocks • citations between inventors in different firms	• R&D alliances • litigations • licensing • equity arrangements and other contracts • supply chain • joint projects • joint membership in consortia	• patent citations • joint patent applications • proximity between organisations in competences, technologies, markets, etc.
Intra-organisational	*Links can be:*	• informal networks (friendship or advice) in or across business units • inventor joint publications • project co-work • citations between inventors in the firm	• knowledge flows between departments or SBUs	• knowledge or competence maps • interdependence between projects, products, modules

concentrated in the network, how knowledge clusters are linked and who the critical actors are. Zooming in can reveal the micro-processes of tie formation, their maintenance and how tie content influences processes like knowledge transfer. For example, one of the challenges of sponsoring an innovation is to distinguish influence from similar tastes. Do people in a group have similar adoption patterns because they are influenced by each other? Or do they form a group in the first place because they share similar tastes? Distinguishing these two effects is important when deciding how to promote an innovation. These questions can be better addressed by having a good understanding of how ties form – in other words by zooming in on the network. Deciding when to zoom in and when to zoom out is not always straightforward, and I will explore this further in Chapter 5.

Figure 3.2 clarifies the network horizon concept at the intra- and inter-organisational levels. The upper part of the figure shows the inter-organisational level of analysis and the part below the intra-organisational level. At both levels the network horizon broadens as one moves up (inter-organisational) and down (intra-organisational).

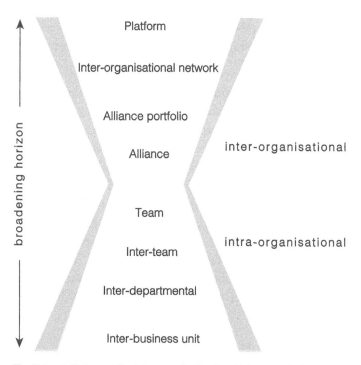

Figure 3.2   The Network Horizon at the Intra-organisational and Inter-organisational Levels
Note: Narrow parts illustrate *zooming in* at the micro-level, broader parts show *zooming out* to take into consideration aggregate networks.

3.3   The Upper Network Horizon: Inter-organisational Level

The term network can have two different meanings in inter-organisational research. The first refers to a specific governance structure, the 'network-based organisation'.[2] The second uses the term network in a generic way, forms where all governance can be represented as networks.

Research on the network-based organisation emphasises the gradual transition that has taken place in the organisation of economic activities over the last three decades, from vertically integrated corporations towards networks of small and flexible firms. Trust between firms and sharing of resources and knowledge have been the hallmarks of this form of governance. These networks are facilitated by the development of a common language among member firms, signalling legitimate and illegitimate behaviour, as well as reputation and status. One of the characteristics of these persistent networks is trust, which reduces the costs of opportunistic behaviour. This form of governance has been associated with embeddedness, signifying that economic relations are inseparable from social contexts.[3] The nature of links in a network usually varies from short-term, arm's-length relations to long-term or renewed partnerships. Oliver (1990) identifies six motives for inter-organisational relations:

- **Necessity:** organisations sometimes form ties to meet legal or regulatory requirements. For example, a common strategy for multinational companies looking for foreign market entry is to find a partner in the host country. This is sometimes regulated by host governments, obliging firms to form alliances with a local partner for technology transfer.
- **Asymmetry:** refers to the use of power or influence of one organisation over another. Resource scarcity may induce firms to exercise power or influence over other firms that have the scarce resource. For example, a corporation can form a board interlock with a financial institution to have access to credits and other financial resources.
- **Reciprocity:** refers to collaboration and cooperation rather than the exercise of power (horizontal rather than vertical links). Reciprocal motives

---

[2] On the nature and characteristics of network forms of organisation, see Jones, Hesterly and Borgatti (1997) and Powell (1990).

[3] Smelser and Swedberg (2005: 3) define economic sociology as 'the application of the frames of reference, variables and explanatory variables of sociology to that complex of activities which is concerned with the production, distribution, exchange and consumption of scarce goods and redources'.

lead to alliances when partnerships are formed with a common and mutual interest in sharing resources and knowledge.

- **Efficiency:** refers to the effort to improve the internal input–output ratio. When market-based exchanges are more efficient than vertical integration (known as the make-or-buy decision), organisations partner to economise on costs.
- **Stability:** organisations may form alliances as an adaptive response to uncertainties. In particular, in industries characterised by rapid technological change, firms form alliances with others to pool knowledge and information about technologies and markets.
- **Legitimacy:** organisations form alliances to improve reputation, image and prestige.

The importance of each of these motivations varies according to strategic, economic, institutional and technological conditions. For example, in uncertain and highly competitive industries, reciprocity and stability can be important motives, whereas in the case of joint ventures in biotechnology there is an asymmetry effect, where larger firms exercise organisational control over smaller firms (Kogut, 1988). The major schools of thought in explaining inter-organisational networks as a form of governance are explored further in Boxes 3.1, 3.2 and 3.3.

The second way in which the term network is used in inter-organisational research is as a structural way to represent relations. According to this use of the term, all organisational forms and governances can be viewed as networks, without referring to a network as a specific form of governance. Relationships between organisations can be strategic alliances, participation in consortia or trade associations, relations within the supply chain, licensing agreements, patent litigation – and other types of relationships that can be expressed in the form of networks.

The upper part of Figure 3.2 shows four levels of the network horizon.

3.3.1 Alliance Level

The narrowest network horizon at the inter-organisational level is a single alliance.[4] In Figure 3.1 an example is the tie between E and C. At this level ties can be mergers and acquisitions, licensing and cross-licensing

---

[4] For strategic alliance management see Das (2012).

Box 3.1 Networks and Transaction Cost Theories

In transaction cost economics (TCE), the choice between markets and hierarchies depends on transaction costs (Williamson, 1975). In market contracting, transactions are non-repetitive and involve standardised products; there is technological stability, and communication is carried out by means of prices. In a hierarchy, assets are tightly controlled and all transactions are internalised. Once resources are committed under pure market exchange, irreversibility and specificity render parties vulnerable to possible opportunistic behaviour in the future (known as the hold-up problem). In addition, because of bounded rationality and uncertainty, future conditions cannot be predicted in advance. These factors increase the transaction costs of pure market exchange, especially when exchanges are carried out on a more frequent basis. Firms are created to economise on such transaction costs. In TCE, the network is a hybrid form between a market and a hierarchy. Networks are neither as rigid as hierarchies, nor as flexible and anonymous as a market exchange. Rather, network governance is 'a select, persistent and structured set of autonomous firms engaged in creating products or services based on implicit and open-ended contracts to adapt to environmental contingencies and to coordinate and safeguard exchanges' (Jones, Hesterly and Borgatti, 1997). TCE has been criticised on several grounds. The central place of opportunism in TCE shifts attention away from trust and the embeddedness of economic relations in social contexts. TCE's focus on efficiency disregards strategy and the organisational learning aspects of networks. In addition, most authors have pointed out that in the face of rapid economic and technological change, TCE represents a static cost trade-off analysis that cannot be used to explain dynamic gains from networks.

Further Reading

Özman, M. (2009). Inter-firm Networks and Innovation: a Survey of Literature. *Economics of Innovation and New Technology*, 181, 39–67.

Powell, W. (1990). Neither Market Nor Hierarchy: Network Forms of Organization, *Research in Organisational Behavior,* 12, 295–336.

Thorelli, H. B. (1986). Networks: between Markets and Hierarchies. *Strategic Management Journal,* 7, 37–5.

---

agreements, R&D alliances, marketing alliances and others. Three stages in alliances can be distinguished: formation, operation and outcome (Das and Teng, 2002). As far as their effect on innovative capabilities is concerned, the most important part of alliances is related with learning and each stage of an alliance is characterised by different learning processes (Das and Kumar, 2007). The strength of an alliance tie is revealed by resource commitment, timespan, repeatability and trust between firms; alliance strength is an

---

Box 3.2 Resource-based and Knowledge-based Theories

According to the resource-based view (Wernerfelt, 1984), an organisation is a bundle of resources and the most common motive for collaborating with others is resource complementarity. The knowledge-based view regards an organisation's key resource as knowledge. Grant (1996b) explains organisations in terms of the coordination they provide to integrate the specialist knowledge of individual members. Markets cannot maintain this coordination because knowledge is tacit and immobile, and production requires individual specialists. In these approaches, firm boundaries are explained in terms of organisational capabilities. When complementary capabilities require tight coordination that an organisation cannot provide, intermediate solutions may emerge, such as licensing, alliances and joint ventures. In other words, organisations are not self-sufficient – they collaborate to access each other's resources and reduce uncertainty. In sectors where interrelatedness is high, technological complementarities are a significant motive. Other motivations include access to markets and shorter innovation periods. For example, in biotechnology, the complexity and multi-disciplinary character of the knowledge base are key factors that draw firms into external collaborations. The knowledge base is dispersed and collaborations often link large pharmaceutical firms, which offer market access opportunities, with small firms that can provide new scientific and technological approaches. Appropriability conditions are also important in determining collaborations. Gulati and Singh (1998) have found that the more coordination costs are related to interdependence, and the weaker the appropriability regime, the more firms are likely to have structures with high hierarchical control.

Further Reading

Das, T. K., and B. S. Teng (2000). A Resource-based View of Strategic Alliances. *Journal of Management*, 26(1), 31–61.

Pfeffer, J., and G. Salancik (1978). *The External Control of Organizations: A Resource Dependence Perspective*, New York, NY: Harper and Row.

Wernerfelt, B. (1984). A Resource-based View of the Firm. *Strategic Management Journal*, 5(2), 171–80.

---

important element of the effectiveness of knowledge transfer mechanisms. Alliance management capabilities are dynamic capabilities controlling the extent to which organisations are able to leverage previous alliance experiences by acquiring and internalising new knowledge, deepening their existing knowledge and increasing their ability to select partners and operate alliances in an effective way in the future. Alliance management will be more fully covered in Chapter 6.

Box 3.3 Networks and the Learning Perspective

The learning perspective is another theoretical stream that explains inter-organisational collaborations. Organisations collaborate with each other not only because they lack resources and need access to those of others, but in order to learn from each other. Powell, Koput and Smith-Doerr's (1996) seminal work in biotechnology places organisational learning at the centre of the literature of networks. Distinguishing between exploration and exploitation in organisational learning, the former refers to 'experimentation with new alternatives', and the latter to the exercise of 'refinement and extension of existing competencies, technologies and paradigms' (March, 1991). According to Powell, Koput and Smith-Doerr (1996), organisational learning depends both on access to new knowledge and on having the capacity to use and build on it. Networks enable firms to explore new knowledge effectively and to complement it by building on their own internal knowledge. Collaboration between firms not only enhances learning about new developments but also strengthens internal competencies; for this reason, the 'locus of innovation' can be found in learning networks (Powell, Koput and Smith-Doerr, 1996). Both the learning approach and networks are explored further in Chapter 7.

3.3.2   Alliance Portfolio

The next level in the network horizon is the alliance portfolio of an organisation. In the network of Figure 3.1, the alliance portfolio of E includes A, B, C and F. An alliance portfolio includes all the alliance partners as well as the ties between them. For example, A and B have a tie so the information that E obtains from both might be redundant. But C and F are not connected, so E may have access to novel information from its ties with each of them. Managing an alliance portfolio involves coordinating different partnerships, overseeing and leveraging their complementarities and differences.

3.3.3   Inter-organisational Networks

Zooming further out from portfolios, we reach the network level. In this level a wide range of organisations in a certain industry or technology field are included (Section 4.1.2). In the small-scale network at the bottom-right of Figure 3.1, the organisations are shown as nodes and the links between them show alliances. An important concept at the network level is structural embeddedness, which refers to the informational benefits that firms can access through the structural position they occupy in the network (Gulati, 1998; Rowley, Behrens and Krackhardt, 2000). Their position in the network has implications for resource, knowledge and market access, learning and knowledge transfer, or innovative performance.

3.3.4   Platform

The next level in the network horizon is platform. At this level different types of population and their interactions are included (firms, customers, suppliers, etc.). Baker and Faulkner's (2002) inter-organisational network illustrates this level; they represent networks across three populations (suppliers, producers and buyers) and the multiple types of relationship that characterise ties between them.

This level includes multi-sided platforms (MSPs) with indirect network externalities between different populations, which are most often complementors and final users.[5] An MSP is defined as 'one who creates value primarily by enabling direct interactions between two or more distinct types of affiliated customers' (Hagiu and Wright, 2011). Platforms are sometimes based on a proprietary technology surrounded by a range of different types of actor supplying complementary products and services to the platform. For example, the video games industry is an MSP consisting of game editors, game designers, console manufacturers, customers and so on. Sony's strong relations with game developers played a major role in the success of its video game platform PlayStation. Halving the industry norm licensing fees and making its development platform easily accessible made the development of games much cheaper and easier.[6]

3.4   The Lower Network Horizon: Intra-organisational Level

The lower part of the network horizon in Figure 3.2 shows intra-organisational networks. At this level network analysis can be used for many purposes. The structure of intra-organisational networks depends on factors like the strategic priorities of organisations, organisation of tasks, organisational structure, task-related information flows and culture. So, even within the same field of activity the structure of intra-organisational networks can differ significantly. Box 3.4 describes the informal networks inside three European municipalities: Rotterdam, Copenhagen and Barcelona.

Analysis of intra-organisational networks is also beneficial during the implementation of organisational change projects, like the introduction of

---

[5] On the essentials of product platforms, see Meyer and Lehnerd (1997) and Gawer and Cusumano (2002).

[6] See, for example, Rochet and Tirole (2010) for an analytical model of indirect network externalities in multi-sided markets. For complementor strategies, see Yoffie and Kwak (2006). Tie formation processes between different actors in platforms are covered in Chapter 11.

Box 3.4 The Network Structure of the Municipalities of Copenhagen, Barcelona and Rotterdam

Project LIPSE (Learning Innovation in Public Sector Environments) is funded by the seventh framework programme of the EU (FP7). It identifies the barriers to and drivers of social innovation in the public sector in eleven EU countries. In one part of the project, SNA has been used to map the network structures of workflows and information networks in a few European cities (Lewis and Ricard, 2014; Lewis et al., 2014). The strategic access information network was formed by posing the following question:

> Looking back over the last six months, who did you go to most when you wanted to get strategic information about something in the municipality (including background information not yet available in reports)? List up to five people either inside or outside the municipality and indicate each person's position and organisation or relationship to you. (RR1: 53).

The resulting networks are shown in Figures 3.3, 3.4 and 3. 5. According to the research results, in Copenhagen, which scores highest in terms of social innovation performance, level 2 managers are the most well connected to important others; in Rotterdam it is the directors (senior) and in Barcelona the politicians, followed by level 2 managers. The Barcelona network shows a very clear core-periphery structure, in which the core seems to be composed of the higher-level hierarchy. At the same time, the networks of central actors have more closure, which may imply limited access to diversity. The Rotterdam network is composed of densely connected pockets with shortcuts between them and brokers who are senior directors dispersed throughout the network. The Copenhagen case is quite different. First, it has separated divisions, in which intra-divisional communication is higher. In addition, middle managers have a mixture of open and closed ties in their immediate networks, giving them access to diversity as well as the advantages of closure, which is often considered beneficial for innovation performance.

---

a new management system, change of key personnel, adoption of a new technology or a major reorganisation. For one thing formal change also brings change in informal networks (see Chapter 10). Understanding how informal networks respond to formal change can be critical for the successful implementation of change.[7] In most cases people are resistant to organisational change projects. Informal networks can be influential in coping with resistance. Here, boundary spanners who bridge silos within an organisation can play a critical role in disseminating information, overcoming uncertainties or resistance to change. In Figure 3.1, consider Omar and Tom or Betty and Barney, who bridge different groups (or departments) inside C.

---

[7] See, for example, Kleinbaum and Stuart (2014) and Gulati and Puranam (2009).

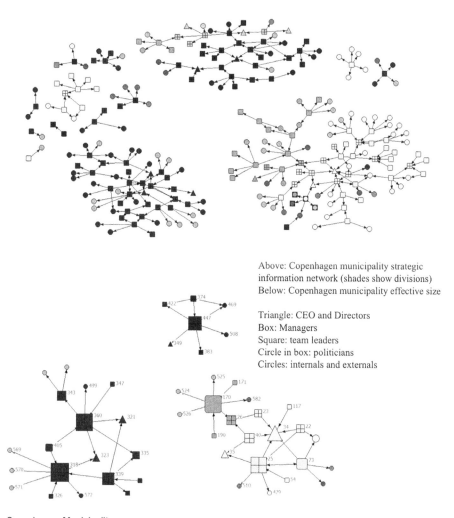

Above: Copenhagen municipality strategic
information network (shades show divisions)
Below: Copenhagen municipality effective size

Triangle: CEO and Directors
Box: Managers
Square: team leaders
Circle in box: politicians
Circles: internals and externals

Figure 3.3   Copenhagen Municipality

3.4.1   Teams

The first level of the network horizon involves team formation for specific
tasks or projects. In Figure 3.1, network E-a can be taken as a project team.
One of the factors that influence team performance is diversity, especially in
projects where creativity or task-specific problem-solving skills are required.
Team diversity can be represented in acquired characteristics (education,
knowledge background, etc.) or inherent characteristics (age, gender, race, etc.).
While different dimensions of diversity are often considered beneficial for
creativity, the nature of a task, complexity, tacit knowledge or increased need

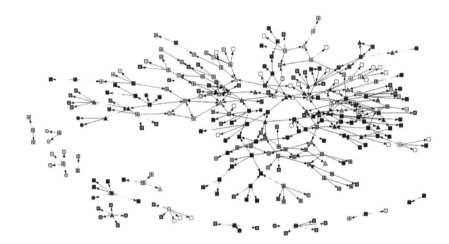

Above: Rotterdam municipality strategic information network
Below: Rotterdam municipality effective size

Triangle: CEO and Directors
Box: Managers
Square: non-leaders
Circle in a box: all others (politicians and lower levels)

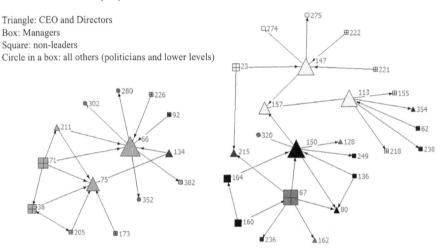

Figure 3.4   Rotterdam Municipality

for conflict resolution can also call for more homogeneous teams to facilitate communication between members. These issues will be explored in Chapter 7.

3.4.2   Inter-team Relations

Explaining inter-team relations at the design and innovations consultancy IDEO, Kelley (2001) writes about the benefits of an open culture and seamless communication between teams. At IDEO, teams that are

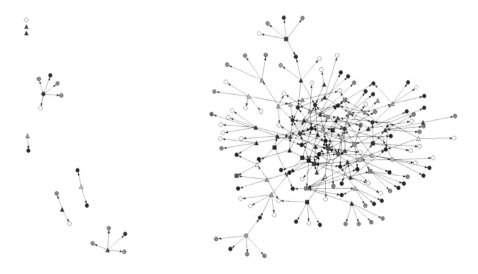

Above: Barcelona municipality strategic information network
Below: Barcelona municipality effective size
Triangle: Level 1 Directors   Box: Managers   Square: Team leaders   Circle: no information

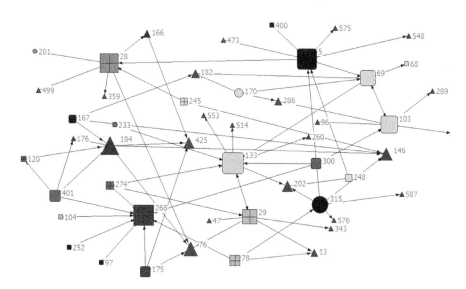

Figure 3.5   Barcelona Municipality

experienced in different industries are encouraged to communicate with each other to ensure the cross-pollination of ideas and knowledge. An open culture facilitates analogous thinking, where concepts, ideas or solutions in one domain can be applied to problems in different domains. The specialisation of different teams in different industries often makes communication between them difficult. As a result, teams can become largely isolated from each other resulting in impermeable knowledge bubbles. In this case, boundary spanners are better positioned to spot opportunities for innovative recombinations across different groups (Burt, 2004). They also have an important role in referring people to each other when there is a need to complement diverse capabilities.

Boundary spanners also have an important role in bringing external knowledge inside an organisation. For example, in the network shown in Figure 3.1, Mike in E works with Mia in F, making him a boundary spanner for organisation E (Mia herself is also a boundary spanner for organisation F). In some cases knowledge accessed and acquired outside the organisation might be difficult to integrate inside, depending on people's openness and the extent to which the boundary spanner has effective internal network links. For example, Figure 3.1 shows that Mike has two links in his department but Mia has only one (although her alter is quite central). For Mike's knowledge to be diffused and integrated in other departments, organisation E needs channels between department b and others.

3.4.3   Inter-departmental Relations

The third level in the network horizon involves relations between departments. The lack or weakness of inter-departmental ties can be a serious impediment to innovations. Successful innovation requires integration of user needs, market segments, technological trends or distribution systems (Dougherty, 1992). When the insights provided by different departments are not integrated effectively, departmental thought worlds can form a barrier to effective collaboration between people and prevent the synthesis of people's diverse experiences in the innovation process. Departmental thought worlds refer to the processes by which people in the same department (R&D, manufacturing, sales, etc.) develop common and shared understandings about a particular aspect of the innovation process and are unable to think outside them or share them with other departments. Segmented interpretive schemes and selective filtering by departments can inhibit effective collaboration. Dougherty (1992) describes departmental thought worlds as distinct ways in which technology-market links are interpreted by departments, in terms of future expectations in uncertain markets, critical aspects of the product development process and the way people understand product development itself.

In periods of crisis, informal networks can play an important part in resolving conflicts, which often arise through formal networks that dictate co-working patterns. Crises often provoke uncertainty, to which people respond by increasing commitment to their cohesive networks and trusted peers and reducing cooperation with other sub-units (Krackhardt and Stern, 1988). In this way crises increase the possibility of conflict in the organisation. Krackhardt and Stern (1988) find that organisations are more effective in handling crises when there are friendship ties across departments.

3.4.4   Strategic Business Unit Networks

The broadest level in the network horizon is links between business units in multi-unit firms. Relations between strategic business units (SBUs) are critical for the transfer of best practices that can enable significant cost savings. For example in BP's peer assist programme (Hansen, 2009), business unit heads and engineers are encouraged to ask for problem-solving and technical advice from other similar business units. Weak inter-unit ties can speed up the search for information but stronger ties are needed for joint problem-solving, especially when knowledge is complex, context-specific and tacit (Hansen, 1999). In other words, for more effective inter-unit ties communication channels should be aligned with the nature of what is communicated. An SBU's links with other units are also correlated with its innovative performance. In the case of two companies in very different sectors – food manufacturing and petrochemicals – Tsai (2001) found that the centrality of a business unit is an important source of its innovative performance.

Discussion Questions

1. What is meant by level of analysis, unit of analysis and network horizon in network management?

2. Find examples for the following:
   a. An intra-organisational network with nodes as artefacts
   b. An intra-organisational network with nodes as persons
   c. An inter-organisational network with nodes as persons
   d. An inter-organisational network with nodes as groups
   e. Market-level network with nodes as groups.

3. Why is it sometimes necessary to zoom in, and at other times necessary to zoom out of networks?

4. What can be taken as the links, nodes, level of analysis and network horizon, in the following situations:
   a. Analysing your organisation's knowledge and specialisation and how it evolved in the last five years.
   b. Improving creativity in your organisation.
   c. Spreading the word in the neighbourhood.
   d. Managing a new product development team that is designing a wearable to measure sports performance. You aim to find alternative uses for the product.
   e. Promoting sustainable consumption in a community.

4 | Social Network Analysis for Innovation Networks

Any fact becomes important when it's connected to another.

Umberto Eco

> In this chapter we explore the basics of social network analysis, and introduce some essential mathematical notation. We go through some of the commonly used social network metrics and methods in innovation studies, for example, node-based metrics, knowledge mapping, and some well-known global network structures. We understand why and how these methods are used by providing contextual examples. Some data sources in innovation networks, like bibliometric data, strategic alliance data, and data collected through surveys and interviews, are explained. Finally, some key debates in social network theory are introduced.

SNA refers to a range of techniques in graph theory, used to analyse network structure. Over the last fifty years, methods for analysing social networks have developed rapidly. There are many valuable sources on social network analysis and a range of (mostly free) network analysis software.[1]

This chapter looks at SNA techniques and three ways in which they are used in innovation studies. The first uses node-based SNA metrics to analyse the positions of individual actors (firms, individuals, teams and so on) in a network, and how these metrics are related to the nodes' characteristics, behaviour or performance. The second is detecting subgroups, or clusters, with certain characteristics within a network, for example, groups in which people

---

[1] Borgatti, Everett and Johnson (2013); Wasserman and Faust (1994); Brass et al. (2014); see also Robert Hanneman's webpage (http://faculty.ucr.edu/~hanneman/nettext/, accessed 5 July 2016). Online documentation is very rich for the following software packages: UCINET (Borgatti, S.P., Everett, M.G. and Freeman, L.C. (2002) Ucinet for Windows: Software for Social Network Analysis. Harvared, MA: Analytic Technologies; PAJEK (Batagelj, V. and A. Mrvar: Pajek – Program for Large Network Analysis. Home page: http://vlado.fmf.uni-lj.si/pub/networks/pajek/); iGraph in R platform (Csardi G, Nepusz T. (2006) The igraph software package for complex network research, InterJournal, Complex Systems 1695 (http://igraph.org).

have dense networks within technology domains that are closely related to each other or important patents in the evolution of a technology. The third is exploring the implications of global networks for a given purpose. For example, which network structures are the most appropriate for knowledge diffusion? Which networks deter creativity? In this third category, the focus is on global network characteristics, like density, small-world coefficient and centralisation. Finally, some central debates in social network theory have implications for innovation networks, and these are covered in the last section of this chapter.

4.1   Network Data Sources in Innovation Studies

Various data sources can be used to construct and analyse innovation networks at the inter-organisational, intra-organisational and market levels. Commonly used data sources for inter-organisational networks are strategic alliance databases, patent data, data on project partnerships, litigations, board interlocks, underwriting syndicates and interviews and surveys.[2] Survey and questionnaires and market research are used as data sources for the diffusion of innovations and user behaviour, but in recent years social media data sources have been increasingly used.[3] Intra-organisational network data are often collected through sociometric questionnaires to map friendship or advice networks in related units of an organisation, or among inventors or scientists in an area of interest.[4] (Some examples of commonly used survey questions are reproduced in the Appendix.) Archival sources are also used.[5] Bibliometric data are commonly used in innovation and in science and technology studies; other sources of archival data include conference or event participations, e-mail (or other electronic) correspondence and membership of clubs and associations.

---

[2] Some commonly used strategic alliance databases are as follows: MERIT /CATI, SDC Platinum. For biotechnology, BioScan, Core, Recap. For comparison of these databases see Schilling (2008). Patent litigation data sources are MaxVal, Lexmachina. Commonly used patent databases are USPTO and EPO/PATSTAT; for project data in Framework programs see CorBIS. Also see the website of complex networks by Mark Newman for some open data on networks (www-personal.umich.edu/~mejn/net data/, accessed 5 July 2016).

[3] See Appendix for examples of survey questions according to different purposes. Some studies using online data sources are: instant messaging in Yahoo (Aral, Muchnik, Sundararajan, 2009); Twitter (Bakshy et al., 2011; Romero et al., 2011); Facebook (Goel, Watts and Goldstein, 2012). For the evolution of social networking sites (SNS), see Ellison and Boyd (2013) and Kane et al. (2014).

[4] An initial sociometric analysis of scientists in a field was made by Diana Crane in 1969, where she detected 'invisible colleges' in which scientists are more densely involved in collaborations than scientists in other fields. See Crane (1969).

[5] See Borgatti, Everett and Johnson (2013) for discussion of archival and sociometric data.

4.1.1   Bibliometric Data

Bibliometric data provide detailed information about scientific publications and patents. Patent data give rich insights about the knowledge bases of firms, the sources of their knowledge, their inventive output, knowledge flows between firms and their environment, and their competitive positioning in the technology space. Patent analysis yields important insights in guiding firms' strategic decisions (Ernst, 2003). Patent data are also used to map knowledge dynamics in regions. Examples include inventors' mobility,[6] knowledge flow between inventors within and outside regions, inter-firm collaborations and the evolution of regional knowledge.[7] Patent data are also used for mapping the nature and evolution of technology domains.

While patent data are widely used, there are downsides in using them to analyse innovation networks. First, patents are output-based measures and a firm's knowledge base is not necessarily revealed by its patents. For example, in the telecommunications sector, firm knowledge is embedded in routines and operational procedures, and there is far less patenting intensity than in other science-based sectors like chemicals. Also, patents measure inventions, not innovations.[8] The commercialisation of inventions requires the capability to integrate effective funding, design, marketing and manufacturing, which are not reflected in patents.

As Figure 4.1 shows, patents measure only a small part of the innovation space. The extent of patenting depends on the industry and firm strategies. In industries where knowledge is codified, innovations are easily imitable, R&D requires large capital investments and patents correspond directly to products (like pharmaceuticals), patenting intensity is higher. On the other hand, there is likely to be less propensity to patent where knowledge is tacit, imitation difficult, products draw on several patents and product life cycles are short, as observed in high-tech sectors such as information communications technologies (ICT) (Orsenigo and Sterzi, 2010). Process innovations also tend to be patented less than product innovations (Arundel and Kabla, 1998). Some firms use patenting strategically to prevent other firms entering

---

[6] For example, Agrawal, Cockburn and McHale (2006) show that knowledge spillovers are also a feature of inventors' previous localities, pointing to the role of social capital.

[7] On patent networks in regions, see Owen-Smith and Powell (2004). Ter Wal (2013) analyses the evolution of networks in life sciences and information technology in Sophia Antipolis through a patent-based network analysis (see Terwal and Boschma, 2009, for a review).

[8] See Griliches (1990) for a review and evaluation of using patent data for innovation. See also Gambardella, Harhoff and Verspagen (2008), PATVAL: 'The Value of European Patents: Evidence from a Survey of European Inventors', available at http://ec.europa.eu/invest-in-research/pdf/download_en/patval_mainreportandannexes.pdf, accessed 5 July 2016).

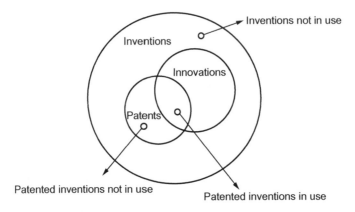

Figure 4.1   The Relation between Inventions, Innovations and Patents
Source: Basberg (1987)

a specific technology domain. For all these reasons, it is important to be cautious when interpreting results obtained from patent-based analysis.

4.1.2   Boundary Specification

Boundary specification is about sampling in network data.[9] Laumann, Marsden and Prensky (1989) distinguish three generic boundary specification strategies.

- **Positional approach:** this considers the attributes of actors and network membership criteria, for example, employment in an organisation or a strategic alliance in a predetermined domain or industry. Initially an industry or organisation is selected, and only members of this set are included in the network.
- **Event-based strategies:** actors are selected on the basis of their participation in a pre-defined set of activities, for example, industry fairs, conferences or similar. Because there is the risk of missing important actors in the network if they do not attend these events, as many events as possible are included in the sample.
- **Relational strategies:** here, the main criterion is connectedness. The researcher begins with a few actors and gradually expands the network sample by name generators, suggested by the initial respondents. Knoke and Yang (2008) list four procedures that can be used in relational strategies. In the *reputational method*, some pre-selected experts are asked to nominate a set of actors. *Snowball sampling* begins with a small set of actors who nominate

---

[9] See Marsden (2005) for reviews of important issues involved in network data collection.

others with whom they have a specific relation. In the *fixed list method*, a pre-defined list of actors is provided and the respondents are asked to indicate their ties on the list. With *expanding selection*, respondents are asked to identify as many ties as they can, without being restricted to a pre-defined list.

Risks of Omission. One of the important issues in survey design is the risk of omitting actors. Kossinets (2006) analysed the effects of three common reasons of omission in bipartite networks: poor boundary specification, non-response and fixed-choice name generators. Kossinets found that all these could have different but serious effects on social network metrics. In particular, clustering and assortativity coefficients (i.e. the tendency of similar nodes (in terms of an external interia like degrees) to be connected to each other) can be overestimated as a result of fixed-choice designs and poor boundary specification, and under-estimated as a result of non-response or inaccurate responses from participants.

Boundary Specification in Bibliometric Data. The boundaries of data depend largely on the research question. In some fields, a specific technology class is already defined on formal patent classification systems like World Intellectual Property Organization (WIPO) International Patent Classification. For example, in analysing semiconductor networks only the patents that belong to the semiconductor patent class can be included, as a patent in this field includes the relevant technology class. In other cases, technology domains may not be well defined and may include several patent classes together. In this case, a possible strategy is to contact experts, collect keywords and detect the relevant patents based on text mining. Focusing only on patents in a specific technology is likely to exclude the underlying know-ledge it draws on (upstream), as well as the fields it influences (downstream). For example, assuming that the core set includes patents granted in the field of semiconductors (which has a specific technology class) would exclude patents that influence the knowledge base of this field. To analyse knowledge flows between different technologies it is necessary to include patents that are cited by the core set of patents, as well as patents that cite the core set.

4.2 Basic Notation

In the following three sections, some commonly used social network metrics in innovation studies are introduced. While it is commonplace to utilise social network software to calculate these metrics in social network analysis, some of the basic formulae are presented here, to give a better understanding of how they are used in innovation network analysis.

The basic form of social network data is an adjacency matrix, which can be expressed as matrix A of size n × n, where n denotes the number of nodes (or vertices), and $a_{ij} = 0$ if there is no edge between vertices i and j. If there is an edge between them, $a_{ij} > 0$. In some cases, there is only information that a tie exists between i and j, then we take $a_{ij} = 1$. In other cases we may have information (or we derive information) about the weight of a tie between two nodes. For example, in a co-inventor network, the nodes are inventors and there will be a link between two inventors if they publish a patent together. Then a weighted link between two inventors may refer to the number of patents they have published jointly. If they have co-authored three patents, then, $a_{ij} = 3$. In what follows, unless specified otherwise, I take binary values of a_{ij}, where $a_{ij} = 1$ if there is a tie between i and j, and 0 otherwise.

A tie between two nodes i and j can be directed or undirected. For example, patent citation networks are by definition directed. A tie between the cited patent and the citing patent denotes the direction of the flow of knowledge, indicating that the knowledge in the old patent was used in producing the new patent. Obviously, an old patent cannot cite a newer patent. In a strategic alliance network ties are usually not directed, because an agreement is signed mutually by two organisations. An advice network is directed as well, as there are sources and recipients of advice. Most of the network metrics given below should be corrected as necessary when the network is weighted and/or directed. To illustrate these, Figure 4.2 shows four network configurations, and corresponding adjacency matrices, depending on whether a network is weighted, directed, or not.

4.3   Focus on the Node

Nodes can be firms, inventors, teams, individuals or artefacts (see Table 3.1). In innovation studies, sometimes we need to assess the importance of a node. Importance can be defined in different ways, for example, a node's closeness to other nodes, its potential to influence others, its control of information flows or the extent to which it bridges different parts of the network. Node-based measures are commonly used in innovation studies according to different purposes.

4.3.1   Prominence of Nodes in Advice Networks

Advice networks are directed networks where there is a dispatcher and a recipient of advice. They are important in the way jobs get done in

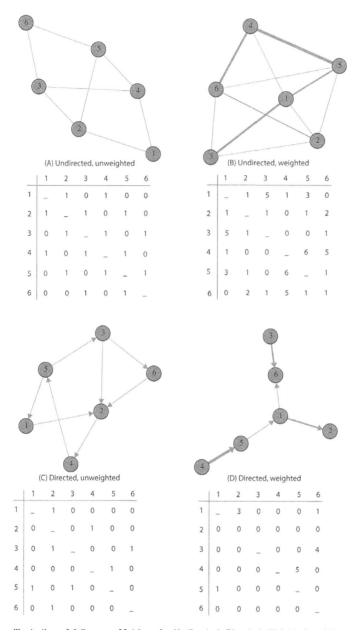

Figure 4.2   Illustration of Adjacency Matrices for Undirected, Directed, Weighted and Unweighted Networks

organisations, because most formal organisation charts do not reveal informal advice flows. Advice can be finding solutions to problems, validating solutions, gaining legitimacy, seeking information sources or gaining new insights on a problem (Cross, Borgatti and Parker, 2001). Degree centrality is a commonly used metric to evaluate the role of people as dispatchers and receivers of advice. In particular, in directed networks, indegree centrality can be used to measure an actor's importance as a knowledge source and technical advisor. High indegree centrality means that many others address the focal actor for advice. An actor here can be an individual or business unit in the organisation (Tsai, 2001). Degree centrality is the number of links a node has (Bonacich, 1987).

$$dc_i = \sum_j a_{ij}$$

where $a_{ij} = 1$ if a tie exists between i and j and zero otherwise. Figure 4.3 shows a hypothetical undirected network and the corresponding node-based

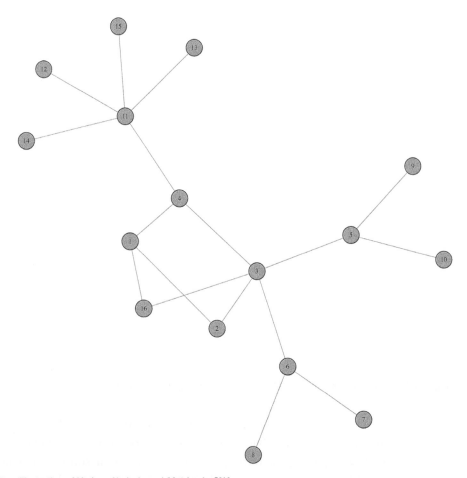

Figure 4.3   Illustration of Various Node-based Metrics in SNA

Table 4.1 Centrality Measures of Network in Figure 4.3

Node	Constraint	Degree	Closeness	Betweenness	Eigenvector
1	0.3	3	0.024	6.50	0.68
2	0.5	2	0.024	2.33	0.59
3	0.2	5	0.034	69.50	1.00
4	0.3	3	0.032	52.33	0.77
5	0.3	3	0.026	27.00	0.46
6	0.3	3	0.026	27.00	0.46
7	1	1	0.019	0.00	0.16
8	1	1	0.019	0.00	0.16
9	1	1	0.019	0.00	0.16
10	1	1	0.019	0.00	0.16
11	0.2	5	0.027	50.00	0.52
12	1	1	0.020	0.00	0.18
13	1	1	0.020	0.00	0.18
14	1	1	0.020	0.00	0.18
15	1	1	0.020	0.00	0.18
16	0.5	2	0.024	2.33	0.59

metrics are given in Table 4.1. In Figure 4.3, the highest degree centrality belongs to nodes 3 and 11, each of which has five ties.

4.3.2   Knowledge Brokerage

Innovation is most often the recombination of existing but disparate elements of knowledge. To measure the extent to which a node is an intermediary in this process, various brokerage metrics are used. Brokerage is a central notion in innovation and we will return to it in later chapters. Nodes can be inventors linking other inventors, patents linking distant knowledge domains, or firms bridging different industries through their alliances. Three metrics –Burt's constraint, ego network density and effective size – are commonly used to assess whether a node is well positioned to broker activities, and to measure the extent to which a node's ties are connected among themselves.

- **Burt's constraint:** measures the extent to which entrepreneurial opportunities that might otherwise be obtained are constrained as a result of dense connections between ties (Burt, 1992). As Burt (1992: 55) puts it, 'Your entrepreneurial opportunities are constrained to the extent that you have invested the bulk of your network time and energy in relationships that lead back to a single contact.' For a node i, the extent to which it is constrained by alter j is given by:

$$c_{ij} = \left(p_{ij} + \sum_q p_{iq} p_{qj} \right)^2 \quad i \neq q \neq j$$

where p_{ij} refers to the proportion of network time and energy i spends on j, in the time and energy i spends on all contacts. The total constraint on i from all network contacts is:

$$c_i = \sum_j c_{ij} \quad i \neq j$$

In the network in Figure 4.3, the least constrained nodes are 3 and 11, as most of their ties are not connected among themselves.

- **Ego network density (cliquishness):** measures the extent to which a node's ties are connected among themselves. It is given by:

$$cl_i = \frac{\sum_j \sum_k a_{jk}}{n_i(n_i - 1)} \quad \forall j, k : a_{ij} = 1, a_{ik} = 1$$

where n_i is the number of ties of node i. Here, $n_i(n_i - 1)$ measures the maximum possible number of links that can exist in i's network, if all of its ties are connected to each other. The numerator measures the actual number of links between ties. The higher the density of the ego network, the more i's ties are connected, reducing opportunities for brokering across disconnected parts of the network.

- **Effective size:** Burt's (1992) effective size is another measure of openness of the ego network. It is given by the following:

$$es_i = \sum_j \left[1 - \sum_q p_{iq} m_{jq} \right] \quad \forall j, q : a_{ij} = 1, a_{iq} = 1$$

where p_{iq} is the proportion of i's network time and energy invested in the relationship with q, and m_{jq} is the marginal strength of j's relation with contact q (interaction with q divided by the maximum number of j's contacts with others). When j is connected to none of i's other contacts, there is no redundancy and the expression inside the bracket will be equal to 1. Therefore when there is no redundancy in i's ego network, effective size will be equal to the number of contacts of i.

4.3.3   Prominence in Cross-boundary Knowledge Flow

One of the measures of interest is the extent to which a node is connected to the outside compared to the inside. For example, a firm in an industry or region, a team in a firm or an individual in a group may have most of its links inside and fewer with the outside. This balance has implications for the flow of knowledge across boundaries. Some studies have found that firms in an industrial region that have a combination of local and global ties (with others outside the region) have better innovation performance. In the same way, inventors who are connected both within and outside a firm are better positioned to bring knowledge to the firm from outside. For these purposes, Krackhardt and Stern's (1988) E-I index, which measures the dominance of external over internal ties of a node i, can be used.[10] It is given by:

$$ei_i = \frac{e_i - i_i}{e_i + i_i}$$

where e_i and i_i denote the number of external links and internal links of node i respectively. The index ranges between -1 and 1 and a value close to 1 indicates that node i has more external than internal links.

4.3.4   Social Influence

Social influence indicates the degree of power an actor has to shape the attitudes of others. As I explore in more detail in Part III, social influence is important in persuading others to adopt a technology in the market or in shaping others' attitudes towards a novelty. Various SNA techniques can be used to measure social influence, of which degree centrality and brokerage measures are the most common. At the same time, it is important to distinguish social influence from the potential to diffuse information. Often units with high indegree centrality have an immediate impact on diffusing information to a wide audience (hubs, for example). However, social influence is concerned with the power of an individual to *change* others' attitudes and behaviours.

The significance of an actor in diffusion depends on the extent to which a network becomes disconnected on the actor's removal (Borgatti, 2006). The greater the number of disconnected components following removal, the

---

[10] Note that, knowledge brokerage metrics can also be used for this purpose depending on the aim of the analyst.

more critical a node is in terms of ensuring a path between others, which in turn is critical for diffusion.

4.3.5   Controlling Information Flow

Sometimes we need to measure a node's potential to control information flow in the network. These might be critical suppliers who are effective at diffusing information in urgent situations or people inside an organisation who can control the diffusion of information to others. Closeness centrality and betweenness centrality are useful metrics to assess the ability of a node to control diffusion of information in the network.

- **Closeness centrality for speed of flows:** closeness centrality measures the average distance of a node from all other nodes in the network (Sabidussi, 1966; Freeman, 1979). Nodes with high closeness centrality are important because of their role in controlling the speed of information flow in the network. In this calculation, the geodesic distance between a node and all others is included. Geodesic distance between nodes i and j measures the minimum number of intermediate ties between node i and node j. Diameter of a network measures the maximum of the geodesics between all pairs. Table 4.2 gives the shortest paths between all the nodes in the network in Figure 4.3.

  The closeness centrality of node i is found by:

$$cc_i = \frac{1}{\sum_j d(i,j)}$$

  where $d(i,j)$ refers to the geodesic distance between i and j. In the network of Figure 4.3 the highest closeness centrality belongs to nodes 3 and 4. Note that nodes 3 and 11 have a high degree centrality but node 11's closeness centrality is lower than that of node 3, as it is quite distant from nodes 7–10.

  Closeness centrality can also be used to assess the extent to which a firm is dependent on others for information (Powell, Koput and Smith-Doerr, 1996). Firms with high closeness centrality are less dependent on others, as they have more control over the flows in the network.

- **Betweenness centrality for accuracy:** betweenness centrality measures how many times a node i lies in a geodesic connecting two nodes in the network. Nodes with high betweenness centrality have more control over

Table 4.2 Shortest Paths for the Network of Figure 4.3

	1	2	3	4	5	6	7	8	9	10	11	12	13	14	15	16
1	0	1	2	1	3	3	4	4	4	4	2	3	3	3	3	1
2	1	0	1	2	2	2	3	3	3	3	3	4	4	4	4	2
3	2	1	0	1	1	1	2	2	2	2	2	3	3	3	3	1
4	1	2	1	0	2	2	3	3	3	3	1	2	2	2	2	2
5	3	2	1	2	0	2	3	3	1	1	3	4	4	4	4	2
6	3	2	1	2	2	0	1	1	3	3	3	4	4	4	4	2
7	4	3	2	3	3	1	0	2	4	4	4	5	5	5	5	3
8	4	3	2	3	3	1	2	0	4	4	4	5	5	5	5	3
9	4	3	2	3	1	3	4	4	0	2	4	5	5	5	5	3
10	4	3	2	3	1	3	4	4	2	0	4	5	5	5	5	3
11	2	3	2	1	3	3	4	4	4	4	0	1	1	1	1	3
12	3	4	3	2	4	4	5	5	5	5	1	0	2	2	2	4
13	3	4	3	2	4	4	5	5	5	5	1	2	0	2	2	4
14	3	4	3	2	4	4	5	5	5	5	1	2	2	0	2	4
15	3	4	3	2	4	4	5	5	5	5	1	2	2	2	0	4
16	1	2	1	2	2	2	3	3	3	3	3	4	4	4	4	0

information flows in the network as they have more intermediary positions than nodes with low betweenness centrality. It is given by:

$$bc_i = \sum_{j<k}(g_i(j,k)/g(j,k))$$

where $g(j,k)$ refers to the number of shortest paths (geodesics) between nodes j and k, and $g_i(j,k)$ is the number of these geodesics containing node i. For example, in Figure 4.3, node 4 has only three ties but its betweenness centrality is close to that of node 3, which has five ties. Note that nodes 5 and 6 lie in all paths connecting nodes 7–10 to the rest of the network so they also have high betweenness centrality.

4.3.6 Buy-in Ties

Some studies find a negative correlation between an individual's ability to implement a creative idea and coming up with the idea in the first place. These are very different, as implementation often depends on accessing critical resources, validating through others' approval and building coalition with the help of prominent actors in the network. Buy-in relations help the pursuit of initiatives (Podolny and Baron, 1997). Various structural network metrics, like brokerage and centrality, can be used for this purpose (see Chapter 9). Network cohesiveness and the normative content of network ties reveal the extent to which intrapreneurs (entrepreneurial managers within an organisation) access resources.

Eigenvector centrality, also called Bonacich (1972) centrality, is a structural metric that measures connections with prominent actors and the extent to which a node's alters are central in a network. It can be used as a measure of proximity to prestige (Wasserman and Faust, 1994). It is given by:

$$ec_i = \lambda \sum_j a_{ij} e_j$$

where λ is a parameter required for finding a nontrivial solution. In Figure 4.3, nodes 3, 4 and 1 have the highest eigenvector centrality. Note that node 1 has low betweenness centrality but its eigenvector centrality is high because it is connected to one important node (4) and also to nodes 2 and 6, which have high eigenvector scores (because they are connected to node 3).

The eigenvector centrality of a firm can be used to assess firm value and to measure the extent to which an entrepreneurial firm is connected to prominent others (Hochberg, Ljungqvist, and Lu, 2007).

4.3.7   Detecting Important Patents

In citation networks the nodes are patents (or publications) and a direct link between two nodes means that one patent cites the other (usually the direction of links shows the direction of the knowledge flow, meaning that an incoming link is from the cited patent). Citation networks can be used to reveal the importance of patents or publications.[11]

Citation Count. One way to measure the importance of a patent is through direct citation count (the degree centrality of a patent in the citation network). If a patent is cited intensively by other patents, it is deemed to contain important knowledge that is used in the patents that cite it.[12] By their very nature, patent citation networks have a time bias, as older documents have a greater chance of being cited. Although newer patents may be technologically and scientifically important, they may not be cited in the short term.

---

[11] For patent citation analysis in innovation studies see Jaffe, Trajtenberg and Romer (2005).

[12] The citation network approach has its roots in the work of Solla de Price (1965). For the relation between economic value and citations see, for example, Hall, Jaffe and Trajtenberg (2005).

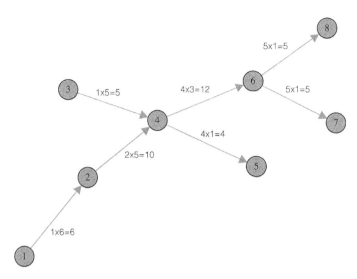

Figure 4.4   An Example of Patent Connectivity Analysis

Therefore one of the problems in comparing citations received by two patents is related to the time issue, since it is difficult to distinguish whether a patent is cited more because it is older or because it is important (Sanditov, 2006).

Connectivity Analysis. One way to detect important patents in the evolution of a technology is patent connectivity analysis, based on the algorithm developed by Hummon and Doreian (1989). This is an efficient algorithm as it narrows down the set of patents to the most important. The idea is that the knowledge contained in each patent draws upon the knowledge contained in a set of previous patents. Among many patents granted, which have been influential in the cumulative development of knowledge in a field? Two procedures yield similar results: the search path node pair (SPNP) method and the search path link count (SPLC) method.[13] Figure 4.4 shows the SPNP calculation on a simple patent citation network, involving eight patents. Direction of edges shows knowledge flow; for example, patent 4 cites patents 2 and 3 (uses the knowledge in those patents). Next, the importance of each edge is calculated. For example the importance of edge 4–6 is found by multiplying the number of 'downstream' patents ('1', '2', '3', '4') by the number of 'upstream' patents ('6', '7', '8') = 4 x 3. In other words, there are

---

[13]   Verspagen (2007); Batagelj (2003); Fontana, Nuvolari and Verspagen (2009).

twelve distinct pairs of patents that are linked by edge 4–6. The main path is selected by considering all starting points and proceeding along the edges with maximum value. Starting from node 1, the main paths are 1–2–4–6–7, 1–2–4–6–8 and starting from node 3, the main paths are 3–4–6–7, 3–4–6–8.

Downsides of Using Patent Citation Data. One of the problems with using citations is that they can be added by applicants' attorneys or patent examiners. As a result, citations may not reveal accurately the knowledge spillovers between inventors themselves, that is, the knowledge actually used in the production of new knowledge. Moreover, while highly cited patents are considered technologically or scientifically valuable, citations may not reveal the extent to which a patent is *commercially* valuable. Hall, Jaffe and Trajtenberg (2005) found evidence that there is a correlation between highly cited patents and their economic value. In addition, the EU PatVal project explored the invention process in Europe, focusing on the extent to which inventions, measured by patents, yielded economic value. According to the PatVal results, three factors contribute to the barriers between inventions and innovations: first, commercialising an invention requires assets that the inventor may not possess; second, some patents lie dormant in corporate labs and are never used; third, some patents are only applied for strategic reasons, for example, to block rivals. According to the results of the PatVal project, around 35 per cent of European patents are unexploited (Gambardella, Harhoff and Verspagen, 2008).

4.3.8   Finding Breakthrough Inventions

Citation weight of patents can also reveal the extent to which a patent is a breakthrough invention (Ahuja and Lampert, 2001). Patent analysis does reveal that breakthrough inventions are more likely to draw on other domains than the firms' established fields of research, and on emerging technologies (Ahuja and Lampert, 2001). For example, Schoenmakers and Duysters (2010) find that there is a correlation between the radicalness of an invention and the extent to which it draws on a combination of unconnected domains. Uzzi, Mukherjee, Stringer and Jones (2013) found that highly cited papers are likely to include elements of conventional knowledge from earlier work as well as unusual combinations, and that multi-author articles are 40 per cent more likely to be published that single-author articles. Distance also has a positive effect on citations; for example, Nomaler, Frenken and Heimeriks (2013) found that citation impact increases with geographical distance between countries.

4.4 Detecting Cohesive Subgroups

Cohesive subgroup detection is useful for large-scale data that indicate some aggregate patterns, as well as for understanding how innovations diffuse in a population. A cohesive subgroup in a network means that the members of the subgroup are more closely connected to each other than to others outside the group.

For example, groups of firms that collaborate or compete intensively with each other in a certain industry can be detected in alliance networks using subgroup detection techniques. Gomes-Casseres (1996) defined these alliance networks as constellations within which groups of firms compete. In Asian economies, new terms were coined to describe these powerful networks, like the Japanese *keiretsu* or the Korean *chaebol*.

Informal cohesive subgroups can also be detected with these techniques. Identifying these subgroups is important because their members tend to share similar attitudes or tastes. A good understanding of cohesive subgroups is useful for obtaining help or advice, diffusing information, building coalition or marketing.

Detecting cohesive subgroups is not easy, especially in large and complex networks. However, most software packages include sophisticated subgroup detection algorithms. Some commonly used subgroup definitions are:

- **Clique:** a clique is a maximally connected sub-graph of three or more nodes (Wasserman and Faust, 1994). Luce and Perry (1949) defined a clique as a subset of nodes all of which are connected to each other and where no other node in the network is connected to all members of the clique. In Figure 4.5, nodes 1, 2, 4 and 1, 2, 3 form two cliques. Node 4 is not connected to all the nodes in clique 2 (1, 2, 3), so it has no place in clique 2. Node 3 is not connected to all nodes in clique 1 (1, 2, 4), so it has no place in clique 1. One of the useful characteristics of cliques (depending on the aim) is that they overlap. For example, in Figure 4.5, nodes 1 and 2 have a place in both cliques. The extent to which cohesive subgroups overlap due to common members can be used as a measure of the intensity of inter-group interactions (Özman, 2010).

- **n-clique and n-clan:** the concept of n-clique is based on the idea that all members in a cohesive network should be relatively reachable by all other members. Based on this criterion, an n-clique is defined as a maximal sub-graph in which all nodes included are reachable by all other nodes in maximum n intermediate ties (Alba, 1973). For example, the network in Figure 4.5 is a 2-clique, as all nodes in the network can reach each other in at most two steps. An n-clan is a maximal sub-graph with diameter less than or equal to n.

- **k-plex:** another definition of a subgroup in a network is based on the number of nodes to which each node in the group is connected. A k-plex is a maximal sub-graph in a network in which each node is adjacent to no fewer than n_s-k other nodes in the sub-graph. For example, in a 2-plex composed of five nodes, all nodes should be connected to at least three other nodes. As k reduces, the sub-graph becomes more cohesive. Here, the k parameter needs to be specified by the analyst in advance.
- **k-core:** while k-plex is based on the number of acceptable absent links, a k-core is based on the number of ties that nodes should have in order to be included in the subgroup (Seidman, 1983). In the *k-core* method, the nodes are included according to whether their connections satisfy a minimum threshold of k in the network.[14] For example a 3-core group means that the group should be defined in such a way that each node is connected to at least three other nodes. The network in Figure 4.5 is a 2-core group, as all the nodes have at least two ties to all other members.

One of the advantages of these metrics is that the analyst has the chance to set the level of cohesiveness desired. For example, in k-plex lower values of k indicate increased cohesiveness. However, sometimes we want to detect subgroups without having to set the number or size of clusters in advance.[15] For this case, an alternative is the community detection algorithm developed by Girvan and Newman (2002), which is based on gradually removing edges with high betweenness centrality from the graph. Each time, the quality of the resulting subgroup division is evaluated by an index of modularity (Newman, 2006).

4.5   Knowledge Mapping

Network analysis is useful in mapping the knowledge base and collaboration patterns in firms, industries or regions. For this purpose bibliometric data can be used.

---

[14] For the k-core method, see Doreian and Woodard (1994); for sampling in survey data and snowball sampling see Frank (2005); for expanding selection and fixed list selection, see Doreian and Woodard (1992).

[15] This type of problem is called community detection (Newman, 2006).

4.5.1   Inventor Collaborations

Co-invention (or co-authorship) networks are derived from bibliometric data, showing a link between two inventors/scientists if they worked jointly on a patent, or if they co-authored a scientific paper (Newman, 2001). Co-invention networks are derived from two-mode data. In networks derived from two-mode data (also called bipartite networks) there is a set of actors (in this case, inventors) and a set of events (in this case, patents). When two actors are affiliated with the same event, the actors are assumed to have a tie.

Figure 4.6 illustrates how co-invention networks are constructed. Inventors are shown as 1–13, patents as a–e, and applicants show firms, A–D. In the co-inventor network shown in Figure 4.6, a link between two inventors exists if they co-authored a patent together. For example, inventors 1 and 3 have a tie, because their names appear on patent a. Likewise, inventors 8–11 all appear on patent d, so they form a fully connected sub-network.

In co-inventor networks a social tie is *assumed* between inventors, although this tie may not be properly defined as a social tie, but as a 'proxy for unobserved social ties' (Borgatti and Halgin, 2011b). These networks show the rate of collaboration between inventors and the positioning of inventors in inter-organisational or intra-organisational networks. They enable the identification of the actors who occupy key positions in the network (Lissoni, Llerena and Sanditov, 2013). They reveal places in the networks where collaboration is sparse, signalling potential brokerage opportunities, and also show who the brokers are likely to be. Co-invention networks can also be used to observe evolution of collaboration networks.

There are several downsides to using these networks. For one thing, important actors who contribute to inventions but whose names do not appear in patent data can be missed out. There is also the risk of omitting multiple relations between the same inventors (like simultaneous co-patenting and friendship). Some of the problems associated with secondary data sources are also associated with primary data collection techniques, especially if some crucial actors fail to participate in a field survey (Knoke and Yang, 2008) or are excluded by the researcher. Because co-invention data are derived from two-mode data, the network metrics and their statistical features are significantly different from normal one-mode data. For example, measures like centrality and clustering coefficients can be augmented spuriously (Vernet, Kilduff and Salter, 2014).[16]

---

[16] For further issues involved in analysing affiliation networks, see Borgatti and Halgin (2011a); Vernet, Kilduff and Salter (2014); Borgatti and Everett (1997).

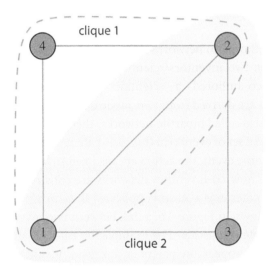

Figure 4.5   Illustration of Subgroups in SNA

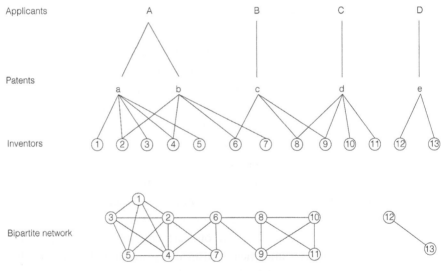

Figure 4.6   Deriving a Co-invention Network from Two-mode Data on Patents and Inventors
Note: When two inventors work jointly on a patent, a link is placed between them in the inventor network.
Sources: Newman (2001) and Balconi, Breschi and Lissoni (2004)

4.5.2 Analysing the Knowledge Base of Firms by Co-occurrence of Technological Domains

These networks are constructed by the co-occurrence of keywords or techno-logical classes in patents (or other documents). For example, two technology classes are linked if they co-occur together in a patent. When co-occurrence is conducted for the set of patents of a firm, or patents in a region, the network shows how different knowledge elements are linked. Co-occurrence networks may be useful in search processes, as they can pinpoint weakly linked areas open to novel connections or show domains that are often linked in patents. Co-occurrence networks give an insight into the extent to which firm know-ledge is localised, indicated by strong coupling between a range of related technologies.[17] Highly localised knowledge can limit the firm's search space and its ability to recognise distant and potentially valuable opportunities. Box 4.1 compares the knowledge base of Intel and Advanced Micro Devices (AMD), based on research by Yayavaram and Ahuja (2008).

Figure 4.7 shows the knowledge base structure of the leading light emitting diodes (LED) company, Cree, during three separate periods, as revealed by its patents. Here the nodes are patent classes and there is a link between two nodes if they appear together in a patent. As the knowledge base of the firm expanded throughout the whole period (1995–2012), it can be seen that previously distinct domains were gradually linked, some of the domains became central in the network (light emission), and the network was increas-ingly integrated around two technologies: semiconductor equipment and electric discharge tubes. As this example shows, patent data can be useful in mapping the knowledge base of a firm.

Co-occurrence networks often contain a very large number of patents, so the network of sub-classes is likely to be fully connected, that is, it is likely at least one patent will include any two sub-classes. This makes it difficult to uncover pairs of sub-classes, which are more likely to be used together than randomly selected pairs because they are more closely related. Different cohesive subgroup algorithms can be used to cope with this difficulty. A minimum threshold number of co-occurrence between two classes can be imposed, so that weakly related sub-classes are not included in the co-occurrence network. Cohesive subgroup detection techniques can be used to identify strongly linked patent sub-classes. For example, Dolfsma and

---

[17] For example, using co-occurrences of classes between patents, Breschi, Lissoni and Malerba (2003) constructed a matrix of relatedness between different technological areas.

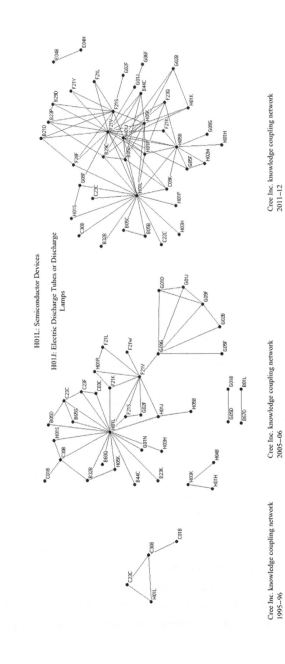

Figure 4.7 Cree Inc. Knowledge Network in Three Periods

Leydesdorff (2011) used a k-core algorithm to analyse nanotechnology clusters in India and the Netherlands.

4.5.3 Analysing Technology or Industry Evolution

Sometimes the analyst is interested in analysing the nature of a technological domain, how it is related to other domains and the characteristics of its knowledge base.

Defining Technological Domains. Technological domains can be analysed using bibliometric data sources. Here are some examples of characteristics that can be explored to analyse the knowledge base of technological domains. (These can also be used to analyse the knowledge base of firms, regions, countries, etc., depending on the initial set of patents chosen.)

- **Breadth of knowledge base:** refers to the number (range) of different subjects that a particular domain draws upon. One way to measure breadth is to count the number of distinct patent classes in a patent document and evaluate the nature of the knowledge base statistically.
- **Depth of knowledge base:** refers to the concentration of a few knowledge domains (or subjects). A deep knowledge base indicates greater specialisation.

Box 4.1 The Knowledge Base Structure of Intel and AMD

Yayavaram and Ahuja (2008) have compared the structure of the knowledge bases of Intel and AMD, analysing how they 'couple' distinct knowledge elements. A 'coupling' between knowledge elements happens when a firm routinely uses the elements together, from a belief that they will work well together, possibly based on successful past experimentation with that combination. The authors construct networks so that there will be a link between the two technological classes if they both appear on a patent document granted to the firm. The intensity of this coupling (i.e. the number of patents) reveals the strength of the coupling and indicates the firm's knowledge base structure. This study has found that firms differ significantly in terms of their coupling patterns, even when the same technology classes are included. In a regression study, the authors have also found that knowledge bases that are nearly decomposable (those with discernible but weakly linked clusters) produce more useful inventions, as revealed by the number of citations received. Figure 4.8 shows that Intel's knowledge base is almost decomposable.

Box 4.1 (cont.)

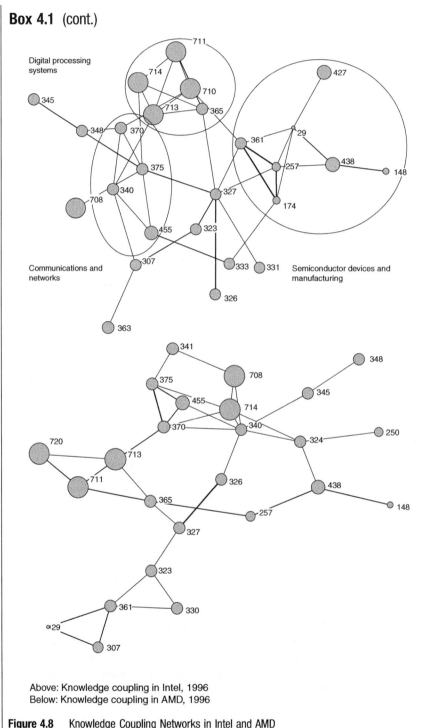

Above: Knowledge coupling in Intel, 1996
Below: Knowledge coupling in AMD, 1996

Figure 4.8   Knowledge Coupling Networks in Intel and AMD
Source: Yayavaram and Ahuja, 2008

- **Pervasiveness of knowledge base:** measures the extent to which the domains spread across different technological classes. This dimension is used to assess the diversification of a domain.
- **Complexity of knowledge base:** Sorenson, Rivkin and Fleming (2006) used the rarity of a particular combination of sub-classes in a patent as a measure of its complexity. The higher the number of sub-classes in a patent, and the less each sub-class had been used with others in the past, the more interdependent the patent, which can be taken as a measure of the complexity of its knowledge base.
- **Scientific base:** to what extent does a technology domain draw upon scientific knowledge? One of the ways this can be measured is to calculate the extent to which scientific publications are cited by the patents in the domain.
- **Dispersion among innovators:** how concentrated is innovative activity in a field among countries, regions or firms? To what extent are a limited number of firms responsible for the evolution of the domain? These questions can be answered by using a measure of concentration, like the Herfindahl index, using the applicant name or region name in a patent.
- **Self-citation of the field:** the extent to which patents in a specific domain cite other patents from the same domain indicates the cumulation of knowledge in the domain.
- **Entry of new firms:** the extent to which patents in the field are granted to new entrants yields insights about the extent to which disruptive innovations are likely to occur in the domain.

Domain Analysis by Co-occurrence Networks. Co-occurrence networks can also be used to define and analyse the characteristics of emerging domains for which there is no pre-defined technology class. For example, by analysing a patent pool consisting of eco-inventions and ICT, Cecere et al. (2014) examine the characteristics of this technological domain, its pervasiveness, its scientific roots, the contributions made by countries and firms to its development and also its sub-fields. Co-occurrence networks can also yield insights about the complexity or novelty of patents.

Domain Analysis by Citation Networks. The historical, industrial and geographical clustering of innovation was explained in Chapter 2. Citation networks can be used to show this clustering, as they reveal the *selectiveness* of knowledge flows. Knowledge flows are not homogeneously distributed among subjects and geographies, and network analysis can be used to reveal the geographical concentration of knowledge flows, the extent of domain specificity or time biases. There is rich evidence that knowledge spillovers have a strongly localised nature and are more concentrated among actors within geographical borders (Jaffe, Trajtenberg and Henderson, 1993).[18] Citation patterns are also largely domain-specific, where probability of citation within a domain is higher than the probability of citing a patent outside a domain.

4.6 Focus on Global Networks

The global structure of networks gives some insights into a variety of innovative capabilities, like the extent to which the network cultivates and sustains creativity, speed, the effectiveness of knowledge diffusion in the network and the concentration of power.

4.6.1 Creativity and Recombination Capacity

Small-world Network. In 1967, the American social psychologist Stanley Milgram published the results of a series of experiments he had conducted in the US, in which he showed that, on average, any two people are separated by a path length of six intermediaries (Milgram, 1967). In Milgram's experiment, randomly selected people from Nebraska and Kansas were given letters addressed to a person in New York. They were expected to send the letter directly to the addressee if they knew him on a first-name basis, or send it to someone they thought might know the final target and whom they knew on a first-name basis. Few of the letters actually reached their destination; for example, in one experiment the rate was 64 out of 296. But among the 64 that arrived, the average number of intermediaries was six (hence the term, 'six degrees of separation'). Another of Milgram's findings was that some people played a central role in passing the letters. For example, in one experiment a significant number of chains went through a clothing merchant called 'Mr. Jacobs', who was in the neighbourhood of the target. This experiment revealed that people were actually much closer than expected, thanks to shortcuts that connected distant networks. There were also central people in the network (hubs) who were important in connecting distant people.

---

[18] Breschi and Lissoni (2009) find that mere geographical proximity does not explain citations and that social proximity and inventor mobility should be taken into account.

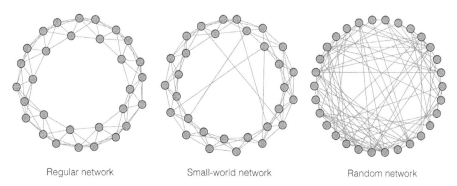

Regular network   Small-world network   Random network

Figure 4.9   Illustration of the Small-world Network Structure between Regular Networks and Random Networks

Nearly thirty-five years later, Milgram's experiment was repeated by Dodds, Muhamed and Watts (2003), who used e-mail chains and had eighteen targets in different countries. Interestingly, they found on average nearly the same number of intermediaries, between five and seven. But contrary to Milgram's findings, there were no hubs through which the majority of messages passed in the network. In this later study, professional acquaintances were the most important in passing messages.

Watts and Strogatz (1998) were the first to systematically explore small-world networks in mathematical terms. Small-world networks are character-ised by two parameters, clustering coefficient and path length. Figure 4.9 shows three networks. The first is a regular network with a high clustering coefficient, in which each node is connected to the nearest four nodes, with most of their links also connected to each other. In this graph, paths between nodes are long. In other words, reaching one node from another requires passing through several intermediaries. The last network shows quite the opposite, a random network in which the clustering coefficient is low but there are many shortcuts between nodes. Watts and Strogatz (1998) demon-strate that the small-world region lies somewhere between these two networks. The figure in the middle shows a small-world network, with high clustering, but short paths due to shortcuts that link one part of the network to the others. Small worlds, which lie in between these two extremes, are characterised by high clustering (nodes have high ego network density) but also low average path lengths, thanks to shortcuts between distant agents. Many real-world networks have been shown to have small-world characteristics.[19] In Chapter 7,

---

[19] Some examples for small-world characteristics in the real world: co-authorship (Newman, 2001); co-invention and academic inventors in France (Lissoni, Llerena and Sanditov, 2013). See also Davis, Yoo

I show that small-world networks have the advantage of high-quality knowledge transfer, due to clustering, and novelty potential, due to shortcuts between distant nodes.

The small worldliness of an observed network can be evaluated by calculating the small-world ratio (Davis, Yoo and Baker, 2003). This ratio compares the observed network's clustering coefficient (CC) and path length (L) with another network with the same number of nodes and ties but where the links are distributed randomly. It is given by:

$$Q = \frac{CC/CC_R}{L/L_R}$$

In general small-world networks have higher clustering coefficients than random networks $(CC \gg CC_R)$ and a path length that is approximately equal to the random network $(L \approx L_R)$.[20] One of the concerns in two-mode data is that the clustering coefficients can be augmented spuriously. Box 4.2 shows a method to compute the small-world ratio for two-mode data (Newman, Strogatz and Watts, 2001).

Scale-free Network. Most real-world networks have asymmetric degree distribution; that is, some nodes have more ties than others. In scale-free networks, this asymmetry is very strong and the degree distribution of the nodes follows a power law (Barabasi and Albert, 1999). In other words, a very small number of nodes have a very high number of ties and the vast majority of nodes have very few ties. Barabasi (2002) notes this in the case of the World Wide Web. One of the mechanisms behind this is preferential attachment in network growth, or the well-known Matthew effect ('the rich get richer and the poor get poorer'), where nodes with a large number of ties are more likely to attract new ties than others.[21] Preferential growth has been studied under the rubric of scale-free networks, which have been used to explain a variety of real-world structures involving hubs (Solla de Price, 1965; Barabasi and Albert, 1999). While hubs can be found in some networks like

---

and Baker (2003) for board interlocks; Fleming, King and Juda (2007) for Silicon Valley co-invention networks. For a review see Uzzi, Amaral and Reed-Toschas (2007).

[20] Note that the numerical value of Q depends on the size of networks, so this coefficient can be rescaled (cf. Gulati, Sytich and Tatarynowicz, 2012), or the threshold value is set according to the size of the network (cf. Baum, Shipilov and Rowley, 2003).

[21] Note that if there is growth without preferential attachment, the degree distribution is exponential, as early nodes by definition attract more ties as they have been in the network longer than recent nodes. Only when there is preferential attachment, that is, when new nodes connect to nodes with high degree centrality, do we obtain power law degree distribution.

Box 4.2 The Small Worldliness of Networks Involving Two-mode Data

The statistical properties of bipartite networks are different from those of unipartite networks (Borgatti and Everett, 1997). Converting two-mode data to one-mode data (as shown in Figure 4.6) can be technically challenging if we are interested in the small worldliness of networks. Consider the example of co-inventor networks: if seven inventors are listed on a patent document (cf. seven nodes affiliated to the same event), these seven inventors will all be connected when the co-inventor network is constructed, forming a clique. The creation of many such cliques can result in an overestimation of clustering, thus increasing the small worldliness of one-mode networks derived from two-mode data (Uzzi and Spiro, 2005; Uzzi, Amaral and Reed-Tsochas, 2007; Lissoni, Llerena and Sanditov, 2013). To cope with this problem, benchmark random networks should also be constructed from two-mode data (Newman, Strogatz and Watts, 2001). When this is done, two features of the observed network (the average number of events per node and the average number of nodes per event) should be used to generate random networks.

To compute the CC of the observed network to be used in benchmarking, the following equation has been proposed by Newman, Strogatz and Watts (2001):

$$CC = \frac{3 \times \text{Number of triangles in the network}}{\text{Number of connected triples of vertices}}$$

The numerator is the number of pairs of inventors with a common acquaintance (a third inventor they are both linked to). The denominator is the total number of triads, in which at least two links exist. This CC measures the extent of between-team clustering – that is, the extent to which the two patent teams overlap. This CC, which ranges between zero and 1, corrects for the clustering bias observed in bipartite networks, and can be used when benchmarking against the generated random graph.

---

the World Wide Web, where they play an important role in the diffusion of information, there is little evidence that they are a source of influence on others in adoption decisions. There is more about this issue in Chapter 11.

4.6.2 Concentration of Power

Sometimes we need to assess the extent to which power is concentrated in the network. Studies show that networks composed of a core and a periphery can have both positive and negative implications for innovative potential. In a core-periphery network core members are densely connected to each other and peripheral members are loosely connected to the core and among themselves. This is measured by degree of network centralisation.

The centralisation of a group of nodes is found by:

$$DC = \frac{\sum_i (dc^* - dc_i)}{(n-1)(n-2)}$$

where dc_i is node degree centrality and dc^* is the largest observed value among all nodes. Degree centralisation takes into account the dispersion of degree centralities around the most central node in the network. If there is a large difference, that is, high asymmetry in terms of degree distribution, centralisation tends to be greater.

Centralised advice networks can be disadvantageous as core members' time and efforts are often limited, especially if they are in higher hierarchical levels. Centralised advice networks also reveal an uneven distribution of knowledge within the organisation. When helpers are at higher hierarchical or tenure levels, peripheral members can be less aware of who knows what in the organisation (Singh, Hansen and Podolny, 2010). Innovative performance in a core-periphery network is better when teams include members from both the core and the periphery (Cattani and Ferriani, 2008).

4.6.3   Interaction Intensity

The density of a network indicates the relative number of realised links compared to the total number of links possible, were all nodes connected to each other (complete network). Dense and sparse networks indicate the number of interactions between nodes in a network. Depending on the tie content, the density of a network may indicate cohesion, that is, the extent to which members are held together in a network (Friedkin, 2004).[22] Cohesion can be taken as 'the resultant of all forces acting on the members of a group to remain in the group' (Festinger, 1950: 274).

Density. In an undirected graph, density is given by:

$$d = \frac{\sum_i \sum_j a_{ij}}{n(n-1)}$$

Note that density is an aggregated measure and does not show the distribution of links.

---

[22] Cohesion is discussed widely. Here we focus on the social network perspective and social psychological approaches. For a review, see Friedkin (2004).

Clustering Coefficient. The CC of a network is calculated by taking the average of ego network densities over the entire network. It is given by:

$$CC = \frac{\sum_i cl_i}{n}$$

where cl_i is the ego network density of node i.

4.6.4 Speed of Knowledge Diffusion

The average path length in a network can be used to measure the speed of diffusion between nodes: the shorter the average path length, the higher the speed of diffusion. This is given by the network-level average of path length between all pairs in a network:

$$L = \frac{\sum_i \sum_j d(i,j)}{n(n-1)}$$

where $d(i,j)$ is the shortest path length between nodes i and j.

Table 4.3 summarises the use of SNA to analyse innovation networks.

Table 4.3 Synthesis: SNA for Innovation Networks

Node-based measures	Prominence in advice networks
	Prominence in cross-boundary knowledge flow
	Social influence
	Buy-in ties
	Controlling information flow
	Brokerage
	Detecting important patents
	Finding breakthrough inventions
Cohesive subgroups	Constellations
	Relations between subgroups
	Technology or industry evolution
	Knowledge base of firms, regions, industries
Global network	Creativity
	Concentration of power
	Cohesion and knowledge transfer
	Speed of diffusion
Knowledge mapping	Inventor collaborations
	Knowledge base of organisations and regions
	Technology or industry evolution

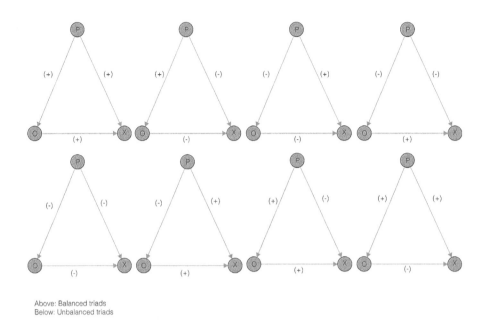

Above: Balanced triads
Below: Unbalanced triads

Figure 4.10   Balanced and Unbalanced Triads in Heider's (1946) POX (Person, Other, and X) Schema

4.7   Some Important Topics

This section covers some central debates in the development of the field of social network analysis. These discussions are often referred to in research on innovation networks and are worth a closer look.

4.7.1   Balance Theory and Homophily

Heider (1946; 1958) defined balance theory in four short phrases: 'My friend's friend is my friend, my friend's enemy is my enemy, my enemy's friend is my enemy, my enemy's enemy is my friend'. In other words, in a triad, only two states are in balance: three positive ties, or two negative and one positive tie (see Figure 4.10).[23] Balance theory is about cognitive consistency and two of its components are reciprocity and transitivity (Kilduff and

---

[23] See Cartwright and Harary (1956) for the graph theoretic notion of balance theory. They state that if balance theory strictly holds, in balanced state there will be two cliques in a network: positive ties within group and negative ties between groups. Various authors explore balance theory in the SNA context, including Davis (1963); Hummon and Doreian (2003); Kilduff and Tsai (2003); Kadushin (2012).

Box 4.3 Dyadic Network Data and the QAP

When dyadic network data are used, the QAP is preferred to ordinary least squares (OLS) regressions (Krackhardt, 1988), as these can give biased results. For example, taking the dependent variable in a regression as the probability of a link between the two actors (dyad), we might want to know how their similarities in various dimensions (age, education, common friends, etc.) could influence the likelihood of a tie formation between them. Often, in such cases, dyads have a link to each other. For instance, if A is linked with B and B is linked with C, it is likely that A is linked with C. In such cases, errors will be correlated, generating inflation or deflation in standard errors. In the QAP, a standard multiple regression analysis is performed across corresponding cells of the dependent and independent matrices. Rows and columns of the dependent matrix are then randomly permuted and the regression model is recomputed. The main advantage of the QAP is that it provides robust results in comparison to the results of the standard procedure followed by OLS.

Tsai, 2003). Actors prefer friendship ties to be reciprocated (Newcomb, 1961) and prefer transitive triads. Balance theory has been used to explain tie formation, as it maintains that groups tend towards balanced structures over time (Hummon and Doreian, 2003).[24] One of the problems encountered in the econometric analysis of dyads is that they are often not independent from each other. Quadratic assignment procedure (QAP) can be used to address this problem and is explained in Box 4.3.

As an illustration of balance theory, Figure 4.10 shows Heider's (1946) POX schema. P is a person (ego), O is the other (person) and X is a subject or a third person. For example, if P likes O, and has a positive attitude towards X, then P would prefer O to have a positive attitude towards X as well. P is under tension (or stressed) when O is negative or indifferent towards X. Heider distinguished between four balanced and four imbalanced cases (Figure 4.10).

Homophily is the process through which similar actors form more ties than would be expected by chance (Lazarsfeld and Merton, 1954; McPherson, Smith-Lovin and Cook, 2001). It is reflected in the old saying, 'Birds of a feather flock together'. As actors interact more over time, they begin to resemble each other, presenting a 'chicken or egg' problem. The homophily rule can help explain tie formation patterns and actors' attitudes, tastes and beliefs. Kadushin (2012: 20) summarises four ways in which homophily happens: (1) similar people come together; (2) people influence one another and in the process become alike; (3) people end up in the same place; and

---

[24] See, for example, Sytch and Tatrynowicz (2014) for the inter-organisational level.

(4) once they do, the place itself makes them grow alike. The last two items are related to what Feld (1981) called 'social foci', which are 'social, psychological, legal or physical entit[ies] around which joint activities are organized (e.g. workplaces, voluntary organizations, hangouts, families, etc.)' (Feld, 1981: 1016). Actors tend to grow alike because they attend the same social foci.

Homophily processes are important in various innovation-related issues both inside and outside organisations. For example, marketing might be interested in the answer to the question whether people in a cohesive network have similar adoption patterns because they have similar tastes, or because they are influenced by each other (Aral, Muchnik and Sundararajan, 2009). A number of questions arise in the context of organisational and inter-personal networks. Are homophilous ties between organisations better for performance and, if so, under which conditions? Which dimensions of homophily explain inter-organisational tie formations? In intra-organisational networks, what aspects of homophily lead people to ask for advice, or explain friendship patterns (Ibarra, 1992)? Can leaders' strong identification with others similar to them jeopardise organisational performance (Zahra and Eltantawy, 2009)? We will turn to these questions in the remaining chapters of this book.

4.7.2   Strong and Weak Ties

Granovetter (1973) defined strong ties as the 'combination of the amount of time, the emotional intensity, the intimacy (mutual confiding) and the reciprocal services which characterise the tie'.

In social network analysis, the weight of a tie ($a_{ij} > 0$) often indicates tie strength. For example, the number of patents issued by two inventors, the physical distance between two units, the number of alliances between two organisations, the number of e-mail exchanges between two co-workers, the number of times two words appear together in patent abstracts – all these are different ways in which the strength of a tie between two nodes can be expressed. Usually the strength of one node's tie with another is normalised with respect to the total strength of all its ties.

The importance of weak ties, as Granovetter (1973) argued, is that they are more likely to give access to a distant and unfamiliar network, which can bring new opportunities. Granovetter (1973) showed that bridging ties connecting two otherwise separated networks are necessarily weak. He based this premise on Heider's (1958) balance theory. If a bridge between two nodes is a strong tie, then the other alters of the nodes should also be connected, for the balance condition to be satisfied. But then it would no longer be a bridging tie, therefore bridges are by definition weak ties. Later on Burt (1992) refined this analysis stating that what matters is not the weakness or the strength of a tie, but the extent to which it connects otherwise unconnected networks. Burt (1992) explains that tie weakness is a correlate rather than a condition of a bridging tie. At the same time, ties in dense networks are likely to be strong – but not necessarily so.

The conceptualisation of strong and weak ties is relevant to many areas of innovation studies. In particular, research shows that strong ties are better for the transfer of tacit knowledge, as actors are more motivated to share knowledge and communicate with others with whom they have strong ties (Reagans and McEvily, 2003; Hansen, 1999). Weak ties, on the other hand, can give access to novel perspectives and diverse opinions and opportunities.

4.7.3   Closure and Structural Holes

There has been a long-standing debate about types of network position that are rich in social capital (this is discussed further in Chapter 6). Social capital is the value that actors derive from social structure that they can use to achieve their interests (Coleman, 1988). Debate focuses on two network positions in particular, as sources of social capital: cohesive networks (higher triadic closure) and networks rich in structural holes (Burt, 1992). Closure stresses the positive performance impacts of dense and closed networks (Coleman, 1988). Supporters of closure maintain that opportunistic behaviour is mitigated by the embedded relations in cohesive networks, where frequent, often face-to-face, interactions facilitate rich knowledge exchange and build trust. A common language is developed within closed networks, facilitating knowledge exchange and increasing efficiency in terms of the time and cost of negotiation (Uzzi, 1997). On the other hand, too much embeddedness can have counter-effects; for example, it can render actors vulnerable to external shocks or insulate them from novel knowledge sitting elsewhere in the network (Uzzi, 1997). Proponents of structural holes argue that dense and closed networks result in redundant knowledge exchange, since the same actors interact frequently. Burt (1992) argued that actors should fill structural holes and bridge otherwise disconnected networks. Such weak ties can have the advantage of creating access to novel knowledge from diverse sources (Rowley, Behrens and Krackhardt, 2000).

These bridging relations are sometimes referred as network range, meaning the breadth of diverse knowledge domains accessed through them (Reagans and McEvily, 2003). This debate between structural holes and cohesive networks has resulted in a very rich stream of research. While some researchers find that the effect depends on external conditions (Rowley, Behrens and Krackhardt, 2000), others stress the complementary nature of both network positions (Uzzi, 1997).

4.7.4   Structural and Regular Equivalence

Equivalence refers to the similarity between the network position of two nodes (Lorrain and White, 1971; Burt, 1976). Two actors have a regular equivalence when their positions in the network are similar, although they need not be connected to exactly the same nodes and can even be part of different networks. For example, in this meaning of equivalence two middle managers in different organisations would be equivalent to each other. In Figure 4.3, nodes 8 and 9 are equivalent, although they are not connected to the same nodes. Structural equivalence, on the other hand, means that two nodes are connected to the same nodes in the network, regardless of whether or not they are connected to each other. For example, in Figure 4.3, nodes 2 and 16 are structurally equivalent, as they are both connected only to nodes 1 and 3. Their positional metrics in Table 4.1 are also identical. In Table 4.1 nodes 8 and 9 have the same network metrics, not because they are connected to exactly the same nodes (like nodes 2 and 16), but because they have regular equivalence, occupying similar positions in different parts of the network. Equivalence can help explain social influence (Burt, 1987). When there is uncertainty, people tend to observe others who occupy similar social positions to theirselves. A well-known example is the study carried out by Coleman, Katz and Menzel (1966) on diffusion of the broad-spectrum antibiotic Tetracycline in the US. The initial explanation for the rapid diffusion of the antibiotic was based on cohesion in the networks of physicians, who were influenced by what their close colleagues were doing. On the other hand, Burt (1987) argued that people in cohesive networks are not necessarily influenced by one another, while structurally similar positions tend to trigger similar behavioural patterns.[25]

---

[25] The case of Tetracyline was studied by many researchers. Van den Bulte and Lilien (2001) showed how marketing effects were influential in the diffusion of the medicine.

4.7.5   Structure and Agency

The network approach has been criticised for its early emphasis on structural position, with the implication that the role of individuals' actions, performance and behaviours is not taken into account adequately (Emirbayer and Goodwin, 1994). However, many recent studies have addressed the micro-processes of tie formation, asking: Why do actors form ties? Whom do they select as alters? How do these decisions depend on context, personalities, nature of industries, or complementarities and compatibilities between people, organisations? These issues are covered in Chapter 12.

Also, as a French proverb puts it nicely, 'One bee does not make a swarm'. In other words, tie formation at the micro-level and networks at the macro-level are related but different processes. Tie formation is related to an individual action (bee), while the whole network is related to the way in which the decisions of numerous individuals (bees) form certain macro patterns (swarm) that constrain and enable the actions and behaviours of individuals (bees). One stream of research analyses the dynamics of whole networks over time, addressing questions like: How do networks change over time according to different contexts? What factors give rise to the emergence of certain network structures, like core-periphery networks? How do short-cuts form in networks, connecting otherwise disconnected clusters? Is network change stable? What factors drive change in network structure? These issues are addressed in Chapter 13.

It is important to remember that network dynamics is different from network evolution. As Doreian and Stokman (1997) point out, network evolution requires understanding the rules governing the sequence of change over time. While studies on network evolution explain network dynamics in terms of an understood mechanism, they do not highlight the role of actors' deliberate actions (or strategy) in shaping their network positions. In short, to have a better understanding of agency in networks, micro-processes and macro outcomes should be taken together, as they are interdependent. Networks constrain and enable individuals, and individuals' combined decisions give rise to networks.

Agent-based simulations directly take into account this feedback between structure and agency. In these models, networks evolve as agents make self-interested decisions about whom to connect with. As they form ties, the resulting networks constrain and enable their actions, which in turn shapes their decisions about whom they will connect with in the future. Therefore adaptation and learning is incorporated in these models, which yield insights into how networks evolve in different, otherwise unobservable, parameter spaces. The essential idea in these models is that explanations of aggregate patterns have to take into account interactions among heterogeneous agents, the way they evolve over time, and how they endogenously shape agents' choices in return.

Discussion Questions

1. What are the different network metrics that can be used to measure brokerage?

2. What is the difference between different centrality measures?

3. Give examples of different contexts in which
   a. We are interested in identifying cohesive subgroups in a network
   b. A network exhibits small-world characteristics
   c. A network exhibits both small-world and scale-free characteristics.

4. Can you imagine cases in which the following do not hold:
   a. A strong tie cannot be a bridge that connects two (otherwise unconnected) clusters
   b. We have very limited control over our networks, and our networks determine our behaviour and achievements
   c. Friend of my friend is my friend
   d. Birds of a feather flock together?

5　Managing Innovation Networks

Strategies are to organisations what blinkers are to horses: they keep them going in a straight line, but impede the use of peripheral vision.

Henry Mintzberg

In this chapter we focus on the scope of network management. We introduce a comprehensive network management model. We highlight the domains in which network management is useful, and explore the benefits of network management in each domain. We also highlight how network management is related to major decision variables in innovation management. These are types and sources of innovation, R&D intensity and the timing of innovation. This chapter also addresses the question of why different sectors have different strategic alliance network structures. Finally, we revisit the network horizon, and explore the factors that determine the trade-off between the costs and benefits of zooming in and zooming out of networks. In doing so, we understand how the technological, institutional, market and firm specific factors shape this trade-off.

In many ways innovation is in tension with strategy. Innovation is serendipitous and uncertain and technological change is seldom, if at all, under the control of a single organisation. The flexibility to adapt to environmental contingencies is an indispensable competence, and strategies can slow down this adaptation, especially in rapidly changing environments. It is no wonder that Quinn (1985) described innovation management as 'controlled chaos' and Mintzberg observed that strategies impede the use of 'peripheral vision' (Mintzberg, 1987). In fact, it is precisely this peripheral vision that is indispensable for innovation and where a network approach is most valuable: in recognising opportunities, increasing variety, accessing resources and timeliness in the face of uncertainty and sponsoring the diffusion of innovations in dynamic environments.

Mintzberg and Waters' (1985) incrementalist approach suggests a continuum of strategies ranging from the most deliberate to the most emergent.

Deliberate strategies are those in which the distinction between formulation and implementation stages is most clear-cut: there is a detailed plan, followed by pre-programmed implementation. Deliberate strategies leave little space for coping with uncertainties and are better suited to stable environments. As strategies move along the spectrum from most deliberate to most emergent, the distinction between formulation and implementation phases becomes fuzzy. At the far end of the spectrum strategies are realised ex post, without prior plans.

For most firms network management and network strategy are either emergent or completely non-existent. However, a non-existent strategy does not necessarily imply failure (Mintzberg and Waters, 1985; Inkpen and Choudhury, 1995). Research has found the correlation between the success of a strategy and its deliberateness (or even its existence) to be weak. A lack of network management does not imply that network benefits will not accrue: it simply implies the absence of regular processes and routines to sustain network advantage in the long run. Without network management, the benefits gained from networks and collaborations will be at best the result of chance events. Positive chance events are more likely with a systematic network perspective (as Pasteur observed, 'Chance favours only the prepared mind'), so developing network management capabilities increases the chances of leveraging network advantage in a sustained manner. Network management is about making informed decisions, taking into account the implications of networks and the ways in which decisions will shape networks in the future.

This chapter focuses on the main elements of managing innovation networks. Four dimensions of innovation management are linked with networks: type of innovation, intensity of R&D, sources of innovation and timing.[1] In the final part of the chapter, the network horizon (see Chapter 3) is revisited to address the question of how managers decide which level of network horizon to take into account. What external and internal factors influence the trade-off between distant and proximate network horizons?

5.1   What is Network Management?

Despite its potential benefits, for most organisations network management is unexplored terrain. There is little evidence that organisations actually oversee

---

[1] For innovation management see Tidd and Bessant (2013). For decision variables in innovation management see Zahra and Das (1993) and He and Wong (2004).

their position in a network and select partners accordingly. However, those that are more aware of their position in a network are more likely to obtain privileged positions (van Liere, Koppius and Vervest, 2008).[2] There are several reasons for this. First, network management requires a good understanding of social network analysis and theory, as well as analytical tools for data analysis, which require training and resource allocation. This can be especially challenging for small organisations that lack resources. Second, most organisations also face difficulties in changing people's mindset towards a relational way of seeing innovation (overseeing complementarities and synergies between different elements, organisations or people). Third, there are often barriers to openness and resistance towards collaboration: people may hesitate to share and exchange information. Fourth, networks are not completely manageable; they tend to form in a self-organising manner, so that the position of actors in a network depends on decisions made by others. The network shown in Figure 5.1 is an example of this. Node C is positioned as a cut-off connecting two clusters through its connections with B and G. If B or G withdraws, the network position of C changes significantly, and it becomes a peripheral rather than a strategically important member of the network.

The term network management suggests direct interventions, like selecting partners, severing links, motivating or discouraging ties and so on. But network management actions are much broader than these: many innovation-related activities change networks and are influenced by them. The barriers to adopting a network view of innovation can be overcome once these interrelations are better understood. Figure 5.2 shows the stages of innovation network management based on the innovation network box introduced in Chapter 1.

5.1.1   Aims of Network Management

Network management is useful in a number of areas.

Change Management. The implementation of change projects can be challenging in organisations and research shows that only around 30 per cent succeed (Kotter, 2007). One problem is employees' resistance to change, which may be rooted in perceived uncertainty about the project, the

---

[2] They find that this effect is even stronger when there is higher heterogeneity in awareness.

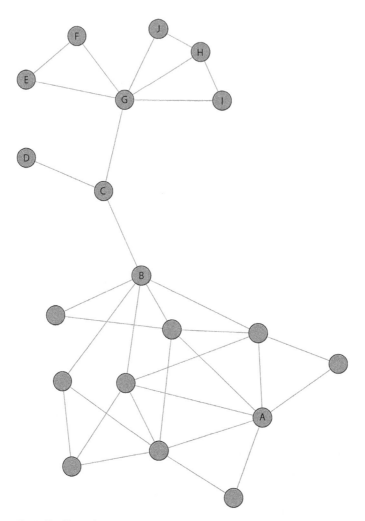

Figure 5.1   Illustrative Network

conditions that will follow change, concern about losing access to valuable resources and a general tendency to preserve the status quo. Network analysis can be used to identify potential sources of resistance and build coalition to reduce uncertainty. For these purposes, informal networks in an organisation are mapped (Cross, Ernst and Pasmore, 2013).

For example, in Figure 5.1 one question of interest is who can influence people's opinions and attitudes? Some studies show that actors like C are more influential, since they enable coalition-building between groups. Other studies point out that central actors like G or A are more influential, as they reach many others. Which node in the network is likely to be more effective

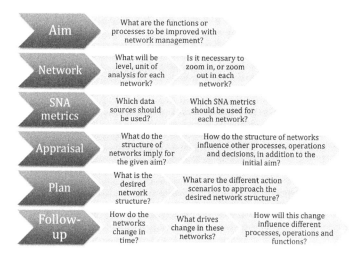

Figure 5.2   Innovation Network Management Model

in coalition-building depends on the nature of the change project as well as how ties are defined. For example, Krackhardt (1992) showed that advice and friendship networks have different impacts when it comes to convincing others about a change project. This is covered in Chapter 10.

Fit between Informal and Formal Networks. In most organisations informal networks determine how work actually gets done. A recent McKinsey report[3] found that in many industries, including manufacturing, services and the public sector, informal networks almost never follow formal organisational charts and so managers often fail to guess correctly who turns to whom for advice. Such key people can be detected with network analysis, as social network studies have shown (Cross and Parker, 2004).[4] Moreover, the extent of fit between formal and informal networks can have implications for organisational performance. For example, centralised formal networks, where people often turn to a few core members, can create inefficiencies, as core members' time and resources are limited. Informal advice networks can complement these formal ties by increasing the efficiency of workflows.

---

[3] McKinsey, 'Tapping the Power of Hidden Influencer', 18 March 2014 (www.mckinsey.com/business-functions/organization/our-insights/tapping-the-power-of-hidden-influencers, accessed 19 July 2016).
[4] Krackhardt (1992) explains the failed results of the unionisation process in a firm using detailed social network analysis. Krackhardt found that one reason for the failure of the union was the selection of an enthusiastic but inefficient representative in the company who was not a central actor in either an advice or friendship network.

Creativity Management. An important process underlying creativity is the recombination of diverse insights and ideas. Diversity in teams is frequently cited as a critical success factor but research shows that too much diversity can be accompanied by communication problems. In addition, the overall network structure in an organisation also has implications for creativity. For example, small-world networks foster creativity, as they strike a balance between diversity (which brings novelty) and similarity (which facilitates communication).

Knowledge Management. Dosi (1988:1126) defines a knowledge base as 'the set of information inputs, knowledge, and capabilities that inventors draw on when looking for innovative solutions'.[5] An organisation's knowledge base is the collective knowledge that is stored, shared, disseminated and assimilated by its members in a distributed way. Network analysis can help demonstrate what an organisation knows, how its knowledge is distributed among departments or individuals and how its knowledge base evolves over time. Applying network analysis to knowledge management helps map the knowledge and expertise of groups or people in large organisations with multiple competences. It can also reveal the flow of knowledge into and out of an organisation, identifying people who are critical to cross-border knowledge exchanges and those who span departmental silos. It can help increase the effectiveness of inter-departmental knowledge-sharing by showing where blockages occur, sources of inefficiencies and spotting critical actors or groups that can increase the effectiveness of knowledge flows.[6]

Partner Selection. The strategic orientation of firms is often reflected in the network positions they occupy in alliance networks. For example, Dittrich and Duysters (2007) showed the way Nokia's alliance portfolio reflected the company's strategy in the face of a changing technological environment, namely its transition from an exploitation-oriented to an exploration-oriented learning strategy. It is easy to find this sort of evidence, especially for large firms. However, alliance portfolios do not always reflect strategic priorities, in the short term at least. This might be because of a gap between the way management selects partners in practice and its strategic priorities in

---

[5] A narrower definition of knowledge base refers to the knowledge and competence domains of inventors active in the R&D process. These competences can be measured by secondary data sources like patent citations (Fleming, 2001) or co-occurrence networks (Yayavaram and Ahuja, 2008).

[6] On managing knowledge networks, see Johnson (2009).

innovation. For example, radical innovations call for new partnerships and access to distant domains but firms may prefer to retain their existing partners, because of trust relationships and joint experience. Network analysis can help spot where to look for partners that will be the best fit for an organisation's strategic innovation priorities.

Transfer of Capabilities. The three levels in the network horizon that have implications for capability transfer are strategic alliance, alliance portfolio and network. If we assume that the network in Figure 5.1 shows a strategic alliance network within an industry, the positions of firms in the first (lower) cluster are advantageous because cohesive networks usually mean better quality of information and easier knowledge transfer. On the other hand, their positions are disadvantageous because they lack access to diversity. The firm B enjoys both benefits. It is part of a cohesive network and through its connection with node C has access to knowledge in the second (higher) cluster. But the extent to which these network positions yield advantages depends on many other factors. Converting industry relations into networks yields important clues about how to manage learning processes effectively, according to environmental conditions.

Industry and Competitiveness Analysis. Network analysis can be applied to the evolution of a technological field, detecting the major patents and leading firms that contribute to its evolution. It can also be used to evaluate the positioning of organisations vis-à-vis others in the network and to identify strategic groups or constellations (Gomes-Casseres, 1996). In an early study, Stuart and Podolny (1996) analysed the evolution of the technological positions of Japanese semiconductor firms in networks, illustrating the proximate positions of consumer electronics companies (Sony, Sharp, Matsushita, Sanyo) on the one hand and those of computing devices (NEC, Hitachi, Toshiba, Fujitsu) on the other. They showed how the positioning of Mitsubishi gradually moved from one group to the other through its changing competences.

Supply Chain Management. In supplier networks, mapping the network positions of second- and third-tier suppliers yields interesting insights into the critical yet unrecognised role some of them play. Kim, Choi and Dooley (2011) analysed the supplier network of Honda Acura and detected the vital role played by a third-tier supplier (HFI) that was connected to prominent suppliers in the Honda network, yet whose strategic role had gone largely

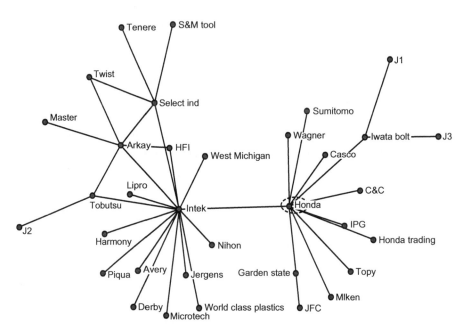

Figure 5.3   Supply Network of Honda Acura, and the Critical Importance of HFI
Source: Kim, Choi and Dooley, 2011

unnoticed. They noted the critical role of this firm in timely identification and resolution of system-level operational problems in the network (see Figure 5.3).

Diffusion of Managerial Practices. When markets are uncertain, organisations are likely to mimic the behaviour of others (DiMaggio and Powell, 1983), exchange with others who occupy similar positions and also rely more on others with whom they have exchanged in the past (Podolny, 1994). In addition, when market information is unavailable, actors rely on the information revealed by others' status in the network (Podolny, 1993; 1994). According to social network theory, equivalence and prominence may trigger similar behaviours and attitudes (Burt, 1987). For example, in Figure 5.1 nodes J and I are both connected only to nodes H and G, making them structurally equivalent and giving them a similar social status in the network. Another mechanism of mimicry works through prominence; that is, actors may observe and mimic others whose prominence is revealed by a central network position (for example, node G in Figure 5.1). In cohesive networks actors are influenced by the attitudes of others in a closed network. For example, most of A's connections are connected to each other, which increases the likelihood that common attitudes and behaviours are observed in A's network. A network perspective increases awareness of the way search processes diverge from or converge on others occupying similar positions or from those in the same strategic block.[7]

Marketing. Information about products diffuses through networks. Moreover, networks are important in adoption decisions, as people often turn to their peers to ask for advice and information, and their decisions are often influenced by others in their networks or elsewhere. Network analysis yields clues about the potential influentials in a market or community.

Decision-making. In a McKinsey study conducted among 2,207 executives in 2009, 60 per cent reported that bad decisions were made as frequently as good decisions. The study found that by increasing the quality of the decision-making process itself, an increase in returns of up to 7 per cent was likely.[8] Cohesive networks with strong ties between members may result in cognitive biases in decision-making. For example, in Figure 5.1, node A is a central actor in the first (lower) cluster and its only access to external information is from the nodes in this cluster. All these members are largely connected to one another, forming a cohesive network. This means that an opinion can be increasingly shared and agreed upon between them, preventing their exposure to alternative views. So to what extent is the feedback received from these connections precise and reliable? Are there biases involved that might lower the quality of decisions taken? Diversity in feedback networks can considerably reduce this risk. A positive feedback mechanism embedded in a network may mean that an inferior routine is increasingly favoured at the expense of more peripheral or niche areas that might be ignored.

Venture Capital and Entrepreneurs. Networks give off signals about the status of their members (Podolny, 1993; 1994). Podolny (1993) highlighted the importance of status revealed by the social networks of investment banks, finding that higher-status banks could borrow at lower costs. Such signals

---

[7] Examples are Stuart and Podolny's (1996) research on Japanese and US firms, as well as Nohria and Garcia Pont (1991) on strategic blocks.

[8] Lovallo and Sibony (2010). For cognitive biases in decision-making, see Tversky and Kahneman (1974) and Kahneman, Lovallo and Sibony (2011).

can be critical to the decisions venture capital firms make when selecting entrepreneurs to fund. With better awareness of such signals, venture capitals can improve the quality of their decisions and entrepreneurs can build networks in an informed way, depending on the resource needs that characterise different start-up phases.

Implementation of Innovation. Studies show that where access to resources is critical, networks effective in the generation of ideas and recognition of opportunities differ from networks that help implement ideas. Social network theory explains which type of network position is better for which purpose in entrepreneurship, intrapreneurship and building coalitions for innovation projects. For example, Baer (2012) showed that the more novel an inventor's idea, the higher the positive effects of the inventor's strong buy-in ties and networking ability within a firm, on the chances of implementation.

5.1.2   Which Network?

This step involves deciding which networking level to focus on (intra-organisational, inter-organisational or market level), and how to define network nodes. Of course, several types of network can be analysed simultaneously and specific data can be used for various purposes. For example, if an organisation is interested in the fit between informal and formal networks and its effects on performance, analysis of an internal advice network can be carried out alongside an analysis of co-working networks. An advice network can also be used to identify influential people in an organisation. The information an advice network reveals can be complemented by an analysis of patent networks, and so on. As well as determining levels and units of analysis, it is also necessary to decide whether to zoom in or zoom out of the network to take a bird's-eye view. Zooming in often requires refined data collection about the qualitative attributes of ties and actors. Zooming out implies overseeing a broader range of actors and ties and collecting qualitative data may not be feasible. Later in this chapter we will consider some decision-making criteria for zooming in or zooming out depending on a variety of external conditions.

5.1.3   Social Network Analysis

A critical decision is determining what social network metrics to apply to the task at hand. The correspondence between different processes and relevant network metrics is explored in detail in the later chapters of this book. Depending on what type of SNA metrics is chosen, data collection is carried out. (Some major sources of data are described in Chapter 4.) The nature of data needed and the resources available will affect the time needed for data collection, which can be done in the short term or span several weeks if, for example, individual interviews and surveys, etc., are necessary. Once data collection is complete software tools are used to map social relations in the form of networks.

5.1.4   Appraisal

What are the implications of the results of network analysis for the initial aim? How do networks influence various procedures in innovation? What factors give rise to networks? Throughout this book we will see what different network positions and structures imply for different purposes, and in Part IV we will examine what lies behind networks. It is important to remember that every network structure can have a different implication, depending on the initial aim.

5.1.5   Planning

The extent to which network interventions can be carried out depends largely on the network horizon and level of analysis. The larger and more complex a network, the more difficult it becomes to lay out a desired structure and intervene in it. Nevertheless, it is feasible to sketch out an idea of a desired network structure and gain some insight into the kinds of actions that will be needed to achieve it. At the intra-organisational level, sketching a desired network structure is easier, as are network interventions. In some cases network management does not involve direct network interventions but is used to analyse existing situations.

5.1.6   Follow-up

Network management is a continuous process, not a once and for all activity. It requires monitoring the way network interventions change outcomes and putting in place routine processes to ensure regularisation of all the steps described here. For maximum effectiveness, changes in networks should be observed over time so that organisations can develop an understanding of the factors behind network change and how the evolution of networks is related to performance outcomes.

5.2 Innovation Types and Networks

Different types of innovation have different implications for innovators' networks.

5.2.1 Product and Process Innovations

Studies reveal that product and process innovations are better carried out with different types of alliance partner. The role suppliers and customers play in process innovation is often emphasised, while collaborations with universities, research labs and customers are highlighted in product innovations.

Process Innovations. During in the development of the Honda Accord, manufacturing costs were reduced by around 25 per cent as a result of innovative ideas from suppliers working with Honda engineers and knowledge-sharing applied to a number of design problems (Liker and Choi, 2004). The connections between the suppliers themselves also increased their innovative contributions to the value chain, as they shared technical information or jointly developed new parts (Choi and Krause, 2006).

Users play an important role in process innovations by recognising needs and inventing solutions through trial and error and experimentation during the production process (Von Hippel, 1976). A historical example is the joint venture between Ford Motor Company and Pilkington Brothers Glass, which resulted in a process innovation in which the previously separate casting and annealing processes were combined. This resulted in a considerable productivity increase in plate glassmaking, which ultimately strengthened the market for gasoline-powered car design (Utterback, 1994). Pilkington's complementary knowledge about its own expertise came from a user (Ford) outside the glass industry.

In the pharmaceutical sector, Procter & Gamble has initiated a systematic programme in which customers participate in finding solutions to particular problems (Dodgson, Gann and Salter, 2006). Similar practices have been observed in the steel industry (Nakamura and Ohashi, 2008). They find that user innovation accounts for approximately 40 per cent of total factor productivity in the basic oxygen furnace process.

Cross-industry Collaborations. A critical network management capability is maintaining the autonomy and diversity of suppliers, while ensuring their identification with the network.[9] A possible negative side-effect of suppliers' contributions to process innovations is that the focal firm may become dependent on its suppliers for innovation. Moreover, supplier knowledge is generally at the component level and contributes to efficiency increasing process innovations rather than breakthroughs. During recent years, automotive firms have increasingly outsourced their R&D to suppliers and in the process have lost their capability to develop breakthrough innovations themselves, with the risk that they are becoming largely dependent on their suppliers' innovative capabilities. BMW followed an unconventional strategy with its cross-industry alliance with a 'non-supplier' (Gassman et al., 2010). The authors show how BMW reduced its dependence on its established suppliers for innovation by introducing a driver-controlled computer system (iDrive) in collaboration with the haptic technology firm Immersion. Indeed, vehicle manufacturers are increasingly turning to cross-industry collaborations to innovate, in response to a host of technical and regulatory challenges as well as suppliers' lack of knowledge in platform-based application programming interfaces (APIs).[10] In a study of Canadian firms, Li and Vanhaverbeke (2009) report that cross-industry collaboration with suppliers helped generate breakthrough innovations.

Product Innovations. For product innovations, universities, research labs and customers can be the most effective partners. In the early phases of technology life cycles in particular, access to new scientific knowledge is a critical input in innovation. Belderbos, Carre and Lokshin (2004) find that in rapidly changing technological environments R&D-intensive firms tend to form collaborations with universities in developing new products.

Examples from open innovation strategies show how different stakeholders contribute to product and process innovations through 'knowledge brokers'. Knowledge brokering refers to the systematic procedures firms use

---

[9] The innovative potential of the network largely depends on the cooperative strategies of the integrator. According to the 2014 survey of the consultant group Planning Perspectives Inc, suppliers rank Honda and Toyota as the best firms in terms of collaboration quality. On the other hand GM is ranked worst automaker, in terms of trustworthiness, communication skills and IPR protection. On the governance of buyer-supplier relations in new product development, see Sobrero and Roberts (2002).

[10] For example, Chevrolet Spark collaborated with Internet radio specialist Livio. Livio's process innovation is a connection application that can be used with many mobile and automobile platforms. See Newcomb (2012).

to find novel ideas about new product concepts or to solve problems related to innovation. One well-known example is Procter & Gamble's Connect and Develop programme, where knowledge brokers have a central role in searching for solutions, new insights and potential partners. Knowledge brokering is increasingly used for business process innovations as well, since business processes often have common characteristics across different contexts. For example, a European bank used innovative ideas from amusement parks, supermarkets, department stores and traffic control planning systems to find solutions to the problem of customer queueing (Billington and Davidson, 2010).

5.2.2   Radical and Incremental Innovations

Dahlin and Behrens (2005) identify three characteristics of radical innovation: novelty, uniqueness and impact on future technologies. Radical innovations are likely to change the competitive positioning of firms in an industry, while incremental innovations build on existing competences, reinforcing the position of established firms in the market (Abernathy and Clark, 1985).

Alliance Portfolios and Radical/Incremental Innovations. A firm's alliance portfolio shows the balance between exploration and exploitation (related respectively to radical and incremental innovations) in its innovation strategy (Beckman, Haunschild and Phillips, 2004). An exploration strategy calls for diversity in the alliance portfolio, as well as partners that are distant from the focal firm in terms of their competences. Radical innovations are associated with a broad knowledge base that includes diverse and unrelated elements. In other words, major leaps in innovation call for distant rather than local search activities.

Conversely, an exploitative alliance portfolio consists of partners with similar technological competences, homogeneous partner profiles, strong ties and long-term relationships. Localised search activities are more likely to increase incremental innovation capabilities. But there is a trade-off: as Cohen and Prusak (2001) put it, 'the ties that bind can also become the ties that blind', and in this case strong ties can deter firms from radical innovations. Radical innovations are associated with brokerage positions in networks, since novelties can emerge from bringing previously unconnected elements together (Granovetter, 1973; Burt, 1992). At the same time, cohesive networks, where trust, common knowledge and experiences govern relations, are more effective for deep knowledge transfer (Hansen, 1999).

Intra-organisational Networks and Radical Innovations. At the intra-organisational level, formal and informal networks also have implications for the explorative and exploitative nature of innovations. Jansen, Van Den Bosch and Volberda (2006) found that the centralisation of networks is correlated with fewer exploratory and more exploitative innovations. Centralisation reduces the quality and quantity of innovative ideas because it is in tension with non-routine problem-solving processes, reducing the likelihood that people in the organisation will search for innovative solutions and ideas. The authors also find that higher connectivity in informal networks increases explorative innovations – but only up to a point. Beyond a threshold level, connectivity reduces explorative innovations, as cohesive networks tend to exclude divergent perspectives.

Radical Innovations and Network Change. Existing networks also change as a result of radical innovations. Barley (1986) carried out an ethnographic network study in two radiology departments in the US before and after the adoption of computerised tomography (CT) equipment. He shows how the power distribution in networks changed as the new and disruptive CT technologies reduced the need for the expertise of tenured radiologists and increased the power of newly recruited CT specialists in the organisation. (We will learn more about network changes due to organisational change in Chapter 10.)

5.2.3 Architectural versus Component Innovations

New product development requires two types of knowledge: one is concerned with how different components are integrated to form a coherent whole; the other with the individual components of a system (Henderson and Clark, 1990). Innovations that reconfigure the way components are linked together, without major changes in the components themselves, are called architectural innovations. Improvements or novelties in components, without any alteration in the interfaces between them, are termed component innovations. Architectural and component innovations can be both incremental and radical and are usually associated with different networks (Henderson and Clark, 1990). Collaboration with suppliers is critical for quality improvements in component innovations, while collaboration with customers is important for architectural innovations, since customers can give insights about how the architecture of a system can be reconfigured to address a different need.

The modularity of a product system has an impact on the extent to which architectural innovations can be pursued through partnerships with suppliers and customers. In modular systems, interfaces are clearly defined, so that the specialisations of different firms can be integrated into the system. However, modular systems can also prevent breakthrough innovations, because modularity enables partners to specialise on individual components, reducing the possibility of a radical change in the overall product architecture (Fleming and Sorenson, 2003). We will learn more about modular product architectures and how they can define relations between producers in Chapter 8.

5.3   R&D Intensity and Networks

In many sectors there is a strong correlation between R&D intensity and involvement in strategic technology partnerships (Freeman, 1991; Hagedoorn, 1995). Figure 5.4 shows the firms involved in innovation in Organisation for Economic Cooperation and Development (OECD) countries, distinguishing between R&D active firms and firms with no R&D. It shows

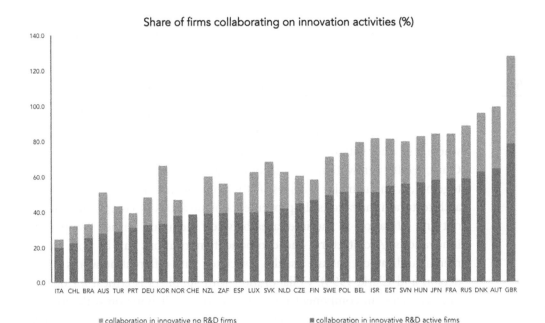

Figure 5.4   Collaboration Patterns in OECD Countries according to R&D Intensity
Source: OECD STI Scoreboard 2013

that despite wide differences between countries, collaboration mostly takes place among R&D active firms.

5.3.1 Absorptive Capacity and Network Advantage

The importance of R&D intensity in inter-organisational networks is related to absorptive capacity, which is the 'ability of a firm to recognise the value of new, external information, assimilate it, and apply it to commercial ends' (Cohen and Levinthal, 1990). Organisations' internal capabilities and their access to external knowledge are largely complementary. R&D intensity is critical in gaining network advantage because it enhances absorptive capacity, facilitating the acquisition of knowledge and capabilities from partners. In other words, absorptive capacity increases the potential to leverage network positions.

For example, Tsai (2001) found that the centrality of a business unit increases innovative performance when the unit has higher absorptive capacity. Shipilov (2009) found that the extent to which firms can make use of structural holes in a network depends on their absorptive capacity in dealing with heterogeneous information from diverse sources.

5.3.2 Cognitive Distance between Partners

Learning from partners depends largely on the cognitive distance between them, which is directly influenced by R&D intensity. While some degree of knowledge similarity is necessary for two organisations to be able to understand and communicate with each other, too much similarity can restrict the potential for novelty, since the two partners do not have much to add to each other's knowledge. Absorptive capacity is critical in determining this optimal cognitive distance between two firms.[11]

5.4 Sources of Innovation and Networks

Firms are turning increasingly to external sources of knowledge and innovation, as the growing popularity of open innovation indicates (Chesbrough, 2003).

---

[11] For the inverted-U relation between knowledge transfer and partnerships, see Mowery, Oxley and Silverman (1998); Schoenmakers and Duysters (2006); Nooteboom et al. (2007).

5.4.1   Sectoral and Country Differences

The preference for internal or external sources of information, and specific sources of external information, are dependent on sectors and institutions. Figure 5.5 shows the importance attached to internal and external information sources by firms in selected OECD countries and Table 5.1 shows the breakdown of information sources within some selected sectors. In science-based sectors like pharmaceuticals, chemicals and mining, external sources of information from universities, scientific publications and professional and industry associations are more important. Laursen and Salter (2006) find that in science-based sectors and medium- to high-technology sectors like chemicals, firms access a broad range of sources for innovation. In relatively low-tech industries, like paper and printing or textiles, search is often narrower. In other sectors, like telecommunications and computing, suppliers, customers, competitors and other enterprises are significant sources of information. Besides sectoral differences, institutional framework also plays a role, as the heterogeneity in the importance given to various sources of information among OECD countries in Figure 5.5 shows. For example, environmental policies and health and safety regulations in different countries largely shape the relevance of different sources of information.

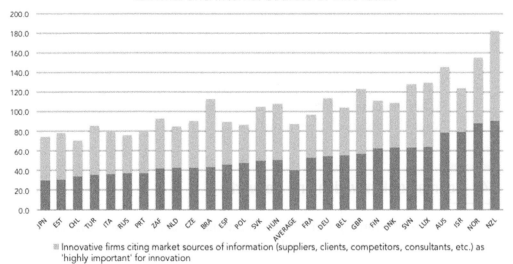

External and Internal Sources of Innovation

▦ Innovative firms citing market sources of information (suppliers, clients, competitors, consultants, etc.) as 'highly important' for innovation

■ Innovative firms citing internal sources of information as 'highly important' for innovation

Figure 5.5   Sources of Innovation in OECD Countries among Innovative Firms
Source: OECD STI Scoreboard 2013

Table 5.1 Sources of Innovation by Sector

	Customers from the private sector	Customers from the public sector	Competitors or other enterprises	Conferences, trade fairs, exhibitions	Within the enterprise	Government, public or private research institutes	Scientific journals and technical publications	Universities	Professional and industry associations	Suppliers
Mining and quarrying	23	9	19	15	52	7	14	15	12	32
Manufacture of food products; beverages and tobacco products	24	6	13	13	44	5	8	6	8	28
Manufacture of textiles, wearing apparel, leather	34	9	13	18	48	4	9	4	6	26
Manufacture of wood, paper, printing	25	12	13	20	43	4	10	4	7	30
Manufacture of chemicals and chemical products	27	9	13	16	54	8	19	11	10	24
Manufacture of basic pharmaceutical products and preparations	25	14	17	24	62	14	25	18	11	28
Manufacture of computer, electronic and optical products	32	9	14	18	58	7	10	10	5	23
Manufacture of electrical equipment	33	12	15	21	50	4	10	8	11	32
Manufacture of machinery and equipment	35	11	16	20	53	6	11	10	7	25
Manufacture of motor vehicles	29	12	16	14	54	5	13	9	9	20
Waste collection, treatment and disposal activities; materials recovery	15	11	12	11	48	4	5	5	8	25
Construction	19	10	12	14	41	5	8	9	7	29

Table 5.1 (*cont.*)

	Customers from the private sector	Customers from the public sector	Competitors or other enterprises	Conferences, trade fairs, exhibitions	Within the enterprise	Government, public or private research institutes	Scientific journals and technical publications	Universities	Professional and industry associations	Suppliers
Wholesale and retail trade	25	10	17	16	45	8	11	5	8	29
Information and communication	30	14	15	14	60	4	12	8	7	22
Publishing activities	22	15	17	12	52	4	8	3	5	19
Telecommunications	33	13	21	21	55	4	11	8	7	35
Computer programming, consultancy	33	16	15	15	64	5	13	9	8	20
Financial and insurance activities	25	10	21	7	62	2	6	3	10	26
Architectural and engineering activities; scientific research and development; advertising and market research	27	10	12	14	52	9	17	11	9	22

Source: OECD STI Scoreboard 2013

5.4.2   Range of Information Sources

Looking at UK firms, Laursen and Salter (2006) found that the range of different sources of innovation (breadth of search) is curvilinearly related to innovation performance. In other words, while the diversity of external sources has a positive effect, too many external sources of innovation increase coordination costs and a balance between external and internal sources has to be found. Co-inventor networks and inventor mobility patterns can reveal knowledge flows in and out of firms. For example, Fleming and Marx (2006) map the networks of inventors in Silicon Valley, demonstrating both the collaboration patterns between inventors and the mobility of inventors between firms (see also Fleming and Frenken, 2007).

5.5   Innovation Timing and Networks

A major innovation management decision is the timing of entry into new markets. A firm's network strategy can influence the success of new market entry.

5.5.1   Timing in Standards-based Industries

In standards-based industries, the utility of a technology depends on its widespread adoption. A common strategy of technology-owning firms is to form partnerships early on with a wide variety of actors in the industry (customers, other firms, suppliers, research institutes, etc.) to strengthen the installed base of their standard/technology. A variety of early partnerships means firms can benefit from network effects in strengthening the standard and increase its adoption as the market matures. Early partnerships with producers and suppliers of complementary goods gives a critical strategic advantage in developing a standard within a technical community. The network position of firms determines the extent to which they can access different stakeholders. For example, Soh (2010) looked at local area networks in the US and found that central firms with high ego network density (see Chapter 4 for ego network density) that adopted an open strategy of knowledge-sharing achieved better innovation performance than other closed central firms.

In standards-based industries, firms' alliances and intellectual property rights (IPR) strategies can determine the dominant standard that will be adopted later on. An example of this is Motorola's strategy during the early 1990s when the GSM standard was being set in Europe (Bekkers, Duysters and Verspagen, 2002). Two factors played a central role in the evolution of the GSM market: the first was Motorola's aggressive patenting and licensing strategy as a holder of numerous essential patents;[12] the second was Ericsson's strategic and central network position in controlling the flow of information in the network. Motorola selected firms that it cross licensed its technologies strategically so as to influence the standardisation process, and its cross-licensing partnership with Ericsson helped it obtain a central position in the strategic alliance network.

5.5.2   Early Access to Information

First-mover advantages and disadvantages can be critically dependent on firms' early access to information through networks. The position of a firm in a strategic alliance network is related to the timing of its entry in an emerging product market. For example, Lee (2007) considered mobile telephony and analysed the impact of the network position of firms in terms of the quality, quantity and diversity of information they accessed. In the early phases of a technology life cycle in particular, access to information can be a critical determinant of later success by reducing market and technological uncertainties. While a cohesive network and repeated interactions with partners increase the *quality* of information accessed, they can have a negative impact on firms' *flexibility* in adapting to novelties. This trade-off can be managed with a network strategy where firms balance existing networks and new partners.

5.5.3   Industry Life Cycle

According to the industry life cycle approach (Utterback, 1994; Abernathy and Utterback, 1978), in the introduction phase of industry evolution, product innovations are more common than process innovations. As a dominant design emerges, product innovations slow down and process innovations intensify. This is because later on, competitive pressures and increased entry by new firms call for efficiency gains in production processes.

---

[12] An essential IPR is one in which the standard will work only with the knowledge or technology involved in it. Therefore both before and after a standard is established, an essential IPR has a great strategic value (Bekkers, Duysters and Verspagen, 2002).

In mature phases of the industry life cycle, with the emergence of a dominant design, the assemblies, sub-assemblies and components of the product system, as well as production processes, are largely shaped. In this phase product innovations are often made to complementary products that support the existing dominant design. In other words, the types of partnership that yield strategic advantages to firms depend on life cycle stage and innovation type (product or process). In addition, established networks give incumbents a strategic advantage, because links with suppliers and distributors can act as a barrier to the entry of new firms.

5.6   Revisiting the Network Horizon

In this section we will explore the factors that help organisations decide whether to zoom in or zoom out of networks.

A broad network horizon allows diverse elements to be incorporated into an organisation's vision rather than focusing on a limited part of it. In general, a broad network horizon is considered beneficial for innovation performance, particularly for generating radical innovations or break-throughs (Burt, 2004). But broadening horizons has a cost in terms of the cognitive resources required to understand and manage them; uncertainty and the risks involved in forming new ties with actors that are not proximate also have to be taken into consideration. The broader the network horizon, the more complex it is to analyse and manage networks.

Figure 5.6 illustrates this trade-off. The network horizon is shown in the horizontal axis, and costs (benefits) in the vertical axis. As the network horizon is broadened, the costs of network management increase exponentially. These costs are related to the increased complexity of processing more information and higher coordination costs. Some of these cost items are tangible, for example, the cost of data collection and processing and information and training about social networks. At the intra-organisational level costs are also higher as the network horizon grows, for similar reasons. One important challenge is management's ability to interpret data (Daft and Weick, 1984). A wider horizon means more information to collect, process and analyse and the challenge of interpretation can be daunting. When it comes to information, more is not necessarily better, since there is always the risk of information overload in organisations (O'Reilly, 1980).

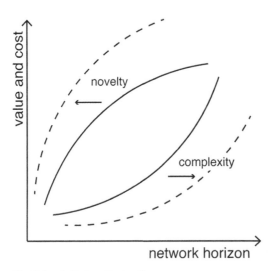

Figure 5.6   The Network Horizon Trade-off
Note: As network horizon broadens (as one zooms out of the network), complexity of the network increases, and so does the potential for novelty.

A number of factors contribute to the difficulty of managing networks as the network horizon expands.

- **Complexity:** networks inside and outside organisations are often complex. It takes computational effort to unravel their exact structure, including data collection and analysis.
- **Dynamics:** networks are continuously in a state of change and most organisations have little direct control over their structure.
- **Routines:** an organisation's existing routines, procedures and processes may not be suitable for incorporating distant, unfamiliar actors and technologies in the decision variables revealed by a broad network horizon.
- **Bounded rationality:** the broader the network horizon the more difficult it is to understand the complex interactions between elements. A more attainable target is to focus on a few partners because as a network grows, so too do inaccuracies in interpreting and appraising patterns of interdependence.
- **Consent of different parties:** a broad network horizon gives the opportunity to detect potentially useful partners but the willingness of other firms to engage with the focal firm is a further challenge. Even if new potential partners are detected, forming and sustaining a (successful) partnership is an uncertain process. Successful criteria are especially

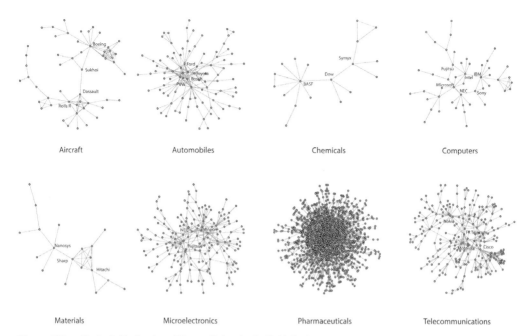

Figure 5.7   Strategic Technology Alliance Networks in Eight Sectors
Note: The networks show the largest connected components.
Source of data: MERIT-CATI database

important here because of the potential for opportunism when partners are strangers to a firm's existing network.

The next question is what factors influence the trade-off between the costs and benefits of broadening the network horizon? Under what conditions do the benefits outweigh the costs? What are the external and internal factors that determine the balance?

5.7   Complexity and Novelty Trade-off: Institutional, Technological and Firm-specific Factors

An analysis of network structure reveals similarities and differences between industries. Figure 5.7 shows the networks of strategic technology partnerships between firms in eight sectors, during the years 2004–6.[13] The network measures are given in Table 5.2.

---

[13] The source of these data is MERIT-CATI on strategic technology alliances. Only the largest connected components are shown.

Table 5.2 Network Measures for Alliance Networks in Eight Sectors

	Automobiles	Aircraft	Chemicals	Materials	Pharmaceutical	Computers	Micro-electronics	Telecom
Number of nodes	261	86	277	276	1814	137	306	450
Number of links	285	127	186	227	2390	118	387	601
Links per node	1.09	1.48	0.67	0.82	1.32	0.86	1.26	1.34
Number of alliances	194	55	169	161	2280	93	268	330
Centralisation	0.192	0.208	0.420	0.245	0.0368	0.145	0.107	0.091
Number of nodes in the largest component	96	52	19	19	1307	48	179	224

Among the eight sectors, the most intensive R&D partnerships are in pharmaceuticals (by a considerable degree), microelectronics and telecommunications. The structure of the latter two networks is highly alike and can be explained by similarities in their knowledge bases and the relatedness of the two sectors. Materials and chemicals also share structural similarities, except that the existence of BASF in the chemicals sector significantly increases the centralisation of the network compared to materials. Chemicals and materials networks are also remarkable for their high fragmentation; the proportion of firms in the largest connected cluster, as shown in Figure 5.7, is lower than other industries – only nineteen firms out of 277 (chemicals) and 276 (materials). There is a discernible core-periphery structure in the automobiles network, revealed by the high centralisation coefficient; the network core is composed of firms like BMW, Daimler, Ford and the leading parts supplier Bosch. The aircraft sector is composed of two noticeable clusters, connected by the alliance between Russian military aircraft producer Sukhoi and Dessault Aviation in 2003 for the purpose of developing a supersonic administrative plane. There are four clusters in the computers network, connected by alliances between the industry leaders (Fujitsu, Microsoft, Intel, NEC, IBM and Sony) that take place at the network centre.

Why can we observe these differences and similarities between networks in different industries? The factors that give rise to them can be categorised as institutions and major events, technologies and markets, and organisation-specific. It is difficult to untangle the effects of these factors, largely because they co-evolve with the networks and are highly complex. In Chapter 13, we will look at the evolution of networks in different industries in more detail, as well as the factors that govern evolution. Here, we will examine insights about the three categories of sources for different network architectures.

5.7.1   Institutions

Financial systems, policy context, forms of competition, legal systems and culture all play a role in the way actors relate to each other when generating innovations.[14] For example, in their study of the history of the computer industry, Cloodt, Hagedoorn and Roijakkers (2006) underline the role of European-level policies that aimed to diminish the dominance of US firms in domestic markets, which intensified partnerships among European firms. In biotechnology, the instability of the capital markets in the 1980s and the stock market collapse in 1987 drove entrepreneurial biotechnology firms to enter into partnerships with large pharmaceutical companies, which influenced network structure to a large extent (Roijakkers and Hagedoorn, 2006). European-level policies to combat problems related to the environment have been influential in many different kinds of collaboration between various stakeholders. Policy frameworks also determine the way that organisations benefit from privileged network positions. For example, Vasudeva, Zaheer and Hernandez (2012) find that corporatism influences the impact brokerage positions have on firm performance. Firms make better use of brokerage positions in corporatist contexts. To interpret sectoral differences in networks it is necessary to have a good understanding of how the institutional context promotes relations between actors or inhibits them, and how actors benefit from networks.

Other factors that influence sectoral differences in networks are technology and market-related and organisation-specific (Table 5.3). These factors shape the extent to which it is necessary for management to zoom in or zoom out of networks.

---

[14] The institutional approach to innovation studies developed during the mid-1990s, particularly within the systems of innovation area (see Chapter 2). On this, see Edquist (1997).

Table 5.3 Factors that Influence the Network Strategy Trade-off

Institutional Factors, Major Events, Macro-economic Conditions	
Technology and market-specific	Economies of scope
	Uncertainty
	Modularity
	Heterogeneity in consumer tastes
	Industry life cycle
	Network externalities
	Knowledge base (complexity, breadth, depth)
Organisation-specific	Absorptive capacity
	Size and diversity
	Network management experience
	Innovation strategy

5.7.2   Technology and Market-specific Factors

Economies of Scope. These refer to the extent to which a competence can be used to meet different market needs.[15] Some industries are characterised by rich economies of scope, for example, the software industry, in which software modules can be reconfigured easily to address user needs in different markets. As an example, 3M's innovative capabilities are largely rooted in the way it applies adhesive technology to a range of different products.[16] Large and diversified firms can have an advantage in exploiting economies of scope, by applying the knowledge in one business unit to the operations of other business units. However, the coordination costs of broadening the intra-organisational network horizon are also increased. In general, the advantages to be gained by expanding the network horizon (exploiting new markets, recognising opportunities for innovation) will justify higher coordination costs when there are rich economies of scope.

Heterogeneous Consumer Preferences. The extent to which economies of scope can be exploited successfully depends on how variety is valued in the market. In platforms, standardisation facilitates the generation of variety by ensuring the seamless integration of the elements produced. For example,

---

[15] The notion of economies of scope refers to economising through variety. Its origins date back to Panzar and Willig (1981) and the concept is used to explain related diversification activities of firms, where firms economise through using one competence in a range of different areas. Henderson and Cockburn (1996) show that large firms in drug discovery have more opportunities to make use of economies of scope by utilising spillovers internally and externally.

[16] Arndt (2006).

in the video games industry, standard interfaces defined by console manufacturers attract diverse game developers to design games for platforms, which ultimately increases the variety of games offered. A broad network horizon, which takes into account the interactions between different sides of the market and their networks, is useful where utility depends on variety.[17]

Modularity. The elements of a modular system can be mixed and matched in different configurations. With inter-organisational modularity, each firm is specialised in a different element of the system (Schilling, 2000). Although modularity increases efficiency by enabling these specialisations, it can also inhibit breakthrough innovations because of a low level of communication between producers. A broader network horizon will help with the reconfiguration of interfaces and architectural innovations and enable better oversight of the different parts of the system and the ways in which they are connected.

Knowledge Base. When the knowledge base of an industry is broad and complex, broadening the network horizon can be both beneficial and costly. One advantage of complexity is richer technological opportunities, as there are more recombinative possibilities. On the other hand, complexity makes it more difficult for actors to access and understand each other's knowledge. For example, Sorenson, Rivkin and Fleming (2006) found that when knowledge is not complex, the distance between the source and recipient of knowledge is irrelevant, because even if the social distance is great, the recipient will still have access to knowledge. When knowledge is highly complex, distance between recipient and sender is still irrelevant, because it is difficult for both parties to access the other's knowledge.[18] However, at an intermediate level of knowledge complexity, the social distance between recipient and sender becomes significant, as a short social distance increases the quality of access to knowledge. In this case a narrow network horizon will help knowledge communication and a broad network horizon will help identify complementary knowledge residing in distant parts of the network.

---

[17] See Gawer (2014) on platforms, economies of scope and innovation.

[18] They measure the knowledge complexity of a patent by the ease with which its domains (sub-classes) can be used together with other domains, by analysing the sub-class's co-occurrence with others in earlier patents.

Stage in the Industry Life Cycle. A broad network horizon is useful in the initial phases of an industry life cycle, in order to help organisations recognise technological opportunities in distant markets. The initial phase of an industry life cycle is characterised by product innovations that might yield early market share, and such innovations are better generated by access to diversity. A broad network horizon in the initial phases of an industry life cycle will also mean better reception of market signals about evolving technologies, and help an organisation cope better with uncertainty. In mature phases of an industry life cycle, product innovations give way to efficiency-oriented process innovations. There are fewer benefits of adopting a broad network horizon at this stage, since available opportunities for product innovations are saturated. While these call for a narrower network horizon, focusing on the proximate network and efficiency increasing process innovations, there is a risk of losing flexibility. Christensen's (1997) notion of disruptive innovations refers to the ability of firms to recognise opportunities in market 'fringes' and users' unmet needs. Late entrants may gain market share by recognising and exploring these niche segments and needs, while incumbent firms may miss distant market opportunities because they are entrapped in existing networks. Therefore in the later stages of an industry life cycle, an organisation will benefit from having a balance between a narrow and broad network horizon.

Network Externalities in User Markets. A broader horizon enables the development of complementary products in a product system, increasing the utility of the technology for users and strengthening its installed base. A wider network horizon that takes into account the links between users and the producers and suppliers of complementary goods will attract diverse actors to a platform with network externalities. The case of GSMs is an example: Ericsson's network position yielded advantages in information control within the network that were very useful in the development of the standard (Bekkers, Duysters and Verspagen, 2002). Broadening the network horizon is beneficial when there are network externalities.

Uncertainty. Uncertainty and turbulence in an industry increase new tie formation between new partners and reinforce ties between existing partners, depending on the nature of uncertainty. Beckman, Haunschild and Phillips (2004) find that firms facing market uncertainty tend to reinforce existing ties and those facing firm-specific uncertainty tend to broaden their networks. Yet the impact of tie reinforcement depends on the overall network structure. There is evidence that reinforcing existing ties within a tightly bound cohesive network reduces the innovative performance of firms in technologically turbulent industries.[19] This is because embeddedness in cohesive networks, when the technology and the market are in flux, reduces the extent to which firms are informed about developments elsewhere in the industry. In this case, the benefits of broadening the network horizon increase. At the same time, organisations receive better quality information more rapidly through strong ties, which is beneficial during periods of uncertainty and flux (Aral and Van Alstyne, 2011). Therefore, a balanced focus on both proximate and distant networks is beneficial.

5.7.3   Firm-specific Factors

Size and Diversification of Organisation. As organisations grow the complexity of networks in and around them also increases. Diversification increases the costs of coordination between different business units. This is because businesses may have different resource needs and conflicting strategic priorities, which add to the complexity of network management. But at the same time there are benefits of broadening the network horizon to make use of cross-synergies between different business units. Diversification enables the leverage of existing networks in different areas. Coherence in the knowledge base and relatedness among different business units can reduce the costs of taking a broad network perspective, because knowledge-sharing is facilitated.

Incremental or Radical Innovation Strategy. Explorative strategies that increase the likelihood of radical innovations are better implemented by broadening the network horizon because radical innovations call for the recombination of distant elements. However, focusing on the qualitative dimension of links between proximate partners is more helpful for an incremental innovation strategy, which requires improvement of existing competences and deep knowledge exchange, both of which are more effective between familiar partners.

---

[19] Rowley, Behrens and Krackhardt (2000) test this for the case of semiconductors and steel industries and find a negative interaction effect between the cohesiveness of the network and tie strength in semiconductors. Goerzen (2007) finds that repeated ties in the face of uncertainty reduce innovative performance.

Absorptive Capacity. Firms with higher absorptive capacity are more likely to cope with the information processing costs associated with increased network complexity, reducing the costs of a broad network horizon. They are also more capable at using their network positions to their advantage (Shipilov, 2009)

Experience in Network Management. Powell, Koput and Smith-Doerr (1996) found that the more R&D collaborations a firm had, the greater its number of non-R&D collaborations. In other words firms can cope better with complex networks as they gain more experience in R&D collaboration. Therefore the complexity and costs of a broad network horizon are expected to decrease as organisations gain experience.

First Mover or Follower? While first-mover firms perform better in developing a major technology, research shows that followers are more likely to address niche markets and adapt an innovation to the needs of different market segments. Therefore the benefits of a broader network horizon will in general increase for follower firms.

Discussion Questions

1. How does network management contribute to competitive advantage?

2. As far as network management is concerned:
   a. What are the difficulties in managing networks?
   b. What are the purposes of network management?
   c. What are the main stages in network management?

3. You are the director of a non-profit organisation, that aims to diffuse ecological practices in primary schools in the region. How would you use network management? Which networks would you consider? How can you use situational and interventionist network management? (For situational and interventionist network management, see Chapter 1.)

4. Why are there sectoral differences in alliance network structures?

5. In deciding the timing of entry in a market with network externalities, in which ways can inter-organisational networks be leveraged?

PART II

Search Processes

Alliances, Networks and Learning

Wisdom lies neither in fixity nor in change, but in the dialectic between the two.

Octavio Paz

In this chapter we explore the role of networks in learning and capability transfer in inter-organisational networks. We look into exploration and exploitation processes in learning, and consider how their balance, termed as ambidexterity, is related to alliances, alliance portfolios, and an organisation's positioning in global networks. We highlight various factors that shape the trade-off between the benefits of cohesive alliance networks and filling structural holes in an alliance network.

Most of the time learning in alliances is difficult, frustrating and necessitates effective management of knowledge transfer. The case of New United Motor Manufacturing, Inc. (NUMMI) shows how General Motors learned about the Japanese lean production system through knowledge transferred from Toyota to NUMMI, and then from NUMMI to GM (Inkpen, 2008). The NUMMI automobile manufacturing plant[1] was a joint venture between GM and Toyota, operating between 1984 and 2010 in Fremont, California. Initially, GM faced many challenges in establishing effective knowledge channels to bring external knowledge back into the firm. For one thing, there was strong resistance to a joint venture with Toyota from GM engineers, who felt their own capabilities were under threat. GM-based advisors who were appointed to NUMMI were insufficiently prepared to take the knowledge back to GM and implement what they had learned at NUMMI. Few people in GM were open to the new knowledge they brought back because it challenged the firm's existing operational routines. Faced with these problems GM set up new channels to improve knowledge transfer. Advisor training and rotation programmes were implemented, in which all advisors were assigned GM tutors and regular visits to NUMMI were

---

[1] NUMMI was acquired by Tesla Motors in 2010.

organised. These processes were facilitated by the formation of a Technical Liaison Office, which over time became the core element of building up alliance learning capabilities in GM.

The case of NUMMI highlights how intra-organisational networks can be aligned during the formation of an alliance. There are many barriers to learning from alliance partners: resistance inside the organisation to new knowledge, difficulties in communicating with a partner, concerns about the leakage of valuable knowledge, problems related to heterogeneous knowledge endowments, and so on. The challenges faced in managing a single alliance are increased by the fact that organisations are usually involved in more than one alliance at a time, which necessitates overseeing the synergies between different partners. Alliance portfolio management has therefore become a critical managerial capability for building effective channels of learning. An alliance portfolio is essentially an egocentric network, embedded in a larger network of organisations. Focusing solely on the alliance portfolio misses the big picture of the broader network, where the position of an organisation has important implications for its learning. Various levels of network horizon are at stake and network management involves overseeing the complementarities between them.

In this chapter we look at organisational learning at three levels: the dyadic level, where a single alliance is managed; the alliance portfolio level, concerned with all alliance partners; and the network level, which includes firms in the industry. Through alliances, organisations learn about partners, how to manage alliances, a specific technology or task, industry dynamics, protection of valuable knowledge, and how to learn (Anand and Khanna, 2000). What are the critical issues to consider at different network levels, to increase the chances of building and sustaining effective networks for learning?

6.1   Organisational Learning

There are two dimensions to organisational learning: exploration and exploitation (March, 1991).

6.1.1   Exploration and Exploitation

Exploration is about discovering the unknown, experimenting with new alternatives and increasing variety, while exploitation aims at refining and extending existing competences, technologies and paradigms (March, 1991: 85). A vast number of studies on exploration and exploitation address questions ranging from how organisations explore and exploit, whether exploration and exploitation are substitutes, which domain of activities they cover, or whether they are useful constructs at all.[2] Lavie, Stettner and Tushman (2010) state that when distinguishing between exploration and exploitation, the main reference point should be an organisation's existing knowledge base. Exploitation is associated with all activities that build on and strengthen an organisation's existing competences. On the other hand, exploratory activities deviate from an organisation's existing competences and knowledge base.

A useful categorisation of exploration and exploitation is provided by Li, Vanhaverbeke and Schoenmakers (2008), who distinguish three domains in which organisations explore and exploit: scientific, technological and the market. In these domains organisational learning takes place on a spectrum ranging from activities that are most familiar to the organisation (i.e. exploitative) to least familiar (i.e. exploratory). In addition, the notion of 'familiarity' can be cognitive, spatial or temporal (Li, Vanhaverbeke and Schoenmakers, 2008). For example, forming an alliance in the same geographical region or in the same field of activity is respectively spatial and cognitive exploitation. On the other hand, alliances formed across industries and nations are exploratory. 'Temporal' refers to the recency of investment. Exploitative investments are related to recent activities, whereas exploratory investments are those made when a firm launches a search about an activity undertaken in the past. For example, large pharmaceuticals engage in alliances with biotech companies to put previously discarded experimental compounds through a series of new tests. These tests might result in discovering new treatment areas for a compound that went unrecognised when it was first found (Li, Vanhaverbeke and Schoenmakers, 2008).

6.1.2   Ambidexterity

An organisation's internal routines and procedures can be oriented towards exploration, exploitation or both. Excessive exploration can be destructive if it comes at the cost of exploitation, that is, allocating resources to increase efficiency and improving what is already known (Levinthal and March,

---

[2] For more about the usefulness of this framework, see the debate in the DRUID Conference 2012: 'Let it be resolved that this conference believes that the exploration/exploitation trade-off is a helpful metaphor, but has little value in informing research that is relevant to organisations/managers.' The full debate can be found at www.druid.dk/streaming/ds2012/onsdag/links.htm, accessed 7 July 2016.

1993). Exploratory activities have risky returns, are uncertain and their results are often obtained in the long run. On the other hand exploitation is safer because it concerns short-term returns and there is less inter-temporal variety in performance. In his original essay, March (1991) highlighted the trade-off that organisations face in their choice between exploration and exploitation, stressing the importance of balancing the two strategies. This is organisational ambidexterity (Tushman and O'Reilly, 1996). Consistent research reveals that ambidexterity is associated with higher innovative performance and that successful firms balance exploration and exploitation through time and across different domains (Lavie, Kang and Rosenkopf, 2011). For example, Stettner and Lavie (2014) found that balancing exploration and exploitation across internal organisation, alliances and acquisitions enhances performance; Uotila et al. (2009) found that there is an inverted-U relationship between exploratory weight and financial performance to which R&D intensity contributes positively.

Yet ambidexterity can be difficult to realise because exploration and exploitation are usually based on distinct incompatible routines, which implies that they can be mutually detrimental.[3] Whether organisations can follow such distinct routines simultaneously depends on whether exploration and exploitation compete for resources. The more exploration and exploitation draw upon non-scarce resources the more they can be balanced (Gupta, Smith and Shalley, 2006).

An organisation's external links with other organisations are important sources for both exploration and exploitation. In this sense, the management of an individual alliance, composition of the alliance portfolio and an organisation's position in the industry network have implications for both activities.

6.2 Learning at the Dyadic Level

Figure 6.1 shows a hypothetical network in which nodes are organisations and links the alliances between them. The pair of organisations (17, 11) is a dyad in the network (D), and the light shaded area (P) illustrates the alliance portfolio of 17. For now, we will focus on three aspects that are critical for learning at the dyadic level: strength of ties, knowledge overlap between firms and alliance management capabilities.

---

[3] One point of view supports the idea that exploitation and exploration are substitutes – that is, one is conducted at the expense of the other. See, for example, Benner and Tushman (2002).

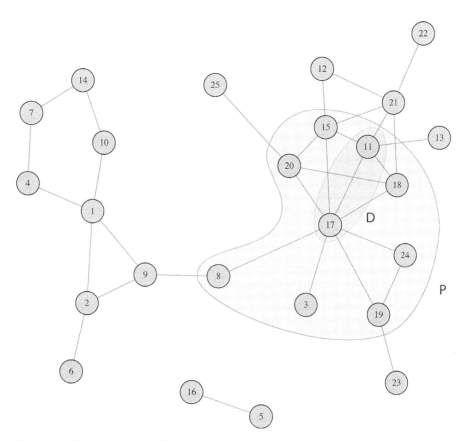

Figure 6.1   Illustration of Dyad, Portfolio and Network Levels
Note: D shows a single strategic alliance, P shows firm 17's portfolio of alliances.

6.2.1   Strength of Ties

In Figure 6.1, the 17–11 dyad is embedded in a cluster composed of nodes 15, 18, 20, 21. In this sub-network the information that 17 receives from its connections is likely to be redundant, as most of its partners are also connected to each other. Intuitively a dense social structure implies strong ties between organisations. On the other hand, sparse networks, or the lack of common partners between two organisations, generally implies weak ties (Granovetter, 1973), as indicated by the tie 17–8 in the network in Figure 6.1.[4] Granovetter (1973: 1361) defined strong ties as

---

[4] Ties in cohesive networks are not necessarily strong. See Chapter 4 for a discussion.

the 'combination of the amount of time, the emotional intensity, the intimacy (mutual confiding), and the reciprocal services which character-ise the tie'.

In inter-organisational alliances there are some indicators about the extent to which a tie between two organisations can qualify as strong.[5] One of these is alliance type. Whereas marketing and licensing alliances are often con-sidered weak ties, technology development, R&D alliances and equity-based arrangements like joint ventures are often considered to be strong. The duration of a partnership, the extent to which it is repeated and high resource commitments are also signs of a strong tie. Strong ties are usually associated with trust among organisations, an essential ingredient in learning.[6] On the other hand, weak ties refer to arm's-length alliances in which knowledge-sharing is limited, relations are usually short-term and resource commit-ments are limited. Contracts that allow partners to abandon an alliance at any time are also considered weak ties (Duysters and de Man, 2003), as they may reflect the avoidance of deep resource commitments (see the case of BMW in Box 6.1).

The strength of a tie is important for organisational learning because it gives a hint about whether an alliance is predominantly explorative or exploitative (Hagedoorn and Duysters, 2002). Strong ties are often better for exchanging fine-grained and tacit knowledge between partners, as a common understanding about the issues at stake is valuable for effective exchange.[7] Having prior joint experience is useful for this purpose; parties will understand each other when developing solutions to prob-lems, solve conflicts and participate equally in knowledge exchange. Exploitative alliances are usually in core technological areas of the firm and exploratory alliances in non-core activities (Vanhaverbeke et al., 2009).

---

[5] See Marsden and Campbell (1984) for a classic article on measuring tie strength.

[6] For type of alliance and tie strength see Powell (1990), Nohria and Garcia Pont (1991), Koza and Lewin (1998); for Nokia, see Dittrich and Duysters (2007) and Duysters and de Man (2003). See Larson (1992) and Parkhe (1998) on trust, and Das and Teng (1998) and Gulati and Sytch (2008) on familiarity and trust. See Uzzi (1996) on the transfer of fine-grained information and knowledge with strong ties. Levin and Cross (2004) examined how trust mediates the relation between strong ties and knowledge transfer. See Zaheer, McEvily and Perrone (1998) on the distinction between inter-organisational and inter-personal trust. See McEvily and Tortoriello (2011) for a survey and discussion of measuring trust in organisational research.

[7] Hansen (1999) finds that in an electronics firm, tacit knowledge is transferred better through strong ties in inter-unit relations. Smith, Collins and Clark (2005) find in the cases of 72 high-tech companies that strong ties between members are critical in the knowledge creation capabilities of firms, and that the number of ties (network range) is not significant.

Box 6.1 The BMW and Immersion Alliance

The case study of an alliance between BMW and the company Immersion carried out by Gassman et al. (2010) illustrates the role of strong and weak ties and dyadic and portfolio-level alliance strategies in learning. In the late 1990s, BMW came up with the idea of introducing iDrive to its BMW7 series. iDrive was a radically new approach, involving an integrated control concept with a computer-like screen and control devices. However, BMW's R&D engineers did not have the know-how to develop this radically new module, which involved the integration of a number of new technologies and advanced software programming capabilities. Approaching its own network of suppliers first, BMW could not find any firm that could help in developing the technology. Looking outside, BMW found the Silicon Valley-based firm Immersion, which had developed the haptic feedback technology, TouchSense™. This was clearly an explorative alliance for BMW: the technology had the potential to be used in iDrive but there were also many uncertainties. The two firms had completely different knowledge bases: Immersion knew nothing about cars, while BMW had no knowledge of the technology, nor any idea of whether it could be used in cars. There were also issues of trust: Immersion was a 'stranger' to BMW, and BMW had to risk trusting another company with unknown capabilities. Moreover, the business models and strategies of the two companies were vastly different because of sectoral differences. For these reasons, BMW did not initially commit all of its resources; instead, it signed a temporary contract with Immersion. Later, as the two companies worked together, what had initially started as a weak tie developed into a relationship of trust. Gradually, BMW increased its commitments and decided to use haptic technology. BMW also involved other suppliers, with whom it had strong, long-standing ties, in its network. These suppliers were important because they possessed deep knowledge of automotive components and modules that both Immersion and BMW lacked. This case study shows that both its strong ties with an existing supplier network and its exploratory alliance and weak tie with Immersion gave BMW access to a new technological domain that proved critical in introducing this innovation.

Because exploitation is concerned with deepening existing competences, the ability to communicate task-specific, complex and tacit knowledge is a key aspect of exploitative alliances. Strong, committed, repeated relationships in which partners trust each other in terms of declaring their resources openly are considered better for exploitation. Joint problem-solving between organisations is particularly important, as it enhances the positive relationship between trust and capability acquisition (McEvily and Marcus, 2005).

One of the challenges firms face is the trade-off between openness and the risk of valuable knowledge leakage. Firms use various mechanisms to protect their knowledge, including patents, secrecy, selective revealing and limiting the scope of alliances.[8] Laursen and Salter (2014) find that while appropriation mechanisms can be useful for signalling the quality of a firm's competences, too much protection reduces variety in the breadth of collaborations and can hamper innovation potential.

Weak ties differ from strong ties in that they are not frequent, alliances function at arm's length and alliance partners are not the firm's usual partners. Originally, Granovetter (1973) associated weak ties with novelty because they are more likely to give access to a distant network. In exploratory alliances firms look for novel perspectives and know-how unlike their own. Using these insights, we can predict that the tie 17–11 in Figure 6.1 is likely to be an exploitative alliance. On the other hand, tie 17–8 is likely to be exploratory, giving 17 access to a completely different network from its dense sub-network.

6.2.2   Knowledge Overlap between Firms

Over time strong ties may weaken and weak ties get stronger (or fade away altogether). As a tie between two organisations gets stronger through repeated or long-term alliances, the knowledge bases of the organisations themselves are likely to begin to resemble each other.[9] This convergence means that the organisations' potential to contribute to each other's knowledge declines and there will be less and less to learn from each other as the alliance proceeds. Alliances can have diminishing marginal benefits over time because knowledge transfer and learning at any point depends on the partners' *relative* knowledge levels. Research shows that the relation between learning and common knowledge is likely to follow an inverted-U pattern, as shown in Figure 6.2.[10] When there is little overlap between organisations' knowledge bases, there is little they can learn from each other because of mutual misunderstanding. At the other extreme, when organisations are too

---

[8] See Henkel (2006) for selective revealing strategies in open innovation. Oxley and Sampson (2004) discuss limiting the scope of alliances as a solution to the risk of such hazards in R&D cooperations.

[9] Empirically, the complementarities between firms are measured in terms of similarities or differences. A commonly used measure has been the non-overlapping niches between two firms' products, which is based on the difference (Gulati, 1995; Chung, Singh and Lee, 2000; Rothaermel and Boeker, 2008). In other cases, measures that focus on the similarities between firms look at firms' technological base (Mowery, Oxley and Silverman, 1998; Vanhaverbeke et al., 2009); similarities in overall innovative potential (Rothaermel and Boeker, 2008); the strategic groups that firms belong to (Nohria and Garcia Pont, 1991); similarities in management practices (Lane and Lubatkin, 1998) and coherence in knowledge bases.

[10] For the issue of inverted-U, see Schoenmakers and Duysters (2006); Nooteboom et al. (2007); Mowery, Oxley and Silverman (1998).

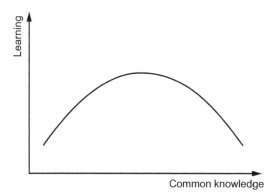

Figure 6.2   The Relation between Knowledge Commonality and Learning Potential between Two Actors

similar they can add little to each other's knowledge base. Hypothetically, there should be an intermediate level of knowledge overlap, where learning is highest. This mechanism is similar to homophily in the case of inter-personal networks, which we examined in Chapter 4. Similarity between organisations can drive tie formation but too much similarity inhibits further learning.

The evolution of relative knowledge levels depends on the absorptive capacity of organisations, the nature of knowledge exchanged, previous alliance experience and the nature of the alliance. The higher the absorptive capacity of partners and the more experience they have of alliance management, the sooner diminishing returns can be expected to set in (Nooteboom et al., 2007). For more complex alliances that are wider in scope, the time and energy partners allocate to understanding each other are greater and diminishing returns take longer to set in. The nature of an alliance (exploitative or exploratory) also has an effect. For example, Nooteboom et al. (2007) find that the positive effect of cognitive distance on the novelty value of an alliance is higher for exploratory than for exploitative alliances.

6.2.3   Alliance Management Capability

Learning in alliances depends strongly on firms' previous experience of alliance management.[11] Unfortunately, experience in alliances does not accumulate as effectively as experience in standard processes like manufacturing activities (Duysters et al., 2012) Firms learn at different rates:

---

[11] For alliance management capability, see Das (2012); Anand and Khanna (2000); Hoang and Rothaermel (2005); Reuer, Zollo and Singh (2002); Zollo, Reuer and Singh (2002); Kale and Singh (2009). For managing the balance between competition and cooperation between different partners, see Faems, Janssens and Van Looy (2010).

learning-by-doing depends on a variety of firm-specific factors, like the proficiency of individual employees, coordination inside the firm and the extent to which people in the organisation can leverage others' knowledge (Reagans, Argote and Brooks, 2005).

Das and Kumar (2007) distinguish between three learning processes in alliances, each of which has different strategic outcomes, depending on the stage of alliance. They are partner-specific, content and alliance management learning. Partner-specific learning is intensive in the formative phase of an alliance, when positive experiences will increase the motivation to repeat ties with the same partner in the future. Content learning occurs during the operationalisation of an alliance and is related to organisations' ability to acquire and internalise knowledge from their partners. Finally, alliance management learning is the dynamic capability of profiting from alliance experiences; while this process is embedded in all stages of an alliance, it is intensified in the content learning and outcome phases.

One of the critical issues in developing alliance management capabilities is the extent to which individuals' experiences in an alliance are transferred and leveraged effectively by others inside the firm. Learning is not guaranteed, when the experiences of those actively involved in alliances are neither effectively integrated nor institutionalised inside the organisation. Here, integration refers to the transfer of knowledge from individuals to the group, and institutionalisation to the transfer of knowledge from the group to the organisation as a whole (Heimeriks, Duysters and Vanhaverbeke, 2007). An example of the failure to integrate knowledge within an organisation was the difficulty experienced by GM-based advisors at the start of the NUMMI joint venture, described at the beginning of this chapter.

Boundary spanners play a critical role in the way external knowledge is integrated within an organisation by sharing and disseminating learning processes, resolving conflicts and bridging diverse opinions between groups. These groups can be research teams, departments or SBUs. Increased inter-group communication within an organisation is likely to reduce inter-group conflict and smooth the transfer of experiences between groups. In Chapter 3 we saw how departmental silos, or thought worlds, can prevent cross-fertilisation of ideas between departments. Intra-firm networks are important for sharing and disseminating the knowledge and experiences obtained from different alliance partners (Heimeriks, Klijn and Reuer, 2009). A key factor in overcoming interpretive barriers in learning caused by departmental silos is to develop an organisational context that allows innovators to build on the unique insights offered by different perspectives.

Table 6.1 summarises issues of organisational learning at the dyadic level.

Table 6.1 Learning in Organisational Dyads

Factor	Indicator	Implication
Tie strength	• Long duration of partnership • Repetition of ties • High resource commitment • Strategic technology alliances • Equity arrangements	• Strong ties are better for tacit and complex knowledge transfer and indicate trust • Weak ties are better to access diverse, novel information
Knowledge overlap between partners	Various indicators of overlap can be used: see Box 6.4 for some measures of diversity and similarity commonly used for this purpose	• An intermediate level of knowledge overlap is better for learning
Alliance management capability	• Previous alliance experience • Integration and institutionalisation of external knowledge inside the organisation • Efficiency in time and effort spent in searching for partners • Returns from alliances	• Learning is faster • Makes better use of privileged network positions

6.3 Learning and Alliance Portfolios

An alliance portfolio is an egocentric network, composed of a focal organisation (ego), its partners (alters) and the ties between them.[12] In Figure 6.1, the alliance portfolio of node 17 is shown by the light shaded area P. The importance of an alliance portfolio stems from the complementarities, overlaps and interdependences between an organisation's different alliances. Managing an alliance portfolio effectively requires resources to be allocated so that the various complementarities and synergies between partners can be leveraged and duplication and redundancy avoided[13] (Hoffman, 2005). Also, by managing the composition of an alliance portfolio, firms can balance the exploration and exploitation dimensions of organisational learning. For example, Box 6.2 describes how the strategic repositioning of IBM was reflected in its alliance portfolio throughout its history (Dittrich, Duysters and de Man, 2007).

[12] When the network analysis is carried out from the perspective of focal node (ego), we also use the term ego network, which has the same meaning as an egocentric network.

[13] Hoffman (2007) distinguishes between three portfolio management strategies: stabilising strategies focusing on the exploitation of competences; shaping strategies aiming at exploration; and adapting strategies aiming at understanding and interpreting the environment to reduce uncertainty.

Box 6.2 IBM Transformation

Dittrich, Duysters and de Man's (2007) case study on IBM shows how its strategic repositioning during the 1990s was reflected in its alliance portfolio (see Figures 6.3a, 6.3b and 6.3c). Facing growing market pressure at the beginning of 1990s, IBM shifted its strategic priorities; from having been a vertically integrated computer company, it began to move towards services and software. During the period 1991–2, most of IBM's alliances involved microprocessors for PowerPCs and associated software. These were its core competencies and its alliance portfolio reflected an exploitation strategy. During 1996–7, this portfolio began to change, as the complexity of its network configuration increased through more multiple partnerships. These alliances were both exploitative (for example, a microchip-based alliance with Toshiba and Motorola) and also exploratory, as IBM entered into new alliances to source Internet and ebusiness-related products and services. The JV, developed with Netscape, Sony, Oracle and Nintendo, illustrates this strategic trend. Finally during 2001–2, IBM's portfolio reflected an increasing focus on telecommunications, with partners such as Cisco, Nortel Networks, Nokia, Ericsson and NTT DoCoMo. The evolution of IBM's alliance portfolio reflects how structural repositioning was achieved not only internally but also by changing the nature of its portfolio from predominantly exploitative alliances to a portfolio that included exploratory alliances in new fields.

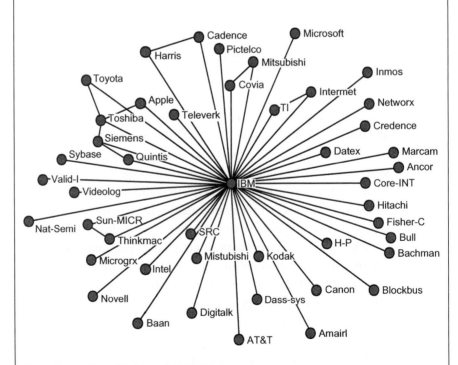

Figure 6.3a   Alliance Portfolio of IBM 1991–2
Source: Dittrich, Duysters and de Man (2007)

Box 6.2 (cont.)

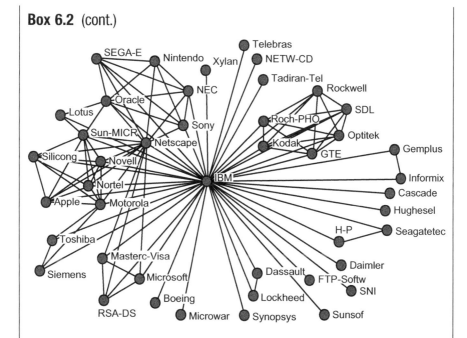

Figure 6.3b Alliance Portfolio of IBM 1996–7
Source: Dittrich, Duysters and de Man (2007)

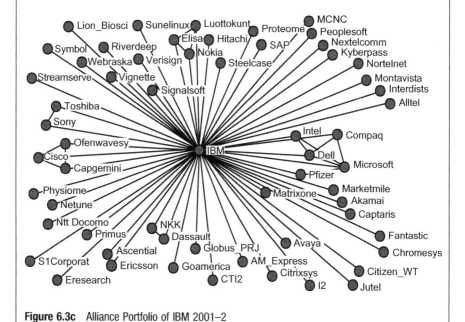

Figure 6.3c Alliance Portfolio of IBM 2001–2
Source: Dittrich, Duysters and de Man (2007)

6.3.1   Portfolio Diversity

Diversity among the partners and portfolio complexity are particularly important variables for managing learning through alliance portfolio management. But as Goerzen and Beamish (2005) find, only a small proportion of firms manage diversity successfully in their international alliance portfolios. A diverse alliance portfolio can increase opportunities to explore different domains but, at the same time, diversity increases coordination costs. The higher the capability of an organisation to manage complex portfolios, the more effective its learning processes will be. However, if complexity increases too much, the costs of managing it can outweigh the benefits, reducing the effectiveness of knowledge transfer and its successful integration inside the organisation.

There are three dimensions to diversity within an alliance portfolio:

- **Partner diversity:** type, size, age or other partner-specific characteristics.
- **Tie diversity:** type of agreement (equity, marketing, research, distribution, joint venture, etc.), duration of agreement or other tie-level parameters.
- **Pairwise diversity:** a comparative measure of similarities or differences between the focal organisation and its ties.

In all three of these dimensions we need to consider the *proportion* of a certain category relative to others (for example, the proportion of research labs in the portfolio) or the *dispersion* of different categories throughout the portfolio as a whole (for example, is there a balanced distribution of different partner types?). While partner-level and tie-level diversity do not take into account the characteristics of the focal organisation, pairwise diversity is a comparative measure that takes the *dispersion of distances* between the focal firm and its partners. An example is the dispersion of the knowledge overlap between partners and the focal organisation.

Partner Diversity. Partner diversity concerns the type, location, size, age, industry or innovative capabilities of partners. Three types of organisation have the most significant effects on learning: universities and research labs, peers or competitors, and suppliers and customers. In general, partner diversity is positively associated with innovative capabilities as it provides access to a greater breadth of cognitive resources, which is relevant in search processes. For example, Duysters and Lokshin (2011) looked at Dutch community innovation surveys (CIS) and found that firms at the frontier of innovation have broader alliance portfolios (i.e. a variety of partner types) compared to their imitators. Another dimension of partner diversity is the weight of local versus international partners in the portfolio. A greater number of international partners is associated with better chances of entering foreign markets (Duysters and Lokshin, 2011); however, such diversity can also reduce firms' learning capabilities due to cultural and institutional differences (Lavie and Miller, 2008).

Partner diversity is also related to the type of innovation pursued. Incremental innovation capabilities are associated with a more homogeneous alliance portfolio and radical innovations with a more diverse one (Oerlemans, Knoben and Pretorius, 2013). Similarly, partner diversity is better suited to exploratory innovation because it enhances access to non-redundant knowledge (Phelps, 2010; Lavie and Rosenkopf, 2006).

Tie Diversity. Ties within a network can be defined in terms of their strength, type of agreement or level of commitment. The dominance of strong ties in an alliance portfolio is generally associated with exploitative activities and dominance of weak ties with exploratory search activities. A balanced innovation strategy involving both exploration and exploitation requires both types of tie in the portfolio.

Notwithstanding the numerous benefits of diversity for innovation, research consistently shows that too much diversity in an alliance portfolio increases the costs of coordination and reduces innovative performance. This is because increased diversity needs to have dedicated alliance management functions in place to benefit from the synergies, complementarities and conflicts between organisations in the portfolio. Most studies predict that there is an inverted-U relationship between the diversity of alliance partners and organisations' innovative capabilities.[14] At the same time, developing alliance management capabilities is likely to offset the increased coordination costs of diversity (Duysters et al., 2012).

Pairwise Diversity. Pairwise similarities between a firm and its partners can also be used as an indicator of a portfolio's exploratory or exploitative weight.[15]

---

[14] Goerzen and Beamish (2005) find that firms that have either very homogeneous or extremely diverse partners enjoy better economic performance in international joint ventures. De Leeuw, Lokshin and Duysters (2014) show that diversity in partner types has an inverted-U relation to radical innovations.

[15] See, for example, Cecere and Özman (2014) for technological distance with partners. Darr and Kurtzberg (2000) find that strategic similarities increase the knowledge transfer.

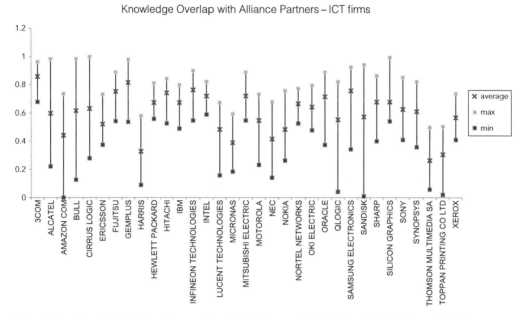

Figure 6.4   Knowledge Overlap between Selected ICT Firms and their Partners in their Alliance Portfolio

The extent to which partners are technologically distant from an organisation is an indicator of exploratory innovation (Nooteboom et al., 2007) and recombination search (Ahuja and Katila, 2001). Luo and Deng (2009) measured this type of diversity in a study of a dedicated biotechnology firm (DBF), identifying the percentage of partners in the firm's alliance portfolio that were also DBFs (this corresponds to pairwise similarity in type of partner). The authors found that this proportion has an inverted-U relationship to the innovation performance of a firm; that is, as the weight of similar firms in the portfolio increases beyond a threshold, the innovation contribution of partnerships starts to fall.

As an example of pairwise diversity in alliance portfolios, Figure 6.4 shows the maximum, minimum and average technological distance between selected firms and their partners in the ICT sector. These values are based on the comparison between the technology fields that appear on the patents granted to firms and those of their partners. As Figure 6.4 shows, some firms have more homogeneous portfolios, with little dispersion in the distance between the focal firm and its partners. Other firms have a wide dispersion in partner knowledge, ranging from partners with a very high overlap to those with little overlap with the focal firm. For example, Sandisk is remarkable in that it has both very proximate partners (with high knowledge overlap with Sandisk) and distant partners (low knowledge overlap), reflecting a high dispersion in its alliance portfolio. The partners of some other firms exhibit low dispersion in terms of the overlap in common technologies. For example, Infineon's partners have a high overlap with the firm while Harris, Thomson, and Toppan are remarkable for having a low overlap with the partners in their alliance portfolios. A dispersed alliance portfolio is better for allocating resources to deepen knowledge in common areas and for also learning about novelties from distant firms, as in the case of BMW's alliance with Immersion, described in Box 6.1.

The effects of dispersion in a portfolio also depend on stages in the technology life cycle. Jiang, Tan and Thursby (2010) find that in the late phases of a cycle, incumbent firms can benefit from a portfolio in which they and their partners have a high dispersion of pairwise similarities. In this way, firms can receive novel information from their distant partners and also have the opportunity to deepen knowledge with similar partners. In the late stages of technology life cycles, distant firms can help recognise opportunities in niche market segments.

A critical technical issue in assessing similarities between an organisation and its partners is to make sure that the characteristics of the overall firm population are taken into account. When there is high similarity among a population of firms, a homogeneous alliance portfolio reflects the population rather than a specific strategic choice. Box 6.3 explains how to tackle this problem. Another issue is how to choose among a wide range of available diversity and similarity metrics. Box 6.4 explains some commonly used similarity and diversity measures and their characteristics.

6.3.2   Ties between Partners

Another characteristic of an alliance portfolio that has implications for learning is the extent to which a focal organisation's (ego) partners (its alters) are connected among themselves. From a learning perspective, cohesive portfolios in which partners are also connected are good for the transfer

Box 6.3 The Ego Network and Whole Network Data

Collecting data on a whole network can often be a cumbersome process. Burt (1984) suggested that collecting data on a focal actor and his or her network (egonet) could facilitate this process and reveal many structural features. In analysing the similarity and diversity of partners in an alliance portfolio, it is important to acknowledge the risk of selection bias. Borgatti, Everett and Johnson (2013) have explained why ego network data drawn from whole network data are better than personal network research designed to avoid this bias. When data are drawn from a whole network, it is possible to see the overall characteristics of the population, and to observe nodes with which the ego firm does not have a tie. Researchers are then able to examine whether the similarities between two firms are due to a preference for similar partners or to population characteristics. Consider Figure 6.1. If we had data only about the partners of node 17 and not about the rest of the network, we might draw biased conclusions about the similarity between 17 and its partners; we would not be able to see how similar node 17 is to other, unconnected nodes in the network. Having data from the whole network gives us the ability to observe characteristics of the firms node 17 does not have a tie with. Yule's Q may be used to address this problem (Borgatti, Everett and Johnson, 2013: 273). In Figure 6.1, out of twenty-five firms in the network, firm 7 has eight partners. Suppose that four of these partners are the same type of organisation as firm 7, and four of them are different, as shown in Figure 6.5. Of the remaining sixteen firms in the population that firm 7 does not have a tie with, eight are similar and eight different (Figure 6.5).

Figure 6.5   Yule's Q

Yule's Q is given as: $Q = \dfrac{ad - bc}{ad + bc}$

which is zero in this case. This means that node 17's partners represent the population of all other nodes in the network, in terms of their similarity with node 17.

Box 6.4 Measuring Similarity and Diversity

This box provides some measures of diversity and overlap for measuring firm-based capabilities, knowledge bases and market or technological similarities between firms.

Blau index: measures the dispersion of a variable over different categories. High values indicate the increased evenness of the variable.

$$B = 1 - \sum p_i^2$$

where p_i measures the proportion of category i in the population.

Teachman/Shannon entropy index: another measure of diversity across different categories.

$$E = \sum p_i \ln (p_i)$$

Euclidian distance: measures the distance between two vectors of size n.

$$D = \sqrt{\sum (x_i - y_i)^2}$$

where x_i and y_i refer to the characteristics of x and y in dimension i.

Cosine index: measures the overlap between vectors x and y in n dimensions. It takes a value between zero and 1. Higher values indicate a higher overlap.

$$\cos = \frac{\sum x_i y_i}{\sqrt{\sum x_i^2} \sqrt{\sum y_i^2}}$$

Jaccard index: can be used to measure the overlap between sets A and B. The general format is:

$$J = \frac{A \cap B}{A \cup B}$$

of high-quality information and tacit knowledge. On the other hand, sparseness of the ego's network is beneficial in terms of an organisation's access to novelty. Studies find that a balance between the two is better for learning. For example, the network surrounding node 17 in Figure 6.1 is composed of four clusters of nodes that are not connected to each other: nodes 11, 15, 18 and 20 form a dense sub-network; nodes 24 and 19 form a triad with node 17; node 3 has one connection (17), implying its dependence on node 17, and finally node 8 gives node 17 access to a distant and completely independent network. Box 6.5 gives details of how to calculate ego network density.

We saw in Chapter 4 that dense networks with many redundant links among partners are the most effective at transferring tacit knowledge. Toyota is famous for sustaining routines to transfer highly tacit knowledge by encouraging links between its suppliers. Dyer and Nobeoka (2000) describe how Toyota established a strong knowledge-sharing network. The key initiative was to establish relationships among the suppliers themselves. The Toyota network, although highly centralised, includes multiple relations between suppliers, which facilitates the transfer of tacit knowledge through increased opportunities for deep, face-to-face knowledge-sharing and the development of a common language, helpful in solving technical problems. In doing this, Toyota held direct competitors at bay and introduced a rotation scheme to maintain diversity among partner firms.

Table 6.2 summarises learning in the context of alliance portfolios. It is important to remember that focusing on the portfolio level captures only part of the network. Alliance portfolios are embedded in a larger network of organisations, which also has implications for learning.

Box 6.5 Calculating Ego Network Density in an Alliance Portfolio

Let us calculate the ego network density of nodes 17 and 11 in Figure 6.1 as an illustration of the extent to which the networks surrounding nodes 17 and 11 are sparse. If all eight partners of node 17 were connected to each other, we would have (8 x 7)/2 links between the eight partners. Out of these twenty-eight possible links, only five links have been realised: 15–20, 11–15, 11–18, 18–20 and 19–24. Therefore, the density of the alliance network of node 17 is 5/28. In Figure 6.1, node 11 is structurally embedded in a network formed by nodes 15, 17, 18, 20 and 21 and its network is largely cohesive, having a high ego network density (except for 12, which does not belong to the group). Node 11's network is largely closed. Node 11 has five partners; if all the links between them were realised, there would be 5 x 4/2 = 10 links between partners. Out of these ten possible connections, four have been realised: 15–17, 15–21, 17–18 and 18–21, giving an ego network density of 4/10 = 0.4, which is larger than that of node 17.

Table 6.2 Learning through Alliance Portfolio Management

Factor	Diversity Type	Indicator	Metrics (see Box 6.4)
Diversity of portfolio	Partner-level diversity	• Type of partners • Location of partners • Industry of partners • Size of partners • Age of partners, etc.	• Central tendency (the proportion of a certain type relative to others) • Dispersion of different categories in the portfolio
	Tie-level diversity	• Strong/weak ties • Types of tie (marketing, manufacturing, distribution, research, information, equity) • Duration of ties	
	Pairwise diversity	• Proximity between an organisation and partners (technological, cognitive, market-based, spatial, etc.)	• Measures of similarity, distance or overlap • Dispersion of these measures across partners
Ties between partners		• Highly dense ego networks can be an advantage for supply chain networks, to cope with unforeseen contingencies and for increased learning • Highly dense ego networks can be disadvantageous for accessing novelty	• Burt's constraint • Ego network density • Effective size

6.4   Learning in Networks

As Box 6.3 explains, the whole network level and the ego network level are complementary. An ego network takes a focal organisation and its partners, as well as the ties between the partners (in an ego network, second or higher tiers are sometimes included as well). On the other hand, a whole network shows ties in a certain industry, technology or geographical district. For example, in Figure 6.1 the first degree ego network of node 17 is shown by the shaded area P; the second degree ego network would include partners of the partners in P (which are not partners of 17) and so on. Nodes 16 and 5 are not connected to node 17, but they are included in the network level. If we focus only on the portfolio level, nodes 8 and 13 are equivalent. However, by expanding the network horizon, the strategic importance of the ties with nodes 8 and 13 is better distinguished. Here, node 17's tie with node 8 gives 17 access to a distant network, whereas its tie with 13 is isolated from the rest of the network.

6.4.1 Contingency and Balance Perspectives

In Chapter 4, we explored one of the enduring debates in the network literature, which is what type of network provides a rich source of social capital: closure or structural holes? The proponents of closure stress that a cohesive network is a source of social capital, since it facilitates trust-building and knowledge-sharing between partners and increases the access to other members' resources and capabilities (Coleman, 1988), ultimately increasing the innovation potential. On the other hand, Burt (1992) maintains that structural holes fill gaps in a network to bridge otherwise disconnected parts and are an important source of social capital.[16] For example, in Figure 6.1, nodes 8 and 9 have bridging ties linking otherwise unconnected clusters in the network and so have access to opportunities that would have been inaccessible to both.

There are two principal perspectives on ways to reconcile the debate between brokerage and closure. The first is a *contingency perspective*,[17] which claims that the benefits of a network position depend on environmental conditions. The second is a *balance perspective*[18] that highlights the complementarities between both sources of social capital (Reagans and McEvily, 2008) and promotes a network position that is cohesive in some places and sparse in others. In this sense, node 17 in Figure 6.1 is in a balanced position:

---

[16] Ahuja's (2000) longitudinal study within the international chemicals industry examined how the network position of the firm influences its innovative output. A firm acquires two kinds of benefit through networks. First, firms access the resources (physical, skills, knowledge) of other firms; second, networks enhance firms' access to outside developments, for example a major technological innovation. Ahuja's findings suggest that structural holes have a negative impact on innovative output; indirect ties (enhancing knowledge spillovers, without the cost of maintaining links) and direct ties (enhancing access to resources and knowledge spillovers) have a positive effect on a firm's innovative output. McEvily and Zaheer (1999) study metal-working workshops and find evidence in favour of non-redundant, infrequent and geographically dispersed bridging ties for competitive advantage. Inkpen and Tsang (2005) focus on different networks (cluster, intra-cooperation and strategic alliances) and investigate how knowledge transfer can be facilitated in different types of network with respect to different dimensions of social capital. In the case of the global steel industry, Koka and Prescott (2002) outline different dimensions of social capital and demonstrate that each dimension has a different impact on firm performance (information flow dimensions, like volume, diversity and richness).

[17] Burt (2000) and Rowley, Behrens and Krackhardt (2000). Their findings for the semiconductor and steel industries reveal that weak ties are beneficial for exploration, especially in uncertain technological environments, and that strong ties are beneficial for exploitation, where uncertainty is low and competitive pressure is high.

[18] See, for example, Uzzi (1997); Reagans and McEvily (2003). Tiwana (2008) highlights the complementarities between strong and bridging ties for knowledge integration. Shipilov (2005) finds that the combination of both types of tie is not beneficial in Canadian investment banks, mainly because of the nature of investment banking, where a mixed relational strategy may provoke confusion and increase competitive pressure.

it is part of a cohesive network through its ties with nodes 11, 15, 18 and 20, and its non-redundant contacts with the nodes 8 and 3, 24 and 19 (within the shaded area P). In two studies, Uzzi found that networks composed of a mix of arm's-length and embedded ties are better for performance in the apparel industry (Uzzi, 1997) and commercial banking (Uzzi, 1999). A balance of both positions is beneficial in terms of the safety, fine-grained information transfer and trust that embedded ties confer and the adaptability and novelty conferred by arm's-length ties. In his well-known study of the New York fashion industry, Uzzi (1997: 57) highlights the paradox of embeddedness: 'the same processes by which embeddedness creates a requisite fit with the current environment can paradoxically reduce an organisation's ability to adapt' mainly by decreasing diversity, reduction of non-redundant ties and sometimes causing over-embeddedness. Over-embeddedness can be caused by the inability of the firm to change its network portfolio, a state that Kim, Oh and Swaminathan (2006) term 'network inertia'.

6.4.2   Brokerage and Learning Performance

In Chapter 13, the antecedents of brokerage positions will be covered in more detail. Here, we look at some factors that shape the way brokerage is related to learning and innovation performance in inter-organisational networks.

Absorptive Capacity. Cohesive and dense networks are better suited to the transfer of tacit knowledge, while codified knowledge can be transferred even within arm's-length relationships, when the ties between actors are weak or infrequent.[19] The greater an organisation's absorptive capacity, the better use it can make of brokerage positions to increase its capabilities to deal with heterogeneous, tacit and complex knowledge. In the banking sector, Shipilov (2009) found that firms with a higher absorptive capacity, revealed by a wider scope of experience across different markets, benefit more from filling structural holes in a network to help them deal better with heterogeneous information.

Institutional Framework. The way brokerage is exercised and perceived, and the effects it has, depend on culture and institutions. Most of the studies that support established theories about brokerage are based on information

---

[19] Cowan, Jonard and Özman (2004); Llerena and Özman (2013); Hansen (1999); Smith, Collins and Clark (2005).

and data about Western economies. However, some studies show that social capital is culture-specific. For example, Bian and Zhang's (2014) analysis of the corporate social capital in the Chinese *quanxi* culture shows that a strong tie is highly personalised, incorporates kin sentiments and develops through mutual favours across time. It is characterised by very strong reciprocal support and dependence between parties and is highly associated with firms' increased economic performance.[20] Institutions also shape the effect of brokerage on innovative performance. Cultural contexts may vary in the way brokerage is perceived. For example, Xiao and Tsui (2007) find that the collectivist, cooperation-oriented and communal sharing values that dominate Chinese culture do not fit with the way brokerage and structural holes operate in Western business contexts, where they are likely to bring network advantages. Brokerage benefits in inter-organisational networks may also depend on corporatism. For example, looking at fuel cell technology alliances Vasudeva, Zaheer and Hernandez (2012) found that the effect of brokerage on innovative performance is higher for alliances where the firm or some of its partners come from corporatist countries.

Stability of the Industry. Uncertainty and technological turbulence increases the need to access information from diverse sources. Rowley, Behrens and Krackhardt (2000) found that bridging positions in a network bring greater advantages when the environment is unstable and network closure is more beneficial when turbulence is low. At the same time, there is a trade-off between the novelty of received information and the rapidity with which it can be accessed. While bridging ties help when accessing novelty, the flow of information between them is often slow and its content less reliable than strong ties in cohesive networks (Aral and Van Alstyne, 2011).

Time. Not only is the rate at which actors access information slow but the privileges conferred by structural holes are also often temporary. As Burt (2002) suggested, bridging ties can have high rates of decay as the benefits that accrue to brokers stabilise or subside over time. For example, Soda, Usai and Zaheer (2004) studied Italian TV series teams and found that the privileges conferred by structural holes in the past do not persist for a long time, whereas the positive effect of network closure lasts longer. Gulati, Sytch and Tatarynowicz (2012), looking at the computer industry, found that brokerage positions are not sustained and the small worldliness of networks

---

[20] See Luo, Huang and Wang (2012).

is temporary. Perry-Smith and Shalley (2003) proposed that the creativity benefits of brokerage positions in intra-organisational networks subside over time; as a result, the central network position of a creative individual with many weak ties gradually becomes a cohesive network with strong ties.

Nature of Task. The kinds of benefit that accrue through brokerage depend on the nature of the task. While bridging ties can help access diversity, they can be inadequate when creative ideas are being put to practice, whereas strong ties with the holders of valuable resources can be critical in the latter phase (Obstfeld, 2005; Perry-Smith, 2006). Bridging ties can help generate ideas but may not be helpful for their subsequent diffusion, depending on whether the holder of a bridging position actually exercises brokerage. For example, technical experience and knowledge are often correlated with holders of bridging positions but individuals with superior track records may not be so willing to use their position strategically for their own and others' benefits (Fleming and Marx, 2006). Bridging ties can help accumulate status but can also dampen firms' market performance (Shipilov and Li, 2008). Obstfeld (2005) distinguishes between 'tertius iungens' and 'tertius gaudens' positions. *Tertius iungens* refers to a brokerage position that prioritises coordination between a focal actor's different partners; *tertius gaudens* is a position where brokering advantages are obtained by 'playing off' partners against each other (Burt, 1992). Obstfeld's case study of engineers in a large automotive manufacturing plant showed that of the two positions, *tertius iungens* explains involvement in innovation.

Brokerage positions are beneficial for routine tasks but might be inefficient for innovative and new tasks that require deeper knowledge-sharing (Moran, 2005). Vanhaverbeke et al. (2009) found that the impact of partner redundancy on innovation depends on the type of innovation (exploratory or exploitative) the firm aims for. Sparse networks can be better for exploratory innovation, dense networks for exploitative innovations. Gargiulo, Ertug and Galunic (2009), using data on investment bankers, found that the effects of network closure depend on whether the actor is a knowledge acquirer or a knowledge provider. A sparse network is advantageous for an actor who is a knowledge provider, as the actor has the freedom to play off different partners and gain brokerage benefits. But when an actor is a knowledge acquirer, a dense egocentric network is better; the existence of common third parties induces partners to invest more time and energy in relations with a focal actor.

Interactions with Other Network Metrics. Brokerage benefits also depend on the other network metrics surrounding the bridging tie. Bridging alone may not be enough for innovative performance. Successful bridging positions are usually complemented by strong ties and coordination capabilities in the networks surrounding the bridge (Tortoriello, Reagans and McEvily, 2012). For example, Tortoriello and Krackhardt (2010) carried out a study in the R&D department of a large multinational and found that it was the Simmelian ties around a bridge that yielded advantage.[21] A Simmelian tie is a bridging position with ties to a common third party. In Figure 6.1, the link between nodes 9 and 1 is an example. Both these nodes have a common tie with node 2; at the same time, the tie between them is a bridge that connects the two main clusters in the network. Several studies point to the complementarity between centrality and brokerage. Consider node 17 in Figure 6.1. It has a bridging tie in the network through its connection with node 8 and it also has a high degree of centrality in its network. Some studies find that centrality and brokerage reinforce each other's effect on innovative performance.[22]

The effectiveness of brokerage also depends on network type. Wang et al. (2014) looked at the effect of an inventor's position in two types of network: one a co-invention network and the other the inventor's knowledge network (that is, the inventor's use of technology sub-classes jointly in a patent). The authors find that an inventor's exploratory invention (using a technology class in the firm for the first time) is negatively related to the inventor's degree centrality in the collaboration network. Degree centrality in the knowledge network has an inverted-U relationship to the inventor's exploratory invention capabilities. This means that, if an inventor often uses a specific technology class together with several other knowledge elements (centralised knowledge network), then the inventor's exploratory invention capabilities rise only up to a point, after which they start falling.

The multiplexity[23] of ties in a network can also reinforce learning and capability transfer (and vice versa). For example, Mahmood, Zhu and Zajac

---

[21] For Simmelian tie theory see Simmel (1950). Krackhardt (1999) defines a Simmelian tie as a dyadic tie embedded in a clique.

[22] See, for example, Nerkar and Paruchiri's (2005) research on a network analysis of inventors in DuPont. They find that there is a positive interaction effect between an inventor's centrality and brokerage role, in the use of an inventor's knowledge by others in the department. Yang, Lin and Peng (2011) also find that the joint brokerage and centrality of two firms moderates the relation between the firms' learning strategy and their acquisitions. An exploration strategy is more likely to result in an acquisition and joint brokerage with the other firm strengthens this relation.

[23] Multiplexity refers to the number of different social connections between two actors.

(2011) show that the relations between board members of firms interacted significantly and positively with firms' buyer-supplier alliances, as far as their impact on R&D capability transfer was concerned.

6.5   Revisiting the Network Horizon

Figure 6.6 shows which levels of network horizon are relevant in managing learning and capability transfer at the dyadic (single alliance), alliance portfolio and inter-organisational network levels.

At the dyadic (single alliance) level the relative knowledge levels of partners are an important determinant of learning. When knowledge overlap (or similarity) is too high, partners make only limited contributions to each other's knowledge. When knowledge overlap is too low, learning can also be limited because partners can have difficulty communicating. These insights have been observed in different contexts.

At the alliance portfolio level, organisational learning depends on the way different alliances complement each other over time and across different projects and domains. Alliance portfolio diversity can be evaluated according to partner type, nature of ties or pairwise comparisons. Diversity provides access to exploratory opportunities but too much diversity reduces the cognitive capability to transfer knowledge between parties and requires close network management. A closed network is more effective for high-quality information, trust and knowledge-sharing.

As far as intra-organisational networks are concerned, an important point is how externally accessed knowledge is shared, disseminated and recombined with people's existing knowledge. Departmental thought worlds can hamper the effectiveness of internal knowledge creation mechanisms. Boundary spanners are individuals who have substantial links to the external world (outside the group), so that they usually play an important role in how external knowledge is disseminated to local people (Tushman and Scanlan, 1981; Allen and Cohen, 1969). Boundary spanners and inter-departmental broker ties are important in integrating knowledge accessed externally and in institutionalising this knowledge throughout the organisation.

As Figure 6.6 shows, each level of analysis contributes to achieving a balance in organisational learning and complements the other levels. The information hidden in the network is not revealed at the ego network level, and information at the ego network level is not revealed in each alliance.

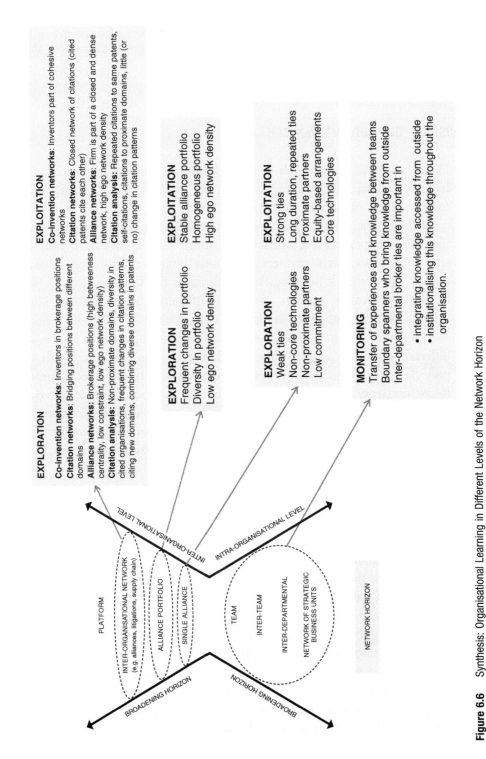

Figure 6.6 Synthesis: Organisational Learning in Different Levels of the Network Horizon

A balanced learning strategy can also be achieved over time. For example, an organisation might be predominantly involved in exploitation alliances at one particular period, and in exploratory alliances at another. Balanced learning can also be achieved in different domains – exploitation in some, exploration in others (Lavie and Rosenkopf, 2006). This is important to note because industrial, technological and market conditions can make either strategy better in a certain period or domain. We reviewed these conditions in discussion of the network horizon trade-off in Chapter 5. The benefits of overseeing the wider network can be increased or reduced through factors like modularity, heterogeneity in consumer preferences, network externalities, knowledge and absorptive capacity.

Discussion Questions

1. What are the important factors in managing:
   a. Learning in dyads
   b. Learning in portfolios
   c. Learning in networks?

2. Explain the contingency and balance perspectives in the structural hole – closure debate.

3. How does the nature of a task determine the effect of brokerage for learning in networks?

4. By considering the positions of firms in a strategic alliance network, can we have some insights about their learning strategies (exploration/exploitation/ambidexterity)?

7 Creativity and Networks

Creativity is thinking up new things and innovation is doing new things.

Theodore Levitt

Both individual traits and the social environment play an important role in creativity. In this chapter we focus on the role of networks in fostering or inhibiting creativity. In particular, we focus on four managerial activities: forming teams; monitoring brokerage roles; monitoring informal networks, and accessing diversity at the inter-organisational level. Diversity and recombination are especially important in creativity, and we highlight the networks that are more likely to sustain these. We also explore different brokering roles, for example, consultant, coordinator, liaison and boundary spanner, and how these influence creativity. Finally, we see how, at the network level, small-world networks and core-periphery networks have implications for creativity.

'Durable, engineered and permanent – those are in opposition to idiosyncratic, delicate, ephemeral.' These are the words US artist Janet Echelman uses to describe the challenge she encountered when asked to build one of her giant fishnet sculptures on the waterfront at Porto in Portugal (see Figure 7.1).[1] Creating a sculpture that gives the same feeling as the fluidity of a fishnet but could survive ultraviolet rays, pollution, salt, wind and traffic was a challenge that her skills and knowledge as an artist were not sufficient to master. This led to her collaboration with Peter Heppel, an engineer specialised in lightweight structures and aerodynamics. The combination of Echelman's art and Heppel's technical expertise resulted in steel structures 40 metres in diameter that flow like fishnets on the coast at Porto.

Janet Echelman's work is unique but two more general lessons about creativity can be drawn from her story: exposure to distant worlds and the recombination of distant elements. Janet Echelman had no expertise in

---

[1] See TED Talk by Janet Echelman, June 2011: www.ted.com/speakers/janet_echelman, accessed 7 July 2016.

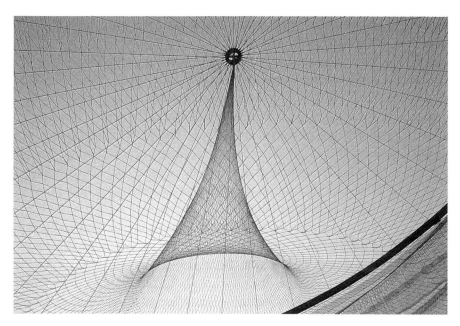

Figure 7.1　Janet Echelman's Sculpture *She Changes*, Porto, Portugal (courtesy Studio Echelman)

fishing. A Fulbright scholarship took her to India, where she had the idea of creating giant fishnet sculptures as she watched fishermen on the beach. However, she did not have the technical knowledge to combine two opposing worlds – 'durable, engineered and permanent' versus 'idiosyncratic, delicate and ephemeral'. This led to her collaboration with engineer Peter Heppel, in which these two contrasting worlds were recombined.

In Chapter 6, we focused on inter-organisational relations in search processes. This chapter deals with creativity in search. Creativity is about the way in which the interaction of ideas and knowledge between individuals sparks novelties that can turn into useful products or services. In creativity, inter-organisational and intra-organisational levels are complementary. The former is about new knowledge that spans organisational boundaries, while the latter is about how this knowledge is integrated within the organisation to conceive creative ideas.

7.1　The Individual and Social Sides of Creativity

Research on creativity bridges the individual and social sides of innovation. As Csikszentmihályi (1996: 23) puts it, creativity 'does not happen inside people's heads, but in the interaction between a person's thoughts and a sociocultural context'. Creativity is not confined to producing goods or pieces of art; we can be creative in our work by generating novel ideas, processes and solutions (Perry-Smith and Shalley, 2003). Here, novelty is defined as something new and useful to the context to which it is introduced (Amabile, 1983). As Amabile states, 'creativity can be regarded as the quality of the products or responses judged to be creative by appropriate observers' (Amabile, 1996: 33). In other words, creativity is context-dependent and the extent to which something is found to be creative changes over time. Prior knowledge, task motivation and skills are essential parts of the novelty generation process (Amabile, 1983).

The systems view of creativity stresses the cultural and social dimensions of the process (Csikszentmihályi, 1999) as well as the organisational context (Woodman, Sawyer and Griffin, 1993; Amabile, 1983). While creativity has long been seen in the psychology literature as an individual trait, today hardly anyone denies the importance of social context in understanding the sources and effects of creativity. Recombining unrelated elements does not take place in a vacuum; it happens through collaborations that permit analogous thinking, that is, applying a technique, idea or method from other domains to solve a problem.[2]

In this chapter we will explore the role networks play in coming up with new ideas and finding novel solutions to problems. The second part of the process, implementation, is covered in Chapter 9.

7.2   Recombination, Diversity and Complexity

Creativity is the ability to come up with alternatives, think outside the box and see issues from different perspectives. Ideation refers to the processes of novelty generation and communicating novelty to others. The role networks play in these processes is to provide three major building blocks of creativity: recombination, diversity and complexity. Diversity is accessed, elements are recombined and complex knowledge is shared and disseminated through networks.

7.2.1   Recombination and Analogous Thinking

Schumpeter (1934) identified resource recombinations as the principal aspect of the innovation process. Recombination means that no idea arrives out of

---

[2] See Johnson (2010) for historical examples on creativity.

nowhere; new knowledge is essentially created by combining elements of existing knowledge. The more diverse, distant and unrelated the knowledge to be combined, the more likely it is that the novelty will be radical in nature (Schoenmakers and Duysters, 2010). On this, Hargadon (2003) gives the example of the Reebok pump shoe. The Design Continuum's team came from diverse backgrounds, which helped them to come up with the idea of applying the technology of medical IV bags to the design of the air pump mechanism in the shoe. Analogous thinking is a psychological heuristic often used in creating novelties. Biomimicry illustrates this process well, as explored in Box 7.1.

In general, we all tend to bring different domains into association when attempting to solve problems. However, exposure to the source of analogy significantly increases the extent to which such associations are made, as the experiment by Gick and Holyoak (1980) showed. In their experiment, Gick and Holyoak analysed the process of analogous thinking, encouraging people to apply the solution to a military problem (an account of an attack on a village fortress) to the problem of how to treat a malignant tumour without harming the patient. Gick and Holyoak showed that people should have at least some idea about which field to form an analogy with when solving a problem. Exposure to diversity increases the probability that a source of analogy will be found in the creativity process. The more diverse opinions, values, ideas and knowledge domains people are exposed to, the more possibilities there will be to find analogies between different domains or

---

Box 7.1 Fireflies and LEDs, Cockleburs and Velcro

In her 1997 book, Janine Benyus coined the term 'biomimicry', to describe innovation inspired by nature (Benyus, 1997). Benyus provides a rich array of examples of cases in which scientists have been inspired by nature to develop solutions to problems in a wide range of domains. A recent example involves research carried out by a team of scientists from Belgium, France and Canada (Hurst, 2013). They discovered that the specific structure on the abdomen of a firefly helps it emit more light. They used the same shape on the exterior of gallium nitride LEDs, resulting in an approximately 55 per cent increase in the brightness of LEDs.

Another example is the case of Velcro. Henry Petroski, in his book, *Innovation by Design* (Petroski, 1996), describes how, in 1948, George de Mestral returned from a walk in the Alpine woodlands and realised that his dog's hair was covered with cockleburs, which he had some difficulty removing. When he looked at them through a microscope to see how they stuck the way they did, he had the idea of using them as the model for an alternative to the conventional zipper (Petroski notes that de Mestral was not a stranger to invention, having received a patent for a toy aeroplane at the age of twelve).

to bring different areas into association.[3] In other words, there is a direct relation between diversity and recombination; the more variety in a system, the more alternative recombination paths (Weitzman, 1998) people will come up with.

7.2.2 What Kind of Diversity?

Diversity is a broad term, so the question of what kind of diversity is important for creativity is highly relevant.

- **Technological diversity** increases a firm's innovative potential by maintaining the availability of a broad set of alternative recombination paths.[4] For example, Miller, Fern and Cardinal (2007) found that knowledge transfer among divisions in technologically diverse firms increases the impact of inventions on subsequent technologies developed. Leten, Belderbos and Van Looy (2007) detect a curvilinear relationship between technological diversity and innovative performance; too much diversity increases coordination costs but coherence of technological areas reduces them (see Chapter 6 on the effect of diversity on learning and capability transfer).
- **Cultural diversity:** most studies find that cultural diversity has a positive effect on creativity.[5] However, cultural diversity can be a 'double-edged sword' (Milliken, Bartel and Kurtzberg, 2003). On the one hand it can increase innovative potential, thanks to the synergies formed through the integration of different viewpoints, as culturally diverse teams can make better use of information (McLeod, Lobel and Cox, 1996). On the other hand, cultural diversity can have negative effects on creativity, due to difficulties in resolving conflicts, identifying with the group and communication problems (Milliken, Bartel and Kurtzberg, 2003).[6]
- **Diversity in knowledge backgrounds** is generally useful for creativity. However, too much diversity can inhibit knowledge-sharing, because when common knowledge is limited people have difficulty communicating their own knowledge. In addition, exposure to too much diversity through

---

[3] For analogical thinking see Kalogerakis, Lüthje and Herstatt (2010); Gavetti and Rivkin (2005); Gassman and Zeschky (2008).

[4] Fleming (2002) and Carnabuci and Bruggeman (2009).

[5] For a discussion and overview of diversity and creativity see Milliken, Bartel and Kurtzberg (2003).

[6] Note that up to a certain level, conflict and dissent have a positive impact on creativity. Nemeth and Nemeth-Brown (2003) discuss how conflict and dissent can also be useful for creativity. On this, also see Sutton (2001).

numerous weak links can cause distraction and loss of focus, lowering the level of mental energy allocated to creative activities (Perry-Smith and Shalley, 2003).

7.2.3 Complexity

Complexity is important in creativity in two ways. The first is the complexity of job design. According to previous research, complex and challenging jobs enhance people's intrinsic motivation and consequently their creativity (Oldham and Cummings, 1996; Hackman and Oldham, 1980). Here complexity implies jobs with high levels of autonomy, skill variety, identity, significance and feedback (Oldham and Cummings, 1996). The second is related to the interdependences between the different knowledge elements that characterise a problem space. To the extent that stronger interdependence brings about more intensive interactions between innovators, realising cross-cutting synergies between elements may bring about creative outcomes.

In the next sections of this chapter, we will focus on how structural network properties relate to creativity, beginning with brokerage, which is both a structural position and a process (Borgatti, Brass and Halgin, 2014). In general, brokerage is associated with higher creative potential (Burt, 2004) because brokering between different contexts increases the chances of recombining these contexts in creative ways. The second network property is cohesiveness. If brokerage is important for diversity and recombination, cohesiveness is important for the transfer of complex and tacit knowledge between actors.

Finally, we will look at two global network structures that have implications for creativity, core-periphery and small-world networks.

7.3 Brokerage and Ideation

Brokerage positions in a network can be advantageous for creativity, depending on whether there are the mechanisms to sustain brokerage and how it is exercised.

7.3.1 Sustaining brokerage

The sustainability of brokerage relates to the extent to which it is a permanent factor in the way tasks are organised. Brokerage benefits tend to subside rapidly but for creativity it is better if brokerage is sustained through the

---

Box 7.2 3M

The company 3M often appears in innovation-focused case studies. This is partly because its culture and organisational routines are highly oriented towards creativity and innovation (Govindarajan and Srinivas, 2013). Every year, for example, it organises the Tech Forum, an event at which scientists from different laboratories around the company can regularly meet, present and discuss their work. It also has a Technical Council that meets regularly to discuss progress on projects. In one of these councils, the Post-it inventor Spencer Silver talked about the weak adhesive technology that he had accidentally developed. One of those attending the meeting, Stephen Fry, realised that this adhesive could be useful as a bookmark in his choir hymnbook. Later on, Fry applied for funding to create the Post-it note.

Another 3M practice is the '15% rule', which stipulates that every employee should spend up to 15 per cent of his or her time pursuing their own selected projects. The formation of new ventures is encouraged because it enables inventors to form their own teams within the company; if the project fails, team members can go back to their previous positions in the firm.

R&D at 3M is organised around various kinds of labs. Corporate labs focus on basic research, while division labs form a bridge between basic research and the market. Through access to a very rich database of technical reports written by 3M researchers, scientists easily can find out who worked on a related problem in the past. For example, some years ago 3M introduced a product called the Filtek Supreme Plus, which combined two contrasting features of dental fixtures: strength and polishability (Scanlon, 2009). During the development of this product, Sumita Mitra used the database to find another 3M scientist whose previous research on nanoparticles was just what he needed.

---

formal organisation of work. A person occupying a bridging position may not maintain it for long due to the saturation of creative opportunities. For example, Perry-Smith and Shalley (2003) introduce the spiral model of creativity and networks drawing upon Lindsley, Brass and Thomas's (1995) spiral model of efficacy. They show that initial weak ties and boundary spanning positions trigger an individual's creativity. As that person becomes more central in the network, he or she may move from a network of weak ties to one with strong embedded ties. This embeddedness will constrain creativity as the person is distracted by his or her centrality.

In the organisation of work, rotation programmes can be introduced to sustain brokerage positions. Fleming (2002) showed that the rotation of engineers between projects at Hewlett Packard enabled their experiences to be used in new and completely different areas. The result of this rotation was the ink-jet printer. A similar reasoning is valid at the inter-firm level. For example, in the case of Silicon Valley, mobility of inventors between companies largely contributed to the diffusion of knowledge and creativity, by bringing new knowledge into companies through earlier contacts (Almeida and Kogut, 1999). Box 7.2 shows how creativity and innovation is managed in 3M.

7.3.2 Brokerage Roles

Brokerage benefits depend on the extent to which a person in a brokerage position in a network actually exercises brokerage activities. Just as the same actor can exercise different brokering activities over time (see Box 11.2 in Chapter 11 for an example), different people can become brokers in an organisation temporarily. Here it is important to distinguish between brokerage as a *process* (what the broker actually does) and brokerage as a *position* (purely structural) (Obstfeld, Borgatti and Davis, 2014). As a position, brokerage is structural and describes network positions in which a structural hole is filled (see Chapter 4 for a reminder of the different metrics used for structural holes). As a process, brokerage describes the *type* of activities in which a broker is involved. Four types of brokerage role have implications for creativity; one of these is at the inter-organisational level, and the others are at intra-organisational level (see Tables 7.1 and 7.2).[7]

Consultant. The consultant position refers to organisations that, by the very nature of their operations, have richer opportunities to exercise recombination by associating diverse domains. The organisational routines of professional service providers like advertising agencies, consultancy services, software companies or design firms are oriented towards devising customised and client-based solutions, where the clients usually belong to different industries. In the network in Figure 7.2, A fills a consultant position, where it has the chance to recombine experiences with different types of organisation B–F with which it has ties.

A famous case study of knowledge brokers was carried out on the design firm IDEO by Hargadon and Sutton (1997). In this acclaimed work they showed how the experiences of people working with clients in one industry were transferred to other projects in the firm. Because brokerage positions reveal otherwise unseen opportunities they are important sources of social capital (Burt, 2004). Hargadon and Sutton show that creativity is fostered through IDEO's brokering activities, linking distant universes. The consultant position is an opportunity particularly for firms that span multiple markets, where associations between different fields are a source of inspiration (Hargadon, 1998).

Because people become experienced about different industries, establishing channels to share this knowledge, and finding alternative ways to look at

---

[7] See Fernandez and Gould (1994) for these and other brokerage roles.

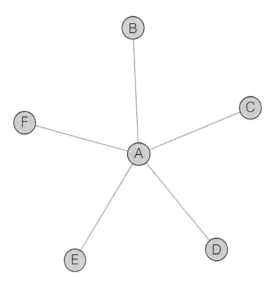

Figure 7.2 Consultant Brokerage Position

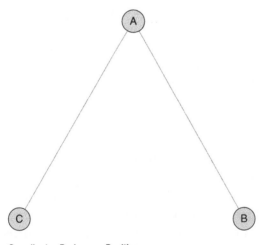

Figure 7.3 Coordinator Brokerage Position

problems inspired by other contexts become possible when consultant firms can transfer best practices internally. This is done through coordination, liaison and boundary spanning.

Coordinator. Figure 7.3 illustrates the coordinator role. Here, C goes to A for advice about how to approach a certain problem. A is not experienced in this domain but knows that B worked on a similar issue in the past (C knows that A is likely to refer him to someone else). In this case, A brokers a meeting between B and C, taking the *tertius iungens* (third coordinating party) role in the network. B connects to C through A's brokerage. In this case, it is irrelevant whether B and C were already or previously structurally connected. The point is that C did not know that B was working on a related topic. A (the broker) enabled C's needs to be matched with B's knowledge. Obstfeld (2005) gave an example of similar brokerage in the engineering division of an automotive producer. He documented how *tertius iungens* status increases innovation performance when ego network density is high (where there is an absence of structural holes in the ego network – in our example, a network where nodes C and B are also connected). Access to different people enables a coordinator to detect occasions when the knowledge and experiences of one group might benefit another. If the two alters are not connected, the coordinator has the unique advantage of foreseeing useful links for the transfer of best practices within an organisation. The coordinator acts as a source of information about who knows what, increasing the chances that there will be effective knowledge-sharing.

Liaison. Liaison, the third brokerage role, is shown in Figure 7.4. In this case, node A has weak links with B, C and D, who belong respectively to three

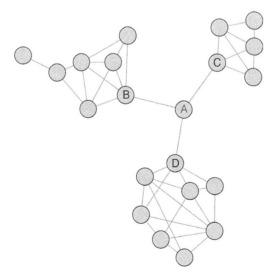

Figure 7.4   Liaison Brokerage Position

cohesive and otherwise unconnected teams (i.e. they are connected only through A). In this case, A does not belong to any of these groups and can potentially access three silos in an organisation, without being constrained by any pressure to conform to the dominant views of any one of them. Therefore A has more chances to develop a unique vision and synthesise others' views.

An individual whose connections are diverse, with weak ties, is more autonomous, does not have to conform to the expectations or interests of a certain group and is not under pressure to comply with the norms of a particular social structure. Within a cohesive network, beliefs, values, tastes or opinions are likely to converge, reducing the possibilities for generating novelty. In other words, knowledge is more homogeneous within groups than between them, and a liaison can benefit from the diversity accessed, increasing opportunities for recombination. Another advantage of liaison is that autonomy increases the creative potential of individuals and flexibility in the way they approach issues (Woodman, Sawyer and Griffin, 1993).

However, a disadvantage of the liaison position is possible lack of trust from others. For example, in an open community case, Fleming and Waguespack (2007) find that people who hold liaison functions need more physical interaction with others, to compensate for the lack of trust that accrues from not being part of a group. They also find that being a boundary spanner between different technical fields significantly increases the likelihood of being a leader in open source communities.

Boundary Spanner. Figure 7.5 shows a boundary spanner. Node A is part of a cohesive group whose members are connected with strong ties. A is the only node with access to the external nodes (B, C, D). In this case A is the gatekeeper who carries knowledge across boundaries.[8] An example of gatekeepers are the 'technology entrepreneurs' in Procter & Gamble's Connect and Develop programme. Huston and Sakkab (2006) describe these gatekeepers as senior level people who are specialised in distinct areas and are responsible for scanning the outside world (users, other companies, start-ups, etc.) for solutions to problems or new product ideas. They form networks with people outside the firm and maintain relations with a wide range of actors to connect internal ideas with the external world. Boundary

---

[8] Allen and Cohen's (1969) research on an R&D lab and Tushman (1977) are two initial systematic studies of the innovation networks in an organisation. See also Tushman and Scanlan (1981).

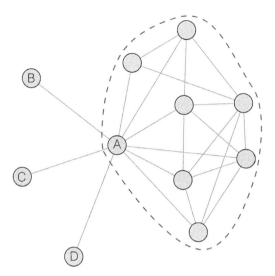

Figure 7.5 Boundary Spanner Position

spanners also have an important role in communicating with users and integrating users' ideas, inventions or insights into internal innovation processes.

7.4   Strong Ties, Cohesion and Creativity

While brokerage is relevant for diversity in the network, cohesive networks and strong ties help to *process* this diversity effectively, that is, sharing, disseminating and adapting it to a specific context.[9] To do this, an organisation needs effective knowledge transfer channels between people in order to arrive at alternative solutions to an existing problem. Transfer of best practices between organisation members is sometimes impeded by complicated relations between sender and receiver (Szulanski, 1996). Trust-based cohesive networks, within which team members communicate readily and openly with each other, facilitate the sharing of resources and knowledge.

---

[9] Note that this chapter takes a structural approach to creativity in relation to networks. For theoretical foundations of creativity in groups, see Paulus and Nijstad (2003).

7.4.1   Cohesive Networks

Cohesive networks help to develop group-based norms – values that are shared by the members in the group – which makes the diffusion of knowledge smoother within a group than between groups. Opportunistic or undesirable behaviour is unlikely to arise, because news about such behaviour travels fast, forestalling members' likelihood to indulge in it. Cohesive networks are usually characterised by strong links between members.[10] One reason for this is that people are more motivated to transfer knowledge to one another when the tie between them is strong and they share a common language (Reagans and Mcevily, 2003). Strong ties are also effective in transferring best practice between members. For example, in a sociometric study conducted in the development department of a software firm, Sosa (2011) found that dyadic ties, characterised by a broad range of task-related issues shared between two people, are more likely to yield creative ideas.

7.4.2   Trade-off between Cohesion and Sparseness

There is a fundamental trade-off in the efficacy of cohesive networks for creativity. Novelty depends on diversity, yet diversity is at odds with cohesiveness.[11] In other words, cohesiveness can have a negative impact on creativity, due to conformity pressures, or convergence in cohesive groups (see, for example, cognitive biases like group polarisation and groupthink discussed in Chapter 9). People communicate better with like-minded others, but as they communicate more and more, they become even more like-minded and diversity diminishes. In this sense cohesion can act as a barrier to creativity, mainly due to pressures that network members may feel to reach a consensus and conform to the ideas that emerge, inhibiting divergent thinking[12] (Janis, 1972). Therefore, strong ties are usually considered to have a negative impact on creativity, because people with strong ties can have convergent views on issues that may reduce their ability to come up with alternatives.

[10] Note that this does not exclude the possibility that there can be strong ties outside a cohesive network and weak ties within it.

[11] See the introductory chapter in Paulus and Nijstad (2003) for an overview of this trade-off in the context of groups and creativity.

[12] This phenomenon is often referred to as groupthink. See Nemeth and Nemeth-Brown (2003) for possible positive effects of these processes.

7.4.3 Nature of Tasks

These effects of cohesiveness depend on external factors like complexity, task specificity and the tacitness of knowledge.

- **Tacit and complex knowledge:** tacit and complex knowledge are transferred better in cohesive networks (Cowan, Jonard and Özman, 2004; Hansen, 1999). The complexity of a task is often managed by breaking it down into modules that are allocated to individual teams, especially in modular product systems. In general, increased interdependence between modules implies deeper interactions and knowledge-sharing between specialised teams (see Chapter 8). Highly cohesive teams may prevent effective sharing of knowledge between teams. In this case, boundary spanners with strong ties that cut across groups play a critical role in maintaining communication between teams.
- **Task specificity:** research shows that the more people share specific and marginal interests, as opposed to interests shared by the greater part of the population, the more likely they are to form a tie. For example, Adamic, Buyukkoten and Adar (2003) studied the users of an online student centre at Stanford University in California and found that two students are more likely to be friends if their interests overlap, and even likelier if those interests are in a specific or niche subject. People can be more motivated to share their knowledge in cohesive networks when tasks are highly specific, compared to teams that work on more general areas.
- **Balancing cohesion and diversity:** cohesion can have a positive impact on creativity when it is balanced by some source of diversity in the group (although this may not be sustainable in the long run, as group members grow more alike). Because diversity is an important ingredient of creativity, different forms of diversity have been extensively researched.[13] Fleming, Mingo and Chen (2007) show that, when the participants in a cohesive group come from diverse *backgrounds*, cohesion in the group will foster creativity. The background of team members is significant as a moderating factor: drawing upon a wide breadth of previous experience increases the positive impact of cohesiveness on creativity (see Box 7.3).

Similar reasoning also applies at the dyadic level. For example Aral and Van Alstyne (2011) show that when strong ties have 'higher channel bandwidth', meaning that more diverse information flows through them,

---

[13] See Harrison and Klein (2007) for measuring diversity in organisations. The dimensions of diversity can include nationality, ethnic background, gender, educational background, tenure, cultural values, problem-solving orientations, personality and others (Milliken, Bartel and Kurtzberg, 2003).

Box 7.3 Making Engineers and Medical Doctors Work Together: CIMIT

The Center for the Integration of Medicine and Innovative Technology (CIMIT) is a multi-institutional organisation founded in 1998 by a group of four collaborating institutions in the Boston area: Massachusetts General Hospital, Brigham and Women's Hospital, MIT and the Draper Labs.[1] The idea behind CIMIT was an ambitious one, to make engineers and physicists work together to solve health problems. Despite facing many difficulties and challenges, today CIMIT is a vibrant organisation with over 500 projects funded since its foundation. CIMIT's original aim was to make MIT and the Massachusetts General Hospital work together on pressing problems that required a wide breadth of knowledge, beyond the scope of specific disciplines. This was not an easy task; for one thing, MIT and the hospital had dominant conservative cultures that made it difficult to bring together people willing to share knowledge, understand each other and develop a common language.

When asked about the major challenges they encountered, Joseph Vacanti, co-programme leader in CIMIT, said that when discussing their work, specialists from different backgrounds had to be able to describe everything they did, regardless of how technical it might be, in language that an eleven-year-old could understand (Dillon, 2001). Another challenge was to decide which model of interdisciplinarity to adopt – whether to promote collaborations between diverse disciplines, or to train hybrid people, knowledgeable about a wide range of subjects. As the founders have explained, excellent work in engineering and medicine involves dramatically different types of thinking and information. For this reason, a collaborative model based on joint creativity was adopted. Jonathan Rosen, who directed the CIMIT Office of Technology Implementation until 2006, has explained that this was largely related to the type of task undertaken: some medical technology tasks required deep specialisation, while others needed a broad range of understanding and knowledge from various people (Dillon, 2001). These collaborations were facilitated by the leaders, who spent a great deal of time finding overlaps between researchers, and also by weekly forums in which physicists and engineers educated each other and came up with new ideas. When communicating, it was very important for researchers to be open about the gaps in their knowledge. Their shared passion for solving problems was the glue that held them together.

[1] www.cimit.org, accessed 7 July 2016.

---

novelty is not confined to weak ties but can also be accessed from strong ties, depending on the range of issues shared between two people. Sosa (2011) obtains a similar result in the case of a large software firm, where he finds that strong ties are a source of creativity, depending on the extent to which the tie brings diverse areas of knowledge.

So far, we can see that brokerage positions and roles are largely associated with diversity-generating processes, and cohesive networks and strong ties are associated with the effectiveness of knowledge-sharing and transfer between people. Cohesiveness and brokerage are both needed for creative outcomes, depending on the nature of knowledge and task. For cohesive networks to foster creativity, some source of diversity in the network is essential. At the same time, for diversity to foster creativity, mutual understanding and some commonality between network members are necessary (see Tables 7.1 and 7.2). We arrived at a similar conclusion in Chapter 6, with the discussion about the complementarity between brokerage and cohesion.

Table 7.1 Creativity at the Intra-organisational Level

Network Horizon	What to Look for	Indicators	Implication
	Tie strength between team members	Previous experience of working together Overlap or diversity in knowledge/background between team members	Strong ties imply increased motivation to share knowledge Strong ties help develop a common language
Team	Diversity of team members	Diversity in the range of areas shared (tie bandwidth) Diversity in other dimensions (age, sex, nationality, etc.)	Diversity at one or more levels is relevant for incorporating different perspectives or facilitating analogous thinking
Inter-group	Brokerage *Coordinator*	People who initiate ties between others by detecting their common experiences and/or knowledge	Play an important role in advice networks Valuable source of information in forming teams
	Brokerage *Liaison*	People who are not identified with any cohesive subgroup but who have strong connections with existing subgroups	Can cross-check and confirm an idea with people who belong to different thought worlds Are usually more autonomous than people in groups
	Brokerage *Boundary spanner*	People who are part of a group but also have ties outside the group	Critical role in bringing new insights and knowledge from outside the group Critical role in implementation, gaining legitimacy, through their ties with people outside the group

Table 7.2 Creativity at the Inter-organisational Level

Network Horizon	What to Look for	Indicators	Implication
Alliance portfolio	Brokerage *Consultant*	Serving different types of client, industry or alliance with diverse types of partner	Possibility to recombine knowledge accessed from external partners; possibility for analogous thinking
Network	Small-world network (also applies to intra-organisational level)	Cohesive subgroups, with shortcuts between them	Combines advantages of cohesiveness with advantages of diversity
	Core-periphery network (also applies to intra-organisational)	Densely connected core, weakly connected periphery	Centralised network can inhibit even diffusion of knowledge and reduce the effectiveness of advice and information seeking
			Decentralised networks are better for diffusion of knowledge and advice and the transfer of best practice between members
			Network positions between core and periphery have advantages, e.g. accessing novelties from the periphery, leveraging connections with the core in implementation
			Teams composed of the core and periphery are better
Platform	User complementor, supplier networks	Appointing boundary spanners	Searching, collaborating and bringing in creative ideas from users outside the organisation
		Coordinating user networks	Forming a platform to coordinate interactions between users

---

Box 7.4 Collaboration 'in', Solitude 'out'… or Not?

In an interview published in the MIT Technology Review (Dizikes, 2011), Noam Chomsky talks about Building 20 at MIT, where his office was located for several years:

> 'Building 20 was a fantastic environment,' he says. 'It looked like it was going to fall apart. There were no amenities, the plumbing was visible and the windows looked like they were going to fall out. But it was extremely interactive. At [the Research Laboratory of Electronics] in the 1950s there was a mixture of people who later became [part of] separate departments – biology and computer science – interacting informally all the time. You would walk down the corridor and meet people and have a discussion.'

Building 20 was built in a hurry in the 1940s as temporary accommodation for a radiation lab. Later, it housed diverse groups, departments, labs and activities before being demolished in 1998. In recent years, we have witnessed an increasing tendency to design workspaces to facilitate chance encounters between diverse people in an organisation (see Box 1.1), together with an increase in incentives designed to make people collaborate internally, externally and internationally. The effect of collaboration on successful output has been well documented, as has the importance of face-to-face interactions in innovation. However, there is another side to the coin. According to some people, creativity requires solitude; an over-emphasis on collaboration in work environments can be inhibiting to some researchers. This view seems to resonate with many people, judging from the success of Susan Cain's bestselling book *Quiet*, about the creative potential of introverts and the value of solitude (Cain, 2012). A recent HBR article (Congdon, Flynn and Redman, 2014) claims that many people now criticise open plan designs. However, it is not the concept that is wrong but the fact that it is often poorly executed. Innovation requires neither excessive remoteness, nor continuous interactions to promote creativity. One of the challenges facing every business, depending on the nature of its work, is to find the right balance between solitude and collaboration.

We have been considering how collaboration fosters creativity. However, there is a counter debate that claims solitude, rather than collaboration, fosters creativity. This is discussed in Box 7.4.

7.5 Global Network Structures and Creativity

7.5.1 Small-world Networks

Small-world networks (see Section 4.6.1) have a dual function. They accommodate effective knowledge transfer between people in clustered parts of the network and promote diffusion and diversity through shortcuts that convey knowledge between clusters. Various studies confirm the positive impact a small-world network structure has on creativity in the network.[14] In particular, small worlds have been shown to generate the highest rate of knowledge growth, because the diffusion of knowledge is more effective with small worlds than within clustered or random structures (Cowan and Jonard, 2003). However, knowledge growth also depends on the absorptive capacity of actors (Cowan and Jonard, 2004); random networks perform better when actors have high absorptive capacity, as they can cope better with the heterogeneous and diverse information they receive. But when absorptive capacity is low, small worlds perform better as they combine clustering, which enables transfer of tacit knowledge, and shortcuts, which access diverse knowledge.

In their study of Broadway musicals between 1945 and 1989, Uzzi and Spiro (2005) devised the Q parameter, which measures the extent to which teams of artists had previously worked together on other musicals. High levels of Q connote strong connections between team members based on prior experience. Low levels signify unfamiliar members. They found that the most creative musicals were made up of groups with an intermediate Q level, that is, a combination of people with strong ties and strangers to the group. Their reasoning was that when the same team works together repeatedly, creativity is reduced because they tend to repeat elements from previous work. Teams with new connections, on the other hand, bring new perspectives and novelty to productions.

Fleming and Marx (2006) carried out a network analysis of patent co-inventions in the Silicon Valley region. In DEC and Hewlett Packard networks, they highlighted the role played by one inventor (Stewart) in bridging three separate networks through his collaborations. They explained that his technical capabilities resulted in many managers asking him for advice, and accessing the perspectives he brought from other parts of the network. In this study, the authors showed that in both Silicon Valley and the Boston region, intra-firm small worlds grew into inter-firm small worlds over time. In these giant patent collaboration networks, technical gatekeepers like Stewart kept the network connected by providing shortcuts between different clusters.

---

[14] There is also some evidence that small worlds may not be as efficient as assumed. For example, Fleming, King and Juda (2007) find that, while both clustering and short path lengths tend to increase patenting capacity in the Silicon Valley and Boston regions, there is no interaction effect between the two parameters. Note that patenting capacity is not a measure of creativity although there is a correlation. Creativity may not be reflected in the patents and might be reflected in patent novelty. For the measurement of novelty value patents see Schoenmakers and Duysters (2010).

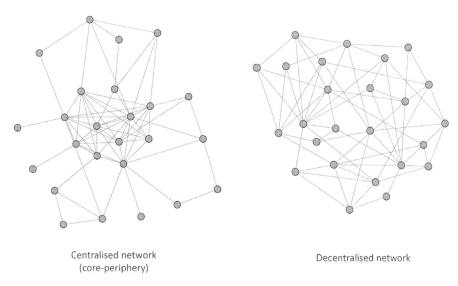

Centralised network
(core-periphery)

Decentralised network

Figure 7.6   Core-periphery (Centralised) and Distributed (Decentralised) Networks

Note that technical gatekeepers do not necessarily engage in brokering roles. They usually display academic and technical excellence but the extent to which they function as 'coordinators', recognising potentially fruitful connections in the network, is not guaranteed. What is more, technical gatekeepers can represent human resource challenges in an organisation. A technical gatekeeper may or may not facilitate the diffusion of knowledge. On the one hand, as shortcuts in the network, they are in a favourable position to diffuse knowledge between different technical clusters in the network. On the other hand, technical gatekeepers possess unique knowledge and they may find it difficult to communicate it to others. In a cohesive technical group, communication is relatively easy; however, the unique positioning of a broker between diverse groups implies that the communication of technical issues may be much less straightforward.[15]

7.5.2 Core-periphery Networks

Figure 7.6 shows two networks. In the first, we can clearly distinguish a core-periphery structure. Core members have higher centrality and are more

[15] See Fleming and Marx (2006) for some examples in Silicon Valley firms.

densely connected to each other than members on the periphery. Peripheral members are sparsely connected to each other and loosely linked to the core. If we assume that these networks illustrate advice networks in an organisation, it is possible to see that in the network on the left, peripheral members depend largely on core members for advice. In the second network, the centrality of network members is distributed more or less evenly throughout the network. The distinction between these two structures has some implications for creativity, especially in advice networks (see Box 10.3 for the characteristics of an advice network). Within an organisation, distributed advice networks (like the second one in Figure 7.6) reflect a social structure best suited for the even diffusion of knowledge among members. For example, in the case of professional service firms that serve clients from a broad range of industries, distributed intra-organisational networks facilitate the sharing of experiences between people who are specialised in a specific client profile. In the case of the design firm IDEO, Amabile, Fisher and Pillemer (2014) found that help-givers and help-receivers are not confined to certain hierarchical levels but are distributed evenly throughout the company, which is largely fuelled by an open and collaborative culture. However, this is not the case in most organisations. For example, Singh, Hansen and Podolny (2010) show that those people on the periphery of an organisational network, because their social position or tenure is disadvantageous, are less aware of who knows what; therefore, they tend to connect with other people on the network periphery rather than those in the core who might guide their search more effectively. As a result, for a variety of factors, the core and periphery of a network can be connected weakly. The authors emphasise the need to cross social boundaries when asking for and receiving help.

Research shows that when networks are centralised, beneficial network positions occur between the core and the periphery. Cattani and Ferriani (2008), in their analysis of the Hollywood film-making industry, found that individual creativity is higher when someone is positioned between the core and the periphery. A person connected to the periphery can access ideas in the fringes of the social system, which can be more creative due to the periphery's independence from the tight social structure and norms that characterise the core. At the same time, a person connected to the core can access resources for legitimising and implementing creative endeavours. Therefore, groups that involve members from both the core and the periphery of a network are often most suited for innovation.

Discussion Questions

1. Why is diversity useful for creativity?

2. Explain different brokerage roles, and how they can play a role in fostering creativity.

3. Explain the trade-off between cohesion and diversity as far as they influence creativity in an organisation.

4. A recent network analysis in your organisation revealed that information flow networks exhibit the following network structures. How would you form a project team if you want to foster creativity?
   a. Small-world network
   b. Core-periphery network.

Users, Product Systems and Networks

If you want to build a ship, don't drum up the men to gather wood, divide the work, and give orders. Instead, teach them to yearn for the vast and endless sea.

Antoine de Saint-Exupéry

The nature of a product system, in terms of its complexity, modularity and underlying knowledge base, shapes the interactions between innovators. In return, these interactions shape the innovation process. In this chapter we explore how these aspects of a product system influence the communication between innovators. We define modularity, and explain the design structure matrix as a tool to map the interdependence between elements of a system. We also explore how firms interact with users to increase innovative potential. We distinguish between three forms of user engagement through networks: firstly, when an organisation creates a platform with which users may interact; secondly, when it appoints knowledge brokers; and finally the open source model, in which a community of users jointly participate in the creation of the product.

The nature of a technology or product system has an important role in the way innovators interact and communicate with each other. The complexity of a product system, its modularity and the nature of the knowledge base largely shape the ways in which producers exchange knowledge and resources and organise production. Therefore understanding how different aspects of a product system influence networks is important in order to align networks effectively with new product development.

A product system can be analysed along three dimensions according to the involvement of different actors. The first is backstage, concerned with the design and manufacturing of products through the networks of producers. The second is the involvement of users in the design of the products, where networks between users and producers are critical. The third dimension is user-only networks, through which knowledge about the product system diffuses and products are adopted. In this chapter, we take a closer look at the first two of these dimensions, namely the relation between the nature of a product system and how it fits with interactions between producers, and interactions between users and producers.

8.1 Modularity

Modularity is an important aspect of a product system and has implications for interactions between innovators. The effective coordination of different modules in a product system is vital to avoid scheduling problems and increased costs and to ensure the timely flow of information and resources. One way to achieve this is to ensure a fit between the interdependence of modules in a product system and the communication between producers, whose tasks are allocated according to different parts of the product. Network analysis can be used to monitor this fit and determine the actions to be taken to ensure that communication and information flows are neither redundant nor insufficient vis-à-vis the architecture of the product system.

8.1.1 What is Modularity?

The origins of modularity date back to Simon's (1962) analysis of managing complex systems by splitting them into modules. His example of two fine watchmakers, Tempus and Hora, is well known. Simon explains why, as Hora prospered, Tempus became poorer and poorer and eventually lost his shop:

The watches the men made consisted of about 1,000 parts each. Tempus had so constructed his that if he had one partly assembled and had to put it down – to answer the phone, say – it immediately fell to pieces and had to be reassembled from the elements. The better the customers liked his watches, the more they phoned him, the more difficult it became for him to find enough uninterrupted time to finish a watch.

The watches that Hora made were no less complex than those of Tempus. But he had designed them so that he could put together sub-assemblies of about 10 elements each. Ten of these sub-assemblies, again, could be put together into a larger sub-assembly; and a system of 10 of the latter sub-assemblies constituted the whole watch. Hence, when Hora had to put down a partly assembled watch in order to answer the phone, he lost only a small part of his work, and he assembled his watches in only a fraction of the man-hours it took Tempus.

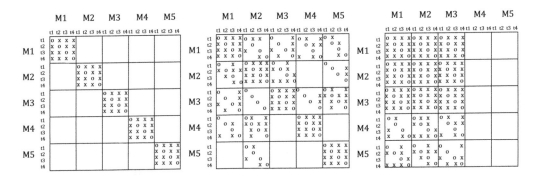

Figure 8.1   Three DSM Matrices

Note: From left to right: DSMI independent modules, DSMII integrated system, DSMIII core-periphery system.

Schilling (2000: 312) defines modularity as a 'continuum describing the degree to which a system's components can be separated and recombined'. Ulrich (1995) defines modularity as the one-to-one mapping between components and the functions of a system.[1] Through modularity, end users can generate additional value by mixing and matching components to satisfy different functional requirements. In this way the modularity of a system can be a source of product variety for users. A common method of mapping the structure of a product system and analysing its modularity is the design structure matrix (DSM).

8.1.2   Design Structure Matrix

The DSM is a method of analysing the interdependence between the modules in a product system. Figure 8.1 shows three hypothetical DSMs of a product system.

The product system in Figure 8.1 consists of five modules with four tasks in each. A cross sign indicates that a particular task in a row is dependent on the corresponding task in the column. In DSM I, each module is independent from all the other modules or does not depend on others. DSM II, on the other hand, shows a relatively more integrated product system, where tasks in each module depend on tasks in other modules. For example, t2 in module 3 depends on t3 in module 5, and so on. A DSM matrix can be represented as a network in which nodes are tasks and a link between two nodes shows their

[1] On modular product systems, see Garud and Kumaraswamy (1995).

interdependence. DSM III shows a core-periphery product system, where there is a strongly inregrated core composed of modules 1, 2 and 3, and peripheral modules 4 and 5 that are dependent on the modules in the core.

DSM is used to map the architecture of software platforms. For example, McCormack, Rusnak and Baldwin (2006) used DSM to analyse the structure of the first releases of Linux and Mozilla open source software. Mozilla originated in the proprietary source code of Netscape, which released its source files in 1998 with the primary aim of developing and improving the code using contributions from other software developers. A secondary aim was to increase the modularity of the source code, as it was too tightly coupled to permit independent contributions to be made to specific source files without changing other elements. The authors found that the structure of the two platforms varied significantly in terms of the extent to which a change in a source file propagated through the system, necesitating changes in other source files. Specifically, they found that a change in a Mozilla source file could impact three times as many source files as a change in Linux, which was more loosely coupled. However, as Mozilla developed further as an open source code its modularity also increased.

The degree to which a change in a source file necesitates potential changes in other source files can be measured by the propagation cost (McCormack, Rusnak and Baldwin, 2006). The idea behind propagation cost is to analyse direct and indirect interdependences between matrix elements. Direct interdependences are revealed by the ties between elements in networks, while indirect interdependences are derived by analysing the path length between elements, using reachability metrics in SNA.

8.1.3   Modularity and Product Performance

Modularity has implications for the performance of product systems and the organisational structure of teams, firms and industries. Producers benefit from the increased efficiency of modular designs, where different product designs can be created using a few platforms. A classic example is the redesigning of the product line by Black & Decker in the 1970s (Lehnerd, 1987). The new design of the electric motor was modularised and all interfaces were standardised so that various power tools could be used with the same electric motor with only minor changes in its structure. Lehnerd (1987) explains the significant cost savings achieved, increased efficiency, lower material waste and greater opportunities for new product development that this redesign enabled.

But there is also trade-off where the performance of products and modularity are concerned. When modular product systems are accompanied by a modular organisational structure, where each firm or team specialises in specific modules within the system, independent innovations can be applied in different modules without having to change the overall product architecture. But this independence comes at a cost, because the possibility of an overall breakthrough innovation in the whole product is reduced (Fleming and Sorenson, 2003). Moreover, as a design rule, optimising the performance of individual modules does not necessarily (and in fact in most cases does not) optimise the performance of the system as a whole (Utterback et al., 2006).

The relation between modularity and product system performance depends to a large extent on how modularity is accompanied by the organisation of tasks. Often, task organisation both shapes and is shaped by the architecture of a product system. For example, in the case of Linux and Mozilla, McCormack, Rusnak and Baldwin (2006) conclude that the organisation of tasks in the two software platforms (one open source and the other proprietary at the point of first release) largely determined the architecture of the product systems: Linux was far more loosely coupled than Mozilla, where teams worked at the same location. However, over time, Mozilla was increasingly organised according to an open source logic, with distributed contributions from many developers, and also became a loosely coupled system. In the next section we address the question of the relation between modularity and the organisation of tasks at the team level and in relation to outsourcing production.

Modularity of the product system requires effective coordination of tasks. In complex product systems, like aircraft or motor vehicles, the architecture of the system can govern the patterns of communications between teams responsible for the design of different modules. In this case, the interdependence between modules shapes interactions.

8.1.4 Teams

Returning to the example of the Black & Decker, when the company realised a fundamental redesign of its production line to incorporate double insulation in all its machines, radical changes in organisation of tasks were also needed. One of these was increased collaboration between manufacturing and design engineers in order to meet the new design requirements while reducing manufacturing costs. New product development was put on hold for some time and design engineers were placed in the manufacturing department.

Sosa, Eppinger and Rowles (2004) highlighted the problem of a possible misalignment between design interfaces and interactions between the teams that produce them. If two modules share a design interface, the teams responsible for the modules are expected to interact. However, in their analysis of the PW4098 derivative aircraft engine developed by Pratt and Whitney, Sosa, Eppinger and Rowles (2004) showed the difficulties of achieving this perfect match, examining two types of misalignment. The first is the absence of team interactions when there is a design interface, and the second the absence of a design interface when there are team interactions. The authors used the network approach as a diagnostic tool to visualise the product architecture, analyse team interactions and identify where and why misalignment occurs. They found there were numerous reasons behind the misalignment in the case of PW4098: much-needed cross-boundary interactions were more likely to be missed than interactions within groups; the most complex and critical interfaces absorbed attention at the expense of less critical interfaces; and teams interacted mainly through intermediaries rather than directly.

The network approach can also be used for diagnosing similar misalignments in non-modular product systems. For example Kratzer, Gemuenden and Lettl (2008) carried out research on interactions between different institutions in space telescope development projects. They found that informal communication networks are much denser and more stable over time than formally ascribed design interfaces.

8.1.5   Outsourcing and Knowledge Transfer

Does Modularity Increase Outsourcing? In general, modularity is likely to increase the outsourcing of modules rather than in-house production (Sanchez and Mahoney, 1996). For one thing, modularity reduces the need for intensive knowledge-sharing as long as there are clear interfaces. When this is the case, knowledge-based theories of the firm (Grant, 1996a) predict that reduced need for knowledge-sharing will reduce outsourcing costs. Moreover, firms will be more flexible in selecting suppliers and can switch between suppliers easily, in cases of conflict or low performance (Garud and Kumaraswamy, 1995). Outsourcing can also benefit modular innovation, leveraging the innovative capabilities of many firms without the necessity of in-depth knowledge transfer and reducing coordination costs (Langlois and Robertson, 1992). Looking at the impact of modularity on the industry, one perspective is that modular product systems are accompanied by increasing autonomy and loose coupling between firms (Sanchez and Mahoney, 1996; Langlois and Robertson, 1992).

Baldwin and Clark (1997) state that modularity facilitates outsourcing, which is an opportunity for firms to access relevant technical expertise they may not themselves possess. But there are contradictory views claiming that modularity is not necessarily associated with increased outsourcing. Hoetker (2006) looked at software firms and found that while modularity gives firms the flexibility to switch between suppliers, it does not increase outsourcing. In other words, modularity is accompanied by weak ties with suppliers ex post, that is, once the decision to outsource is made.

Does Modularity Increase Inter-firm Knowledge Transfer? Supplier relationships in modular product systems are an important opportunity for firms to deepen their component-level, and sometimes system-level, knowledge. In complex product systems like vehicle manufacture, millions of components are integrated, each requiring specialised knowledge and skills. As a result organisational relationships range from arm's-length supplier relations to informal and close-knit ties in the form of joint module designs. As far as learning effects are concerned, the more intensive the interactions between suppliers and integrators, the more opportunities there are for learning.

Modularity may induce outsourcing but this does not mean that the extent of knowledge transfer between firms will be higher. In fact, modularity augments producers' autonomy and may reduce knowledge flows between firms (Pavitt, 2005). To the extent that modules are kept proprietary by a systems integrator, and suppliers are provided with explicit interfaces in the form of blueprints, the extent of learning will depend on the assembler's strategy of interaction with suppliers (Mikkola, 2003; Pavitt, 2005). There is evidence that closer relationships with suppliers, permitting the exchange of tacit knowledge, contribute to the learning process and that joint product design results in improvement in the performance of the overall product architecture (Sobrero and Roberts, 2002).

The difference in managerial approach between Japanese and American vehicle manufacturers is frequently mentioned. Japanese firms mostly outsource 'black box' components that permit increased knowledge flows between firms, while American firms outsource 'detailed controlled' components, meaning that learning opportunities are more limited (Clark and Fujimoto, 1991; Womack, Jones and Roos, 1990; Mikkola, 2003).

Firms need to evaluate modularity carefully. On the one hand deep interactions with suppliers can stimulate innovative insights, but on the other, modular systems increase efficiency as they enable firms to reap the benefits of specialisation.

Through modularity, different product designs can be created using a few platforms, integrating the diverse capabilities of different firms. Modular product architectures in downstream markets can result in a variety of complementary products supplied by different vendors, as in the case of video games.[2] In some instances, where the technology does not have a stand-alone use, the utility users derive from products relies solely on complementary products. Video games and computers are examples in which stand-alone uses are weak or even non-existent.

8.1.6   Modularity and Platforms

Gawer (2011: 45) defines platforms as 'building blocks (they can be products, technologies or services) that act as a foundation upon which an array of firms (sometimes called a business ecosystem) can develop complementary products, technologies or services'. In this sense, a primary characteristic of a platform is the presence of multiple firms. Platforms usually have a hub-and-spoke network structure, in which the platform owner is the hub. The main links in the network are connections to the hub and relations between and among complementors and customers. When there is the potential to create additional value through network effects (usually the case in platforms), expanding the installed base of the platform is a prior concern underlying many collaborations in the industry. This can happen in four ways:

- **Collaborations to increase modularity:** a modular product system facilitates the entry of complementary goods and service providers, inducing firms to enhance the modular features of a system. A positive feedback loop between a large number of participants strengthens the market share of the core technology. An example is Apple's modularisation strategy with iTunes. Its partnerships with major recording companies enabled it to sell tracks through its iTunes network, one of the forces behind the widespread adoption of the iPod music player.

---

[2] On modularity and tie formation patterns, see Özman (2011).

- **Collaborations to join forces:** firms may be involved in alliances with other firms to support a standard (Hill, 1997). An early example is the VHS videocassette, where Matsushita licensed its technology to a range of consumer electronics companies, which ultimately contributed to the widespread adoption of VHS as a standard format. In a similar vein, when Sony and Philips partnered to combine their compact disc standards into one it triggered a bandwagon effect and the joint CD audio player technology was adopted by the whole market. Gnyawali and Park (2011) analysed the evolution of 'coopetition' between Sony and Samsung in creating liquid crystal displays; their collaboration created greater value, for which both companies competed for a larger share.[3]

- **Collaborations to develop compatible products:** firms can be involved in alliances with other firms to develop new technologies compatible with a platform, especially in the early phases of development. IBM's leader position in the computer industry was very effective in the shift from 150 mm to 200 mm wafers used in the fabrication of integrated circuits. IBM collaborated with major equipment suppliers and invested heavily in research. Having early access to critical equipment resulted in an active role in setting standards, a source of competitive advantage in the market (Chesbrough, 2003). Another example is the Sun Microsystems workstation design (Garud and Kumaraswamy, 1993). The authors show how Sun Microsystems adopted an open standard that it enabled other firms to access and expanded its market share through network effects.

- **Hub-complementor relations:** hub firms are usually involved in myriad interactions with complementors to expand the installed base of a platform. Examples are Microsoft's relations with its software providers and Google's cloud-based Enterprise system. Complementors also benefit from these interactions and their tie formation patterns reflect their different strategic concerns. Venkatraman and Lee (2004) identified several patterns related to developers' decisions to develop video games for a specific platform. As Figure 8.2 shows, game developers could choose to connect exclusively to certain platforms but in the majority of the cases they formed ties with more than one platform. The likelihood of a game developer forming ties with a certain platform is increased by the newness of the platform and its embeddedness in the network.

---

[3] On platforms, see Gawer and Cusumano (2002).

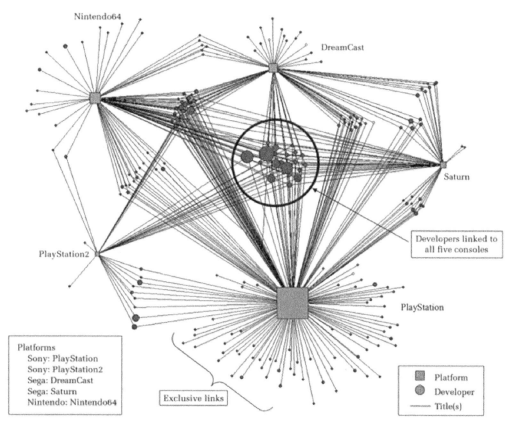

Figure 8.2   Network Structure of Video Game Platforms
Source: Venkatraman and Lee (2004)

8.2   Interactions with Users

One of the problems commonly encountered in innovation is the failure of producers to understand user needs. User participation in the innovation process has been intensifying in recent years. Figure 8.3. shows different ways of interacting with users. The vertical axis shows whether users are *directly or indirectly* involved in innovation. The horizontal axis shows whether use involvement is *systematic* or *sporadic*.

8.2.1   Direct Involvement of Users in Innovation

A firm may create specific opportunities for users to find new applications for existing technologies, come up with ideas for new designs or devise solutions to problems.

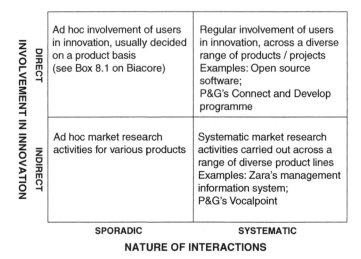

Figure 8.3   Interactions with Users

The direct involvement of users in innovation can be systematic and continuous, carried out regularly across a diverse range of products. An example is Linux, where hundreds of thousands of users are involved in the design of different modules of the code. Open source software projects like Linux have a core-periphery network structure. Another example is Procter & Gamble's Connect and Develop programme, which was initiated in 2001 and has increased innovation by almost 50 per cent. Connect and Develop is a systematic innovation programme based on interactions with external actors. Apart from the active and systematic involvement of users in devising solutions to problems, it involves open networks like NineSigma and Innocentive (Huston and Sakkab, 2006).

Such direct involvement, carried out across a diverse range of products or markets, is seldom a systematic part of innovation processes for many other firms. User involvement is usually confined to specific products or projects and is implemented sporadically. Box 8.1 describes the case of Biacore and the company's strategy to involve users in finding alternative uses for the product, which was originally designed to analyse protein interactions in real time.

8.2.2   Indirect Involvement of Users in Innovation

Users are indirectly involved in innovation through basic market research aimed at tracking their preferences and tastes, and using the data as input in design and new product development. An example of indirect systematic

---

Box 8.1 The Role of Users in Biacore

Biacore is a product used to analyse protein interactions in real time. Harrison and Waluszewski (2008), in their case study of the manufacturer Biacore, have shown how it mobilised users from universities, other companies and research labs to find new applications for the product, following an unsuccessful initial launch. The Biacore project dates from the 1980s, when it was initiated by Pharmacia Biotech in Uppsala, which specialised in surface plasmon resonance technology (SPR) and was one of the world's largest suppliers of biotech analytical tools. A small project group that soon turned into a spin-off was formed to explore ways to use SPR in biosensor instruments. The main sponsor was allergy specialist Pharmacia Diagnostics, a sister company in the same group. This support was ultimately ineffective, later shaping the design and characteristics of the product and ensuring that they complemented the products made by Pharmacia Diagnostics. This support limited the ways in which the product could be adapted to different markets, addressing different needs. When Pharmacia Diagnostics withdrew, Biacore representatives had to find alternative markets in which the product could be used. Starting from the early 1990s, they worked with a range of users from different sectors to develop insights about potential areas of application. The company successfully set up effective user networks, organising events and creating opportunities in which users could interact with each other and with the company leaders. Biacore researchers often worked directly with users, participating in intensive problem-solving activities in new developmental fields. A database was formed using hundreds of publications on alternative uses of the product, undertaken by the users themselves. These efforts resulted in multiple new applications and increased sales. At the same time, because the cost of commercialisation was also rising, the company underwent a major reorganisation of its marketing function.

---

market research is the clothing firm Zara's management information system. Data about items sold daily are aggregated in a central database every day and used as an input in the rapid cycle introduction of new products. Another example is P&G's Vocalpoint forum, where hundreds of thousands of users provide feedback, exchange opinions on household products and share information and experiences with people in their social networks. Indirect involvement in innovation can also be applied to specific projects; for example, alpha testing of computer software or market research before entry into a market.

8.2.3 Network Structure of User Innovation

Interactions with users in innovation can be characterised by three network structures.

- **Observer hub:** the focal organisation creates and leverages networks among users. This type of network is particularly useful when it is focused on a specific market or product line, so that users have a common context to share ideas and develop insights. Examples are the case of Biacore (see Box 8.1) and P&G's Vocalpoint, an online community of mostly individual households, where consumers share their experiences, ideas and problems experienced with different products. This feedback is used in new product development processes.

- **Appointing boundary spanners:** technology brokers within the firm match the firm's priority innovation areas with external knowledge sources. Boundary spanners are responsible for finding partners who can provide scientific and technological solutions to problems. Once again, P&G provides an example: the technology entrepreneurs in its Connect and Develop programme are based all over the world. The boundary spanner model is best suited to cases where user involvement is systematic, direct and distributed across a wide range of fields.

- **Open source model:** crowdsourcing projects involve massive numbers of users who participate in the development of a project. There are numerous examples, including Wikipedia and open source projects like Linux and Mozilla Firefox. The advantage of crowdsourcing projects is the lack of a bureaucratic organisation; however, coordination costs include the necessity to filter and evaluate contributions. Understanding the social structure of open source is important in order to detect actors whose withdrawal can be critical and to coordinate projects. Several studies find that most open source projects have a core-periphery network. For example Shen and Monge (2011) found that core members tend to connect mainly with each other, while novice developers tend to form ties with others in the periphery. Crowston and Howison (2005) constructed networks by analysing messages for fixing bugs and found that the team structure varies greatly; as projects grow, a decentralised pattern can be observed.

Discussion Questions

1. What is modularity? Can you find examples from different industries?

2. Does modularity increase outsourcing? If yes, what are the advantages and disadvantages for knowledge transfer between firms and innovation?

3. What are different network strategies that firms use in platforms, to make use of network effects?

4. Your organisation is an observer hub. Can you find ways in which users participate
   a. Directly
   b. Indirectly?

PART III

Selection Processes

9 Decision-making, Signals and New Ventures

The range of what we think and do is limited by what we fail to notice. And because we fail to notice that we fail to notice there is little we can do to change until we notice how failing to notice shapes our thoughts and deeds.

R. D. Laing (in Starbuck and Milliken, 1988)

In this chapter, we explore the role of networks in receiving and interpreting information. We look at how the network of an actor can generate cognitive biases, and how these biases can be overcome. We also consider the role of networks as signals, providing information about the inherent quality of actors when information is not readily available. We learn that networks are particularly important in intrapreneurial and entrepreneurial settings, in selecting start-ups or projects to fund, and how they can be used by intrapreneurs and entrepreneurs to increase legitimacy, attract venture capital funding, and advocate innovation projects in an organisation.

With the abundance of information in the environment, one of the problems managers face is how to filter out what is irrelevant, *notice* what information is relevant and *make sense* of it.[1] Networks play an important role in noticing and sense-making; changes in the environment and performance feedback are often received through networks. Because decision-making does not take place in a vacuum, networks can be influential in selecting the areas in which R&D investments will be made, new markets for entry, alliance partners and entrepreneurial firms in which to invest.

Networks are important sources of information for entrepreneurs and also provide the means for them to access resources for the implementation of innovative ideas. Coming up with creative ideas is only one aspect of innovation; implementing those ideas is equally important. Research shows that networks that are effective for idea creation may not be effective for implementation. Some networks provide creative insights through search

[1] On sense-making, see Daft and Weick (1984) and Starbuck and Milliken (1988).

processes and help the identification and recognition of opportunities; other networks help to build coalition and attract the resources needed to bring creative ideas to the market.

In this chapter, we will start by looking at the notion of organisational routines that can cause rigidities in innovation. Then we will focus on some potentially hazardous effects of social networks. Finally, we discuss the role of the entrepreneurship process and networks in implementing innovations.

9.1   Organisational Routines and Selection Biases

Every organisation has established procedures, rules, conventions, strategies and patterns of behaviour that govern the conduct of daily operations and decision-making processes. In behavioural theories of the firm,[2] these patterns are explained using the concept of *routines*. Routines are cognitive patterns or regularities observed in decision-making processes. Organisational routines are similar to the 'if then' rules in business environments (Becker, 2004). Routines are shared collectively; they form and develop through interactions and exchanges among diverse people in an organisation. They are recurrent processes that are invoked regularly and because they are largely context-specific their replication across space and time is often difficult (Nelson and Winter, 1982).

9.1.1   Adaptation and Routines

Organisational learning takes place in response to feedbacks received from the environment about the success or failure of previous routines. Changes in routines can be triggered by a number of factors: observing others, the result of direct experience, search activities or trial and error (Levitt and March, 1988). When existing routines are no longer appropriate (because of changes in the environment or negative performance feedbacks) or when a better routine is found that promises greater advantages, adaptive learning processes foster incremental or radical changes in routines (Gavetti and Levinthal, 2000). However, change can be slow and uncertain, especially when feedback is not received or is interpreted incorrectly, or when environmental change is too rapid (March, 1991). Then, organisations might fail to adapt to external changes and fail to reach their objectives.

---

[2] See Cyert and March (1963); Nelson and Winter (1982).

9.1.2   The Two Faces of Routines

In many ways the notion of routine is a double-edged sword in organisational learning. On the one hand routines save on cognitive efforts and increase efficiency because they reduce the range of options available to managers (Winter and Szulanski, 2001). On the other, they can also be sources of rigidity and cause selection biases. The concept of organisational routines is rather like human habit-forming. Someone who has lived in the same place for many years becomes accustomed to the neighbourhood and no longer needs to take a map when going out. Habit and familiarity save time and effort in finding the way around. In much the same way, organisational routines increase efficiency in search processes in an organisation.

However, routines can also have a dark side. Specialisation can be accompanied by path dependence, and organisations can accumulate experience in inferior procedures, and better procedures may not be sufficiently rewarding for use due to lack of experience (Levitt and March, 1988). An organisation can continuously receive positive feedback from a routine that is not necessarily good, when compared to alternatives, leading to competency traps. These traps are related to the failure to recognise the need for change because signals are perceived through lenses fashioned by past experiences (Daft and Weick, 1984). The dark side of routines can be likened to our difficulties in breaking old habits (for example, continuing to go to the usual bakery even though a better one has opened). Changing habits is easier for some people than for others and sometimes change simply never happens. In a similar way, organisational learning is related to the development of adaptation routines that allow organisations to change their rules systematically based on outside signals (Zollo and Winter, 2002). The ability of organisations to adapt their routines is referred to as the dynamic capabilities of an organisation (Teece and Pisano, 1994).

A typical example of the dark side of routines is the failure of established firms to recognise the need to invest in architectural innovations. Henderson and Clark (1990) show that in Kasper Instruments, a company specialised in photolithographic contact aligners, engineers were unable to recognise the emerging threat from Canon's proximity aligner, which did not appear to differ greatly from Kasper's, but whose components were arranged in such a way that it delivered a radically better performance. As Henderson and Clark (1990) note, what began as a success factor for Kasper (its expertise in contact aligners) became a barrier to its recognition of the better performance of an alternative design. Another example is Polaroid, where managers' cognitive representations of the market prevented them from adapting to the changing environment (see Box 9.1).

Box 9.1 Polaroid and Internal Inertia

The case of Polaroid is significant in demonstrating how managers' cognitive representations of the world can act as barriers to interpreting outside signals, resulting in organisational inertia (Tripsas and Gavetti, 2000). Polaroid was one of the companies that shaped the history of instant photography. Polaroid's response to the transition from analogue to digital imaging was largely shaped by its managers' cognitive representations of the world. The executive management team at Polaroid was broadly static; it was made up of long-term Polaroid colleagues, who were in favour of applying the business models used for instant photography to the case of digital imaging. One problem involved the highly technological and research-oriented mindset of the top management team. Their cognitive models of the outside world did not permit a successful adaptation to the new technological paradigm in imaging technologies. Eventually, an external CEO took over, shifting existing cognitive frames from a technology-driven to a market-driven strategy. As the authors state, 'search processes in a new learning environment are deeply interconnected to the way managers model the new problem space and develop strategic prescriptions premised on this view of the world' (p. 1158).

9.2 Noticing Information and Making Sense of It

Social networks play an important role in how managers form opinions and mental models of their environment.[3] These mental models help frame problems and search for solutions (Tripsas and Gavetti, 2000). Individual decisions depend largely on the information available, which is often passed through social networks. This implies that an individual's position in a social network is one of the determinants of what information is accessed at first hand. When there is a lack of readily available information, actors frequently refer to their social networks to collect relevant information from others. In other words, actors (unintentionally or intentionally) search for mechanisms to reduce their bounded rationality and limited understanding of the environment.[4]

---

[3] For a review see Carley and Behrens (1999). Also see Rice and Aydin (1991) for managers' mental models of the environment.

[4] In one of the classic articles on decision-making under uncertainty, Tversky and Kahneman (1974) explain the three heuristics that people often use in decision-making: representativeness, availability of instances and scenarios, and adjusting from an anchor. They find that these heuristics often involve important biases that can be avoided. Also see Levitt and March (1988) for biases in decision-making, as well as Starbuck and Milliken (1988).

One of the challenges that firms face in innovation is related to noticing available information, rejecting what is irrelevant and interpreting usefulness of information (sense-making). This process can help them select between investments in exploration or exploitation (Starbuck and Milliken, 1988). Organisations face many obstacles when trying to balance exploration and exploitation activities.

- **Failure to interpret environmental signals correctly and competency traps:** as firms gain experience in existing routines, the returns on further exploitation increase (path dependence); in other words, positive feedback and the increased efficiency of an existing routine may come at the expense of investment in learning and adapting to superior routines (March, 1991; Levitt and March, 1988).
- **Failure to pick up signals about environmental change:** competitive environments change over time and some periods are marked by breakthrough innovations that tend to destroy or enhance the competences of incumbent firms (Tushman and Anderson, 1986). The way firms deal with these discontinuity challenges will depend on whether they pick up weak signals in the environment at an early stage (Bessant, 2008).
- **Failure to recognise niche market segments:** incumbent firms may fail to recognise opportunities on the fringes of an existing mainstream market. Christensen's (1997) notion of disruptive innovation is not about its radicalness, but rather about the extent to which it addresses the needs of a niche market segment by creating new bundles or business models (Bessant, 2008).
- **Failure to see recombinant opportunities:** radical innovations are often the result of recombining and associating distant elements. Established frames of thought and mental models may prevent organisations recognising the value of recombinations that are highly divergent from existing models.
- **Internal inertia:** failure to interpret environmental signals can also be explained by managers' cognitive frameworks (Tripsas and Gavetti, 2000). Sometimes organisational adaptation can be impeded by inertia in the way managers form mental models of the world (see Box 9.1).
- **Network inertia:** Kim, Oh and Swaminathan (2006: 704) defined network inertia as 'persistent organisational resistance to changing interorganisational network ties or difficulties that an organisation faces when it attempts to dissolve old relationships and form new network ties'. In this case, the flexibility of an organisation to adapt is reduced. Moreover, learning opportunities diminish, as the knowledge bases of organisations grow increasingly similar.

In tackling these problems, it is helpful to distinguish between the role of networks as a possible source of these problems on the one hand and as a route to valuable information and resources on the other. Depending on their nature, social networks can worsen some problems by filtering out useful information and/or shaping the lenses that individuals use to interpret information. Here the main concern is not receiving objective information but receiving relevant information. As Starbuck and Milliken (1988) state, '[o]ne thing that an intelligent executive does not need is totally accurate perception'. In other words, filtering is necessary and increases efficient decision-making by eliminating noise. Accuracy of information is hardly possible; and even if it were, it could result in inefficiencies because of information overload (Feldman and March, 1981). Given all this, how can social networks be used to reveal relevant information and disregard irrelevant information?

9.3 Networks and Cognitive Biases

Networks can be a source of cognitive biases in decision-making, inhibiting the objective evaluation and processing of externally received information (Cross, Thomas and Light, 2009). Awareness of this network bias can help managers improve decision-making processes.

Underlying the idea that a network is a source of cognitive bias is the premise that markets are essentially social structures (rather than purely economic or anonymous). While relevant and valuable information is often received through social networks, they can also be a source of cognitive bias in decision-making, by filtering out vital information. To avoid this it is necessary to have a good understanding of common biases in social networks (see Table 9.1). In addition, social networks reveal signals about the quality of other firms. In decisions about alliances, mergers and acquisitions, adverse selection problems can arise as a result of information asymmetry between organisations, and various network strategies can be helpful in overcoming them.

9.3.1 False Consensus Effect

While it is often the case that people in local social networks tend to share similar opinions and beliefs, individuals may not be aware of the extent of diversity in their network. One of the cognitive biases related to networks is the false consensus effect, when individuals mistakenly overestimate the extent of consensus with others in their environment (Ross, Greene and House, 1977).

Table 9.1 Decision-making under Uncertainty: Cognitive Biases and Information Asymmetries

Possible biases caused by networks in decision-making	False consensus	Overestimating the extent to which the rest of the people in one's social network are of the same opinion as oneself.
	Bounded awareness	Tendency not to search for, use and share relevant information with others.
	Groupthink	Tendency to develop negative stereotypes towards people outside the group. Tendency to conform to the behaviours of others in a cohesive group.
	Group polarisation	Tendency to take extreme decisions when participating in a group, compared to the case when one is alone.
Inaccuracies in information inputs in decision-making	Signalling social status	Network positions yield information about the social status of actors. Matthew effect and impression management can lead to inaccuracy in evaluating actual resources.
	Inaccurate perception of social networks	Tendency to perceive the network, or one's position in it, differently than in actuality.

Research shows that there is a relation between network characteristics and the intensity of false consensus bias. Goel, Mason and Watts (2010) researched individuals' political opinions on Facebook. In their experiment they found that friends tend to disagree more than they think they do, and the intensity of this bias is nearly twice as high when ties are weak. In another experiment, Flynn and Wiltermuth (2010) showed that on ethical issues, individuals who have high betweenness centrality in advice networks tend to overestimate the extent to which their colleagues share their judgements.

9.3.2 Bounded Awareness

Another bias arises when decision-makers' cognitive frames prevent the perception and processing of information that can have vital consequences.[5]

---

[5] See also Levitt and March (1988) who define scarcity of evidence, blindness to evidence and uncertainty in assessing the relevance of evidence as decision biases.

Bazerman and Chugh (2006) term this *bounded awareness*. Three main factors contribute to bounded awareness: (1) failure to see and *search* for information at first hand; (2) failure to *use* the information because its relevance is not recognised; and (3) failure to *share* the information with others, as a result of which bounded awareness becomes an organisation-wide problem (see Box 9.2). Bazerman and Chugh (2006) discuss the 1986 Challenger space shuttle disaster. Interpreting the shuttle explosion using a bounded awareness lens, they explain how the disaster could have been avoided, had NASA's executives sought further data on the relation between low temperature and the failure of the O-rings in the shuttle's solid rocket boosters. Although this issue had been discussed during a meeting the day before the accident, executives' cognitive perceptions were largely framed by the data at hand. The decision-makers took into account the seven prior launches in which O-ring failure occurred, and in which low temperature was not an issue. Unfortunately, they did not seek for the temperature data in

---

Box 9.2 Trial by Fire

This example describes how two large mobile phone companies, Nokia and Ericsson, were influenced very differently by a fire that took place in a supplier plant in New Mexico on 17 March 2000 (Latour, 2001). During this period, the market for mobile phones was growing very fast; a disruption in supplies could have serious consequences in terms of sales. In the Nokia plant, a rapid diffusion of information about the fire was started by a production planner in the Nokia plant in Finland, who was responsible for overseeing the flow of chips from the Philips plant in New Mexico. In Nokia, the news quickly moved up the hierarchy. Soon, a thirty-person crisis team of chip designers, engineers and top management were working together to devise a solution to the problem. The team took some key actions: they mobilised other suppliers to supply the needed parts, worked with Philips engineers and top management and urged them to devise a solution that mobilised other Philips production plants in the Netherlands. The success of the crisis team was remarkable and the fire remained a trivial event not even mentioned in the Annual Report. However, the case was very different at Ericsson. Inside the company, news about the fire did not travel quickly. When it finally reached the management, it was not taken very seriously. Ericsson did not mobilise other suppliers, nor did it have an intensive knowledge exchange with Philips to find a solution to the disruption in supplies. The result was remarkable: according to Ericsson officials $400 million in potential revenue was lost. Interpreting the events from a network perspective, the case reveals the importance of rapid response to external shocks by leveraging and forming networks, both at the intra-firm and supply chain level. It also reveals how internal information diffusion can influence management decision-making. In addition, it shows how the interpretation of events by two management teams in same-sector firms can be strikingly different.

the seventeen other launches in which no O-ring failure had occurred. Had they considered the data from all the twenty-four launches, they would have realised that the likelihood of successful launches in very cold conditions was very low.[6]

9.3.3   Groupthink

Groupthink is another common source of bias (Whyte, 1952; Janis, 1972).[7] Groupthink occurs when individuals in a cohesive subgroup, who share common opinions and beliefs, develop negative stereotypes towards others outside the group. Groupthink can be a barrier to innovation as it can inhibit the cross-fertilisation of diverse perspectives. For example, groupthink can trigger the development of departmental silos, reduce the effectiveness of managerial decision-making by preventing the incorporation of diverse opinions and give rise to inter-group conflicts (Nelson, 1989). Communication across departmental silos is arduous, increasing the difficulty of solving conflicts. Dougherty (1992) states that to overcome such interpretive barriers, it is essential to develop an organisational context that enables innovators to build on the unique insights of different thought worlds.

9.3.4   Group Polarisation

Group polarisation is another cognitive bias that can be augmented by the social networks of decision-makers (Friedkin, 1999). It arises when the joint decision of a group of people is more extreme than the average tendency of the group before a decision is taken. Decisions taken at executive level in an organisation are often influenced by the feedback received from the board of directors. In turn, the structure of board interlock networks can reveal patterns of decision-making at corporate level and possible biases are likely to emerge.[8] For example, Zhu (2013) showed that board decisions on acquisition premiums exhibit evidence of group polarisation. An acquisition

---

[6] Also see Starbuck and Milliken (1988) for Challenger-type decision-making biases.

[7] A review of Groupthink and other biases related to decision-making in groups can be found in Baron and Kerr (2003).

[8] Board interlocks are important in strategic decision-making processes at corporate level. On networks see Davis (1991) and Mizruchi (1996). Carpenter and Westphal (2001) showed that the involvement of board members in the firms' decision-making processes was shaped by the strategic dimension of their involvement in other boards. For firms operating in unstable environments, membership of other heterogeneous boards predicted the extent to which board members monitored and advised on strategic decisions. Also see Gulati and Westphal (1999) on the formation of strategic alliances. Shipilov, Greve

premium is the percentage difference between the final per-share price paid for a target firm and its initial per-share price. Earlier research showed that cognitive biases in decision-making processes can contribute to high acquisition premiums being set, which has an adverse effect on company performance. According to Zhu's (2013) results, when the average premium experienced by directors is relatively high (low) in the beginning, the final decided premium is even higher (lower).

9.3.5   Dealing with Biases by Managing Networks

Adaptation is a process in which actors adjust their knowledge according to the feedback they receive through networks. The paradox in this process is that we have a tendency to get advice and information from people we trust, to whom we are connected with strong ties.[9] This can cause cognitive biases in receiving and processing information, resulting in deviations from the optimal. For example, in their study of an investment credit bank in the US, Mizruchi and Stearns (2001) found that a cohesive and dense information network of bank employees does not successfully predict the closing of a deal.

Research consistently shows that better decisions are taken and biases are reduced when there is diversity in advice networks, and when they are sparse. Diversity is important because it increases the likelihood of exposure to possibly conflicting views and can validate views obtained from different sources. But there is a trade-off; when resources are limited, increased diversity can be better maintained through several weak links than through a limited number of strong links, as maintaining strong links requires more resources. On the other hand, individuals access more fine-tuned and higher-quality information through strong ties with trusted sources. Cross, Thomas and Light (2009) found that when too many people are involved in decision-making, there is over-communication among employees, too much attention from senior management, too many revisions and inefficient decision-making processes. In the company they studied, Cross, Thomas and Light (2009) found that nearly 60 per cent of people's time was spent on getting advice and opinions from people not actually involved in decision-making.

and Rowley (2010) find that board network interlocks predict the initial adoption of governance practices related to board reform in Canada.

[9] It is difficult to generalise this tendency, however. For example, Flynn, Reagans and Guillory (2010) distinguish between people who prefer high closure and people who do not need it. They find that there are differences between the way these two groups perceive their networks.

They concluded that smaller and dedicated decision-making teams, with a mix of strong and weak ties between them, can help deal with the problems related to networks and poor-quality decisions.

9.4   Networks as Signals

In the economy, information and knowledge diffuse unevenly between actors through networks.[10] Actors often rely on their personal networks, which act as the 'pipes and conduits' of information that reflects members' status (Podolny, 2005). Networks are therefore signalling mechanisms that provide information about the inherent qualities of actors when such information is not readily available, especially in the face of uncertainty. Given that people can use a variety of tactics to leverage social networks to gain legitimacy (Cialdini, 1989; Zott and Huy, 2007), when strategic decisions are based on network signals, they can detract from those that are a better fit with the needs of an organisation.

Recognising networks as signals is relevant in decisions that require information about the inherent quality of a target actor, especially when the decision-maker cannot otherwise access this information. When this happens, there is a risk of information asymmetry between the target and the decision-maker, which may result in adverse selection issues. An example is job markets, where candidates give signals to recruiters that reveal their qualities (Spence, 1973). Other decisions of the same kind include selecting strategic alliance partners, acquisition decisions, venture investments and providing resources for entrepreneurial initiatives. Taking the case of biotechnology between 1988 and 1999, Luo, Koput and Powell (2009) found that hiring scientists was a signal of the quality of firms located in less advantageous positions in networks and helped attract R&D partners as well as financial resources.

By observing networks, actors form opinions and perceptions about the social status of others (Podolny, 1993; 1994). The position of actors in a network gives clues about their qualitative attributes on a range of issues. For example, Podolny (1993) found that banks with higher status could borrow at lower cost. Baum and Oliver (1992) found that the legitimacy of day-care centres in Toronto was largely influenced by the centres' links with institutions

---

[10] See White (1981) for the sociological approach to markets. The earliest treatment of the uneven distribution of information in markets is to be found in Akerlof's (1970) conceptualisation of asymmetric information in his article on the market for lemons.

like churches. Social status is related to the trustworthiness or quality of an actor. For example, firms that have held prominent positions in earlier alliance networks are more likely to attract new partners and their network positions affect the extent to which they can enter foreign markets successfully.

Given that actors can form opinions about others through networks, the way networks are perceived becomes a key issue. To what extent do actors perceive networks accurately? At the same time, how do individuals use networks strategically to increase their legitimacy and achieve success?

9.4.1 Network Perception

When information relevant to a decision is based on network signals, biases in network perception can reduce the quality of the decision. Research reveals that the mental models people use to map the structure of the social networks in which they participate are seldom accurate.[11] For example, Kilduff et al. (2008) found that people are inclined to perceive their friends as far more closely connected than they are in reality, attributing inaccurate small-world properties to their network.[12] Moreover, people who have more accurate perceptions of their networks are found to be more powerful in organisations (Krackhardt, 1990), while the performance of people perceived as central in a network is higher than that of those who are actually central (Kilduff and Krackhardt, 1994). These differences in perception may depend on personality, position and the networks considered. For example, Casciaro (1998) found that the perceptions of people at higher hierarchical levels in both advice networks and friendship networks are less accurate.

It is important to be aware of these biases, because the social status of individuals may not reflect their actual performance. (This differentiates perception from reputation, which is based on actual accomplishments.) When there is no information about the actual quality of an actor, the way the actor is *perceived* in the social structure is more significant in terms of prominence and future performance than the actor's real qualifications.[13] Cialdini (1989: 45) cites a well-known anecdote to support this:

---

[11] See Krackhardt (1987) for cognitive social structures, in which the adjacency matrix has three dimensions: sender, receiver and perceiver. More precisely, $a_{ijk} = 1$ means that k thinks that i sends a link to j. For a review of this stream of research see Brands (2013).

[12] For a synthesis on social networks and perceptions see Ibarra, Kilduff and Tsai (2005).

[13] Spence (1973) used the notion of signals in economic analysis for the first time in his research on the job market. See also Perrow (1961) for prestige of organisations.

At the height of his wealth and success, the financier Baron de Rothschild was petitioned for a loan by an acquaintance. Reputedly, the great man replied, '*I won't give you a loan myself; but I will walk arm-in-arm with you across the floor of the Stock Exchange, and you soon shall have willing lenders to spare.*' Apparently, the Baron was wise in more than matters of finance. He understood an intriguing fact within the psychology of impression management: it is possible to influence how we are viewed by managing information about the people and things to which we are merely connected.[14]

9.4.2   Networks as a Source of Legitimacy for Entrepreneurs

The information asymmetry between decision-maker and target can be exacerbated, given that networks are a means to build legitimacy for entrepreneurial firms.[15] Because entrepreneurs or small business owners want to induce positive reactions in potential investors, their connections with prominent actors in the industry is a way to attract resources as such connections help gain visibility and reputation.

When there is information asymmetry between an investor and an entrepreneur, reputation is an economic asset that yields important advantages (Shapiro, 1983). Underlying this is the belief that prominent firms only engage with high-quality entrepreneurs, so ties with such firms will be a signal of the entrepreneurs' quality to others. If entrepreneurs believe that having access to certain network positions will increase the odds of success, they can work their way towards gaining these network positions. Zott and Huy (2007) found that entrepreneurs use a range of tactics to publicise their network connections and that those who practise this symbolic management frequently obtain more resources than those who do not.

9.5   Entrepreneurship and Networks

Entrepreneurship is embedded in complex social networks that give access to opportunities, support and resources (Aldrich and Zimmer, 1986; Stuart and Sorenson, 2005). Opportunity recognition is especially important in the pre-start-up phase, when identifying market needs and gathering information

---

[14] The classic experiment by Cialdini et al. (1976) revealed that college students tend to associate themselves with successful football teams.
[15] On legitimacy and entrepreneurship see Aldrich and Fiol (1994).

about laws and regulations that might open up possibilities for new ventures. Resource mobilisation is critical during the initial phases of starting up a business, as this is the period when entrepreneurs need money, access to skilled labour and tacit knowledge, especially in high-tech start-ups (Stuart and Sorenson, 2005). In different phases of entrepreneurship, understanding the type of network conducive to success is important, and leveraging networks can significantly increase the odds of success.

9.5.1 Cohesive Networks

Different stages in the entrepreneurial process require different resources, which can be accessed from different types of network (Hite and Hesterly, 2001). At the beginning of the entrepreneurial process (nascent and start-up phases) strong ties with other actors in the industry are likely to provide benefits like emotional support, access to experience and technical expertise. Later on, in the early growth stage of a venture, sparse networks can be more beneficial to sustain businesses (Hite and Hesterly, 2001) and reduce dependence on a few firms.

Earlier links between venture capital firms and entrepreneurs increase the odds of success in new ventures (Shane and Stuart, 2002). Entrepreneurship is a highly uncertain process and when information about a new venture is not available, earlier or existing links between entrepreneurs and venture capital firms reduce the transaction costs that might arise from failure to predict the potential market value of an investment decision. Earlier ties between a venture capital and an entrepreneur reduce perceived uncertainties and can be a signal of trust, breeding further ties in the future. In other words previously successful interactions breed further connections between the same actors, independently of the entrepreneur's intrinsic qualities. For example, Sorenson and Waguespack (2006) demonstrated the existence of this kind of self-reinforcing mechanism in the Hollywood film industry, examining the effects of prior relationships between distributors and producers on the box office performance of films. They showed that distributors tend to favour films produced by previous exchange partners and allocate more resources to them, a factor that should increase the odds of a film's success. However, controlling for this effect, the authors found that such over-sponsored films in fact perform worse than others at the box office.

The impact of tie strength on entrepreneurial success depends on the type of innovation. For example, for radical innovations pursued by industry insiders, strong ties with prominent actors are especially important in building legitimacy. These connections also provide access to other actors later on, in the early growth phases of a venture (Elfring and Hulsink, 2007).

9.5.2   Brokerage

Brokerage positions can help entrepreneurs access a wide range of resources in the network. The extent to which entrepreneurial teams fill structural holes in an external advice network has a positive effect on their performance (Vissa and Chacar, 2009). Centrality in an alliance network often reveals actors' social status and prominence in the network. While the effect of centrality often extends beyond the immediate neighbourhood of an actor, the effect of brokerage is confined to the local context, as its benefits are dependent on many context-specific factors. Guler and Guillen (2010) found that the advantages of brokerage positions in the home country are not transferable to a foreign market, while centrality in the home country has a positive influence on the success of entry to foreign markets. One implication of centrality is that recognition within the network has only a marginal positive effect for central actors, who are already well known. On the other hand, the impact of recognition for a peripheral actor in the network is far more pronounced (Soh, Mahmood and Mitchell, 2004).

9.5.3   Venture Capital Networks

Often a venture is supported by multiple VC firms who complement one another's resources by forming a network (sometimes called a VC syndicate network). In this process, VC firms combine their capabilities and provide joint support for different aspects of a venture by sharing financial risks, market-specific knowledge and technical experience. Reputation and trust are essential factors in holding VC networks together. Firms' network positions signal their prominence and attract new ventures: while VC firms select ventures to invest in, innovative entrepreneurs also use these networks to decide whom to ask for support. Association with a reputable VC firm increases the chances of entrepreneurial success, so highly reputable VC firms receive more demands from entrepreneurs. This enhances VC firms' choice among promising ventures, increasing their odds of success and their reputation in the industry.

Hochberg, Ljungqvist and Lu (2007) identify three reasons why the success of an investment deal is related to VC networks. First, in the context of extreme uncertainty surrounding promising deals, VC firms can share knowledge and expectations in their networks, a factor that raises a venture's odds of success. Second, VC firms tend to invite other VC firms to join promising deals, in the expectation of future reciprocity. Third, as most VC firms' knowledge is specific to a certain sector or location, they can combine their expertise to expand the range of deals they support. At the same time, when the networks of incumbent VC firms are dense and close-knit they can restrict entry by other VC firms and as a result benefit by reducing the prices of deals (Hochberg, Ljungqvist and Lu, 2010).

9.6   Buy-in Ties and Intrapreneurs

Innovation is a socio-political process, strongly linked to access to prominent actors whose support can increase the odds of implementation (Kanter, 1983; Frost and Egri, 1991). Podolny and Baron (1997) defined buy-in ties as those that allow the successful pursuit of initiatives in an organisation. A range of personal traits and social network characteristics are critical to access relevant resources in implementing innovation.

9.6.1   The Role of Networks in Attracting Support

In Chapter 7 we looked at the role networks play in creativity. Networks are also important for the validation of creative projects, advocacy, sponsorship and attracting resources for implementation. If one aspect of the creative process is related to the organisational, institutional and cultural context that supports, nurtures and rewards the production of creative ideas, another aspect is related to the validation of these ideas, that is, evaluating and filtering ideas for implementation. There is a fundamental difference between these two aspects: the former is an act of thinking, of devising alternative ways to approach problems as well as coming up with novel ideas; the latter is about promotion, sponsoring ideas so that they are selected for implementation. In the validation phase the creative idea is no longer a concept: it diffuses, is supported and is implemented (or not). Distinguishing between these two aspects of creativity is important for *measuring* creativity. People in an organisation may have great creative potential but unless their potential finds an environment in which it can function, creative ideas will stay in their minds. Therefore, when measuring creativity the potential for implementation should be taken into account (Csikszentmihályi, 1996). Indeed, Axtell et al. (2000) found that, while the generation of ideas is related to individual and job-specific factors, the implementation of ideas is related to the environment at the group or organisation level.

Networks play an important role in idea generation and implementation, albeit in different ways.[16] The resources and competences relevant to idea generation often differ from those that help put ideas into practice. Unsurprisingly, the kinds of network that help to generate new ideas often do not coincide with networks giving access to advocacy, sponsorship or support for implementation. Networks are also important in promoting, communicating and spreading ideas, and in convincing others about implementation.[17]

Creativity implies novelty, which means that it can often challenge an organisation's core activities and dominant routines. Divergent perspectives always risk far more opposition than those that build on existing norms and routines. Novel ideas bring uncertainty, which can generate scepticism and hesitation, especially among those who want to preserve the status quo.[18] There is some evidence that there is even a negative correlation between creativity and implementation. For example, Baer (2012) found that, as the novelty of a creative idea increases, the person who develops it is less likely to be influential in its diffusion.

9.6.2   Network Positions for Validation

Certain network positions offer privileges in terms of validating and implementing innovations. One of these is brokerage. Earlier, in Chapter 7, we examined the liaison role of brokerage. A liaison broker does not belong to a cohesive group but is not an outsider, either. A liaison has connections with different groups, without belonging to any of them, and has certain benefits for validation. A liaison can cross-check and reaffirm the viability of a venture with diverse contacts in different groups, reducing the likelihood of future conflicts that might inhibit implementation. A liaison broker can also play connections off against each other and enhance career mobility. Burt (1992) highlights the positive relation between career advancement and people who fill structural holes in an organisation.

---

[16] See, for example, research by Ohly, Kase and Skerlavaj, (2010); Baer (2012); Fleming, Mingo and Chen (2007).

[17] See Chapter 11 for networks and diffusion. Networks can be important for social support and centrality in friendship networks is considered an indicator of potential influence (Krackhardt, 1992).

[18] On the relation between the radicalness of an innovation and the likelihood of its adoption see Damanpour (1988).

But taking a liaison position, or having a place in a sparse network, does not necessarily mean that a venture will attract funds or that promotion will follow. Podolny and Baron (1997) draw attention to tie *content*. Buy-in ties are important because they reveal normative information to intrapreneurs about what is likely to be acceptable and what not. Trust-based relations and support from others are necessary to build coalition and access to sensitive information. Therefore it is not only a broker's structural position but also the broker's strong ties with prominent others and closed networks that are important in pursuing initiatives. Baer (2012) showed that the relation between novelty and implementation is rather 'loose', because novelty is likely to provoke opposition, to the extent that it challenges existing norms and activities. In a case study conducted in a large agricultural processing firm, he found that the number of strong ties a person holds, and the motivation to implement, counteract the loose relation between creativity and implementation and significantly increase the likelihood that a creative project will get off the ground.

Discussion Questions

1. What are cognitive biases that networks can exacerbate, and what can be done to overcome them?

2. What are VC syndicate networks, and in what ways do they benefit VC firms?

3. In your organisation (or department) think of who is friends with whom, and sketch the networks as you perceive them. Then carry out a network study to map the real networks (see example questions in Appendix). Are there differences in your perception of networks, and reality? If there are, why do you think they arise?

10 Networks and Organisational Change

It must be remembered that there is nothing more difficult to plan, more doubtful of success, nor more dangerous to manage than a new system. For the initiator has the enmity of all who would profit by the preservation of the old institution and merely lukewarm defenders in those who gain by the new ones.

Niccolò Machiavelli

In this chapter, we focus on how a social network approach can be beneficial in a change management scenario. We learn why it is important to analyse pre-change networks in an organisation, and also how formal and informal networks will adjust following the change programme. We see how pre-change network analysis helps to identify people who can be influential in building coalitions, as well as cohesive subgroups within which people are likely to adopt similar attitudes towards change. Post-change networks are discussed as a means of spotting possible sources of resistance to change, and as providing some insights about the fit between formal and informal networks, where this fit may have implications for performance later on.

One of the uses of the network perspective is managing organisational change, where success usually rests on the participation and commitment of people in the organisation. A change project is usually initiated at the management level but people's opinions, beliefs and attitudes about the change largely form and mature through informal networks. Some people in these informal networks are better positioned to diffuse information, bridge management and employees or persuade others in favour of change. Network analysis also reveals cohesive subgroups, in which people tend to share common attitudes. After a reorganisation, the change in formal networks is often rapid but the change in informal networks can be slow to adjust. This is important in two ways. First, by understanding how change will alter resource distribution, possible sources of resistance in the organisation can be spotted and are most likely to come from those who will lose status or privileged network positions. Second, it is important to understand how organisational networks will change after the event because formal and informal networks are complementary in the accomplishment of tasks and organisation-level goals (Gulati and Puranam, 2009).

In this chapter we begin by exploring some antecedents of organisational change and the role of networks. Next, we will examine why it is important to anticipate how networks will adjust following change. Finally, we will look at the role social influence plays in developing common attitudes towards change. In network terms, influence can be explained by cohesion, structural equivalence or the centrality of actors.

10.1 Why Change?

Organisational change is by gradual or intermittent change in organisational routines. It is related to the way an organisation responds to feedback signals from the environment about its performance and the processes of adapting its routines accordingly. As we saw in Chapter 9, routines economise on cognitive effort and increase efficiency because they govern search activities and reduce the options available to managers. At the same time they can also result in inertia or competence traps, as they often favour the local and familiar rather than discovering and experimenting with novelties. From this perspective, organisational routines seem to favour stability and the status quo. However, many studies show that the inherent nature of routines fosters change. Feldman (2000) observed routines as sources of change, as they cannot be separated from the people who continuously observe outcomes, think and create better ways for routines to be reoriented.[1]

Organisational change refers to 'an empirical of difference, in form, quality or state over time in an organisational entity' (Van De Ven and Poole, 1995). In this chapter our focus is on planned change, or change that is initiated by management executives.[2] There are various examples of this kind of episodic

---

[1] On routines and change, also see Feldman and Pentland (2003). Pentland et al. (2012) draw attention to the point that the notion of action provides another and more useful insight about routines. While the emphasis is usually on human agency, and the role cognitive or behavioural attributes play in changes in routines, they also take into account interactions between humans and artefacts (ICT, information systems, machines, etc.) and maintain that these interactions can be a better starting point to analyse how routines are sources of change, and how they change themselves.

[2] See Lippitt (1958) on planned change. Weick and Quinn (1999) identify episodic changes as intermittent, divergent and transformative change, as compared to incremental or continuous change. For a theoretical discussion of organisational change from the perspective of various schools of thought, see Greenwood and Hinnings (2006), and for a discussion see Seo, Putnam and Bartunek (2004).

change: the introduction of a new technology or management system; changes of key personnel; reengineering projects; major restructuring; introduction of a new business unit. Many organisations have been through important changes during the last thirty years. During the 1980s, a major change initiative was the adoption of ICT; more recently it is digitalisation. During the last decade, organisations have faced important challenges in dealing with the vast flow of data in and around them, incorporating social media into their activities, and restructuring the way they interact with external stakeholders like communities, users, customers and suppliers. Box 10.1 gives an example of how firms can overcome challenges and jumpstart the use of social technologies, based on the research by Guinan, Parise and Rollag (2014).

Change can be driven by a variety of factors that can be both internal or triggered by external developments. For example, change can be driven by the changing basis of competition in an industry, major events or technological developments. Entry into new markets, necessitating the internal reorganisation of logistics, can be prompted by events that increase the attractiveness of certain markets over others. Taking the case of Cisco's reorganisation from a customer-oriented to a technology-oriented structure in 2001, Gulati and Puranam (2009) reported that the main trigger for the IT giant's change was the need to gain cost advantages in a market that had become increasingly competitive following Huawei's entrance, as well as declining demand for their products during the 2000s. Whatever the source of change, networks in and around an organisation play varying roles in recognising the need for change, facilitating or inhibiting it, and determining the final outcome.

Box 10.1 Bringing Social Technologies into Work

Guinan, Parise and Rollag (2014) interviewed over seventy managers in thirty companies to find out how social technologies were introduced in companies. Social technologies refer to a broad range of online means to incentivise exchanges between employees, including blogging, Facebook, Twitter and wikis. The authors report that while 87 per cent of Fortune 100 companies use at least one social media platform when communicating with stakeholders, many enterprises find it difficult to motivate employees to accept and use these technologies to share knowledge and opinions. Most companies face resistance to the active employment of social media at work, although these technologies can be useful for innovation. Their interviews revealed that social technologies are successfully adopted when they are introduced in one of the following ways:

- **Young experimenters:** one of the advantages of starting with young experimenters, who have one to seven years of job experience, is that they are often familiar with social technologies in their personal lives, making it easier to adopt them at work. They are

Box 10.1 (cont.)

more likely to be technically experienced and open-minded, as well as less sceptical about social technologies. One of the disadvantages of employing them as change agents is they are often positioned at the periphery of intra-organisational networks due to their tenure, a factor that reduces their influence and access to the core resources needed to implement new projects related to social technologies. This type of strategy works well in young start-ups and decentralised networks (see Figure 7.6).

- **Middle managers:** the authors find that middle managers have a critical role as change agents, as they are both experienced due to their tenure and likely to be endowed with the skills to master new software tools and interfaces. Their expertise, connections and credibility, therefore, are higher than those of the young experimenters, which makes them suitable for initiating social technologies. This strategy works better for dispersed companies with an increased need to link different functions and divisions, where middle managers can act as bridges in diffusing new tools of communication.
- **Enlightened executives:** the authors found that initiating change through senior managers able to see the potential of new technologies was an effective strategy. The advantage of senior executives is that they have the power to provide resources and training to jumpstart the use of new technologies. One of the challenges is that senior managers may be technology averse, or sceptical of new technologies, which can inhibit their own active use. This strategy works well in aiding the rapid adoption of social technologies.

10.2   Change Management and Networks

In some ways, adopting a novelty in an organisation resembles the diffusion of a novelty among a population of users. One of the common aspects is the role of community influence. An important difference, however, is that while diffusion in a market is bottom-up, diffusion in an organisation is often top-down and as a result a typical reaction is resistance to change. The root cause of this resistance is almost always justified, an issue that it is important to address.

The rate of failure in organisational change is high: only around 30 per cent of change projects are considered successful.[3] Moreover, most failures happen in the implementation phase rather than the initial planning.

---

[3] See Kotter (2007) and Duan, Sheeran anad Weiss (2014).

Executives or managers who initiate change are usually so consumed with the design and technical details of change projects (the relation between the desired state and how to get there) that they tend to underestimate the managerial issues of transition, which are critical in the implementation of a change project (Nadler and Tushman, 1997). Also, while information about why change is needed and what it will look like diffuses through formal networks, it is informal networks that generally shape people's opinions and attitudes towards the change.

The ways network analysis can be used to facilitate change management are summarised in Tables 10.1 and 10.2.

10.2.1   Reallocation of Resources Following the Change

A change project often entails changes in both formal and informal networks. Because most projects entail the reallocation of resources, some people are likely to lose their privileged network positions or access to resources after the change. This increases the likelihood of their initial resistance. According to Kotter and Schlesinger (1979) one of the sources of resistance is losing something of value (for example, power) as a result of change. Resistance can also be rooted in people's fear that their informal networks will change (Lawrence, 1969). To the extent that change entails a reorganisation of tasks and communication flows between people, informal networks are likely to adjust to the new formal organisation over time. The responsiveness of informal networks can have implications for different dimensions of performance (Gulati and Puranam, 2009; Kleinbaum and Stuart, 2014). In addition, depending on the nature of change, certain skills can become more valued in the organisation, as a result of which people

Table 10.1 Questions on Change and Networks

Understanding post-change networks
- How will the fit between formal networks and informal networks change?
- Who is likely to resist? Who will lose power and status in the new organisation?

Understanding pre-change networks
- Who are influential in shaping attitudes of others?
- Are there cohesive subgroups within which people are likely to adopt similar attitudes?
- Who can reach more people to diffuse information and overcome uncertainties?

Table 10.2 The Uses of the Network Perspective in Managing Change

Anticipating post-change networks to detect possible sources of resistance and to evaluate post-change resource allocations	Change benefits people with specific skills and capabilities	
	Change benefits people with specific networking behaviour or network position	
	Change of co-working patterns induces change in informal networks	
Understanding pre-change networks for successful implementation of the change project	Centrality	• Detecting people who can reduce uncertainty, diffuse knowledge about change and help in effective coalition-building
	Cohesion	• Understanding the sources of shared attitudes towards change
		• Detecting cohesive subgroups for information diffusion about the change, as information diffuses faster within groups than between them
	Structural equivalence	• Structural equivalence in inter-organisational networks may explain external sources of change
		• Structural or role-based equivalence between people in an organisation can trigger similar attitudes to change

endowed with these skills will assume more prominent positions in formal and/or informal networks.

Resistance to change is not always intentional and explicit; it can be caused by internal inertia,[4] due to habitual thinking in line with an existing system. Tushman and Anderson (1986), explaining competence-enhancing and competence-destroying technological change, state that one barrier to innovation in established firms is the difficulty in changing existing innovation systems as a result of rigidities in internal communication flows. Organisational routines can be a major barrier to architectural innovations (Henderson and Clark, 1990). Many cases show the difficulties firms face in adapting their workflow to the requirements of an architectural innovation that modifies how components come together. Henderson and Clark (1990) took the example of Kasper Instruments, where the mindsets of photolithography engineers were framed according to existing technology, preventing them from adapting to a new innovation system that was different from their own

[4] Inertia can be caused by many factors; see Weick and Quinn (1999).

but performed better. Taylor and Helfat (2009) underline the importance of organisational ties between and within departments for leveraging complementarities between existing capabilities (exploitation) and the requirements of a new technology (exploration). For example, in IBM's transition from electromechanical computing to electronic computing between 1949 and 1965, middle managers assumed an important role in linking various sub-units within the company (Taylor and Helfat, 2009).

10.2.2   Influence and Pre-change Networks

When managing change it is vital to understand the structure of existing informal networks before a change is initiated. Because information and knowledge about a change diffuses through networks, the social structure of an organisation can determine how people will react to change. Social network analysis can identify people who are likely to be influential in shaping others' attitudes towards change. Management can work with these change agents to build coalition throughout the organisation. Social network analysis can also identify cohesive subgroups in which people can develop shared attitudes towards change, based on their shared values, beliefs and strong feelings of identification with the group. Distinguishing between advice and friendship networks is important when analysing informal networks, as we will see later in this chapter.

For both purposes of using a network perspective – anticipating post-change and understanding pre-change networks – uncertainty has to be taken into account. The uncertainty that people feel about change is an essential aspect of change projects and a major source of resistance to change. Uncertainty is often related to doubt about future events or cause-and-effect relationships in the environment (Bordia et al., 2004).[5] At the individual level of analysis, Bordia et al. (2004) distinguish between three often interrelated sources of uncertainty that people face before change: strategic, structural and job-related. Strategic uncertainty is related to doubts about the usefulness or relevance of the change for the organisation. People may doubt its sustainability in the long run or believe that it does not make sense for the organisation. Structural uncertainty centres on doubts about the reorganisation of tasks, team responsibilities and reporting structures that will follow the change. People often feel ambivalent about the allocation of resources and

---

[5] For an exploration of organisational change from the employee perspective, see Oreg, Michel and Todnem (2013).

new job descriptions that will affect their personal status. Finally, job-related uncertainties arise from people's doubts about the future of their position in the organisation and fears about losing their jobs and access to key resources.

10.3   Anticipating Post-change Networks

There are three main reasons why it is useful to understand how networks adjust following change. First, the new change might be biased towards certain capabilities or skills, as a result of which people who have these skills assume more privileged positions following the change. Second, change is sometimes network-biased, favouring those with specific social relationship patterns or network positions. Third, a change in the formal organisation of work usually redefines co-working patterns, as a result of which informal networks are reconfigured.

10.3.1   Capability Bias

Change can be biased towards certain skills and capabilities, increasing the relative importance of those who have them. Some people may become more central in the formal organisational network, if their skills are favoured by the new system. Barley (1986) carried out an initial study on how the introduction of a new technology changes internal networks. He made an ethnographic network study of two US radiology departments to show how the redefinition of roles after the introduction of a technology changed their social networks. In particular, he showed that the distribution of power changed considerably, favouring newly recruited CT specialists, as the new and disruptive CT technology reduced the need for the expertise of tenured radiologists. Another classic example is the Volvo car plant in Gothenburg, where executives decided to use e-mail to speed up internal and external communication in 1985. Although the number of e-mail accounts rose from 18 per cent to 40 per cent, old habits of using internal mail and telephones persisted and there was no increase in actual e-mail use. The efforts of middle managers and the establishment of support centres in each department helped to overcome employees' resistance to the new means of communication. During this process, ICT assistants became more central in Volvo's networks, compared to their peripheral positions before the change, because people began calling them for help (Rogers, 2003). In another example, Burkhardt and Brass (1990) showed that the early adopters of a technology often increase their power within networks as others seek them out for their knowledge about the technology and to resolve uncertainties. A new technology is one of the main sources of uncertainty in an organisation and people reduce their uncertainty by sharing experience and knowledge through social networks.

10.3.2   Network Position Bias

A change project may also be network-biased, favouring people with specific network positions or social relation patterns more than others. For example, Wu (2014) took the case of a large consultancy firm that introduced a social media tool to locate expertise inside the firm. She found that those with a higher network diversity in the pre-adoption phase could make better use of the social media tool, increasing their performance. Paruchuri and Eisenman (2012) gave another example in which they showed how knowledge search networks changed following a merger between two biopharmaceutical companies. In periods of change, when people face stress and uncertainty, they tend to access the most readily available knowledge, which is often found in more central and prominent inventors. In the case of this M&A, knowledge search networks changed so that central inventors became more central, as people accessed their knowledge more frequently rather than accessing the knowledge of peripheral experts. Change can also induce loss of power in vertical networks. In the case of Brand Corporation in the UK, Balogun, Bartunek and Do (2015) explained how the roles of previously privileged senior managers changed and their power lessened when they became middle managers tied to a centralised European division. The authors explained that this loss of power led most senior managers to resist change strongly and to resign after it was implemented.

10.3.3   Fit between Formal and Informal Networks

Organisational change is usually accompanied by the restructuring of work, which redefines both task-induced relations and informal networks (see Box 10.2).[6] As most change projects involve a redefinition of jobs, co-working patterns are also modified. The formal organisation of work

---

[6] Lincoln and Miller (1979) draw attention to the simultaneous existence of two types of networks, composed of instrumental and primary ties in an organisation, and posit that they might have different causes and consequences. In their work, instrumental ties are closely related to the formal organisation. At the same time, the advice networks mentioned here are not necessarily in alignment with the formal organisation; they connote whom to ask for advice on work-related issues.

Box 10.2 Six Myths of Informal Networks

Cross, Nohria and Parker (2002) have drawn attention to six myths about informal networks in organisations:

- **Communicate more:** some managers tend to think that more communication and denser networks are always better for organisational performance. Given the information overload in organisations, more communication does not necessarily mean more effectiveness. The authors highlight the need to focus on 'who knows what'.
- **Everyone should be connected to everyone else:** network building is a costly process, in terms of time and effort. The quality rather than the quantity of ties is important; SNA is a useful tool for this purpose.
- **We can't do much to aid informal networks:** a good understanding of the relationship between a formal organisation and informal networks is necessary. The authors mention four key organisational dimensions: formal organisation, work management practices (mainly developed through team building), human resources management (HRM) practices and cultural values.
- **How people fit into networks is a question of personality:** the authors point out that research reveals a weak relationship between personality and social network positions (this is an emerging area of research – see Chapter 12). Behaviours can be taught or encouraged through a better understanding of how networks impede or enable effectiveness.
- **Central people who have become bottlenecks should make themselves more accessible:** central people to whom others often turn for advice can impede the flow of work, largely because they tend to be very busy. Information provision and decision-making can be shifted to other people in the network, instead of putting pressure on central people to make themselves more accessible.
- **I already know what is going on in my network:** research shows people have a limited understanding of their networks. Instead of investing in more sophisticated information management systems, companies can increase the awareness of networks in the organisation (see Chapter 6).

---

involves vertical authority networks and horizontal networks through which task-related knowledge and resources flow among peers. The change in fit between formal and informal networks can have implications for success in the post-change phase. Soda and Zaheer (2012) suggest that consistency between individuals' formal and informal networks positively influences their performance.[7] When change reconfigures task-induced networks, the old patterns of communication dissolve, as people no longer work with their

---

[7] Soda and Zaheer (2012) distinguish between authority networks and workflow networks. Inconsistency of sequential workflow networks (when resources, materials or knowledge flow from one party to

previous co-workers. Kleinbaum and Stuart (2014) suggest that the responsiveness of informal networks to change in formal networks is likely to have implications for dynamic capabilities, because informal networks help with the adaptation and coordination of activities. In general, change in formal networks is often rapid, but informal networks can be slow to respond, as people maintain their relations with previous co-workers. For example, in the reorganisation of Cisco Systems from a customer-centred to a technology-centred organisation, cited earlier in this chapter, informal networks were slow to respond to changes. Relationships defined by the old organisational form persisted after reorganisation. This had some positive if unexpected outcomes, since it helped Cisco maintain customer responsiveness together with the new emphasis on cost-effective technology development, as people kept talking to each other to solve problems even though the new organisational form did not require them to (Gulati and Puranam, 2009). Kleinbaum and Stuart (2014) contrast this with the case of *USA Today*, which switched to digital news distribution. A completely separate unit was founded, autonomous and independent of the newsroom culture of the paper (Tushman, Roberts and Kiron, 2005). Here, the responsiveness of informal networks to the newspaper's transition was quite fast. Although people working in the new unit were veterans of the print version of *USA Today*, neither formal nor informal networks between the two units were sustained.

10.4   Understanding Pre-change Networks

What clues does the structure of a social network yield about influence among actors?[8] Three theoretical approaches help address this question: social comparison theory (Festinger, 1954); social information processing theory (Salancik and Pfeffer, 1978); and social influence theory (Friedkin, 1998).

Festinger's (1954) social comparison theory concerns individuals' need to evaluate themselves. When objective evaluation from non-social means is lacking, people tend to compare themselves with others who have similar opinions and attitudes.

---

another) and informal networks harms performance. At the same time, there are both positive and negative effects of consistency between reciprocal workflow networks and informal networks.

[8] In sociology, influence has been taken in relation to the notion of power (French and Raven, 1959).

The social information processing approach (Salancik and Pfeffer, 1978) maintains that the information available to people through their immediate social environment shapes their attitudes. People's beliefs and perceptions depend on what they perceive from the environment to be socially acceptable, receiving cues from their social relations. For example, in an organisation social networks influence the way people receive and interpret organisational knowledge, task mastery or role clarity (Morrison, 2002). People's perceptions of work-related conditions can depend on their social networks (Ibarra and Andrews, 1993; Morrison, 2004).

Friedkin (1998) identifies three drivers of social influence:

- **Cohesiveness:** being part of a cohesive group enforces the similarity of attitudes and beliefs among members.
- **Social comparison:** influence from others whom individuals perceive as similar to themselves.
- **Centrality:** influence from prominent actors in the network.

10.5   Cohesion and Structural Equivalence

Cohesion refers to the extent to which members are held together in a network (Friedkin, 2004).[9] While cohesion does not imply a network in which all actors are connected to each other, network metrics – like density, connectivity or clustering – indicate network structures that foster social cohesion (Friedkin, 1993). The individual attitudes and behaviours of group members towards each other are reminiscent of cohesion in a group.

10.5.1   Cohesion and Influence

Cohesion is accompanied by uniformity of norms and enforces the emergence of standardised beliefs and opinions, which can happen through influence between members. Cohesive groups are often characterised by trustful relations, emotional intensity and reciprocity among members. People in cohesive groups are likely to share similar attitudes towards change. Cohesion implies the convergence of ideas and beliefs in a social group. A sense of belonging and development of an identity are closely linked with small,

---

[9] Cohesion is widely discussed. Here we focus on the social network perspective and social psychological approaches. For a review, see Friedkin (2004).

cohesive networks (Podolny and Baron, 1997). Cohesion can also measure power in an organisation, to the extent that cohesive groups shape people's attitudes (Friedkin, 1993). Cohesion is a source (and outcome) of uniformity among group members due to positive ties that are maintained through identification with the group, and uniformity of beliefs among members. This uniformity can also bring pressure to conform to others' ideas and opinions, increasing group homogeneity. This, in turn, shapes people's views of change and novel projects, through observing and sharing their thoughts with others in the same group.

10.5.2 Strong Ties and Persuasion

People are also likely to be more open to persuasion from those with whom they have strong ties. For example, Battilana and Casciaro (2013) found that the impact of a change agent in coalition-building can be critically dependent on the strength of ties between the agent and others. A change agent's informal networks play an important part in the final outcome. In the case of the UK's National Health Service (NHS) a significant restructuring of the health system was put in place in 1997 to improve the overall quality of healthcare, by increasing cooperation between different professional groups and extending the role of primary care organisations. Battilana and Casciaro (2013) found that the strength of ties between change agents and influential people was a significant factor in the success of these changes. In particular, they reported that when potentially important actors are receptive to change, their strong ties with a change agent are likely to promote positive attitudes to change. But when potentially influential actors are resistant to change, strong ties with a change agent will depend more on the nature of the change itself. The more divergent a change is relative to the existing system, the more likely it is that a negative attitude will be reinforced and even jeopardise the attitude of the change agent, who can ultimately turn against the change. But if a change project is less divergent, actors resistant to change who have strong ties with a change agent can adopt a positive attitude.

10.5.3 Cohesion and Perceived Reduction of Uncertainty

Cohesion is also important in the diffusion of information about a change, especially when people feel uncertain and anxious about its consequences. Here, the *number* of cohesive subgroups and links between them is important, since speed of diffusion largely depends on the barriers faced when group borders are reached. In other words, information is diffused rapidly within a cohesive group but the existence of many cohesive groups, especially if they are characterised by different attitudes and sub-cultures, can inhibit diffusion between them, because ideas can be blocked as they pass from one cluster to another (Valente, 2005). Therefore, links *between* groups can be just as critical for diffusion of information as cohesion within groups, especially in eliminating confusion about change (Cross, Ernst and Pasmore, 2013).

10.5.4   Measuring Cohesion

There are various network metrics to measure cohesiveness. Nearly all measure the extent to which people in a network are connected to each other, either directly or through intermediaries. In general, cohesiveness increases the more individuals' ties are connected to each other as there are fewer intermediaries between people, and the denser the network. However, as Friedkin (2004) underlines, a network that is not dense can also be cohesive because cohesion depends on the *qualitative* attributes of ties, rather than the mere number of ties. The most commonly used metrics are related to the identification of densely connected groups. A cohesive subgroup is one in which group members are more strongly connected to other members inside the group than they are to people outside it. Table 10.3 shows the various metrics that can be used to detect cohesive subgroups in a network (see also Chapter 4).

10.5.5   Structural Equivalence and Mimetic Isomorphism

Another explanation why people tend to behave in similar ways is equivalence of network positions (Burt, 1987; also see Chapter 11). Structural equivalence emphasises that similar roles (network positions) induce individuals to behave in similar ways. For example, middle managers in an organisation will demonstrate similarities because they occupy equivalent network positions. In the context of organisations, the process of mimetic isomorphism can explain why and how certain practices spread in an industry. In organisation theory, mimetic isomorphism refers to a process whereby organisations tend to observe and behave like others they perceive to be similar to themselves, especially when there is uncertainty and rapid change in the environment (DiMaggio and Powell, 1983).

Table 10.3 Synthesis: SNA and Organisational Change

Source of Influence	Measure	Comments
Cohesion	Clique, n-clique, k-plex, n-clan, k-core	For detecting cohesive subgroups (see Chapter 4 for definitions). The level of desired cohesiveness can be set by the analyst, using k or n parameters
	Modularity	Used to detect communities in large networks
	Density	Indicates the overall intensity of connections but as it is an aggregated measure it does not show cohesive subgroups
	EI index	Compares in-group and out-group ties
Structural equivalence	Similar social network positions	Influence due to similar roles: people who have similar positions may behave in similar ways (e.g. middle managers in an organisation)
Centrality	Degree	Immediate effectiveness in diffusing knowledge to large audience
	Closeness	Speed of knowledge diffusion, reducing uncertainty in a timely manner; independence from control
	Betweenness	Controlling information flows; making sure there are no inaccurate information flows
	Eigenvector	Status-related influence; because high eigenvector centrality implies being connected to central others, eigenvectors can be effective in accessing resources in the implementation of change
	Brokerage	Advantages in bridging different silos, resolving conflict among different groups, and diffusing information to eliminate confusion

10.6   Change Agents and Centrality

Another source of influence during change is prominent people in the network.[10] In intra-organisational networks central people, and people who bridge departments, silos or teams, are important because their opportunities to communicate with diverse sub-cultures give them unique opportunities to diffuse knowledge about change and reduce possible uncertainties felt by employees. They can be effective in building coalition during change, thanks to their network position, which allows them to access, influence and communicate with others in the organisation.

---

[10] Central people in an organisation's network can be more influential and even better paid than people in peripheral positions (Pfeffer, 2010).

Centrality has long been considered an indicator of influence and power in social networks (Brass, 1984). Different centrality metrics can have different implications for influence in a network.[11] During organisational change there are broadly two ways in which central actors can be influential: in controlling the dissemination of information about the change project; and in persuading others and building coalition.

- **Degree centrality:** this is the most widespread measure of centrality and refers to the number of an actor's incoming and/or outgoing ties. Cramer, Parise and Cross (2007) underline that while central people may be 'hidden' in formal organisational charts, their impact can be high because many people turn to them for information. In addition, high degree centrality indicates immediate diffusion of knowledge, as central people have a high number of ties.
- **Closeness centrality:** this is related to the extent to which people get *rapid* access to information and their relative independence from others' control (Freeman, 1979). Actors who are central are on average closer to others, either directly or indirectly through intermediaries. Even an actor who is not central, in terms of the number of incoming and outgoing degrees, can still have high closeness centrality depending on whom the actor is connected to. Actors who have a high closeness centrality can play a part in reducing uncertainty through the efficient diffusion of information about issues that may be creating ambiguity around a change initiative. Because time is an important factor in change projects, the longer people remain uncertain about what will happen in the future, the more they will develop negative feelings towards the initiative.
- **Betweenness centrality:** this can be used as a measure of power (Freeman, 1979) but we should be careful about what type of flow characterises the network (Borgatti, 2006). In particular, actors who have high values of betweenness centrality can appear many times in paths connecting two actors in the network (see Chapter 4). Therefore, they are considered powerful in terms of the *control* of information flows between people in an organisation. In the context of change, people who have high betweenness centrality can be important in avoiding the spread of non-accurate information between people, which can often be the case in periods of flux. In addition, high betweenness centrality indicates bridging positions,

---

[11] Centrality measures can be highly correlated. This can arise from the social dynamics in the organisation or as a mathematical consequence of the way they are calculated. See Valente et al. (2008).

which means that these people can be influential in coalition-building among diverse subgroups.

A person filling a structural hole in the network is likely to communicate with different silos more effectively. For example, Cramer, Parise and Cross (2007) identified the important role cultural brokers play in organisations by bridging different thought worlds. In their example of a large consumer products company, the new product development department and support groups are examples of such thought worlds. In particular, Tom is in a support group, responsible for substantiating the company's advertising claims, working with toxicologists and scientists outside the company. Tom's job is to suggest how to reframe advertisements for new products when necessary and to make sure that advertisements are legitimate. In this case, Tom's experiences with product developers, the marketing department and people outside the organisation enabled him to reduce friction between sub-cultures in the firm.

The impact of central agents also depends on the *nature* of change. For example, Battilana and Casciaro (2012) found that people who fill structural holes in a network are better at diffusing projects that diverge from existing practices, due to their capacity to bridge different sub-cultures. They found that influence through cohesion, on the other hand, is associated with diffusion in less divergent and more incremental change projects, where filling a structural hole can have a negative effect on diffusion.

- **Eigenvalue centrality:** this can be used to measure influence in a social network (Borgatti, 2005). It indicates the extent to which an actor's alters are themselves central. Even an actor who is not central can be influential in the spread of an idea if connected to highly central others, by influencing immediate ties, who in turn influence their own ties. If eigenvector centrality measures indirect influence, degree centrality measures immediate influence in a network.

10.7 Advice Networks and Friendship Networks

One of the critical issues in identifying potentially influential people in an organisation is to distinguish between an advice network and a friendship network, as each indicates a different kind of social influence (see Box 10.3 on advice networks). Previous research suggests that the causes and consequences of these two networks differ in an organisation. In an advice

---

Box 10.3 Intra-organisational Advice Networks

Cross, Borgatti and Parker (2001) have distinguished between the following five types of interactions in an intra-organisational advice network:

- **Solutions:** people exchange knowledge that they will use to find solutions to problems. Distinguishing between declarative knowledge (know-what, or knowledge of facts) and procedural knowledge (know-how), the authors find that it is more common for people to turn to others when searching for the latter.
- **Meta-knowledge** involves getting advice from another about where to find information. In this case, the provider of information fulfils a brokering role, by pointing the information receiver to the necessary sources.
- **Problem-reformulation:** in this type of knowledge exchange, the information receiver is able to see the problem in a new light, either from a broader perspective, or by recognising unforeseen dimensions of the problem.
- **Validation:** in some cases, communicating with others about an issue helps to affirm the legitimacy of the problem, especially when the information receiver is uncertain. At critical junctures in projects, affirmation of the course of action taken or solutions found can increase the confidence of the information seeker.
- **Legitimation:** in some cases, getting advice from a respected source increases the credibility of the solution found, especially under conditions of ambiguity, when the quality of a solution is difficult to assess.

---

network, knowledge flow is predominantly task-oriented or professional. Advice-based ties are usually looking for task-related guidance, information or assistance (Sparrowe et al., 2001). The receptor trusts the knowledge and expertise of the informant in a task-related subject. Centrality in advice networks has therefore been associated with power and influence (Brass, 1992; Ibarra and Andrews, 1993).[12] On the other hand, friendship networks are based on affection, and are characterised by shared understandings built over time, reciprocal trust, altruism and a common language. Friendship networks are important in increasing resource-sharing during crises (Krack-hardt and Stern, 1988), in career-related decision-making (Kilduff, 1992) and in resolving conflict, when they cut across group boundaries in an organisation (Nelson, 1989). In principle, advice and friendship networks

---

[12] See Klein et al. (2004) for the personality-related antedecents of being a central actor in advice and friendship networks in an organisation. Advice networks have been associated with job performance (Sparrowe et al., 2001), self-efficacy and attitudes towards technology (Burkhardt, 1994). For example, Seibert, Kraimer and Liden (2001) find that filling a structural hole in a career advice network has a positive impact on performance. Krackhardt (1990) finds that those who perceive advice networks more accurately are judged by others to have greater power.

may overlap, but in practice they do not always do so. For example Brass (1984) found that there is significant overlap between friendship networks and communication networks (flow of information). Burt (1997) found that there is little overlap in the names cited by people in eight different networks.

Some studies reveal friendship networks actually matter more for influence during change. For example, Gibbons (2004) analyses the effect of advice networks and friendship networks in changing professional values like attitudes to work, perceptions about what is ethical and opinions about new practices. She finds that advice networks are built upon existing professional values and so tend to sustain existing systems rather than promote change. Change is more likely to happen through influence in friendship networks.

An example is found in Krackhardt's (1992) classic study of unionisation in a Silicon Valley firm, where he takes these two networks separately. People who are central in the advice network can be quite peripheral in the friendship network, and vice versa. Chris, who is the most central person in the friendship network, cutting across functional and hierarchical boundaries, turns out to be a peripheral actor in an advice network. In Krackhardt's (1992) case study, unionisation failed because of a mismatch between the roles assigned to people and their positioning in friendship networks. Hal was selected to represent the Union in the firm, but Hal was not central in the organisation's friendship network and his attempts to mobilise people were ultimately ineffective. On the other hand, Chris, who was in the most central position in the friendship network, finally withdrew because of cross pressure from different groups who had opposing ideas about unionisation. In these cases, withdrawal from change projects can occur, in which case people in central positions end up supporting no side (Krackhardt, 1992).

Discussion Questions

1. In change management, why is it important to understand:
   a. Pre-change networks
   b. Post-change networks?

2. By analysing a friendship network in your organisation, how can you spot potential change agents that can be influential in advocating change?

3. Can you sketch your advice network and your friendship network (including you, your alters, and the ties between them)? Do these two networks overlap?

4. Why are cohesive subgroups of interest to management during implementation of a change project?

Networks and Diffusion

We are like chameleons, we take our hue and the colour of our moral character, from those who are around us.

John Locke (1632–1704)

In this chapter, we explore the role of networks in the diffusion of innovations, both online and offline. We consider the self-reinforcement process, which is a mechanism whereby adoption of an innovation by some users in a market triggers further adoption, through influence. We explore the characteristics of 'influentials', which refer to those individuals who are able to influence others' attitudes towards a novelty. We learn how social network analysis is used to detect influentials. Network positions, like centrality, brokerage (and node removal), structural equivalence, and cohesive networks associated with diffusion, are discussed. We consider the advantages and disadvantages of using these metrics to analyse a network of potential adopters in marketing activities. Finally, we explore some factors that shape diffusion, and the role that networks play.

'Why do people put solar on their roofs? Because other people put solar on their roofs', read the title of an article in the *Washington Post* on 25 October 2014. This logic of influence and imitation applies to a diverse range of behaviours, attitudes, beliefs, opinions and strategies – as there are numerous contexts in which actors are influenced by the behaviour of others they admire or perceive to be similar to themselves. The findings about solar panels were based on research confirming this influence, controlling for other factors, in Connecticut and California (Bollinger and Gillingham, 2012; Graziano and Gillingham, 2015).

How can the network perspective help us understand the process of diffusion and learn how to direct it? Valente (2012: 49) defines network interventions as 'purposeful efforts to use social networks or social network data to generate social influence, accelerate behaviour or change, improve performance, and/or achieve desirable outcomes among individuals, communities, organisations, or populations'. The network perspective can help us detect potentially influential actors to promote diffusion, understand barriers to diffusion and discover which networks are better for diffusion in a given context.

11.1   Diffusion Studies: From Past to Present

Diffusion studies have a long history in the social sciences.[1] Three major studies have been influential in the growth of this field of research. The first (Ryan and Gross, 1943) points to the *time lag* in innovation diffusion. The authors investigated the diffusion of hybrid corn in two communities in Iowa, finding that diffusion of the technology happened as farmers first tried the hybrid corn by allocating part of their land to the new seed, and then gradually extending it as they became more experienced.[2] The second study (Coleman, Katz and Menzel, 1966) highlights the role of *social networks* in the diffusion process. The authors worked on a project to understand the role of inter-personal networks in the diffusion of the antibiotic Tetracyline among doctors in Illinois. They found that social connections between doctors explained its diffusion. The third study (Lazarsfeld, Bereslon and Gaudet, 1944) stressed the role of *opinion leaders* in diffusion. Their research was later formalised as a two-step communication model (Katz and Lazarsfeld, 1955). Taking opinion leaders as the bridges between the media and the public, the authors found that majority of people are informed by opinion leaders rather than through direct media sources.

Recent research on networks makes increasing use of data available through social networking platforms. Greater product complexity, shorter product life cycles, information asymmetries between producers and users, the growing use of online social networking, as well as the availability of other data sources about customer behaviour have resulted in a fast-growing research field focusing on online diffusion. While offline diffusion studies are mostly about understanding the micro-processes in local (or small-scale) networks, online diffusion models use large databases about the behaviour of individuals.[3] The increasing anonymity on the World Wide Web presents

---

[1] French sociologist Jean Gabriel de Tarde is considered to be the pioneer on the diffusion of novelties (de Tarde, 1890 (2003)). Among initial studies on diffusion, see also Subcommittee for the Study of Diffusion in Farm Practices (1955).

[2] See also Griliches (1957).

[3] On this see Kane et al. (2014).

both constraints and opportunities for researchers. On the one hand the availability of data enables a better understanding of how large-scale adoption (of a behaviour, technology or product) happens. On the other, the larger a network, the further the analyst moves away from the micro-processes (like influence) that underlie diffusion. This increases the need to build synergies between different disciplines, such as sociology, physics and computer sciences, which are complementary to understanding the role of networks in diffusion.[4]

The analysis of the role of network structure in diffusion process should be approached with caution. There are important contingencies, depending on context, that have different implications for diffusion. They include the nature of an innovation and its compatibility with existing systems; network effects; switching costs from old to new technologies; the readiness and the attitudes of people to adopt a novelty; and the medium of diffusion (online or offline). We will cover these in this chapter and also address the following questions: When are people more likely to be influenced by prominent actors and when are they influenced by individuals whose social status is similar to their own or by their peers? If homophily drives tie formation, how can we know whether adoption of an innovation is the result of influence, or happens merely because connected people have similar tastes? Are opinion leaders really effective and if so, in what conditions, who are they and how can we spot them?

11.2 Threshold Models of Diffusion

Broadly speaking, threshold models are concerned with the likelihood of adoption.[5] Threshold models refer to a broad family of models where the underlying premise is that people tend to adopt a novelty depending on the choices of others in a system. Diffusion is sometimes triggered by the mere *number of adopters* in a system. This can happen through three mechanisms:

---

[4] See, for example, an interview by Steven Cherry with Duncan Watts, 17 October 2012: available at http://spectrum.ieee.org/podcast/geek-life/profiles/duncan-watts-from-sociology-to-social-network, accessed 8 July 2016.

[5] The pioneering article in threshold models of adoption is by David (1966), in which he analysed the adoption decisions of horse-powered mechanical reapers by US Midwest farmers in the mid-nineteenth century. In David's model, the threshold was the minimum farm size for which farmers would adopt the mechanical reaper. For a review of threshold models in the context of technological transitions, see Zeppini, Frenken and Kupers (2014).

- **Normative pressure:** this is pressure on actors to conform to the norms, conventions and values shared by people in a social structure. For example, recycling habits in a neighbourhood can spread through people's concerns about others' disapproval,[6] so that as more people acquire recycling habits, the more others in the community are driven to do so as well.
- **Direct network externality:** with direct network externalities,[7] the actual value of what is diffused depends on the *number* of current users. The use of fax machines is a classic example: the more people used them, the more the benefits accrued to all users.
- **Information cascade:** with an information cascade,[8] people willingly disregard their own information sources in favour of observing the behaviour of others. Consider a scenario in which a choice has to be made between two restaurants in an unknown city, one that is very crowded and the other suggested by the tourist guide. Some people will prefer the crowded restaurant to the one listed in the guide. Their choice is based on the rationale that if more people prefer that particular restaurant, their choice is likely to be based on their previous experience. Note that in this case it is the *absence* of information that drives behaviour. The number of people in a restaurant is a 'signal' of quality when there is no other information available.

In all these three mechanisms diffusion occurs through *self-reinforcement*. As more individuals adopt a behaviour, the more others are inclined to do so as well.

11.2.1　Examples of Threshold Models

Many parameters related to diffusion can be incorporated in these models, including individual tendencies to adopt, the extent of adoption in the general environment, the nature of the ties between people, the nature of the novelty and so on.

---

[6] Cialdini (2003) notes that for positive environmental behaviour (like energy conservation), public advertisements that mention how many others take part are effective in spurring positive behaviour, but the opposite applies for negative environmental behaviours: if reminded about how many others do something bad, people tend to repeat the bad behaviour themselves, although the advertisement may give a disapproving signal of the action.

[7] Arthur (1989; 1990).

[8] See Bikhchandani, Hirshleifer and Welch (1992). Sometimes the term 'herding behaviour' is also used; see, for example, Banerjee (1992). Note that the information cascades model can also be considered a 'network effects' model, where these arise not from direct network externalities but from social learning.

An early and famous model of diffusion is the Schelling segregation model (Schelling, 1978). Schelling explained the emergence of 'macrobehaviour' from 'micromotives', through a model in which people's preference for a certain proportion of their neighbours to be the same colour as themselves results in total segregation according to ethnic background in a geographical area. Granovetter (1978)[9] developed a similar model in which he explained the emergence of collective behaviour (like participation in a riot or adoption of a technology) through a threshold model in which people consider the decisions of others in their network when deciding whether or not to participate or adopt.

As an illustration let us consider Arthur's (1989) classic model of two competing technologies under increasing returns to adoption, where agents chose between technologies by considering the choices of others. The model takes two competing technologies, A and B. Assume that agent i's returns from adoption of either technology depend on the number of previous adopters of the technology and i's individual preference for it. In the model the returns of agent i from adopting technology A and B respectively is given by:

$$u_A = a + rn_A$$
$$u_B = b + rn_B$$

Here, n_A refers to the number of agents who have previously adopted technology A, and n_B refers to the number of agents who have adopted B. Agent i's stand-alone preference for technology A, without any other adopters, is given by the parameter a. The marginal utility agent i derives due to one additional adopter of a technology is given by r.[10] It follows that agent i will select technology A if the following condition is satisfied:

$$a + rn_A > b + rn_B$$

Rearranging terms, agent i will adopt A when:

$$n_A - n_B > \frac{b - a}{r}$$

---

[9] See also Granovetter and Soong (1983; 1986) for consumer demand patterns and bandwagons, and Granovetter and Soong (1988) for expressing public opinions and pluralistic ignorance.

[10] The original model is slightly different, where two types of agents are distinguished. Each type has a natural preference for either technology A or B. The model aims to show that early chance events that take place in the adoption process can determine the evolution of the market for two technologies. When this is the case, it is possible that the winning technology emerges independent from its intrinsic qualities. Network externalities are the main mechanism at work in the process.

In other words, agent's choice depends on the balance between:

1. the extent to which adopters of A exceed adopters of B in the system (given by the difference on the left-hand side);
2. the extent to which agent i personally prefers B over A (given by numerator on right-hand side); and
3. how much agent i values a marginal increase in the number of users of either technology (given by r).

For example, even if agent i has a natural preference for technology B ($b>a$), if there is a sufficiently high number of A adopters relative to B adopters, and if agent i's valuation of the number of users is sufficiently high, i can switch its choice to A.

11.2.2 Threshold Model and Networks

In Arthur's (1989) model it is assumed that agents value the decisions of all other agents equally, as revealed by the unique r parameter in i's utility function, regardless of whose choice i considers. Let us assume that agents are located in a network and that agent i is not influenced equally by the decisions of all others in the population, but by the choices made by those she has a tie with. We can then define a vector W_i where w_j gives the weight of the tie between i and j, and $w_j = 0$ if there is no tie between i and j. Here w_j can be any dyadic feature, like structural equivalence, similarity, proximity or other factor that is of interest to the analyst. When we define Y_A as the vector of A adopters, where $y_j = 1$ if j adopted A and zero otherwise, and Y_B as the vector of B adopters, where $y_j = 1$ if j adopted B, then rearranging terms, the equation above becomes:

$$W_i(Y_A - Y_B) > \frac{b - a}{r}$$

In other words, agent i's choices depend on the choices of agents that she is connected to, and the dyadic characteristic that is of interest in diffusion is given in the adjacency matrix W.

11.2.3 Network-related Determinants of Adoption

To explore the impact of network structure on diffusion using threshold models, it is important to distinguish between contagion and adoption. Contagion mimics an epidemic, where the existence of a connection between

i and j is sufficient for its spread from one to the other (Young, 2009). Therefore, in contagion the threshold value is almost always 1, meaning that a single connection with an individual is enough for that individual to be 'infected'. The concept of contagion applies specifically to the diffusion of information. Hubs are effective on social media platforms like Twitter, as followers of a hub get instant information. According to the findings of Bakshy et al. (2011), the largest information cascades are formed by users with the greatest number of followers. Yet, Bakshy et al. (2011) also find that that probability that a hub will create a large cascade is not reliable at all times, and that targeting only a few hubs in a network, to maximise diffusion, may not be effective.[11]

Adoption is different from contagion as it involves making a decision to accept or conform to a behaviour, or a novelty. In other words, adoption implies a conscious decision which also depends on the characteristics of the novelty and how it fits within the context, as well as the characteristics of the population and networks. The following network-related factors are critical in adoption decisions:

- **Number of ties:** the number of people who have already adopted increases the tendency to adopt. A question of interest is the quality versus quantity of those who adopt in a network. Centona and Macy (2007) distinguish between exposure from multiple ties, and multiple exposures from the same tie. They find that exposure from multiple sources is more effective than multiple exposures from a single alter, even if this alter is central or has a bridging role in the network.
- **Strength of ties:** the strength of ties between an individual and others is also influential in the decision to adopt. Young (2009) defines social learning as the extent to which individuals learn about the use of an innovation from their social networks by accumulating evidence about other adopters' experience. Tie strength between individuals in a network is effective in adoption decisions when the innovation involves uncertainties, when it is more radical or more complex than alternatives. In these cases people prefer to learn about others' experiences and collect information about the *use* of innovations before adopting. Such fine-grained information can be better acquired from trusted connections in one's social network.

---

[11] Many studies about online diffusion networks do indeed find that hubs are not necessarily or always effective in diffusion. A study by Kitsak et al. (2010) also confirms this.

Box 11.1 Individuals and Particles: the Ising model

One variation of the threshold model uses the statistical mechanics of ferromagnetic particles, or the Ising (1925) model, used to model binary decisions (adopt–not adopt). In the Ising model, the system is composed of a number of magnetic particles called spins, pointing up or down (a state of 1 or -1) and arranged regularly on a lattice. The temperature of the system and the magnetic field acting on it determines the state of a spin. In low temperatures, spins align with the magnetic field acting on them. At high temperatures, they start to reverse their direction. The function for a magnetic field acting on a spin i is: $m_i = \sum_j w_{ij} z_j$ where w is the strength of interaction between spins i and j, and z_j is the state of spin j. The probability of observing either state for spin i is given by the logistic function:

$$pr(z_i = \pm 1) = \frac{1}{1 + \exp(\mp(bm_i))}$$

Note that, as $b \to 0$, $pr() \to 1/2$. In other words, the magnetic field (or, to use the analogy, the influence field) does not have an effect on the state of i. On the other hand, when $b \to \infty$ and for sign of $m = (-)$, $pr(z_i = 1) = 0$, and $pr(z_i = -1) = 1$. This model gives a range of parameters in which we can incorporate the extent of influence, to see how it impacts patterns of diffusion (Özman, 2005).

Further Reading

Allen, B. (1982). Some Stochastic Processes Exhibiting Externalities among Adopters. *International Economic Review*, 23(3), 595–608.
An, M., and N. Kiefer (1995). Local Externalities and Societal Adoption of Technologies. *Journal of Evolutionary Economics*, 5(2), 103–17.
Follmer, H. (1974). Random Economies with Many Interacting Agents. *Journal of Mathematical Economics*, 1(1), 41–62.

- **Position in the network:** in addition to the number of connections and strength of ties, an actor's position in the network, as well as the global network structure, also influences the likelihood of adoption. For example, small-world networks are found to be more effective for diffusion. In a random network, diffusion is rapid; in a perfectly clustered network, diffusion is very slow since path lengths are longer. Yet diffusion is found to be fast in a clustered network with a few shortcuts connecting distant actors.[12]

Valente (2005) presents the following general model to estimate personal network exposure, taking into account the number and strength of ties (also see Box 11.1 for Ising models of diffusion).

---

[12] On simulation approaches for diffusion on a fixed network architecture, see Cowan, Jonard and Özman (2004); Cassi and Zirulia (2008).

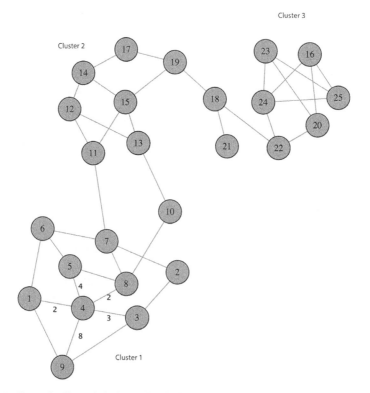

Figure 11.1   Illustrative Network for Innovation Diffusion

$$m_i = \frac{\sum_j w_{ij} y_j}{\sum_j w_{ij}}$$

Here, m_i is the probability that agent i adopts a novelty, w_{ij} shows the strength of tie between i and j, and $y = 1$ if agent j has adopted and zero if not. (As above, W can be a weighted matrix showing any dyadic attribute between i and j, for example, tie strength, similarity or structural equivalence in the network.) This equation permits different structural characteristics of the network to be incorporated. For example, assume that we calculate the adoption probability of node 4 in Figure 11.1. Node 4's ties are, 1, 3, 5, 8 and 9. Assume that 1, 5, 9 have adopted and that the weight of the links is a measure of similarity between nodes. Then, according to the generic model presented above, node 4's probability of adoption is $(2 + 4 + 8)/(2 + 4 + 8 + 2 + 3) = 14/19$. In other words, if similar others in node 4's network adopt the novelty, the probability that node 4 will adopt the novelty increases. In short, incorporating similarity and networks allows the possible influence of each tie to be treated separately.

Some actors in the network can be more influential in diffusion, depending on their network position and the nature of the ties they have with others. Tucker (2008) studied the adoption of video messaging technology among employees in a large enterprise. She found that central and bridging actors are more influential in inducing others to adopt a certain technology with network externalities. This indicates that the utility of adoption depends not only on the number of adopters in a network, but also on who those adopters are.

Another implication of network structure is that the adoption sequence is significant. For example, if the initial adopter in Figure 11.1 is 21, the novelty may not diffuse (unless node 18's adoption is strongly influenced by that of node 21). But if the initial adoption is made by node 15, diffusion may be more effective (and efficient). Based on these insights, in the next sections we will look at the relation between the network structure and diffusion in more detail. We will start by exploring the possible role of an initial set of key players in a population to increase the efficiency and/or effectiveness of the diffusion process.

11.3 Influentials

Rogers (2003: 326) defines opinion leadership as the 'degree to which an individual is able informally to influence other individuals' attitudes or overt behaviour in a desired way with relative frequency'.

11.3.1 Who are Opinion Leaders?

There are numerous criteria by which an opinion leader[13] can be identified, given the range of qualities that enable an individual to influence others.

Timing of Adoption. Initial explanations of opinion leadership focused on the timing of adoption. Rogers (2003) distinguished between early adopters, early majority, late majority and laggards. In some cases the early adoption of

---

[13] Different terms are often used, with slight differences in meaning. For example: influentials (Keller and Berry, 2003); change agents, opinion leaders (Katz and Lazarsfeld, 1955); mavens (Feick and Price, 1987); connectors (Gladwell, 2000); key players (Borgatti, 2006).

a technology is found to be a source of influence. This is because early adopters diffuse information about a novelty early on. Considering the diffusion of 'modern math' teaching methods in Pittsburgh during the 1950s, Rogers (2003) explains that the new – and radical – method diffused throughout the schools through adoption by a few superintendents early on.

The effectiveness of the timing of adoption depends on the *nature* of what is diffused and the network positions of early adopters. For example, when a technology has wide adoption potential, early adopters are often central network members, a factor that can increase their influence (Becker, 1970). On the other hand, when the technology has low adoption potential, early adopters are often on the periphery of the network, a factor that may reduce their influence.

Experience. Another criterion for opinion leadership is experience and expertise in the field. For example, Gladwell (2000) explains that in many cases *market mavens*[14] influence others' opinions through their deep knowledge and experience, as well as interest in a variety of markets.

Distance between Adopter and Opinion Leader. The social or geographical distance between the potential adopter and the opinion leader is also a factor that determines the effectiveness of the latter. In their study of diffusion of medicine, Iyengar, Van den Bulte and Valente (2011) distinguished between the effect of nationally reputed and local opinion leaders. National opinion leaders may be respected for their credibility, expertise or research impact but have less influence on most physicians than local peer opinion leaders. The authors found that physicians like to hold discussions with experts from the same community, who are more familiar and accessible. Other studies have also shown the relative importance of personal recommendations from friends and family, contrary to the common belief that people give more importance to the suggestions of experts. For example, when it comes to choosing between restaurants people value the opinions of their peers rather than those of connoisseurs. Zagat is a popular online platform for restaurant reviews. It was created as a printed guide in 1979 by Tim and Nina Zagat, who collected their friends' reviews of New York City restaurants. At first none of the publishers they contacted was interested in the idea, insisting that

---

[14] See, for example, Coulter, Feick and Price (2002) for heavy use; Godes and Mayzlin (2009) for opinion leaders.

people listen to experts, not to their friends. This proved otherwise, as the later success of Zagat reveals.[15]

Loyalty. Some researchers have stressed the role of loyalty as a criterion for opinion leadership. When technical information is needed, loyal customers can be important sources of diffusion. For example, the people who post frequently on the Apple/Mac technical support website are keen supporters of the brand. However, a study conducted by Godes and Mayzlin (2009) showed that it is not loyal customers of a brand who create the highest buzz for non-technical products (in their case, it was a local bar in the US called Rock Bottom). At Rock Bottom it was mainly customers who went there for the first time, or just a few times, who created the most buzz.

Note that these criteria are not by and of themselves sufficient conditions to be considered opinion leaders. A person with many connections or relevant expertise in a product may not have the personal attributes to be a source of influence. Gladwell (2000) states that an important attribute of market mavens is their genuine unselfish desire to help others. Influential people drive adoption by others, whether they are experts, innovators, early adopters or brokers in their network. To help overcome this difficulty in identifying opinion leaders, SNA can be used to detect them according to their position in a network.

11.3.2   Detecting Opinion Leaders by SNA

Opinion leaders can be detected based on self-designation or through socio-metric means[16] (Rogers and Cartano, 1962; Valente and Davis, 1999). In the first case, people either are asked about their attributes or volunteer to be an opinion leader in promoting a novelty. In the second case social network surveys are carried out, asking people their sources of information about a novelty. Interestingly, Iyengar, Van den Bulte and Valente (2011) found that self-designated and sociometric opinion leadership are only weakly correl-ated. For example, they found that self-designated opinion leaders are less likely to be influenced by others' opinions than those detected through socio-metric means. Sociometric targeting is the process by which a person's likelihood of influencing others is detected through social network analysis, identifying a set of people who are likely influentials and are targeted initially in order to stimulate diffusion among the rest of the population.

---

[15] Zagat was acquired by Google in 2011.
[16] See Valente and Pumpuang (2007) for a summary of various ways in which opinion leaders can be selected, as well as the advantages and disadvantages of each approach.

In diffusion, several sources of influence are at work simultaneously. SNA is useful in detecting potential opinion leaders, as well as understanding other means of influence in a network. Opinion leaders can be effective, but so are cohesive networks in which influence operates between peers and does not depend on a few key players. People are heterogeneous in their decision-making, their tendency to be influenced and their sources of influence. In an early study on referral networks, Reingen and Kernan (1986) found that there were three sources of diffusion in the referral network of a piano tuner in a city: the referrals from an 'expert', in this case the major music store in the area (45 per cent); the strength of social ties between the tuner's customers and their peers (27 per cent); and the tuner's own social network (28 per cent).

A wide range of factors have to be taken into consideration when analysing the diffusion process. Focusing only (or predominantly) on identifying influential people or groups through sociometric analysis can divert attention from other factors. For example, a simulation study by Watts and Dodds (2007) showed that the *tendency* of people to be influenced is critical in diffusion process. Romero et al. (2011) found that potential for influence depends on the degree of a node's passivity in a network. They found that most nodes in Twitter are passive information receivers who do not forward the content to the network. There are additional factors in detecting opinion leaders, which we will explore later in this chapter. First, let us look at some network metrics commonly used to detect opinion leaders.

11.4 Centrality

Detecting opinion leaders through their degree of centrality is a commonly used metric that is frequently debated.

11.4.1 Degree Centrality

Some studies find that nodes with high degree centrality are efficient sources of diffusion in the network (Iyengar, Van den Bulte and Valente, 2011; Yoganarasimhan, 2012). Although it seems obvious that the people with most connections will be better initial seeds, because they reach a larger number of people, this point needs to be considered more carefully. Table 11.1 gives the degree centralities of the nodes in the network shown in Figure 11.1. For example, node 4 has the highest degree centrality but its ties are all in cluster 1, which limits its direct reach to other parts of the network. Looking simply at the number of connections a node has can be

Table 11.1 Centrality Measures of Network in Figure 11.1

Node	Degree	Betweenness	Constraint*
1	3	5.92	0.47
2	2	19.16	0.5
3	3	6.92	0.47
4	5	20.33	0.39
5	3	2	0.44
6	3	25.42	0.33
7	4	98.75	0.25
8	4	46.66	0.32
9	3	1.08	0.63
10	2	27.75	0.5
11	3	100.83	0.33
12	3	11.75	0.33
13	3	36.83	0.33
14	3	14.33	0.33
15	4	135	0.25
16	3	0.83	0.48
17	2	6.75	0.5
18	3	125	0.33
19	3	132.5	0.33
20	3	20.33	0.33
21	1	0	1
22	3	95.33	0.33
23	3	0.83	0.48
24	4	40.33	0.46
25	3	0.33	0.65

Note: * See Section 4.3 for Burt's constraint

misleading; diffusion does not depend solely on a node's number of connections; it also depends on the structure of the broader network surrounding the initial seed, in addition to immediate ties.

11.4.2 Betweenness Centrality

An alternative measure is betweenness centrality, which measures the number of shortest paths between all nodes that pass through a given node (Freeman, 1979). This indicates the extent to which a node lies in the shortest path between all other pairs of nodes in the network. The highest betweenness centrality measures of the network in Figure 11.1 are those of nodes 11, 18, 19 and 15 (in ascending order). For example, although node 4 has the highest number of ties (five), its betweenness centrality is 20.33, less than the betweenness centrality of node 10 (27.75), which has only two ties. Although betweenness centrality is more suited to targeting than degree centrality, there are some issues about its effectiveness. It can be useful in terms of *speed* of diffusion in targeted flows (following the shortest paths in the network), but it is not necessarily a good metric for *maximising* the number of people information reaches. An underlying assumption is that the flow through the network *follows shortest paths* (Borgatti, 2005). But diffusion does not need to follow the shortest path between nodes, if the priority is to *maximise* the *number* of nodes reached.

11.4.3   Problems with Centrality Measures

As an illustration of why betweenness centrality may not be the best metric for selecting opinion leaders, assume that we select a seed in the network based on its betweenness centrality. In Figure 11.1 node 15 has the highest betweenness centrality. Yet if node 15 is removed, all nodes in the network are still connected to each other. This means that diffusion can still take place through other nodes. Node 15 only reduces the distance between other nodes. However, if we remove nodes 18 or 19 (which have less betweenness centrality than 15), the network becomes divided into three and two disconnected clusters respectively.[17] This implies that nodes 18 and 19 might be better at maximising diffusion than node 15. There are even cases in which betweenness centrality can have a negative impact on diffusion. For example, Yoganarasimhan (2012) found that the betweenness centrality of a seed has a negative impact on diffusion on YouTube.

11.4.4   Trade-off between Effectiveness and Efficiency

These points highlight the trade-off between effectiveness and efficiency in diffusion. Efficiency means assuring complete diffusion with a minimum number of ties. Effectiveness means maximising diffusion. Redundancy in the network increases the effectiveness of diffusion but reduces efficiency. Consider node 15 in the network in Figure 11.1. Its existence enables faster diffusion (i.e. it has the highest betweenness centrality). In addition, it is an additional assurance that diffusion takes place, because even if node 15 were absent there is a path between remaining nodes. Therefore, node 15 increases effectiveness but not efficiency. On the other hand, consider nodes 18 and 19.

---

[17] Removing node 18 results in three disconnected parts: clusters (1+2); node 21; cluster 3. Removing node 19 results in two disconnected parts: clusters (1+2); cluster 3.

They are quite critical, because their absence would inhibit complete diffusion in the network. There are no alternative redundant paths connecting other nodes to each other if either node 18 or 19 is absent. Therefore, redundancy in the network is both good and bad, depending on whether one prioritises effectiveness or efficiency of diffusion. Redundancy increases the extent and speed of spread but reduces efficiency; sparseness increases efficiency but reduces path diversity, reducing the probability of complete diffusion.

11.4.5 Core-periphery Network

When the network exhibits a core-periphery structure people in the core can be effective seeds and spread information to the rest of the network. In this case an important point to consider is the *efficiency* of the target group in terms of reaching the maximum number of people, while avoiding redundancies caused by common ties between them. When selecting a set of initial seeds, it is better not to include structurally equivalent nodes in the core set because their ties overlap. Even if they are not structurally equivalent two central actors can have many common connections, so that it might not be efficient to include both in the initial set to reach as many people as possible. For example, Kitsak et al. (2010) showed how the extent of spread in very large networks depends on the distance between spreaders in the network core. When spread originates from a number of nodes in the core, the highest spread occurs when they are not directly linked to each other.

Another point to consider in promoting diffusion in centralised networks is that when the central people are prominent in the social structure, they may be reluctant to diffuse a novelty and more inclined to preserve the status quo (Valente and Fujimoto, 2010). In addition, when a novelty has the potential to alter existing networks and socio-cognitive frames based on the existing system, a condition for sustained adoption is to strengthen networks among the actors in the periphery, rather than between actors in the core and those in the periphery. This is because in centralised networks, clusters among peripheral actors are usually sparse, a factor that may reduce the effectiveness of diffusion.

11.4.6 Endogeneity Problem

In diffusion, a source of the endogeneity problem is the difficulty of distinguishing between the inherent quality of a product and the centrality of its sponsor. Consider YouTube: are some authors more central because the videos they post are of higher quality, or do people tend to like posts by central authors? On this, Godes and Mayzlin (2004) found that word-of-mouth (WOM) is not exogenous; WOM increases future sales of a firm, but past sales also determine the reach of WOM.[18] Salganik, Dodds and Watts (2006) carried out an experiment on an artificially created music market, where users rated the songs that they listened to online. Some of the users were given the option to see previous ratings given for the songs; others did not see the opinions of previous listeners. According to the results, the best songs rarely performed poorly and the worst songs rarely did well. But for the majority of songs the results were not predictable. As more users were shown previous rankings, the predictability of success fell; in other words, under conditions of social influence it became more difficult to predict successful songs in advance because of increased variance in the system.

An alternative approach in detecting possible influentials by SNA is to take the cut points and cut sets in a network, that is, those nodes whose removal from the network results in the highest fragmentation.

11.5   Brokerage and Node Removal

Brokers spanning different contexts can be influential in diffusion in two main ways.

11.5.1   Brokers: Spanning Geographies and Categories

Spanning Geographies. There are many historical cases in which a frequent traveller carries a novelty from one part of the world to another. For example, tennis originated in France in the sixteenth century and is thought to have diffused to the UK (and subsequently to the rest of the world) thanks to military personnel and merchants who travelled between the countries. African-American jazz music came to Europe when James Reese Europe visited France in 1918. Rosen (2009) cites the case of Margot Fraser, an American who discovered cork-soled Birkenstock sandals on a trip to Germany and was so pleased with them that she decided to import them into the USA in 1966. Spanning geographies and connecting otherwise unconnected terrains through travels were much more effective for diffusion before the Internet era, because there were hardly any other way that novelties could diffuse to distant countries.

---

[18] Iyengar, Van den Bulte and Valente (2011), taking the case of a newly launched prescription drug, find that even after controlling for marketing activities, contagion through networks is most effective in diffusion.

Box 11.2 Broker for Diffusing Manga: Kappa Comics

Kappa is a small firm located in the Bologna comics cluster in Italy. It is an Italian comics publishing house founded in 1995. Boari and Riboldazzi's (2014) detailed case study shows how Kappa assumed various brokerage roles throughout its history. Even before the company existed, the Kappa founders were gatekeepers, introducing Japanese manga comics to Italian publishers and distributors, and adapting manga cartoons, as both a new artistic form and a new business, to conditions in the local market. During its second phase, Kappa's role as a gatekeeper continued but its nature changed; this time, it was introducing the graphic novel business model prevalent in Europe and North America to Italy. This new business model involved major new approaches: the content and format delivered to customers changed; the distribution was shifted from specialised comic shops to bookstores; and a new and growing market around graphic novels was gradually constructed. Kappa's gatekeeper role was accompanied by a coordinator role in networks, where the firm started working with young professionals who were passionately interested in manga, and who helped with text editing, translation and graphics. At the same time, the firm was also brokering deals between young Italian cartoonists and major European publishing houses that helped to spread Italian talent throughout Europe. Later on, particularly after 2005, Kappa fulfilled a liaison role in the network by promoting a new business model that involved licensing 'cartoons as a brand'. In this role, it openly shared its experiences of managing the brand Dragon Ball, and helping to spread this new business model among firms in other industries, including toy and game manufacturers, animation studios and television broadcasters.

Spanning Categories. Popular science authors are influential in diffusing scientific discoveries and research to the general public by bridging academic researchers and the rest of the public. Brokers also span groups with similar characteristics. For example, a university professor teaches similar student groups in different universities. Box 11.2 gives an illustration of different brokerage roles, looking at a case study of Kappa Comics in Italy.

11.5.2 Brokers and Diffusion

One of the initial studies to take brokerage as the main source of diffusion was the two-way communication flow model, where an opinion leader was defined as an individual who was exposed to the media more often than the rest of the public. It was found that opinion leaders were better positioned to diffuse information. The theory is that people who occupy bridging positions in a network can diffuse a novelty better because they can reach different communities that do not overlap with each other (Burt, 1999). As Burt (2005: 84) put it, 'opinion leaders are brokers whose conversations trigger imitation across the social boundaries between groups'. Bridging people can be effective seeds when they connect with diverse and even conflicting communities

(Valente, 2012). In addition, they can have an important role in diffusion, especially when the novelty is highly divergent from existing practices and norms in a population (Battilana and Casciaro, 2012).

Table 11.1 gives Burt's constraint measures for the network in Figure 11.1. Note that nodes 15 and 7 have the lowest constraint (0.25) and that their egocentric networks are sparse; none of their alters is connected. As we have seen, targeting by node removal is better for maximising diffusion in a population. For example, nodes 18 and 19 have higher constraint measures but their existence is more critical for maximising diffusion in the network.

11.5.3   Node Removal

Removal of a node or set of nodes is considered a better way to arrive at potentially important nodes for diffusion.[19] One method of detecting which nodes are effective bridges for diffusion is to look at the extent to which the network becomes disconnected as nodes are removed. A cut-point is a node whose removal results in the fragmentation of the network. In Figure 11.1, removing node 19 results in two separate clusters, and removing node 18 results in two clusters plus node 21. If the removal of a node results in a high number of disconnected clusters, it signifies that that particular node is critical for diffusion. However, the size distribution of these clusters is also important and the cut-point measure does not take this into account (Borgatti, 2006). If the size distribution of remaining clusters is heavily skewed when a node is removed, that node is less critical than a node whose removal results in clusters of equal size.[20] If we want to target the right nodes, we have to understand their intrinsic qualities and the costs of seeding. For example, the only difference between the removal of nodes 19 and 18 is node 21, which is disconnected if 18 is removed but not when 19 is removed. Valente and Fujimoto (2010) suggest an alternative measure to identify effective seeds, which is to take a set of people whose removal from a network results in the largest fall in the average path length. This measure can be useful when speed of diffusion, or precision of diffused information, is an important criterion.

---

[19] Borgatti (2006) uses the term key players, distinguishing between those who can be influential in the diffusion of a novelty, and those who need to be removed to avoid the further diffusion of something undesirable. See Borgatti (2006) for other network metrics that are effective in selecting a set of key players under both cases.

[20] It is important to consider, therefore, a set of nodes that are most effective in diffusion. Sociometric notions of cut-sets can be used for finding a set of nodes whose removal results in the fragmentation of the network. But as Borgatti (2006) shows, these measures are not optimal when the aim is to assure diffusion as much as possible because, in these measures, the number of members of a set is fixed in advance. In this case, we do not know the optimum number of members of the cut-set.

11.6   Cohesiveness

Another way in which opinion leaders can be selected is by detecting cohesive components in the network, on the basis that spread happens faster within tightly connected groups than between groups (Granovetter, 1978; Valente, 2005). Increased redundancy in the network implies the existence of alternative routes of diffusion between people, so that even if one path is not activated, others will be. In this way diffusion within a cohesive group is considered more effective than diffusion between groups, where the latter depends on a few people spanning different clusters. Cohesion in a network implies the existence of redundant ties between individuals, as there are often multiple paths between any two nodes. Centola and Macy (2007) list the following reasons why cohesiveness can trigger diffusion:

- **Strategic complementarities:** the costs of adopting an innovation decrease as more people accumulate experience with it, and share their knowledge with potential adopters. In this case cohesive networks promote rapid diffusion of knowledge.
- **Legitimacy of a novelty** increases as more people in a social network adopt the new technology.
- **Credibility of information** increases as people receive the information from multiple sources.
- **Emotional contagion** increases the advantages of cohesion, as certain behaviours amplify as people interact increasingly with each other in social gatherings.

Given the impact of cohesion on diffusion, one targeting strategy is to select random targets in different cohesive subgroups.[21] In doing so, both online and offline diffusion mechanisms should be activated. While knowledge about a product diffuses fast in cohesive networks, online mechanisms are effective for spread between different cohesive groups. Consider, for example, Internet-based broadcasting mechanisms like newsletters, blogs and discussion forums that spontaneously diffuse a local knowledge to distant clusters or geographies. While proximity and face-to-face interactions are obviously

---

[21] Detecting cohesive subgroups is one of the debated areas in social network analysis. On this, see Wasserman and Faust (1994) for classic measures like hierarchical clustering, cliques and others (reviewed in Chapter 4). For an introduction to more recent measures of community detection in large networks see Newman (2012).

effective for information diffusion, ICT can speed up diffusion between groups.

While there is no question that cohesion fosters diffusion, it is also important to consider the underlying mechanism of diffusion. One of the critical issues in cohesive networks is related to the distinction between homophily and influence. Because people with similar tastes are more likely to be connected to each other (see Chapter 4), how can we understand whether the source of diffusion is social influence, or mere similarity of taste among people who are more likely to be directly connected?[22] Aral, Muchnik and Sundararajan (2009) took the case of adoption behaviour of a mobile service application among users connected by a global instant messaging network. They found that most studies overestimate the extent of influence in social networks by about 300 per cent and similarities in tastes explain a significant amount of adoption. The importance of this finding is that the two mechanisms envisage different intervention strategies; when there is strong influence between people, an intervention strategy based on targeting influential people is better. When adoption happens due to similar tastes in a cohesive group, an intervention strategy based on demographic characteristics is better, rather than focusing on networks of influence.[23]

11.7   Structural Equivalence

A critical issue in targeting is to distinguish between cohesion and structural equivalence. Reanalysing diffusion of the antibiotic Tetracyline, which was originally analysed by Coleman, Katz and Menzel (1966), Burt (1987) found that structural equivalence between doctors is a better explanation for its adoption than the cohesiveness of their networks. When actors occupy similar positions in the network (consider nodes 23 and 16 in the network

---

[22] On this see Burt (1987), who distinguishes between social cohesion and structural equivalence in revisiting the diffusion process of the antibiotic Tetracyline, originally analysed by Coleman, Katz and Menzel (1966).

[23] A long-standing issue in diffusion literature is concerned with distinguishing between the impact of social influence and that of external sources of diffusion, like traditional marketing efforts (Valente, 1993; Bass, 1969). For policy-makers this is an important question to determine the allocation of resources between diffusion via interpersonal campaigns and advertisements. Van den Bulte and Lilien (2001), for example, find that studies looking at the social contagion impact on the diffusion of Tetracyline do not take into account marketing; once marketing is controlled for, the influence effect disappears. Valente (1993) found both effects in the case of doctors' prescription of drugs and interpersonal influence in adoption of hybrid corn.

of Figure 11.1, which are both connected to nodes 20, 24 and 25) they are likely to be influenced by each other not because they are part of a tightly connected community, but because they are more likely to compete with each other, due to holding similar positions in the social structure. In the case of Tetracyline, this means that if a colleague prescribes the antibiotic, other doctors are likely to do the same, to avoid being perceived as lagging behind. This is akin to adopting a novelty out of concern for credibility when it is adopted by others in the same social reference group (see Coleman, Katz and Menzel, 1966). Similar mimetic processes explain the diffusion of managerial practices among organisations. Organisations often mimic the behaviour of others in the same strategic group, particularly where there is environmental uncertainty (DiMaggio and Powell, 1983).

11.8 Snowball Targeting

In snowball targeting, seeding is directed towards current users of a product or technology so that they will forward the information to others in their network. Snowball targeting is sometimes used for viral online diffusions. The Hotmail diffusion campaign is an early and a famous example; under every Hotmail message sent from a user was the statement 'get your free e-mail at hotmail.com'. The Hotmail campaign is considered one of the most successful viral campaigns, resulting in the adoption of 12 million users[24] in eighteen months. Some gaming applications on Facebook have performed similarly, for example, Candy Crush Saga, which had an estimated 15 million daily Facebook users in May 2013 and 66 million players worldwide. Players can enhance their game performance (i.e. by 'earning additional lives') by inviting other Facebook friends to join the game. Aral and Walker (2011) distinguished between personal referrals and automated broadcast notifications. An example of a personal referral is receiving a personalised invitation to participate in an event, or to join an application like Candy Crush Saga. An example of an automated broadcast mechanism is when a behaviour, adoption or achievement is broadcast automatically to friends. These two viral marketing strategies increase the extent of diffusion among peers, following a snowball mechanism by which initial adopters take up the novelty, then call in their friends, who call in *their* friends and so on. They

---

[24] See Jurvetson (2000).

either provide direct incentives to adopt or spread information about the application.

11.9   Exploring Contingencies

Notwithstanding that some people have greater influence over people's decisions than others, influence is shaped by a wide range of additional factors that should be taken into account to understand diffusion. The most straightforward is the type of product subject to diffusion. As early as 1955, Katz and Lazarsfeld highlighted the fact that different product groups have different opinion leader profiles (they differentiated between food shopping, fashion, public affairs and movies). More recent studies use data from online diffusion networks. For example, some studies have found that the size distribution of online information cascades depends on the content of information.[25] Box 11.3 describes an experiment conducted on Twitter, revealing how different network structures are associated with different subjects.

In addition, social structure and the nature of an innovation determine people's tendency to be influenced at first hand. The extent to which people are influenced by opinion leaders and the effect of network structures on diffusion depend on the following external factors:

- **Specificity of the novelty:** this refers to the extent to which the innovation targets a broad range of people, as distinct from a niche group. Social influence can be stronger between people who share a rare interest, compared to people who share a more general one, because within-group identification is stronger in the former case. For example, Mehra, Kilduff and Brass (1998) show that the relative rarity of certain groups, like race- and gender-based groups, leads to increased within-group social identification and friendship. Cohesive networks are better for diffusion in these cases.
- **Enabling technologies and complementary products:** the unavailability of enabling technologies and complementary products can significantly slow down diffusion even in cohesive networks. For example, consider the critical role of battery charge stations in decisions to buy an electric vehicle. The existence of complementary products speeds up diffusion, increasing the opportunities that people can mix and match to design customised configurations according to their taste. For example, Gandal, Kende and

---

[25] See, for example, Bakshy et al. (2011) and Cha et al. (2010).

Box 11.3 Content and Network Structure on Twitter

Smith et al. (2014) have found that different network structures are associated with different topics on Twitter. They analyse the networks that are formed as people reply to and mention each other on Twitter, using the words, hashtags and URLs used in tweets. They have identified six different kinds of networks.

- **Polarised crowds** are usually associated with political subjects, where the content is likely to be highly divisive, creating two largely unconnected crowds. In these crowds, the important issue is that polarised groups do not argue with one another; instead, they rely on different information sources and use different hashtags.
- **Tight crowds or networks** are highly interconnected, with only a few isolated participants. This is likely to be the case when the topics relate to professions, hobbies, conferences and other subjects that people share intensively.
- **Brand clusters** emerge when people tweet about brands or celebrities who may attract mass attention. Here, the interesting point is that these networks are largely fragmented. The larger the networks, the more fragmented they tend to be. In other words, these people do not really communicate with each other, they just tweet information.
- **Community clusters** occur when topics form multiple small clusters around a few hubs. For example, global events that attract attention may form multiple clusters of people, each cluster formed around a specific news outlet, and each forming and cultivating its own audience.
- **Broadcast networks** involve people retweeting the news broadcast by major media outlets. These networks have a distinctive hub-and-spoke structure. Members are connected to the hub but generally not to each other. Smaller, more connected groups can form around these hubs to discuss the news.
- **Support networks** also have a hub-and-spoke structure but the hub is usually a firm or institution attempting to resolve a problem with a product or service. These differ from broadcast networks in that they are composed of outward spokes, where the flow of information moves from the hub to unconnected others. In a broadcast network, on the other hand, people reply to the hub, or retweet its tweets, creating inward spokes.

Rob (2000) found that the variety of titles available on CD is a significant factor that determines the adoption of CD players.

- **Riskiness:** when the decision to adopt a technology carries certain risks (for example, a new and radical surgical procedure), or when it requires a significant investment decision, people are more influenced by expert 'megahubs' than by people in their local networks (Rosen, 2009). These megahubs are likely to be more trusted sources, rather than local peers. Contrarily, when products or services do not require risky or large investments, peers are effective.
- **Compatibility:** an important determinant of diffusion is the compatibility of the new technology with existing products. Brokers are more effective

than central network members in promoting diffusion for which compatibility can be a problem; central members can be less open-minded about innovation due to their prominent status, as well as a wish to preserve their power and hierarchical position in the network.

- **Observability:** Rogers (2003) states that the observability of a technology is critical to its diffusion. Observability refers to the extent to which one can observe the performance of an innovation prior to adopting. Cohesive networks, composed of strong ties, are effective for innovations where observability is important. This is because strong ties imply trust and increase the motivation of people to share knowledge with each other.
- **Uncertainty:** social learning is defined as the extent to which a potential adopter accumulates empirical evidence about a certain innovation from his/her network (Young, 2009). In this case, peer experiences are important. Uncertainty increases the extent to which people need to receive information and knowledge from multiple sources. This can be through cohesive networks, which are more likely to involve multiple pathways between people. In addition, similar uncertainties about a technology can also trigger watching and imitating others who are structurally equivalent to the actor.
- **Network effects:** the existence of network externalities speeds up diffusion in general but studies show that the impact of peers who can influence adoption depends on the nature of the ties between them and the potential adopter. Tucker (2008) found that the source of network externalities perceived by an adopter largely depends on the adopter's position in the social network. Central actors are more significant sources of network externalities than others.
- **Medium of influence:** while hubs are important for diffusing information to many people in online networks, cohesive networks are better for adoption. Brokers who have many incoming and outgoing links, like popular bloggers or institutional websites, diffuse information efficiently among heterogeneous user groups. For example, Microsoft Most Valuable Professional (MVP) award winners were very influential in the diffusion of Microsoft's operating system. When people want to collect information about software, or solve a specific problem, the existence of online experts influences adoption.

Discussion Questions

1. In threshold models, the number of adopters in a system influences the probability of adoption. What are the different mechanisms that underlie this behaviour?

2. What are the characteristics of an opinion leader? Can you think of opinion leaders you are influenced by? If yes, why are you influenced by them?

3. What are the cases in which people are influenced by their peers in giving a decision, and those in which they are more likely to be influenced by experts?

4. What are the implications of homophily in tie formation if you want to diffuse an innovation among a population of people?

5. The role of networks in diffusion also depends on some external factors. Explain in relation to the following factors, and give examples for each.
   a. Observability of innovation
   b. Uncertainty of innovation
   c. Riskiness of innovation
   d. Existence of enabling technologies.

PART IV

Behind Networks

PART IV
behind Networks

12 Tie Formation and Dissolution

A way of seeing is a way of not seeing

Gianfranco Poggi

In this chapter, we focus on the micro-level antecedents of tie formation and dissolution in inter-personal and inter-organisational networks. We explore why understanding tie formation and dissolution is useful in innovation management. We learn how individual attributes (for example, experience, knowledge, personality, strategy) and dyadic attributes (for example homophily, proximity, resource complementarities and compatibilities) determine tie formation and dissolution. We also look at how past networks shape patterns of tie formation and dissolution between actors in the future. In particular, we focus on notions like relational pluralism, mimetic isomorphism, and relational and structural embeddedness, as important mechanisms in the way past networks influence future patterns in tie formation and dissolution.

Over the last decade, research on networks has increasingly turned to the micro-processes of tie formation and dissolution, as well as the evolution of networks.[1] Tie formation usually depends on individual attributes (personality traits or the specific resource needs of an organisation), dyadic attributes (homophily or physical proximity) and the structure of the local network around an actor. At the actor level, the emphasis is on the 'agency' side of network formation, as compared to the long-standing focus on the effect of networks on performance and behaviour. As Poggi's quote at the beginning of this chapter suggests, too much focus on the performance effects of networks can draw our attention away from the role of agency in network formation.

Understanding the tie formation process is important for innovation management in a number of ways. For one thing there can be a gap between

---

[1] The following reviews are recommended: Contractor, Wasserman and Faust (2006); Brass et al. (2004) and Rivera, Soderstrom and Uzzi (2010).

what organisations do and the best course of action for a specific objective. Consider an organisation looking for partners with complementary resources and capabilities. How do managers scan the set of possible collaborators? Research shows that physical or social proximity can drive such search processes. But as we have seen in previous chapters, there are myriad contexts in which non-proximate actors can bring significant benefits. Understanding how ties are formed increases awareness about the opportunity costs of established routines in tie formation. Tie formation is the result of search efforts to find the most suitable partners and these efforts may not always be efficient. Hallen and Eisenhardt (2012) define tie formation efficiency as the amount of effort expended to achieve desirable outcomes in partner choice. The least efficient partner search happens when a lot of time and effort is expended only to result in a failed tie formation or an undesirable outcome.

It is also important to understand tie formation in order to sponsor the diffusion of a novelty. In technology adoption decisions, separating influence from homophily has been a challenging issue, as we saw in Chapter 11. If ties between people in a social setting are governed by similarities in their tastes or interests, then marketing activities should focus on demographics, rather than targeting specific actors in the expectation that they will influence others (Aral, Muchnik and Sundararajan, 2009).

Advice and friendship networks play a significant role in the way work gets done. For example, we have seen in Chapter 10 that following a major organisational change, the responsiveness of informal networks in terms of new tie formation and the sustaining of old ties can be important for post-change performance (Kleinbaum and Stuart, 2014). Here, responsiveness refers to the speed with which the informal network adjusts to the formal organisation of work.

Table 12.1 summarises the topics covered in this chapter. A distinction is made between non-network-based and network-based explanations of tie formation. Non-network-based explanations are further broken down into intra-organisational and inter-organisational levels of analysis. At the intra-organisational level the focus is on interpersonal ties and personality, homophily and task-related factors that affect tie formation are explored. In inter-organisational networks, we first distinguish between comparative metrics in a dyad, like proximity, complementarity and resource compatibilities, then further distinguish between organisation or technology-specific factors. In the last part of this chapter we explore the network-based explanation of tie

Table 12.1 Tie Formation and Dissolution

Non-network-based explanations	Inter-organisational	Dyadic factors	• Complementarity in resources • Compatibility of resources • Proximity
		Organisation or technology-specific factors	• Temporal factors • Modularity • Strategy
	Intra-organisational and market (ties between people)	• Personality • Homophily • Workflows	
Network-based explanations	• Organisational fields and mimetic behaviour • Relational embeddedness • Structural embeddedness • Relational pluralism and cross-categorical network effects		

formation, focusing on how past networks determine the way new ties are built or old ties sustained.

12.1   Dyadic Attributes

At the inter-organisational level, resource complementarities and compatibilities, and proximity between organisations in different dimensions, shape the extent to which organisations are motivated to form ties, as well as the way they select partners.

12.1.1   Complementarities

Dyer and Singh (1998: 666) define complementarity as 'distinctive resources of alliance partners that collectively generate greater rents than the sum of those obtained from the individual endowments of each partner'. Innovative capabilities yield higher competitive advantage when complemented with external knowledge. The role of absorptive capacity in this process is critical, as higher in-house R&D investments improve the way firms acquire and build upon knowledge accessed externally (Cohen and Levinthal, 1989). Consequently organisations form ties to access others' resources, as partners bring unique resources and capabilities to a collaboration (see Box 3.2 for resource-based and knowledge-based theories). The recent wave of alliances between high-tech and design companies can be seen in this light. In the case of 'wearable technologies', many recent alliances have been formed to design products to keep track of health-and-fitness related data. Mutual benefits are acquired through these alliances: design companies have access to technological capabilities and technology companies improve the aesthetic appeal of their products. Examples are the alliance between Google and the Italian design company Luxottica, as well as the TAG Heuer, Google and Intel alliance for the development of smart watches.[2]

Interdependence between firms and compatibilities in their products are most pronounced in high-technology industries in particular, a factor that increases alliances significantly (Hagedoorn, 1993; Gulati, 1995). For example, in biotechnology Rothaermel and Boeker (2008) identified fifty-four fields in which firms participate. The extent of non-overlap between two firms' niches were taken to be a measure of complementarity between them, which the authors found to be a significant factor in explaining tie formation between established firms and start-ups.[3]

The alliances between established firms and start-ups are particularly illustrative of complementarities. In the case of biotechnology Rothaermel and Boeker (2008) found that the age difference between pharmaceutical and biotechnology companies is a significant factor explaining the likelihood of an alliance between them. Age difference between firms is also important in architectural innovations (Abernathy and Utterback, 1978). Because the processes and routines in established companies are largely oriented around their existing technologies, pursuing innovations that change the configuration of elements is often hard. Alliances with entrepreneurial firms are often a source of new insights about how to change the architecture of products. For example, the growing importance of energy efficiency in motor vehicles has increased the role of start-ups with the technical capabilities to provide radical solutions, compared to the incumbent firms, whose firm-level

---

[2] 'TAG Heuer, Google, and Intel Get Together to Announce a Conceptual Smartwatch', *PC World*, 19 March 2015; 'Fossil Group and Intel Announce Collaboration to Develop Innovation in Wearable Technology', Intel News Release, 5 September 2014 (see http://newsroom.intel.com/community/intel_newsroom/blog/2014/09/05/fossil-group-and-intel-announce-collaboration-to-develop-innovation-in-wearable-technology, accessed 8 July 2016); 'Intel Partnering with Oakley on Smart Sports Glasses', *Wired*, 6 January 2015 (see www.wired.co.uk/article/intel-oakley-wearable, accessed 8 July 2016).

[3] See also Gulati (1995), Chung, Singh and Lee (2000) and Baum and Singh (1994) for overlap in niches.

routines are largely structured according to traditional vehicle design[4] (see, for example, the case of the BMW and Immersion alliance in Box 6.1). In addition to accessing technical capabilities, complementarities are also important in accessing finance and manufacturing capabilities, especially for entrepreneurial firms (Katila, Rosenberger and Eisenhardt, 2008).

One of the challenges in finding partners is detecting those organisations that can complement the focal organisation's capabilities in the best way. Prior alliance experience, knowing who knows what and investing in internal evaluation capabilities are critical success factors that can increase the chances of matching with better partners (Dyer and Singh, 1998).

Information about who knows what is commonly obtained from organisations' past and current partners. Developing capabilities to find and evaluate potential partners that best complement an organisation is important prior to alliance formation, in order to reduce withdrawal rates later on. Greve, Mitsuhashi and Baum (2013) show that the existence of 'greener pastures' – firms that better complement a firm than its current partners – can increase withdrawals from alliances later on.

12.1.2   Compatibility in Resources

Compatibility refers to the extent to which a technology can function with others without any reduction in performance (Farrell and Saloner, 1985). In the case of organisations, compatibility refers to the match between resources in terms of quality and the extent to which they work well together. In an alliance, resource compatibility is important in four ways: it ensures consistent output quality, increases joint competitive strength, increases production capacity as resources are pooled, and makes it easier to distribute the benefits of an alliance between firms (Mitsuhashi and Greve, 2009). The authors showed that firms are more likely to enter into alliances with others that have resources compatible with their own. Moreover, resource incompatibility can trigger withdrawals. For example, in the case of the global liner shipping industry Greve et al. (2010) found that when deciding common routes to operate together, firms initially consider the compatibility of the ships' speed and age the main criterion, but one of the reasons behind withdrawals turns out to be ship size, which is often not considered in advance.

---

[4] Mann, C., 'Beyond Detroit: On the Road to Recovery, Let the Little Guys Drive', *Wired*, 22 May 2009, (www.wired.com/2009/05/nep-auto/, accessed 8 July 2016).

12.1.3   Proximity

Proximity between organisations in geographical, technological, cognitive, organisational or status-based dimensions are important criteria in partner selection.[5] In general there is strong evidence that proximity increases the likelihood of tie formation.[6] Despite this, in most cases there are diminishing returns to this effect. As organisations become increasingly proximate, it becomes more likely that tie repetition will cease (see Chapter 6). In addition, it is difficult to generalise the positive effect of proximity, because this depends on many contingent factors, including complementarities between different proximity dimensions and the types of proximities considered. One contingent factor is the nature of the industry. For example, when knowledge is tacit, physical proximity is likely to play a role since face-to-face interactions are better for effective knowledge-sharing (Audretsch and Feldman, 1996), as shown by the geographical clustering of industries in different parts of the world. Firms' absorptive capacity and strategic priorities are also determining: when firms have higher absorptive capacity, they tolerate better the communication difficulties that arise from dissimilarities in knowledge bases (Nooteboom et al., 2007), so their chances for collaboration with non-proximate partners increase. In the alliance portfolio of an organisation, proximate partners in one or more categories can be balanced by non-proximate partners in others, which is a way to achieve ambidexterity. In a similar way, organisations can prefer complementary partners that are proximate in one category and distant in others.

In addition to these contingent factors there is the issue of time, where the role of proximity in tie formation depends on the evolution of industries (Balland, Boschma and Frenken, 2015). For example, Balland, de Vaan and Boschma (2013) found that as the video games industry evolves, firms tend to partner with more cognitively proximate firms. Strategy and temporal factors are discussed in more detail in the next section.

---

[5] See Boschma (2005) on different dimensions of proximity. For status similarity, see Podolny (1993). Chung, Singh and Lee's (2000) study on status similarity and alliance formation is based on the syndication behaviours of investment banks, measured by tombstone advertisements.

[6] Some examples are as follows. Cantner and Graft (2006), analysing patent data for inventors in Jena, find that the technological overlap between firms predicts network formation. Stuart (1998) uses patent data to place newly established firms in the technology space (the more overlapping competencies firms have, the closer they are) and finds that closeness increases the possibility of future alliances. In the case of genomics, Cassi and Plunket (2015) find that proximity increases the likelihood of tie formation; and in the Dutch aviation industry, Broekel and Boschma (2011) find that social, organisational, cognitive and geographical proximity explain tie formation.

12.2   Organisation and Technology-specific Factors

Tie formation and dissolution are also governed by the nature of industries and the strategic priorities of organisations.

12.2.1   Temporal Factors

There are three main ways in which tie formation and dissolution patterns depend on time. The first is when tie repetition has diminishing returns. As an organisation repeats its alliances with the same partners, the knowledge bases of the focal organisation and its partners are likely to converge. In other words, partners are likely to become more alike, due to a prolonged period of learning (Mowery, Oxley and Silverman, 1998). This implies that there are diminishing returns to repeated collaborations between the same organisations, since what they can contribute to each other's knowledge reduces over time (see Chapter 6). At the same time the benefits accrued through trust and lower coordination costs may outweigh such negative effects. For example, Beckman, Haunschild and Phillips (2004) found that firms facing market uncertainty tend to reinforce existing ties, and those facing firm-specific uncertainty tend to broaden their networks to incorporate new partners.

The second way in which time matters in tie formation is because the resource needs of organisations change as they evolve. From the early growth of the firm to maturity, an organisation's alliance portfolio is likely to evolve from a cohesive to a sparse network (Hite and Hesterly, 2001). In initial phases the network structure conducive to success is more cohesive and as the firm grows filling structural holes becomes more critical for success. Elfring and Huslink (2007) distinguish between three types of start-ups according to conditions at the time of founding. In the first, the founder is an incumbent in the industry and, as Hite and Hesterly (2001) found, networks initially have strong ties and evolve into increasing numbers of weak ties, spanning structural holes in the network. The second case includes start-ups pursuing a radical innovation, in which case both strong and weak ties are critical at the time of founding. Strong ties are needed for resources and weak ties needed for accessing new opportunities. Over time some of the weak ties are dropped and other weak ties that prove useful are strengthened. In the third type of entrepreneurship, the founder is an outsider to the industry pursuing a radical innovation. In this case the initial phases are characterised by an abundance of weak ties as the firm tries to enter the industry. When a tie with a prominent incumbent is established, network search becomes more focused and existing ties are strengthened.

The third way in which time matters in tie formation patterns is because environmental conditions change. The technological and market uncertainty at the beginning of an industry life cycle is usually accompanied by increased knowledge exchange between firms, in which experts develop a common language that is not yet codified.[7] Through these networks new knowledge is continuously created and diffused among actors, contributing to the emergence of a dominant design (Utterback, 1994). At this stage, an important incentive behind tie formation is the exploration of external knowledge. Because technology development is at an initial phase, firms follow closely developments taking place beyond their boundaries, to *explore* novelties that may shape the future of the product system (March, 1991). In this phase, firms prefer partners that give access to knowledge from distant sources, for exploration purposes (Rowley, Behrens and Krackhardt, 2000). In addition to this condition, if there are strong network effects (see Chapter 11), exploration ties are accompanied by a variety of weak ties (like licensing or marketing) to strengthen the installed base of a technology early on. By investing in start-ups that have the potential to be future supporters of a proprietary technology, firms have the chance to enlarge their installed base. For example, Chesbrough (2003) explains that Intel was investing in start-ups that could strengthen its own microprocessor market in the future by providing complementary products.

12.2.2   Strategy

The strategic priorities of firms are reflected in the evolution of tie formation patterns (see, for example, Box 6.2 on IBM). An exploitation-oriented innovation strategy is likely to strengthen relations in the vertical value chain as firms deepen their existing capabilities and partnerships in design and production. On the other hand, in exploration-oriented innovation strategies, cross-industry links, as well as ties with less familiar partners, are more often observed. Radical or incremental innovation strategies also direct partner selection. While exploratory alliances are more likely to come up with radical innovations, concerns about knowledge leakage in radical

---

[7] On the role of industry life cycle on tie formation, see, for example, Rosenkopf and Tushman (1998); Özman (2008) and Özman (2011). Also see Box 2.3 on the computer industry.

innovation projects can lead firms to select partners with whom they have partnered in the past (Li, Vanhaverbeke and Schoenmakers, 2008). However, this also depends on the extent to which firms are equipped with the means to protect themselves from misappropriation. For example, Katila, Rosenberger and Eisenhardt (2008) found that entrepreneurial firms that protect themselves through secrecy and timing can afford to take more risks when forming ties with corporations.

12.2.3 Product System Architecture

In Chapter 8, we looked at how modularity and the knowledge base can promote increased interactions between firms, but may not indicate increased knowledge transfer between them. Firms form ties with others when final product markets are modular; that is, when the utility of products depends on the existence of complementary products that customers can mix and match according to their preferences. Examples are software or applications for operating systems and video games for various console platforms. In these industries, firms tend to form ties with other organisations for a variety of motives, of which increasing the modularity of a product is one of the most important. For example, Netscape made the source code of its Web browser openly available in 1998, introducing it to the market under Mozilla in order to increase its modularity and ultimate performance by encouraging improvements to be made by distributed software developers. Another motive in forming collaborations is to join forces to support a standard in the market. An example is LEDs. In the early phases of the development of LEDs, leading firms competed intensively to have their proprietary standards adopted by the market and various consortia were formed (for example, Zhaga). Firms can also form collaborations to ensure compatibility between products. An example is Intel. During the 1980s, Intel designed the peripheral component interface (PCI) in a modular way to support the speed of its future microprocessors, and made it open and freely available (Gawer and Cusumano, 2002). The modularity of the PCI shaped the architecture of computers. One of the factors that explain the widespread adoption of PCI was the alliances Intel made to diffuse its standard. Finally, hub firms are usually involved in multiple interactions with complementors in order to increase access to their platform. These interactions can be both cooperative and competitive, as both sides benefit from expanding the market for a platform but also compete in sharing its value (Yoffie and Kwak, 2006). The extent of outsourcing complementary products to third parties depends on the capacity of the firm to invest and the extent to which variety is valued by consumers in a specific market. The more variety is valued, the higher the extent of ties between hubs and complementors will be (Yoffie and Kwak, 2006).

12.3   Inter-personal Networks

At the intra-organisational level of analysis, personality, similarities and dissimilarities, as well as task-related factors, have often been cited to explain tie formation and dissolution. Table 12.1 summarises intra-organisational tie dynamics.

12.3.1   Personality

One question of interest is whether network positions are correlated with certain personality traits. For informal networks in organisations this field of research is relatively recent but it has already provided some insights into the possible associations between some personality traits and brokerage, centrality or strength of ties (Landis, 2015).[8]

Self-monitoring Behaviour.[9] Self-monitoring behaviour refers to the extent to which actors read social cues in the environment and adjust their behaviour accordingly. High self-monitors are like chameleons; low self-monitors are true to their self. High self-monitors tend to be more attuned towards status dynamics in a network, and because they have more accurate perceptions of it, their power and performance may be higher (Flynn et al., 2006; Krackhardt, 1990). Self-monitoring behaviour has been associated with central network positions and enhanced ability to make use of these positions for performance outcomes (Mehra, Kilduff and Brass, 2001). Also, high self-monitors have been found to be better at forming and maintaining ties with groups that are otherwise disconnected, which may give them unique advantages (Caldwell and O'Reilly, 1982; Oh and Kilduff, 2008). But these advantages also depend on the extent to which others in the network perceive high self-monitors to be emphatic (Kleinbaum, Jordan and Audia, 2015).

---

[8] See Landis (2015) for a survey of the literature on this emerging field.
[9] On initial research on self-monitoring behavior, see Snyder (1974).

The Big Five. The big five personality dimensions include extraversion, openness to experience, conscientiousness, agreeableness and neuroticism. Much research has been carried out in these dimensions, and their specific sub-categories.[10] In general, extraversion refers to a person's sociability; openness to experience to flexibility of thought and openness to new ideas and emotions; conscientiousness to vigilance in carrying out tasks; agreeableness to the extent to which a person evokes positive emotional affection; and neuroticism to negative psychological states like anxiety, moodiness or depression. In terms of tie formation patterns, extraversion is found to be associated with large network size, characterised by ties with weak emotional intensity (Pollet, Roberts and Dunbar, 2011).[11] A systematic analysis of the effects of these five dimensions on centrality in advice, friendship and adversarial networks was carried out by Klein et al. (2004). One of their findings indicates that openness to experience is negatively related to friendship centrality. People may not be too fond of open colleagues, perhaps because openness challenges expectations for conformity to values (Klein et al., 2004). The authors also found that low neuroticism is associated with centrality in networks.

Locus of Control. This personality trait draws upon a distinction between internal and external locus of control. The former characterises individuals who have a strong belief that they can control events around them. Individuals with high external locus of control believe that things beyond their control (the environment, fate or other factors) shape outcomes. For example, Kalish and Robins (2006) found that individuals with high external locus of control tend to have weak ties with high closure, whereas individuals with strong internal locus of control tend to bridge structural holes, having networks of strong ties with disconnected alters.

Many issues remain to be addressed in future research. One of these is the association between personality, negative ties and tie dissolution (Labianca, 2014). Another is the extent to which individuals maintain consistent positions across different networks. This is important because consistency would indicate the robustness of personality influence on networks. On this Burt (2012) found consistency in people's network positions across different roles in online networks. Also, previous research reveals that cultural context can

---

[10] See Digman (1990) for the five-factor model.

[11] The effect of extraversion on networking does not seem particularly significant in other studies (Landis, 2015).

be an important factor that shapes the way the self is defined and expressed.[12] In other words, not only do personal traits influence network behaviour, networks and social context also shape how the self is expressed. These issues call for cross-disciplinary research in the future.

12.3.2   Homophily

A widely confirmed explanation for tie formation is similarity between people (as the saying goes, 'birds of a feather flock together'). People tend to connect to others similar to themselves rather than to those who are dissimilar (Lazarsfeld and Merton, 1954; McPherson, Smith-Lovin and Cook, 2001). Categories of similarity that trigger increased connections include social and individual identity characteristics, like race and gender, as well as similarity in norms, beliefs, tastes and values. Homophily can also refer to acquired characteristics, like education or income. Similarities in these dimensions attract people to one another because of trust, ease of communication, mutual understanding and increased expectations of reciprocity, as well as conflict resolution. These advantages also appear to increase with tie strength and the rarity of a source of similarity in a population. For example, in an online social community in Stanford University, Adamic, Buyukkoten and Adar (2003) found that when two students share a relatively uncommon or rare interest, they are more likely to connect to each other. Mehra, Kilduff and Brass (1998) arrived at the same conclusion in the case of race, where two people of the same race in a population dominated by a different race will tend to identify with one another due to their commonality. Different dimensions of homophily have differential impact on connections, according to context, like gender-based homophily in the workplace (Ibarra, 1992), ethnic, gender and occupational homophily in business start-ups (Ruef, Aldrich and Carter, 2003) and inter-personal business ties (Vissa, 2011). At the same time, homophily will be further strengthened because similar people tend to be attracted to similar settings, or common 'social foci' (Feld, 1981). In other words, people tend to form ties with similar others and at the same time they become more similar as they are attracted to similar places.

---

[12] On this, see Triandis (1989). For example, Gudykunst, Yan and Nishida (1987) provide evidence that people in individualistic cultures tend to exhibit higher self-monitoring behaviour than people in collectivistic cultures.

12.3.3   Workflows and Division of Tasks

The formal organisation of work, like reporting structures and task-related correspondences, drives informal networks (Lincoln and Miller, 1979). Within most organisations advice and friendship networks are often more significant in getting work done rather than the relations indicated by formal organisation charts. One question of interest is, whom do people contact for advice in an organisation?

In general the likelihood of asking for advice from someone else is driven by a trade-off between the expected value of the advice and the cost of getting it (Nebus, 2006). This trade-off can be thought of in terms of exploration and exploitation; when a person needs advice, does she turn to people who are experts but whom she doesn't know well (exploration), or is she more likely to contact her existing ties, even though they may not be the most competent (exploitation)? The most favourable case is when these two sets of people intersect and a close contact is also an expert, but this may not often be the case. In other cases, people contact friends of friends to access valuable information (Nebus, 2006).

Affection between people is an important factor in task-related ties. Casciaro and Lobo (2008) carried out a social network study in three different organisational contexts: an academic institution, a large information technology firm and an entrepreneurial computer technology company. They found that asking for task-related help from others depends strongly on affection. When affection is negative, the task-based competences of a target are largely irrelevant, and people prefer not to ask for advice. On the other hand, when there is positive inter-personal affection, people tend to ask for advice even if a target's competence is not the greatest in the organisation.

Physical proximity with others is another important factor that increases the likelihood of asking for advice. Borgatti and Cross (2003) highlighted three conditions that determine when one person will seek information from another. First, to ask for information the information seeker must have accurate information about what the other person knows. Second, the information seeker must value the knowledge and expertise of the other. Third, the information seeker should perceive the other's knowledge as accessible. Physical proximity increases the likelihood of asking others for advice, and this effect is even stronger when people feel they can access others' knowledge and are aware of what the other knows. Even if the information seeker and the target are separated by distance, electronic knowledge management systems and video-conferencing technologies can help to facilitate ties. For example, in the case of

BP's peer assist programme, engineers are encouraged to ask for advice about challenging issues from their peers located in other regions, which is largely facilitated by electronic means (Hansen and Nohria, 2004).

The nature of tasks and knowledge characteristics also shape tie formation patterns. For example, complex and tacit knowledge transfer requires frequent and face-to-face interactions; on the other hand, weak ties can be sufficient for information about who knows what or the transfer of explicit knowledge (Hansen, 1999). In the case of scientific research, the rise in cross-disciplinary work has significantly increased collaborations, because scientists prefer to carry out collaborative work instead of learning a new field (Moody, 2004). Also, increased requirements for funding in large labs, as well as quantitative research in the social sciences, seem to have increased collaborations between social scientists (Moody, 2004).

The summary of antecedents of inter-personal tie formation is give in Table 12.2.

12.4 Network Antecedents of Tie Dynamics

Network-based explanations of tie formation focus on current and past networks to explain future tie formation patterns. From this perspective, ties are maintained and strengthened around current networks of focal individuals or organisations. This pattern can be explained through four processes: mimetism, relational and structural embeddedness and cross-categorical network effects, where networks in one category influence the formation of networks in another.

Table 12.2 Antecedents of Intra-organisational Tie Formation

Personality	Self-monitoring
	Big five
	Locus of control
Homophily	Identity
	Acquired characteristics
	Attitudes, beliefs, tastes
Workflows	Complexity of task
	Affection
	Accessibility
	Physical proximity
	Knowledge about target's competences
	Knowledge characteristics

12.4.1   Organisational Fields and Mimetism

Networks provide a feedback mechanism among organisations over time, resulting in the spread of certain organisational forms. In developing the concept of 'mimetic isomorphism', DiMaggio and Powell (1983) addressed the question why we see similar organisational forms in various contexts. This can be either because similar external stimuli provoke similar attitudes, or because actors imitate others who occupy similar structural positions in the network (DiMaggio and Powell, 1983). This type of behaviour is especially pronounced in the face of uncertainty. Mimetic processes can explain how strategic partnerships have spread among firms since the 1980s (Kogut, 1988). As firms mimic the behaviour of other firms, certain organisational forms or practices can diffuse through a positive feedback mechanism conferred by the network. For example, in many industries, certain periods are marked by increased alliance activity among firms, which can subside later on. Gomes-Casseres (1996) terms this an 'alliance fad', and explains the rise of such alliance activities as a pattern whereby a few firms, in response to technological or competitive forces, enter into alliances, and are later followed by other firms who enter into alliances to gain competitive advantage over their rivals. Box 12.1 explains the role of mimetic processes in corporate social action.

In the case of the automobile industry, Garcia Pont and Nohria (2002) found that the local density of alliances in a strategic group significantly influences the likelihood of new tie formation between firms in the group.[13] In organisational fields, actors are more likely to be influenced by others who have similar structural locations as themselves, for example, membership of the same professional associations, or have similar status. In such cases, mimicry of others is even more pronounced, as organisations tend to give the signal to the environment that they, too, have competences similar to their competitors'.[14] For example, in the case of digital publishing, firms have been undergoing a radical change in business relations. Many large publishing enterprises, faced with the challenge of releasing content through electronic media such as tablets and other smart devices, have realigned their strategies

---

[13] Kenis and Knoke (2002) applied the notion of organisational field to a network of firms, and analysed how various measures of network structure influence the patterns of tie formation among the members.

[14] Some early work in this area is the dynamic analysis of the automotive industry by Garcia Pont and Nohria (2002), who find support for the hypothesis that local mimetism is an important motive for alliance formation. As the number of prior alliances increases, the competitive pressure on similar firms to do the same also increases, as does their likelihood to be involved in collaboration. Partitioning the firms in the network into strategic groups the authors measure the effect of similarity by the local network density of strategic groups.

Box 12.1 Community Isomorphism and Corporate Social Action

Mimetic processes govern the behaviour of organisations in many cases. One such process involves corporate social action. Marquis, Glynn and Davis (2007) have shown the way local communities affect the social action of corporations. Three factors are important in explaining the way in which corporate social action is governed by the local community: cultural cognitive, normative and regulatory factors (Scott, 1981). The nature and form of corporate social action is often shaped by common and accepted ways of acting in a community. For example, the Minneapolis community greatly values culture and the arts, whereas in Atlanta local boosterism governs corporate social actions. While cultural cognitive factors are about 'how things are done around here', normative factors are about 'what is right to do around here', shaping the level of involvement in corporate social action. In Minneapolis, networks of business executives form a tight community in which colleagues enforce norms related to the appropriate level of corporate social action. Relations with non-profit organisations also have a considerable impact on the level of involvement in corporate social action. Regulatory factors relate to local politics, government mandates and government incentives to encourage corporate social action; this can temper or promote social action. Finally, agreement among local corporations about the form and focus of corporate social action is likely to increase the level of involvement in corporate social action.

---

towards developing capabilities in digital publishing. Faced with a completely different business model, most companies went into alliances with major software companies, like the alliance between Condé Nast and Adobe.

Note that networks formed in this way transcend industry borders, and form their own organisational field that both constrains and enables the actions of the organisations that constitute it. In a way organisations become cognitively embedded, so that market borders are collectively defined by shared mental models (Porac et al., 1995). Hagedoorn and Frankfort (2008) call this environmental embeddedness, which induces firms to behave in ways similar to others, to gain legitimacy (Dacin, Oliver and Roy, 2007).

12.4.2 Relational Embeddedness

How do past and current partners influence future tie formation? Firms are more likely to form alliances with previously known partners (Gulati, 1995; Gulati and Gargiulo, 1998). There is strong evidence for the role relational embeddedness plays in partner selection. Tie repetition is more pronounced in uncertain environments (Hoetker, 2005), where organisations face difficulties in predicting the conditions of exchange relations in the market and form relations with previously known partners (Podolny, 1994).[15] Trust, ease

---

[15] Contractor and Wonchan (2002).

of knowledge transfer and the predictability of partners' behaviour are critical assets in uncertain environments. Also, in conditions of uncertainty organisations may refrain from forming long-term contracts to avoid committing resources for extended periods and have the flexibility to change partners depending on developments in the environment (Llerena and Özman, 2013). Although repeated ties can involve increased transaction costs[16] due to frequent contract design, the flexibility benefits of short-term and repeated alliances can outweigh such costs. In general, uncertainty increases tie formation rates but the choice of partner also depends on the type of uncertainty faced. Beckman, Haunschild and Phillips (2004) found that market-level uncertainty shared by firms in an industry is associated with strengthening ties with partners in the firm's portfolio, whereas firm-level uncertainty may trigger new ties.

Whether firms pursue radical or incremental innovation is also an important factor in explaining tie repetition. While radical innovation projects are better carried out with unfamiliar partners who can bring novelties, they also often involve access to core technologies and may run a higher risk of knowledge leakage. If knowledge protection mechanisms are not tight, firms are more likely to repeat partnerships with previously known others (Li, Vanhaverbeke and Schoenmakers, 2008). Moreover, completely unknown partners can be chosen over others that are moderately familiar. This is because acquaintances are not as trustful as friends and they can have greater access to firms' knowledge bases than strangers can. The tendency to form ties with strangers is also strengthened when firms perform below or above their previously determined aspiration levels. For example, in the case of Canadian banks, Baum et al. (2005) found that banks prefer risky connections with strangers, particularly when their performance levels differ from social and historical aspiration levels, that is, the performance feedback of the bank compared to other banks or to its own history. In these cases, organisations can be more willing to take risks.

12.4.3   Structural Embeddedness

The motivation of actors to build transitive, balanced triads depends on a range of factors. For the most part organisations prefer to form transitive triads. In general, structural embeddedness in a network increases the likelihood of tie formation among network members. Gulati (1995) found that the likelihood of collaboration between two firms increases along with the number of third parties both firms know. These results have been confirmed in many studies

---

[16] Uzzi (1997) and Goerzen (2007).

since. The existence of common partners is an important driver of alliance formation because they can provide relevant information about who knows what, refer parties to each other, alleviate concerns about opportunistic behaviour and motivate trustworthiness. Consequently networks formed through third-party referrals are more cohesive (Baum and Ingram, 2002). In the case of inter-firm ties in the steel industry, Madhavan, Gnyawali and He (2004) distinguished between *coordinating motives*, where partners aim to increase value for all the actors in the triad, and *countering motives*, where a transitive triad is formed so that just one organisation extracts value from it. When there is geographical proximity, transitive ties are formed by coordinating motives, whereas in the case of technological groups, transitive triads are more likely to be formed by countering motives. At the same time, third parties can amplify the effect of weak or strong ties between two partners. If a tie is strong, third parties have a positive effect on trust; if ties are weak, they will have a negative effect (Burt and Knez, 1995). While mutually known third parties enhance the likelihood of tie formation, they can also increase the rate of withdrawal from alliances (Greve et al., 2010), because dyads are more stable than triads in networks (see the discussion of balance theory in Chapter 4). While it is less likely that partners will withdraw in dyads, triadic closure can be a destabilising factor in a network, forcing joint exits (Greve et al., 2010). For example, Sytch and Tatarynowicz (2014) found that tie decay in unbalanced triads is more likely than tie formation for triad balancing.

In addition to triadic closure and cohesion, firms that are more central in a network are more likely to enter into alliances (Gulati, 1999). Central firms attract more partners, both from the periphery and from the core of the network. Also, central firms are highly sought after as partners because of their power in terms of their control of and access to resources and their better economic performance. As far as relations between core members of a network are concerned, status homophily is an important factor behind tie formation (Lazarsfeld and Merton, 1954; Podolny, 1994). At the same time, peripheral firms in the network that are not included in the embedded core also tend to form relations with the core, rather than with firms similar to themselves in the periphery (Baum, Shipilov and Rowley, 2003; Ahuja, Polidoro and Mitchell, 2009).

12.4.4   Relational Pluralism and Cross-categorical Network Effects

In some cases, networks in one category shape tie formation and dissolution in other categories (Shipilov and Li, 2014). Relational pluralism is defined as 'the extent to which a focal entity (a person, a team or an organisation) derives its meaning and its potential for action from relations of multiple kinds with other entities' (Shipilov et al., 2014). Relational pluralism may involve multiplex ties, when two actors are connected by different kinds of ties (for example, when two people are both spouses and co-workers) but it may also apply when different types of ties exist between different types of nodes. For example, in Baker and Faulkner's (2002) inter-organisational network (ION) box, there are three types of actors – suppliers, producers and buyers – and seven types of relations characterise the ties – illegal, family, political action, interlocks, underwriting syndicates, strategic alliances and market exchange. Viewing a network from the perspective of relational pluralism is an opportunity to observe how cross-categorical network effects shape the formation (or dissolution) of new ties. For example, Shipilov and Li (2012) show that joint customers of two unconnected producers can lead to the formation of a tie between them. Relational pluralism in board interlocks may shape alliance formation patterns and the nature of alliance portfolios. For example, Beckman et al. (2014) find that heterogeneity and multiplicity in board ties are reflected in the diversity of firms' alliance portfolios. In response to a firm's poor performance, managers are likely to seek advice from executives of other firms who either are their friends or are in structurally similar positions (McDonald and Westphal, 2003). When managers seek each other's advice in strategic decisions, trust is enhanced, which is likely to promote future alliances (Gulati and Westphal, 1999).

Inter-firm ties are also built through relations initiated in industry events like conferences and participation in joint technical committees. The latter play a substantial role in initiating new alliances between firms; people discover opportunities for future collaboration through such meetings. This is particularly the case for firms that do not have prior alliances; joint event participation can compensate for the lack of formal knowledge exchange mechanisms through existing contracts. Rosenkopf, Metiu and Varghese (2001) highlighted the role of communication among mid-level managers within technical committees in cellular service providers. They state that when firms have less prior alliance experience, inter-personal communications among technical committees are instrumental in forging knowledge flow, especially in the formation of future alliances and in partner selection.

Cross-categorical network effects also exist in entrepreneurial networks. The problem of adverse selection refers to information asymmetry about the value and future prospects of the resources of a new venture. When this is the case, relations with prominent venture capital firms signal the legitimacy of new ventures, which influence the extent to which they attract new alliance partners (Gulati and Higgins, 2003; Podolny, 1993; 1994). Two types of networks are important in terms of giving this signal; affiliations with venture capital firms and alliances with prominent firms. Ozmel, Reuer and Gulati (2013) showed that these two networks are redundant. In other words, the positive effect of venture capital affiliations decreases as firms become more prominent in alliance networks. Burt and Merluzzi (2014) provided evidence that status is correlated with network constraint, and that status and constraint are complementary for performance. Actors with high status have higher returns from brokerage positions, and actors with low network constraint benefit more from status-related advantage.

Another field of cross-categorical network effects is patent citation and publication networks. While co-invention and co-authorship networks tend to occur together (De Stefano and Zaccarin, 2013), occupying a central position in one network may come at the expense of a central position in the other (Breschi and Catalini, 2010).[17] Another cross-categorical network effect is where social networks of inventors explain citation patterns between patents (Breschi and Lissoni, 2004; Singh, 2005).

Discussion Questions

1. For innovation management, why is it important to understand tie formation at intra-organisational and inter-organisational levels?

2. Explain what is meant by network-based and non-network-based explanations of tie formation.

3. Explain which dimensions of personality are likely to correlate with which network positions.

4. What are the different ways in which complementarity between two firms can be measured?

5. Explain the following concepts, and find examples for each:
   a. Cross-categorical network effect
   b. Mimetic isomorphism
   c. Relational pluralism.

---

[17] This study was carried out in lasers, biotechnology and semiconductors fields. The authors detect that the two communities are strongly connected. They underline the role of author-inventors who, acting as gatekeepers between two communities, have an important role in knowledge transfer.

No bee is a swarm.

French proverb

In this chapter, we learn how networks evolve in different contexts. We explore why certain regularities in real-world large networks, such as their clustering, the existence of shortcuts between clusters, higher centrality of some actors than others, and also network density, occur. We examine the roles of technology and scientific developments, institutions and geography, past networks and individual attributes in driving network change. We distinguish between structure-reinforcing and structure-loosening network change, and identify the sources of both.

Networks emerge and evolve as actors (people, organisations, groups, etc.) continuously form, dissolve or change ties and, as they learn, accumulate experience and change their characteristics. In understanding network dynamics it is important to distinguish between network change and network evolution. Network evolution refers to the changing dynamics of the network over time as a result of an understood process (Doreian and Stokman, 1997). Whereas Chapter 12 focused on the micro-processes of tie formation, network evolution is a globally observed macro-process. In this chapter, network evolution refers to processes that drive network change from the bottom up, without any coercive or directive mechanisms that act upon networks from the top down.

It is not possible to arrive at universal rules of network evolution, because of the diversity of networks involved in innovation. Sectoral dynamics, regulations and institutions influence network evolution differently across contexts. At the same time, it is possible to observe certain structural regularities across different types of networks. There is certainly a path-dependent dimension in network evolution, where past networks shape future networks. But there are other external factors as well, those which can alter the structure of a network in a radical and unforeseen manner.

As a network evolves its structure may change or remain (more or less) the same. Ties are formed (or dissolved) continuously, so it is highly unlikely that an innovation network will stay the same, even for a short time. Therefore it is better to think in terms of the extent to which change diverges from the existing structure. For example, when a network with many clusters grows through the addition of more clusters, it is not a divergent change. But if the clusters dissolve and form a decentralised, homogeneous network then the change is divergent. A change in network structure refers to the differences observed in its architecture. Mere entry and exit of nodes, new tie formations and dissolutions may or may not change this architecture radically. For example, despite the steady growth of the biotechnology network during the 1980s and 1990s, there was observable structural stability (Orsenigo et al., 1998). In contrast, the computer industry went through significant changes in its network structure throughout its historical evolution (Gulati, Sytch and Tatarynowicz, 2012).

This chapter begins by exploring three structural regularities observed in most large innovation networks and the main factors behind network change. These processes can be inherent to the network itself; exogenous, like major events, institutional or organisational changes and individual attributes; or related to the characteristics and nature of technologies and knowledge.

13.1   Real-world Networks: Bridging, Asymmetric, Clustered, Sparse

It is useful to think of network evolution as an ongoing structural process, reinforcing and loosening patterns of tie formation and decay among a large number of nodes. Some of these ties strengthen the existing network structure. For example, if a network is highly centralised, connections with and among the nodes that make up the core will reinforce the centralised architecture. On the other hand, an increasing number of connections among periphery members will, in time, loosen the peripheral structure. In the long run, such loosening may not change the architecture of the network, only the positions of the actors. As peripheral members start connecting to each other, the periphery of the old network can become the core of a new one, maintaining the centralised structure in the long term.

Unfortunately the evolution of most real-world networks is not as neat as this example. Ties that loosen and reinforce structure tend to occur simultaneously in varying intensities; new nodes enter and some nodes exit and as a result most networks are characterised by ongoing activity. These agitations in the network structure are called 'network churn'.[1] While observing network evolution poses some difficulties for researchers, due to the need for long-term network data and the various tangled factors that tend to change networks, we do have some insights about the process. These are related to regularities observed in various networks and the factors that tend to reinforce or loosen them.

What are these regularities? In most real-world large innovation networks, like patent citation, co-authorship, co-invention or R&D alliances or social media networks, it is possible to observe three structural regularities (Cowan and Jonard, 2009). First, their degree distribution is asymmetric. In other words, some nodes in the network have more connections to other nodes than others. Second, there is local clustering characterised by pockets of nodes that are more densely connected within than between themselves. Third, there are bridging ties that provide shortcuts between these dense pockets. For example, in computer, mobile communications, electronics and pharmaceutical R&D alliance networks, a frequently observed network structure is dense tie formation around prominent firms, where these dense pockets are connected to each other directly or indirectly (see Figure 5.7).[2] Fourth, the larger networks are, the more sparse they become. In other words, as networks grow, it becomes increasingly unlikely that a dense network will be observed. In reality, few ties are actually realised, compared to the maximum number of possible ties that can occur in a network.

Given that most real-world networks are characterised by these properties, the question is what factors tend to sustain and stabilise (weaken and destabilise) the bridging, asymmetric, clustered and sparse (BACS) properties of networks over time, in different contexts? Some of these factors are rooted in the structure of networks. Others are exogenous events that may disrupt or reinforce the stability of a network to varying degrees. In this chapter, we will look at the role of networks, industry events, the intrinsic qualities of actors, institutional and organisational change and technology and knowledge-specific features as main drivers of network change. These are summarised in Table 13.1.

---

[1] Sasovova et al. (2010) define network churn as the volume. composition and pattern of changes in networks over time.

[2] See, for example, Roijakkers and Hagedoorn (2006) on biotech and Rosenkopf and Padula (2008) on mobile communications.

Table 13.1 Some Antecedents of BACS in Networks

	Brokerage	Asymmetric Tie Distribution (Centrality)	Clustering and Density
Technology, science	• Emergence of technological opportunities that increase bridging between domains • Competence-destroying technological change	• Radical innovations that benefit early movers • Basic research (central positions of universities and public research labs)	• Knowledge tacitness • Competence-strengthening innovations • Complex knowledge base • Technological uncertainty increases network density
Institutions, geography	• Labour mobility • Government-sponsored research fields	• Regulations can increase/decrease centrality of some organisations when they are capability biased	• Regulations that motivate similar organisations to collaborate • Geographical proximity • Regulations that favour collaboration • Weak IPR may reduce number of diverse ties
Networks	• Centrality	• Preferential attachment • Matthew effect (cumulative advantage)	• Relational and structural embeddedness increases clustering • Closure and transitivity increases clustering
People, organisations	• Personality-related antecedents (self-monitoring, big five, etc.) • Acquired personal characteristics (prior experience, career track, scientific excellence, etc.) • Size, location of organisations • Innovative capabilities • Strategies		• Favouring friends over strangers increases clustering • Exploitation strategy and incremental innovation strategy increases local clustering

Change occurs because of. . .

13.2 Antecedents of Clustering and Centrality

13.2.1 Self-reinforcing Processes in Clustering

In general, asymmetric tie distribution and clustering tend to be sustained by the factors that give rise to them; in other words, both properties are self-reinforcing. In Chapter 12 we saw how relational and structural embeddedness are likely to motivate further tie formation among individuals, and that the clustering of a network can be thought of as a glue that holds embedded actors together in future networks as well (see Chapter 10 for a definition of cohesiveness). At the dyadic level, due to relational embeddedness, actors tend to repeat pairwise collaborations because trust, common understandings, values and tastes are likely to develop over time. Structural embeddedness is likely to reinforce connections between existing actors, due to reputation, effective transfer of knowledge, fast spread of deviant behaviour, trust or a variety of other internal mechanisms that reduce costs of coordination (Polidoro, Ahuja and Mitchell, 2011). These imply that cohesive and redundant networks tend to be characterised by built-in processes that are likely to reinforce cohesiveness and redundancy even further. Note that there are other processes that may distort these dynamics. As shown in earlier chapters, resource incompatibilities, diminishing returns to learning or over-embeddedness may saturate existing cohesiveness, rendering further collaborations less and less beneficial (especially in the case of inter-organisational networks). Duysters and Lemmens (2003) provided evidence of this pattern in the case of the microelectronics industry. Despite these factors, clustered networks are not likely to dissolve quickly over a reasonable time frame.

13.2.2 Self-reinforcing Processes in Centrality

Similar path-dependent processes also apply to asymmetric tie distribution. There are several reasons for this. One is that the actors at the core of a network may increasingly form ties with each other due to status similarity (Podolny, 1993) and a shared interest in sustaining their central and powerful position in the network. There are also processes in network growth that tend to strengthen their centrality, as revealed by phrases like 'the rich get richer', or 'success breeds success' through the Matthew effect. Solla de Price (1976) termed such processes 'cumulative advantages', whereby past networks provide opportunities for focal actors in the future, either because they consciously make use of their structural positioning, or because they become more attractive to others, or both (Zaheer and Soda, 2009).

Formally, the process through which centrality is strengthened in a growing network is called 'preferential attachment' (Barabasi and Albert, 1999). In this process new nodes that enter the network are more likely to connect to ties that already have a high number of nodes. In turn, this growth can result in a scale-free network structure (see Chapter 4). Preferential attachment growth processes have been detected in diverse networks, both at the individual and organisational levels. For example, international co-authorships, R&D collaborations and patents in biotechnology have been found to follow growth by preferential attachment.[3] While these centrality-sustaining processes are rooted in existing networks, central actors have also *intrinsic* qualities that are correlated with their centrality. For example, as far as inter-firm networks are concerned, in most industries the size distribution of firms is largely skewed and large firms are likely to be involved in more alliances, enhancing their centrality in the industry network.

Clustering and asymmetric tie distribution are likely to be sustained in a self-reinforcing way (although not always) but such historical processes are less likely to govern shortcuts in a network. On the contrary, a bridging tie is by definition an unbalanced tie to the extent that it is not transitive, that is as long as a broker's ties are not connected to each other. Moreover, the advantages that can be accrued from a bridging tie are likely to diminish rapidly over time (Burt, 2002). Therefore one of the questions of interest is about the antecedents and dynamics of brokerage positions (Table 13.4).

13.3 Antecedents of Brokerage

13.3.1 Acquired Characteristics

In inter-personal networks, brokers in different innovative activities seem to have some common attributes related to personality and acquired

---

[3] Wagner and Leydesdorff (2005) find that preferential attachment explains network formation in international co-authorships (although there is no power law distribution, possibly because of institutional context). Another example is the case of R&D collaborations in the IT sector, and where Hanaki, Nakajima and Ogura (2010) find that the network has become more clustered over time; they find its growth is explained by preferential attachment. Powell et al. (2005) detect a scale-free network growth in biotechnology 1988–98. Also see Venkatraman and Lee (2004) for preferential attachment patterns in how game developers select platforms.

Table 13.2 Antecedents of Brokerage (Bridging Ties)

Personality	High self-monitoring is correlated with brokerage
Accomplishments	Scientific and technical success has been correlated with brokerage
Past networks	Central actors more likely to bridge clusters in the future
Strategic actions	The existence of structural holes in a network implies that some actors will fill those structural holes, to fulfil different brokerage roles
Regulations, events and technological developments	Technological developments or new regulations can give rise to new structural holes, yielding new opportunities to connect diverse fields of knowledge
Labour mobility	Increased labour mobility is associated with higher brokerage
Knowledge base	Higher economies of scope in knowledge use

characteristics. One of these is their scientific and technological experience and knowledge. A famous study by Allen and Cohen (1969) compared technical communication networks in two R&D labs and revealed that the central actors in communication networks to whom people frequently turned for advice were more knowledgeable about technical literature and acted as gatekeepers, bringing knowledge to the organisation from the outside. In other studies conducted later on, these results were largely confirmed. Prior career experience, a high number of patents and publications, past performance and certain personality traits have often been associated with brokerage positions and roles (see Table 13.2).[4]

13.3.2 Personality

A possible correlation between certain personality traits and brokerage has also been highlighted. In particular, brokers are likely to be entrepreneurial rather than conforming and obedient, more authoritative and to thrive on change rather than stability (Burt, Jannotta and Mahoney, 1998). Brokerage has also been associated with self-monitoring behaviour (Sasovova et al., 2010). Some

---

[4] Lissoni (2010) finds that brokers have high numbers of publications and patents and that many work with companies. In the case of design and high-tech small and medium enterprise networks in southeast Netherlands, Kirkels and Duysters (2010) find that influential brokers are in non-profit and science sectors. Stam (2010) finds prior career experience important in explaining the antecedents of brokers in open source software. In the case of the Internet Engineering Task Force Community, Fleming and Waguespack (2007) show that open community leaders are highly likely to be technical boundary spanners, involved in many task forces simultaneously. For the case of inventors in biotech between 1976–95, Lee (2010) finds that brokers have superior track records and that once this is controlled for, the positive association between brokerage and performance disappears.

studies find that brokerage positions are more likely to be occupied by high self-monitors (see Chapter 12).

13.3.3   Past Networks

Past network positions are also important in explaining brokerage, although empirical evidence is limited. Certainly, centrality can enhance actors' access to resources, knowledge and markets. Therefore those located in central positions can have greater propensity to form bridging ties in the future, because of their advantage in accessing distant or peripheral actors. Italian TV series production networks confirmed this conjecture. Zaheer and Soda (2009) found that the past centrality of TV series producers tends to explain their propensity to fill structural holes later on. There is also some evidence that organisations that fill bridging positions are more likely to occupy bridging positions in the future (Sytch, Tatarynowicz and Gulati, 2012). This is because the experience of bridging is likely to equip firms with the capability to recognise the value of new bridging opportunities in a network, for which the authors found supporting evidence in the computer industry.

13.3.4   Technological Developments

Technological developments often create new opportunities for brokering across different contexts. Innovative opportunities increasingly lie outside the borders of most industries, giving rise to a growing number of cross-cutting links between different domains, reflected in the structure of networks. Shifting technological opportunities, radical innovations, entry of powerful actors, new regulations, macro-economic conditions and change in tastes and values may trigger the emergence of bridging ties in a network that cuts across different technologies and markets. For example, in the case of biotechnology and pharmaceutical networks, Roijakkers and Hagedoorn (2006) found that new entrants in the network with high technological dynamism were soon likely to play an important bridging role in the network by forming crucial links between networks surrounding pharmaceutical firms that otherwise would not be connected. In the initial periods of development of these networks, firms like Biogen, Genex, Genentech and Amgen filled such bridging roles in the network (Roijakkers and Hagedoorn, 2006). In the history of the computer industry, Gulati, Sytch and Tatarynowicz (2012) explain that during the 1990s there were more opportunities for bridging positions in the network, as complementarities and compatibility requirements between different product systems required cross-cutting ties between these different clusters.

13.3.5   Arbitrage

There can also be instrumental motives behind brokerage. Individuals' intentional behaviours to take advantage of entrepreneurial opportunities, coordinating ties between actors, information arbitrage and firm-level strategies may give rise to brokering activities (Burt, 1992; Obstfeld, 2005). For example, the case of Kappa comics in Chapter 11 showed how the Italian company fulfilled different brokerage roles in the network throughout its evolution, driven by its strategic priorities. Heterogeneity of the management team is also positively associated with a firm's role as a broker in the industry, since it is more likely to make diverse connections (Boari and Riboldazzi, 2014). Baum, Shipilov and Rowley (2003) found that the emergence of brokers in Canadian banks is both chance partnering and control partnering by core (central) firms, to enhance their power and control over the network, a process that also explains brokers and the small-world characteristics of firms in the banking sector.

13.3.6   Labour Mobility and Institutions

Labour mobility and institutions can be significant in explaining brokerage, especially in geographical clusters. Consider the paradox of Silicon Valley and Route 128, explored in the famous study by Saxenian (1994). While both regions were high-tech and areas of innovation in which they worked were largely similar, due to cultural factors like openness, tolerance of failure and a collaborative culture, Silicon Valley and Route 128 followed very different paths of development. Comparing the evolution of inventor networks in both regions, Fleming and Frenken (2007) found that a distinguishing feature of the Silicon Valley network is the way a giant component formed around the 1990s when previously disjointed parts of the network became connected. Investigating why such a pattern of evolution was observed, they point out the role of IBM and labour mobility in connecting these components. In particular, a post-doc programme financed by IBM and essentially aimed at creating 'IBM-friendly' inventors in the region and subsequent collaborations through labour mobility played a significant role in bridging disconnected parts of the network. While the Boston region counterpart of IBM was DEC, the latter's strategy was more closed and proprietary, compared to the open philosophy underlying IBM management. Ter Wal (2013) made a similar observation for the high-tech region of Sophia Antipolis in the south of France. Comparing the evolution of IT networks and networks in the life sciences, he detected completely different patterns of evolution in the two regions, although both networks started with similar structures. In particular, the weight of local spin-offs and start-up firms gradually increased in the IT network. He points out the role of spin-offs acting as bridges connecting inventor clusters, and gradually reducing the path lengths in the network.

The importance of knowledge base and technology raises other factors that may not only trigger brokerage in the network, but also eventually alter the whole network structure. In the next section we consider the role of radical innovations, major events and institutional and regulatory changes that can drive network evolution.

13.4   Sources of Network Change

In inter-organisational networks, industry events and major technological breakthroughs can change the structure of the network due to their potential to change the basis of competition or the redistribution of power in an industry. On this, Madhavan, Koka and Prescott (1998) distinguished between structure-loosening and structure-reinforcing events. While structure-reinforcing events tend to make central (and powerful) actors even more so, structure-loosening events tend to benefit the actors located on the periphery of the network.

13.4.1   Structure-loosening Change

Structure-loosening events tend to alter the existing network so that it diverges from its existing structure, changing the basis of competition. In particular, competence-destroying innovations (Tushman and Anderson, 1986) have the potential to change the network structure significantly and are likely to be introduced by new entrants or peripheral firms in the network, since the existing competences and capabilities of established dominant players can inhibit the introduction of architectural innovations (Henderson and Clark, 1990). When peripheral firms introduce important inventions, they gradually become attractive alliance partners (Ahuja, 2000).

In the case of the music industry, as music sharing in peer-to peer (P2P) networks increased, the critical competences required for music creation and diffusion were no longer confined to traditional studio recording, a factor that changed radically the value of existing competences (Tidd and Bessant, 2013). Instead, the growing importance of competences related to the use of online, specialised recording software altered the structure of networks. Previous competences became obsolete and it became a matter of urgency to acquire new competences within a short time period. This implies that the most desirable competences for partnerships also changed. In the case of the music industry, as in many other cases, the Internet has completely altered the networks that define the sector, with previously peripheral actors now occupying a central role.[5]

Major technological developments are also likely to drive network change at the intra-organisational level. For example, in organisational change we saw in Chapter 10 how the introduction of a new technology in the workplace can alter people's roles, patterns of interaction, the distribution of power and consequently network structure. Following a strategic change initiative or the introduction of a major technological restructuring, the power distribution in an organisation is likely to change.

Events are also important because they may destabilise and introduce uncertainty. Events that increase uncertainty in the industry usually trigger the construction of new ties (Rosenkopf and Tushman, 1998). To the extent that these ties are formed with familiar partners, the overall structure of the network is not expected to change radically. However, when the uncertainty necessitates a change in the composition of firms' alliance portfolios, increasing the weight of novel partners, structural changes in the network are more likely. For example, in the case of biotechnology, Phlippen and Riccaboni (2008) found that increasing uncertainty following the genomic revolution resulted in significant structural changes in the R&D network, triggering new tie formations with new entrants and increasing clustering as firms strengthened partnerships in their local networks. Koka, Madhavan and Prescott (2006) explained that the way uncertainty interacts with resource availability is critical. When the effect of an event is to increase the overall resources available to firms, networks become more dense, increasing tie formations and reducing tie dissolutions.

13.4.2   Structure-reinforcing Change

Incremental innovations are likely to have a structure-reinforcing effect on networks, because their effect is often to improve existing technologies and deepen the use of current competences. Consider the vast number of actors

---

[5] Similar effects of technological change on the nature of networks have been studied in other contexts as well, for example, see Glasmeier (1991) on the changing nature of Swiss watchmakers.

who develop application software for major platforms accessible on mobile devices. These incremental contributions tend to strengthen an existing platform along its initial trajectory. The platform becomes more central as more users join and the number of developers increases as a result.

An existing network structure tends to be reinforced when entry and exit patterns align with the current competences in a network. For example, Cantner and Graft (2006) showed that in Jena, one of Germany's core innovation districts, the inventor network converged towards the core of the network over time, with exits occurring at the periphery and entries strengthening the core competences of the district. In this way the core competences of the region were largely sustained and strengthened with the evolution of the networks of R&D collaborations focused on the core.

13.4.3   Knowledge Base

The nature of the knowledge base also tends to govern how networks evolve. For example, Broekel and Graf (2010) found in the case of German R&D networks that basic research-related alliances have significantly different network evolution patterns from alliances in applied fields. Basic research networks tend to evolve in a more disconnected manner and have a dense core composed of public labs and universities.

Another example of the role of scientific and technological developments in driving network evolution is biotechnology. Orsenigo et al. (1998) showed how the hierarchical evolution of the science base in molecular biology was related to the evolution of network structure. *Originator* firms entered the network by initiating new technological trajectories. The firms already in the network had access to these trajectories through their role as *developers*. In the meantime, firms that had competences in the field of transversal technologies, characterised by the emergence of new generic tools, had a diverse range of partners with no identifiable pattern in their partnership behaviour. In the case of German biotechnology, Ter Wal (2014) found that the impact of geographical proximity as a driver of network change diminished as the biotechnology knowledge regime changed from exploratory to exploitative. In addition, the role of triadic closure as a network change driver increased.

13.4.4   Regulations

Institutional and regulatory factors also shape patterns of network evolution. For example, in the case of the computer industry, Gulati, Sytch and

Tatarynowicz (2012) found that the Internet bubble in 2000 had an important effect on the way inter-firm networks became less diversified and more
consolidated, accompanied by disappearance of bridging positions. In particular, saturation of demand and the increasingly risk-averse behaviour of
computer firms gave rise to the increasing importance of trust and consumer
focus. Government-sponsored research in certain scientific fields, the availability of venture capital and developments in the stock market, as well as
IPR regimes, can have direct effects on the patterns of alliances between
firms, shaping the evolution of networks at the global level. For example,
Bekkers, Duysters and Verspagen (2002) found that in standards-based
industries, especially mobile communication, holders of essential IPR are
likely to have high network centrality in alliance networks. More recently,
increased emphasis on pro-poor innovation policies has significantly
broadened the diversity of stakeholders in innovation networks, by integrating the capabilities of NGOs, local communities and government bodies
alongside universities, public research labs and private firms.

13.5   Sparseness

Most research on network evolution is concerned with the directly observable formation of ties in a network. However, one of the characteristics of
networks is that they are sparse: this means that compared to all the possible
ties that may be formed, only a few ties are actually realised (this is increasingly the case as networks grow) and as networks evolve existing ties are
often not sustained. To understand network evolution, we should also
unravel the factors that give rise to the lack or decay of ties, in effect taking
a negative image of the network. Technically, stochastic actor-based network
evolution models and agent-based simulation models (see Boxes 13.1 and
13.2) incorporate these dynamics in network evolution models and they are
increasingly employed in research.[6]

A balance between tie formation and tie decay, in terms of their intensity
and where they occur in the network, would sustain the existing network
structure. Imbalance, on the other hand, results in a network that diverges
from its existing structure. Some studies find that the rules governing tie
decay are quite different from those that govern tie formation (Rowley et al.,
2005). For example, in the case of biotechnology and pharmaceuticals, Sytch

---

[6] See, for example, Buchmann and Pyka (2013).

Box 13.1 Stochastic Actor-based Models

Stochastic actor-based models are increasingly used in analysing network evolution (Snijders, 1996; Snijders, van de Bunt and Steglich, 2010). These models are particularly useful when there are several observations on different states of a network, observed at regular intervals. Here 'long-term' refers to the number of observations or network waves. Snijders specifies that a minimum of two waves (and preferably more) are necessary for robust results. These models look at network change from one network wave to another, resulting in a range of observations on the evolution of the network. The Jaccard index can be used as a guideline to assess whether there is a significant change between one network wave and the next. This is represented by the following equation:

$$J = \frac{N_{11}}{N_{11} + N_{10} + N_{01}}$$

where N_{11} is the number of ties present at both waves, N_{01} the number of ties created in wave 1, and N_{10} the number of ties dissolved in wave 1 (Snijders, van de Bunt and Steglich, 2010). In this way, stochastic actor-based models directly allow the incorporation of tie decay in the models. The aim of stochastic actor-based models is to understand the significance of a range of factors affecting the evolution of a network. These factors can be related to actors' individual attributes, as well as to the earlier condition of the networks. For example, reciprocity, transitivity and homophily are some common factors used to explain the evolution of a network. Snijders and colleagues have developed the SIENA software to model network evolution using stochastic actor-based models.

---

and Tatarynowicz (2014) find that network evolution is likely to be governed by moving away from unbalanced triads, rather than new tie formation for balance.

In centralised networks, peripheral firms can be dependent on the core because of their low status in the network. At the same time, core firms are more flexible in connecting to the periphery as well as to other core members, as they have incentives to maintain their control over the network. In the long run, one explanation for the lack of further ties between periphery and core is that asymmetry may block peripheral firms from connecting to other members of the core in addition to their existing connections. For example, Ahuja, Polidoro and Mitchell (2009) showed that when the alliances between core and periphery firms are equity-based, central firms may abstain from forming links with peripheral firms that are already involved in alliances with other core firms. In this way, the peripheral firms' disadvantaged situations in the network can be sustained. Therefore the future evolution of a network can be determined not only by the existence or lack

Box 13.2 Agent-based Simulation Models

Agent-based simulation (ABS) models are commonly used to model complex adaptive systems. These models are based on the idea that to explain aggregate patterns, one must take into account the interactions between many heterogeneous actors and the way in which agents and networks co-evolve (Tesfatsion, 2001). ABS models have proved particularly fruitful in the case of network evolution, since they enable the feedback between nodes (agents) and the network they form to be modelled. It is possible to see how networks emerge and evolve as a consequence of actors' decisions, which in turn constrain and shape agents. In ABS models, data are created synthetically in a computer environment. In a typical ABS model, a number of 'agents' are created and allocated characteristics and decision-making rules, in accordance with the research question. For example, a range of ABS models looks at learning, adaptation and network structure. After a population of agents with certain tie formation and deletion rules are coded, simulation runs are performed. In subsequent periods, agents form or inhibit ties; as a result of these interactions, inherent characteristics or rules are updated. In network evolution ABS, networks evolve from the bottom up, permitting the analyst to see what kinds of rules, population characteristics, interaction rules and external and other factors govern the formation of different networks. Because the data are generated in a computer environment, the empirical validity of ABS (the extent to which the model is an appropriate representation of the real system) is a critical issue.

Further Reading

Axelrod, R. (2003). Advancing the Art of Simulation in the Social Sciences. Originally published in R. Conte, R. Hegselmann and P. Terna (eds) (1997). *Simulating Social Phenomena*. Berlin: Springer, 21–40.

Epstein, J. (1999). Agent-based Computational Models and Generative Social Science. *Complexity*, 4(5), 41.

Leigh Tesfatsion's Web page (see http://www2.econ.iastate.edu/tesfatsi/, accessed 8 July 2016) includes many useful resources for agent-based computational economics.

Özman, M. (2010). The Knowledge Base of Products: Implications for Organisational Structure. *Organisation Studies*, 31(8), 1129–54.

of ties but also by the types of ties that characterise it. For example, in the case of biotechnology and pharmaceuticals, the equity-based alliances in the initial phases gradually gave way to contractual R&D alliances in later phases, so that large pharmaceutical firms had flexibility without committing deeply to highly expensive and risky technologies whose ultimate performance was uncertain (Hagedoorn and Narula, 1996). This resulted in networks that became very dense over a short period of time.

As some of these examples show, certain factors tend to increase the density of networks. Uncertainty, industry growth and geographical clustering are the most straightforward. Industry growth implies new entrants in the network. Because larger networks tend to have lower density, the extent to which an industry network becomes denser depends on the rate of tie formation between existing firms as well as with new entrants. When the rate of entry is high compared to the tie formation rate, the network can become sparser. Geographical proximity is also a factor that tends to increase ties between organisations. On the face of it, firms located in industrial clusters have increased opportunities to form ties with each other; but there are other factors at work at the same time that increase the connections between firms in the cluster and those outside, which can ultimately stabilise, or even reduce, network density in a region.

Discussion Questions

1. Explain the following:
   a. Divergent network change
   b. Network churn.

2. What are the three structural regularities observed in large networks?

3. Find examples in which a network changes due to:
   a. A radical innovation
   b. Regulations
   c. A major scientific discovery.

4. Explain how self-reinforcement works in:
   a. Clustering
   b. Centrality.

5. Explain why radical (incremental) innovations are likely to trigger structure loosening (reinforcing) network change? Can you find counter-examples?

Appendix: *Network Surveys*

In social network analysis a name generator is used to collect the names of contacts in a person's network through a series of questions. Name interpreter questions can also be asked in addition, which constitute questions related with the attributes of contacts. In innovation studies friendship and advice network surveys are used to construct informal networks between actors. In addition, information on ties that foster generating new ideas, ties that support new initiatives, social support contacts, and buy-in ties can also be distinguished (Rodan and Galunic, 2004). Besides name generators, position generators are also used. These refer to questions in which positions deemed important in a society are ranked, and participants to the survey are asked whether they know anyone in each of these positions (Lin, 1999). In addition, more detailed questions about each of these contacts are asked. Further investigation of social network surveys can be found in Marsden (2005).

Example survey questions are shown in the table below, according to various properties of name generators.

Properties	Example Questions
Position generator	• 'Here is a list of jobs (show card). Would you please tell me if you happen to know someone (on a first-name basis) having each job?' (Lin, 1999)
Tie strength	• 'How close are you with each person?' (Reagans and McEvily, 2003) *Especially close* *Close* *Less than close* *Distant* • 'On average how often do you talk to each (any social or business discussion)?' (Reagans and McEvily, 2003) *Daily* *Weekly* *Monthly* *Less often*
Network perception	• 'The respondent reported his/her perception of the relationship between two pairs of contacts as "close," "neither close nor distant," or "distant." "Distant" was defined as "two individuals rarely work together, are strangers, or do not enjoy each other's company."' (Batagarjal et al., 2013) • 'Who would X consider to be a personal friend?' (Question is asked to each person, for all other persons separately.) (Kilduff et al., 2008)
Advice ties	• 'Please identify up to twenty people that are important in terms of providing you with information to do your work or helping you think about complex problems posed by your work. These may or may not be people you communicate with on a regular basis and can come from within [the organisation] or outside (e.g., clients, friends in other organisations, former work colleagues, family, etc.).' (Cross and Cummings, 2004) • (Advice in) 'Please indicate from whom in (organisation) you regularly sought advice or information to accomplish your work, independently from what the formal organisation suggests that you do. Please indicate your answer by placing a check on the code to the left of the name or names of people you see in the list below. If there are several people you sought out, then check these several names.' (Soda and Zaheer, 2012) • (Advice out) 'Please indicate who in (organisation) comes regularly to you for advice or information to accomplish their work, independently from what the formal organisation suggests that they do. Please indicate your answer by placing a check on the code to the left of the name or names of people you see in the list below. If there are several people who come to you, then check these several names.' (Soda and Zaheer, 2012) • 'Getting your job done on a daily basis as a manager often requires advice and information from others. Who are the key people who you regularly turn to for information and work related advice to enhance your ability to do your daily job?' (Rodan and Galunic, 2004)

(*cont.*)

Properties	Example Questions
Buy-in ties	• 'New ideas often require support from others without which you cannot proceed. Who are the key people that provide essential support to new initiatives?' (Rodan and Galunic, 2004) • 'Most people turn to others for support when they try to get something done in their organisation, such as implementing a new idea or changing a work procedure. Please write down the names, nicknames, or initials of all people whose support you can count on to move your ideas forward.' (Baer, 2012)
Friendship ties	• 'Consider your relation with each of your colleagues. Can you indicate in what sense you consider that relation as a "friendship relationship"?' [not at all – totally] (De Lange, Agneessens and Waege, 2004) • 'Which colleagues do you consider to be your personal friends?' (Zheng et al., 2010)

References

Abernathy, W., and K. B. Clark (1985). Mapping the Winds of Creative Destruction. *Research Policy*, 14, 3–22.

Abernathy, W. J., and J. M. Utterback (1978). Patterns of Industrial Innovation. *Technology Review*, 80(7), 40–7.

Adamic, L., O. Buyukkoten and E. Adar (2003). A Social Network Caught in the Web. *First Monday*, 8(6).

Agrawal, A., I. Cockburn and J. McHale (2006). Gone But Not Forgotten: Labor Flows, Knowledge Spillovers, and Enduring Social Capital. *Journal of Economic Geography*, 6(5), 571–91.

Ahn, Yong-Yeol, S. E. Ahnert, J. P. Bagrow and A. L. Barabási (2011). Flavour Network and the Principles of Food Pairing. Scientific Report, Scientific Reports 1, Article number: 196.

Ahuja, G. (2000). Collaboration Networks, Structural Holes and Innovation: A Longitudinal Study. *Administrative Science Quarterly*, 45(3), 425–53.

Ahuja, G., and R. Katila (2001). Technological Acquisitions and the Innovation Performance of Acquiring Firms: a Longitudinal Study. *Strategic Management Journal*, 22, 197–220.

Ahuja, G., and C. M. Lampert (2001). Entrepreneurship in Large Corporations: a Longitudinal Study of How Established Firms Create Breakthrough Inventions. *Strategic Management Journal*, 22, 521–43.

Ahuja, G., F. Polidoro and W. Mitchell (2009). Structural Homophily or Social Asymmetry? The Formation of Alliances by Poorly Embedded Firms. *Strategic Management Journal*, 30, 941–58.

Akerlof, G. (1970). The Market for 'Lemons': Quality Uncertainty and the Market Mechanism. *The Quarterly Journal of Economics*, 84(3), 488–500.

Alba, R. D. (1973). A Graph-theoretic Definition of a Sociometric Clique. *Journal of Mathematical Sociology*, 3, 113–26.

Aldrich, H. E., and M. C. Fiol (1994). Fools Rush In? The Institutional Context of Industry Creation. *Academy of Management Review*, 19, 645–70.

Aldrich, H., and C. Zimmer (1986). Entrepreneurship through Social Networks. In D. Sexton and R. Smilor (eds), *The Art and Science of Entrepreneurship*. Cambridge, MA: Ballinger, 3–23.

Allen, T. J., and S. I. Cohen (1969). Information Flow in Research and Development Laboratories. *Administrative Science Quarterly*, 14(1), 12–19.

Almeida, P., and B. Kogut (1999). Localization of Knowledge and the Mobility of Engineers in Regional Networks. *Management Science*, 45(7), 905–17.

Amabile, T. M. (1983). Social Psychology of Creativity: a Componential Conceptualization. *Journal of Personality and Social Psychology*, 45, 997–1013.

(1996). *Creativity in Context*. Boulder, CO: Westview Press.

Amabile, T., C. M. Fisher and J. Pillemer (2014). IDEO's Culture of Helping. *Harvard Business Review*, 92(1–2), 54–61.

Anand, B. N., and T. Khanna (2000). Do Firms Learn to Create Value? The Case of Alliances. *Strategic Management Journal*, 21(3), 295–315.

Aral, S., and M. Van Alstyne (2011). The Diversity-Bandwidth Tradeoff. *American Journal of Sociology*, 117(1), 90–171.

Aral, S., and D. Walker (2011). Creating Social Contagion through Viral Product Design: a Randomized Trial of Peer Influence in Networks. *Management Science*, 57(9), 1623–39.

Aral, S., L. Muchnik and A. Sundararajan (2009). Distinguishing Influence-based Contagion from Homophily-driven Diffusion in Dynamic Networks. *Proceedings of the National Academy of Sciences*, 10, 21544–9.

Arndt, M. (2006). 3M's Seven Pillars of Innovation. *Bloomberg Businessweek*. 9 May 2006.

Arthur, B. (1989). Competing Technologies: Increasing Returns and Lock in by Historical Events. *The Economic Journal*, 99, 116–31.

(1990). Positive Feedbacks in the Economy. *Scientific American*, 262, 92.

Arthur, W. B. (1996). Increasing Returns and the New World of Business. *Harvard Business Review*, July–August 74(4), 100–9.

(2009). *The Nature of Technology: What it is and How it Evolves*. New York, NY: The Free Press.

Arthur, W. B., S. N. Durlauf and D. A. Lane (eds) (1997). *The Economy as an Evolving Complex System II*. Santa Fe Institute Studies in the Science of Complexity, Vol. XXVII. Reading, MA: Addison-Wesley.

Arundel, A., and I. Kabla (1998). What Percentage of Innovations are Patented? Empirical Estimates for European Firms. *Research Policy*, 27, 127–41.

Audretsch, D., and M. P. Feldman (1996). Innovative Clusters and the Industry Life Cycle. *Review of Industrial Organization*, 11(2), 253–73.

Axtell, C. M., D. J. Holman, K. L. Unsworth, T. D. Wall, P. E. Waterson and E. Harrington (2000). Shopfloor Innovation: Facilitating the Suggestion and Implementation of Ideas. *Journal of Occupational and Organizational Psychology*, 73, 265–85.

Baer, M. (2012). Putting Creativity to Work: the Implementation of Creative Ideas in Organizations. *Academy of Management Journal*, 55(5), 1102–19.

Baker, W. (2000). *Achieving Success through Social Capital: Tapping the Hidden Resources in Your Personal and Business Networks*. San Francisco, CA: Jossey-Bass.

Baker, W. E., and R. R. Faulkner (2002). Interorganisational Networks. In J. A. C. Baum (ed.), *The Blackwell Companion to Organisations*, Oxford: Blackwell, 520–40.

Bakshy, E., J. M. Hofman, W. A. Mason and D. J. Watts (2011). Everyone's an Influencer: Quantifying Influence on Twitter. WSDM '11 Proceedings of the Fourth ACM International Conference on Web Search and Data Mining, 65–74.

Balconi, M., S. Breschi and F. Lissoni (2004). Networks of Inventors and Role of Academia: an Exploration of Italian Patent Data. *Research Policy*, 33, 127–45.

Baldwin, C. Y., and K. B. Clark (1997). Managing in the Age of Modularity. *Harvard Business Review*, Sept/Oct, 81–93.

Balland, P. A., R. Boschma and K. Frenken (2015). Proximity and Innovation: From Statics to Dynamics. *Regional Studies*, 49(6), 907–20.

Balland, P. A., M. de Vaan and R. Boschma (2013). The Dynamics of Interfirm Networks along the Industry Life Cycle: the Case of the Global Video Game Industry 1987–2007. *Journal of Economic Geography*, 13(5), 741–65.

Balogun, J., J. Bartunek and B. Do (2015). Senior Managers' Sensemaking and Responses to Strategic Change. *Organisation Science*, 26(4), 960–79.

Banerjee, Abhijit V. (1992). A Simple Model of Herd Behavior. *The Quarterly Journal of Economics*, 107(3), 797–817.

Barabasi, A. (2002). *Linked: the New Science of Networks*, Cambridge, MA: Perseus.

Barabasi, A. L., and R. Albert (1999). Emergence of Scaling in Random Networks. *Science*, 286, 509–12.

Barley, S. R. (1986). Technology as an Occasion for Structuring: Evidence from Observations of CT Scanners and the Social Order of Radiology Departments. *Administrative Science Quarterly*, 31(1), 78–108.

Barnes, J. A. (1979). Network Analysis: Orienting Notion, Rigorous Technique, or Substantive Field of Study? In P. W. Holland and S. Leinhardt (eds), *Perspectives on Social Network Analysis*. New York, NY: Academic, 403–23.

Baron, R. S., and N. L. Kerr (2003). *Group Process, Group Decision, Group Action*. Buckingham, PA: Open University Press.

Basalla, G. (1988). *The Evolution of Technology*. Cambridge University Press.

Basberg, Bjorn, L. (1987). Patents and the Measurement of Technological Change: A Survey of the Literature. *Research Policy*, 16(2–4), 131–41.

Bass, Frank M. (1969). A New Product Growth Model for Consumer Durables. *Management Science*, 15 (January), 215–27.

Batagelj, V. (2003). Efficient Algorithms for Citation Network Analysis. arXiv: cs/ 0309023.

Batjargal, B., M. A. Hitt, A. S. Tsui, J. L. Arregle, J. W. Webb and T. L. Miller (2013). Institutional Polycentrism, Entrepreneurs' Social Networks, and New Venture Growth. *Academy of Management Journal*, 56(4), 1024–49.

Battilana, Julie, and Tiziana Casciaro (2012). Change Agents, Networks, and Institutions: a Contingency Theory of Organisational Change. *Academy of Management Journal*, 55(2), 381–98.

(2013). Overcoming Resistance to Organisational Change: Strong Ties and Affective Cooptation. *Management Science*, 59(4), 819–36.

Baum, J. A. C., and Paul Ingram (2002). Interorganisational Learning and Network Organisations: Toward a Behavioral Theory of the 'Interfirm'. In Mie Augier and James G. March (eds), *The Economics of Choice, Change, and Organisation: Essays in Memory of Richard M. Cyert*. Cheltenham UK: Edward Elgar.

Baum, J. A. C., and C. Oliver (1992). Institutional Embeddedness and the Dynamics of Organisational Populations. *American Sociological Review*, 57, 540–59.

Baum, J., and T. Rowley (2008). Introduction: Evolving Webs in Network Economies. In Joel A. C. Baum and Timothy J. Rowley (eds), *Network Strategy*. Bingley, UK: Emerald Publishing, xiii–xxxii.

Baum, J. A. C., and Jitendra V. Singh (1994). Organizational Niches and the Dynamics of Organizational Mortality. *American Journal of Sociology*, 94, 346–80.

Baum, J., T. Rowley, A. Shipilov and You-Ta Chuang (2005). Dancing with Strangers; Aspiration Performance and the Search for Underwriting Syndicate Partners. *Administrative Science Quarterly*, 50(4), 536–76.

Baum, J. A., A. V. Shipilov and T. J. Rowley (2003). Where Do Small Worlds Come From? *Industrial and Corporate Change*, 12(4), 697–725.

Bazerman, M., and Dolly Chugh (2006). Decisions Without Blinders. *Harvard Business Review*, 84(1), 88–97.

Becker, M. C. (2004). Organisational Routines: a Review of the Literature. *Industrial and Corporate Change*, 13, 643–78.

Becker, M. H. (1970). Sociometric Location and Innovativeness: Reformulation and Extension of the Diffusion Model. *American Sociological Review*, 35, 267–82.

Beckman, C., P. Haunschild and D. Phillips (2004). Friends or Strangers? Firm-specific Uncertainty, Market Uncertainty, and Network Partner Selection. *Organisation Science*, 15, 259–75.

Beckman, C. M., C. B. Schoonhoven, R. M. Rottner and S. J. Kim (2014). Relational Pluralism in De Novo Organizations: Boards of Directors as Bridges or Barriers to Diverse Alliance Portfolios? *Academy of Management Journal*, 57(2), 460–83.

Bekkers, R., G. Duysters and B. Verspagen (2002). Intellectual Property Rights, Strategic Technology Agreements and Market Structure: the Case of GSM. *Research Policy*, 31(7), 1141–61.

Belderbos, R., M. Carre and B. Lokshin (2004). Cooperative R&D and Firm Performance. *Research Policy*, 33, 1477–92.

Benner, Mary J., and Michael Tushman (2002). Process Management and Technological Innovation: a Longitudinal Study of the Photography and Paint Industries. *Administrative Science Quarterly*, 47, 676–706.

Benyus, J. (1997). *Biomimicry*, New York, NY: William Morrow.

Bessant, J. (2008). Dealing with Discontinuous Innovation: the European Experience. *International Journal of Technology Management*, 42(1/2), 36–50.

Bettencourt, L. M. A., J. Lobob and D. Strumsky (2007). Invention in the City: Increasing Returns to Patenting as a Scaling Function of Metropolitan Size. *Research Policy*, 36(1), 1071.

Bian, Y., and L. Zhangs (2014). Corporate Social Capital in Chinese Guanxi Culture. *Research in the Sociology of Organisations*, 40, 417–39.

Bikhchandani, S., D. Hirshleifer and I. Welch (1992). A Theory of Fads, Fashion, Custom, and Cultural Change as Informational Cascade. *Journal of Political Economy*, 100, 992–1026.

Billington, C., and R. Davidson (2010). Using Knowledge Brokering to Improve Business Processes. McKinsey Quarterly, January, 110–12.

Boari, Cristina, and Federico Riboldazzi (2014). How Knowledge Brokers Emerge and Evolve: the Role of Actors' Behaviour. *Research Policy*, 43(4), 683–95.

Bollinger, B., and K. Gillingham (2012). Peer Effects in the Diffusion of Solar Photovoltaic Panels. *Marketing Science*, 31(6), 900–12.

Bonacich, P. (1972). Factoring and Weighting Approaches to Clique Identification. *Journal of Mathematical Sociology*, 2, 113–20.

(1987). Power and Centrality: a Family of Measures. *American Journal of Sociology*, 92, 1170–82.

Bordia, P., E. Hunt, N. Paulsen, D. Tourish and N. DiFonzo (2004). Uncertainty during Organisational Change: Is it All about Control? *European Journal of Work and Organisational Psychology*, 13, 345–65.

Borgatti, S. P. (2005). Centrality and Network Flow. *Social Networks*, 27(1), 55–71.

(2006). Identifying Sets of Key Players in a Network. *Computational, Mathematical and Organisational Theory*, 12(1), 21–34.

Borgatti, S. P., and R. Cross (2003). A Relational View of Information Seeking and Learning in Social Networks. *Management Science*, 49(4), 432–45.

Borgatti, S. P., and M. G. Everett (1997). Network Analysis of 2-Mode Data. *Social Networks*, 19(3), 243–69.

Borgatti, S. P., and P. C. Foster (2003). The Network Paradigm in Organisational Research: a Review and Typology. *Journal of Management*, 29, 991–1013.

Borgatti, S., and D. S. Halgin (2011a). Analysing Affiliation Networks. In J. Scott and P. J. Carrington (eds), *The Sage Handbook of Social Network Analysis*. Cornwall: MPG Books Group, 417–33.

(2011b). On Network Theory. *Organisation Science*, 22(5), 1168–81.

Borgatti, S. P., D. J. Brass and D. S. Halgin (2014). Social Network Research: Confusions, Criticisms, and Controversies. In D. J. Brass, G. Labianca, A. Mehra, D. S. Halgin and S. P. Borgatti (eds), *Research in the Sociology of Organisations*, Volume 40. Bingley, UK: Emerald Publishing.

Borgatti, S. P., M. G. Everett and J. C. Johnson (2013). *Analyzing Social Networks*. UK: Sage Publications.

Boschma, R. (2005). Proximity and Innovation: a Critical Assessment. *Regional Studies*, 39(1), 61–74.

Brands, R. A. (2013). Cognitive Social Structures in Social Network Research: a Review. *Journal of Organisational Behaviour*, 34, 82–103.

Brass, D. J. (1984). Being in the Right Place: a Structural Analysis of Individual Influence in an Organisation. *Administrative Science Quarterly*, 29, 519–39.

(1992). Power in Organisations: a Social Network Perspective. In G. Moore and J. A. Whitt (eds), *Research in Politics and Society*. Greenwich, CT: JAI Press, 295–323.

Brass, D. J., J. Galaskiewicz, H. R. Greve and W. Tsai (2004). Taking Stock of Networks and Organisations: a Multilevel Perspective. *Academy of Management Journal*, 47(6), 795–817.

Brass, D. J., G. Labianca, A. Mehra, D. S. Halgin and S. P. Borgatti (eds) (2014). *Research in the Sociology of Organisations,* Volume 40: Contemporary Perspectives in Organisational Social Networks. Bingley, UK: Emerald Publishing.

Breschi, S., and C. Catalini (2010). Tracing the Links between Science and Technology: an Exploratory Analysis of Scientists' and Inventors' Networks. *Research Policy*, 39(1), 14–26.

Breschi, S., and F. Lissoni (2004). Knowledge Networks from Patent Data: Methodological Issues and Research Targets. In H. Moed, W. Glänzel and U. Schmoch (eds), *Handbook of Quantitative S&T Research*, Dordrecht, Netherlands: Kluwer Academic Publishers.

(2009). Mobility of Inventors and Networks of Collaboration: an Anatomy of Localised Knowledge Flows. *Journal of Economic Geography*, 9(4), 439–68.

Breschi, S., F. Lissoni and F. Malerba (2003). Knowledge-relatedness in Firm Technological Diversification. *Research Policy*, 32, 69–87.

Brock, M., and S. Durlauf (2000). Interactions Based Models. National Bureau of Economic Research Working Papers No. 0258.

Broekel, T., and R. Boschma (2011). Aviation, Space or Aerospace? Exploring the Knowledge Networks of Two Industries in the Netherlands. *European Planning Studies*, 19(7), 1205–27.

Broekel, T., and H. Graf (2010). Structural Properties of Cooperation Networks in Germany: From Basic to Applied Research. Jena Economic Research Papers, No. 2010,078.

Buchmann, T., and A. Pyka (2013). The Evolution of Innovation Networks: the Case of a German Automotive Network. FZID Discussion Papers, No. 70–2013.

Burkhardt, M. E. (1994). Social Interaction Effects following a Technological Change: a Longitudinal Investigation. *Academy of Management Journal*, 37, 869–98.

Burkhardt, M. E., and D. J. Brass (1990). Changing Patterns or Patterns of Change: the Effect of a Change in Technology on Social Network Structure and Power. *Administrative Science Quarterly*, 35, 104–27.

Burt, R. S. (1976). Positions in Networks. *Social Forces*, 55(1), 93–122.

(1984). Network Items and the General Social Survey. *Social Networks*, 6(4), 293–339.

(1987). Social Contagion and Innovation: Cohesion versus Structural Equivalence. *American Journal of Sociology*, 92(May), 1287–335.

(1992). *Structural Holes: the Social Structure of Competition*. Cambridge, MA: Harvard University Press.

(1997). A Note on Social Capital and Network Content. *Social Networks*, 19(4), 355–73.

(1999). The Social Capital of Opinion Leaders, *The Annals of the American Academy of Political and Social Science*, 566(1), 37–54.

(2000). The Network Structure of Social Capital. *Research in Organisational Behavior*, 22, 345–423.

(2002). Bridge Decay. *Social Networks*, 24, 333–63.

(2004). Structural Holes and Good Ideas. *American Journal of Sociology*, 110(2), 349–99.

(2005). *Brokerage and Closure: an Introduction to Social Capital*. Oxford University Press.

(2012). Network-related Personality and the Agency Question: Multirole Evidence from a Virtual World. *American Journal of Sociology*, 118(3), 543–91.

Burt, R. S., and M. Knez (1995). Kinds of Third-Party Effects on Trust. *Rationality and Society*, 7(3), 255–92.

Burt, R. S., and J. L. Merluzzi (2014). Embedded Brokerage: Hubs Versus Locals. In D. J. Brass, G. Labianca, A. Mehra, D. S. Halgin and S. P. Borgatti (eds), *Research in the Sociology of Organisations*, Volume 40. Bingley, UK: Emerald Publishing Group, 161–77.

Burt, R. S., Joseph E. Jannotta and James T. Mahoney (1998). Personality Correlates of Structural Holes. *Social Networks*, 20(1), 63–87.

Cain, S. (2012). *Quiet: The Power of Introverts in a World that Can't Stop Talking*. New York, NY: Crown Publishers.

Caldwell, D., and C. O'Reilly (1982). Responses to Failure: the Effects of Choice and Responsibility on Impression Management. *Academy of Management Journal*, 25, 121–36.

Callon, M. (1991). Techno-economic Networks and Irreversibility. In J. Law (ed.), *A Sociology of Monsters? Essays on Power, Technology and Domination*, Sociological Review Monograph. London: Routledge, 132–61.

Camagni, R. (ed.) (1991). *Innovation Networks: Spatial Perspectives.* London, UK: Belhaven Press.

Cantner, U., and H. Graft (2006). The Network of Innovators in Jena: an Application of Social Network Analysis. *Research Policy*, 35(4), 463–80.

Carley, Kathleen M., and Dean Behrens (1999). Organisational and Individual Decision Making. In A. P. Sage and W. B. Rouse (eds), *Handbook of Systems Engineering and Management.* Hoboken, NJ: John Wiley and Sons, Inc.

Carnabuci, G., and J. P. Bruggeman (2009). Knowledge Specialization, Knowledge Brokerage, and the Uneven Growth of Technology Domains. *Social Forces*, 88(2), 607–41.

Carpenter, M. A., and J. D. Westphal (2001). The Impact of Director Appointments on Board Involvement in Strategic Decision Making. *Academy of Management Journal*, 44, 639–60.

Cartwright, D., and F. Harary (1956). Structural Balance: a Generalization of Heider's Theory. *Psychological Review*, 63, 277–92.

Casciaro, T. (1998). Seeing Things Clearly: Social Structure, Personality, and Accuracy in Social Network Perception. *Social Network*, 20, 331–51.

Casciaro, T., and M. S. Lobo (2005). Competent Jerks, Lovable Fools and the Formation of Social Networks. *Harvard Business Review*, June, 2–99.

(2008). When Competence is Irrelevant: the Role of Interpersonal Affect in Task-related Ties. *Administrative Science Quarterly*, 53, 655–84.

Cassi, L., and A. Plunket (2015). Research Collaboration in Co-Inventor Networks: Combining Closure, Bridging and Proximities. *Regional Studies*, 49(6), 936–54.

Cassi, L., and L. Zirulia (2008). The Opportunity Cost of Social Relations: on the Effectiveness of Small Worlds. *Journal of Evolutionary Economics*, 18, 77–101.

Cattani, G., and S. Ferriani (2008). A Core/Periphery Perspective on Individual Creative Performance: Social Networks and Cinematic Achievements in the Hollywood Film Industry. *Organisation Science*, 19(6), 824–44.

Cecere, G., and M. Özman (2014). Technological Diversity and Inventor Networks. *Economics of Innovation and New Technology*, 23(2), 161–78.

Cecere, G., N. Corrocher, C. Gossart and M. Özman (2014). Technological Pervasiveness and Variety of Innovators in Green ICT: a Paten-based Analysis. *Reseach Policy*, 43(1), 1827–39.

Centola, D., and M. W. Macy (2007). Complex Contagions and the Weakness of Long Ties. *American Journal of Sociology*, 113, 702–34.

Cha, M., H. Haddadi, F. Benevenuto and K. P. Gummad (2010). Measuring User Influence on Twitter: The Million Follower Fallacy. Proceedings of the 4th International AAAI Conference on Weblogs and Social Media, Washington, DC.

Chesbrough, H. (2003). *Open Innovation: the New Imperative for Creating and Profiting from Technology.* Boston, MA: Harvard Business School Press.

Choi, T. Y., and D. R. Krause (2006). The Supply Base and its Complexity: Implications for Transaction Costs, Risks, Responsiveness, and Innovation. *Journal of Operations Management*, 24, 637–52.

Christensen, C. M. (1997). *The Innovator's Dilemma: When New Technologies Cause Great Firms to Fail.* Boston, MA: Harvard Business School Press.

Chung, A., H. Singh and K. Lee (2000). Complementarity, Status Similarity and Social Capital as Drivers of Alliance Formation. *Strategic Management Journal*, 21, 1–22.

Cialdini, R. B. (1989). Indirect Tactics of Impression Management: Beyond Basking. In R. A. Giacalone and P. Rosenfeld (eds), *Impression Management in the Organization*. Hillsdale, NJ: Erlbaum, 45–56.

(2003). Crafting Normative Messages to Protect the Environment. *Current Directions in Psychological Science*, 12, 105–9.

Cialdini, R. B., R. J. Borden, A. Thorne, M. R. Walker, S. Freeman and L. R. Sloan (1976). Basking in Reflected Glory: Three (Football) Field Studies. *Journal of Personality and Social Psychology*, 34, 366–75.

Clark, K. B. and T. Fujimoto (1991). *Product Development Performance: Strategy, Organization and Management in the World Auto Industry*. Boston, MA: Harvard Business School Press.

Cloodt, M., J. Hagedoorn and N. Roijakkers (2006). Trends and Patterns in Interfirm R&D Networks in the Global Computer Industry: an Analysis of Major Developments, 1970–1999, *Business History Review*, 80(4), 725.

Cohen, D., and L. Prusak (2001). *In Good Company: How Social Capital Makes Organisations Work*. Boston, MA: Harvard Business School Press.

Cohen, W. M., and D. A. Levinthal (1989). Innovation and Learning: the Two Faces of R & D. *The Economic Journal*, 99, 569–96.

(1990). Absorptive Capacity: a New Perspective on Learning and Innovation, *Administrative Science Quarterly*, 35, 128–52.

Coleman, J. A. (1986). Social Theory, Social Research, and a Theory of Action. *The American Journal of Sociology*, 91(6), 1309–35.

(1988). Social Capital in the Creation of Human Capital. *American Journal of Sociology*, 94, 95–120.

Coleman, J. S., E. Katz and H. Menzel (1966). *Medical Innovation: a Diffusion Study*. New York, NY: Bobbs-Merrill.

Congdon, C., D. Flynn and M. Redman (2014). Balancing 'We' and 'Me': The Best Collaborative Spaces also Support Solitude. *Harvard Business Review* (October).

Contractor, Farok J., and Ra Wonchan (2002). How Knowledge Attributes Influence Alliance Governance Choices. *Journal of International Management*, 8, 11–27.

Contractor, Noshir S., Stanley Wasserman and Katherine Faust (2006). Testing Multi-theoretical Multilevel Hypotheses about Organizational Networks: an Analytic Framework and Empirical Example. *Academy of Management Review*, 31(3), 681–703.

Coulter, Robin, Lawrence Feick and Linda L. Price (2002). Changing Faces: Cosmetics Opinion Leadership among Women in the New Hungary. *European Journal of Marketing*, 36(11/12), 1287–308.

Cowan, R., and N. Jonard (2003). The Dynamics of Collective Invention. *Journal of Economic Behaviour and Organisation*, 52(4), 513–32.

(2004). Network Structure and Diffusion of Knowledge. *Journal of Economic Dynamics and Control*, 8(28), 1557–75.

(2009). Edge Portfolios and the Organisation of Innovation Networks. *Academy of Management Review*, 34(2), 320–42.

Cowan, R., N. Jonard and M. Özman (2004). Knowledge Dynamics in a Network Industry. *Technological Forecasting and Social Change*, 71(5), 469–84.

Cramer, J. M., S. Parise and R. Cross (2007). Managing Change through Networks and Values: How a Relational View of Culture Can Facilitate Large Scale Change. *California Management Review*, 49(3), 85–109.

Crane, D. (1969). Social Structure in a Group of Scientists: a Test of the 'Invisible College' Hypothesis. *American Sociological Review*, 34, 335–52.

Cross, R., and J. N. Cummings (2004). Tie and Network Correlates of Individual Performance in Knowledge Intensive Work. *Academy of Management Journal*, 47(6), 928–37.

Cross, R., and A. Parker (2004). *The Hidden Power of Social Networks*. Boston, MA: Harvard Business Review Press.

Cross, R., C. Ernst and W. Pasmore (2013). A Bridge Too Far? How Boundary Spanning Networks Drive Organizational Change and Effectiveness. *Organizational Dynamics*, 42(2), 81–91.

Cross, R., N. Nohria and A. Parker (2002). Six Myths about Informal Networks – and How to Overcome Them. *Sloan Management Review* (Spring).

Cross, R,, Stephen P. Borgatti and Andrew Parker (2001). Beyond Answers: Dimensions of the Advice Network. *Social Networks*, 23, 215–35.

Cross, R., A. Parker and L. Sasson (2003). *Networks in the Knowledge Economy*. Oxford University Press.

Cross, R., R. Thomas and D. Light (2009). How 'Who You Know' Affects What You Decide. *MIT Sloan Management Review*, 50(2), 35–42.

Crowston, K., and J. Howison (2005). The Social Structure of Free and Open Source Software Development. *First Monday*, available at http://firstmonday.org/article/view/1207/1127, accessed 15 July 2016.

Csikszentmihályi, M. (1996). *Creativity: Flow and the Psychology of Discovery and Invention*. New York, NY: Harper Collins.

(1999). Implications of a Systems Perspective for the Study of Creativity. In R. J. Sternberg (ed.), *Handbook of Creativity*. New York, NY: Cambridge University Press, 313–35.

Cyert, R. M., and J. March (1963). *A Behavioral Theory of the Firm*. Englewood Cliffs, NJ: Prentice Hall.

Dacin, M. T., C. Oliver and J-P. Roy (2007). The Legitimacy of Strategic Alliances: Institutional Perspective. *Strategic Management Journal*, 28(2), 169–87.

Daft, Richard L., and Karl E. Weick (1984). Toward a Model of Organisations as Interpretation Systems. *Academy of Management Review*, 9, 284–95.

Dahlin, K. B., and D. M. Behrens (2005). When Is an Invention Really Radical? Defining and Measuring Technological Radicalness. *Research Policy*, 34(5), 717–37.

Damanpour, F. (1988). Innovation Type, Radicalness, and the Adoption Process. *Communication Research*, 15, 545–67.

Darr, E. D., and T. R. Kurtzberg (2000). An Investigation of Partner Similarity Dimensions on Knowledge Transfer. *Organisational Behavior and Human Decision Processes*, 82(1), 28–44.

Das, T. K. (ed.) (2012). *Management Dynamics in Strategic Alliances*. Charlotte, NC: Information Age Publishing.

Das, T. K., and R. Kumar (2007). Learning Dynamics in the Alliance Development Process. *Management Decision*, 45(4), 684–707.

Das, T. K., and B. Teng (1998). Between Trust and Control: Developing Confidence in Partner Cooperation in Alliances. *Academy of Management Review*, 23(3), 491–512.

(2002). The Dynamics of Alliance Conditions in the Alliance Development Process. *Journal of Management Studies*, 39, 725–46.

David, Paul A. (1966). The Mechanization of Reaping in the Ante-Bellum Midwest. In Henry Rosovsky (ed.), *Industrialization in Two Systems: Essays in Honor of Alexander Gerschenkron*. New York, NY: John Wiley and Sons, 3–39.

(1985). Clio and the Economics of QWERTY. *American Economic Review*, 75, 332–7.

Davis, G. F. (1991). Agents without Principles? The Spread of the Poison Pill through the Intercorporate Network. *Administrative Science Quarterly*, 36, 583–613.

Davis, G. F., M. Yoo and W. E. Baker (2003). The Small World of the American Corporate Elite, 1991–2001. *Strategic Organization*, 1, 301–36.

Davis, James (1963). Structural Balance, Mechanical Solidarity, and Interpersonal Relations. *American Journal of Sociology*. 68(4), 444–62.

De Lange, D., F. Agneessens and H. Waege (2004). Asking Social Network Questions: a Quality Assessment of Different Measures. *Metodološki zvezki*, 1(2), 351–78.

De Leeuw, T., B. Lokshin and G. Duysters (2014). Returns to Alliance Portfolio Diversity: the Relative Effects of Partner Diversity on Firms' Innovative Performance and Productivity. *Journal of Business Research*, 67(9), 1839–49.

De Stefano, Domenico, and Susanna Zaccarin (2013). Modelling Multiple Interactions in Science and Technology Networks. *Industry and Innovation*, 20(3), 221–40.

De Tarde, Jean Gabriel (1890 (2003)). *Les Lois De L'imitation: Étude Sociologique*. (1890, Felix Alcan Publishing) Reprinted 2003, North Charleston, SC: Booksurge Publishing.

Dhanaraj, C., and A. Parkhe (2006). Orchestrating Innovation Networks. *Academy of Management Review*, 31(3), 659–69.

Digman, J. M. (1990). Personality Structure: Emergence of the Five-factor Model. *Annual Review of Psychology*, 41, 417–40.

Dillon, D. (2001). A Review of CIMIT: an Interdisciplinary, Inter-Institutional Enterprise. GoodWork Project Report Series, No. 23: Internal working paper prepared for the Harvard Interdisciplinary Studies Project.

DiMaggio, P., and W. Powell (1983). The Iron Cage Revisited: Institutional Isomorphism and Collective Rationality in Organisational Fields. *American Sociological Review*, 48, 147–60.

Dittrich, K., and G. M. Duysters (2007). Networking as a Means to Strategy Change: the Case of Open Innovation in Mobile Telephony. *Journal of Product Innovation Management*, 24(6), 510–21.

Dittrich, K., G. Duysters and A.-P. de Man (2007). Strategic Repositioning by Means of Alliance Networks: the Case of IBM. *Research Policy*, 36(10), 1496–511.

Dizikes, P. (2011). The Office Next Door: Casual Conversations among Colleagues Can Prove Surprisingly Fruitful. *MIT Technology Review*, 25 October 2011 (see www.technologyreview.com/s/425881/the-office-next-door/, accessed 7 July 2016).

Dodds, P. S., R. Muhamad and D. J. Watts (2003). An Experimental Study of Search in Global Social Networks. *Science*, 301, 827–9.

Dodgson, M., D. Gann and A. Salter (2006). The Role of Technology in the Shift Towards Open Innovation: the Case of Procter & Gamble. *R&D Management*, 36(3), 333–46.

Dolfsma, W., and L. Leydesdorff (2011). Innovation Systems as Patent Networks: the Netherlands, India and Nanotech. *Innovation-Management, Policy and Practice*, 13(3), 311–26.

Doreian, P., and F. N. Stokman (1997). *Evolution of Social Networks*. Amsterdam: Gordon and Breach Publishers.

Doreian, P., and K. L. Woodard (1992). Fixed List Versus Snowball Sampling. *Social Science Research*, 21, 216–33.

  (1994). Defining and Locating Cores and Boundaries of Social Networks. *Social Networks*, 16, 267–93.

Dosi, G. (1988). Sources, Procedures and Microeconomic Effects of Innovation. *Journal of Economic Literature*, 26, 1120–71.

Dosi, G., and L. Marengo (2007). On the Evolutionary and Behavioral Theories of Organizations: a Tentative Roadmap. *Organisation Science*, 18, 491–502.

Dosi, G., and R. Nelson (1994). An Introduction to Evolutionary Theories in Economics. *Journal of Evolutionary Economics*, 4(3), 153–72.

Dougherty, D. (1992). Interpretive Barriers to Successful Product Innovation in Large Firms. *Organisation Science*, 3, 179–202.

Duan, L., Emily Sheeren and Leigh M. Weiss (2014). Tapping the Power of Hidden Influencers. *McKinsey Quarterly*, 18 March 2014, 1, 116–20.

Duysters, G. M., and A. P. De Man (2003). Transitory Alliances: an Instrument for Surviving Turbulent Industries? *R&D Management*, 33(1), 49–58.

Duysters, G. M., and C. E. A. V. Lemmens (2003). Alliance Group Formation: Enabling and Constraining Effects of Embeddedness and Social Capital in Strategic Technology Alliance Networks. *International Studies of Management and Organisation*, 33(Summer), 49–68.

Duysters, G., and B. Lokshin (2011). Determinants of Alliance Portfolio Complexity and Its Effect on Innovative Performance of Companies. *Journal of Product Innovation Management*, 28, 570–85.

Duysters, G., K. H. Heimeriks, B. Lokshin, E. Meijer and A. Sabidussi (2012). Do Firms Learn to Manage Alliance Portfolio Diversity? The Diversity-performance Relationship and the Moderating Effects of Experience and Capability. *European Management Review*, 9(3), 139–52.

Dyer, Jeffrey H., and Kentaro Nobeoka (2000). Creating and Managing a High-performance Knowledge-sharing Network: the Toyota Case. *Strategic Management Journal*, 21, 345–67.

Dyer, Jeffrey H., and Harbir Singh (1998). The Relational View: Cooperative Strategy and Sources of Interorganisational Competitive Advantage. *Academy of Management Review*, 23(4), 660–79.

Edquist, C. (ed.) (1997). *Systems of Innovation: Technologies, Institutions and Organizations*. London: Pinter Publishers/Cassell Academic.

Elfring, T., and W. Hulsink (2007). Networking by Entrepreneurs: Patterns of Tie Formation in Emerging Organisations. *Organisation Studies*, 28/12, 1849–72.

Ellison, N. B., and D. Boyd (2013). Sociality through Social Network Sites. In W. H. Dutton (ed.), *The Oxford Handbook of Internet Studies*. Oxford University Press, 151–72.

Emirbayer, M., and J. Goodwin (1994). Network Analysis, Culture, and the Problem of Agency. *American Journal of Sociology*, 6, 1411–54.

Ernst, H. (2003). Patent Information for Strategic Technology Management. *World Patent Information*, 25(3), 233–42.

Faems, D., M. Janssens and B. Van Looy (2010). Managing the Cooperation-competition Dilemma in R&D Alliances: a Multiple Case Study in the Advanced Materials Industry. *Creativity and Innovation Management Journal*, 19(1), 3–22.

Fagerberg, J. (2004). Innovation: a Guide to the Literature. In J. Fagerberg, D. C. Mowery and R. R. Nelson (eds), *The Oxford Handbook of Innovation*. Oxford University Press, 1–26.

Fagerberg, J., and B. Verspagen (2009). Innovation Studies: the Emerging Structure of a New Scientific Field. *Research Policy*, 38, 218–33.

Fagerberg, J., M. Fosaasa and K. Sappraserta (2012). Innovation: Exploring the Knowledge Base. *Research Policy*, 41(7), 1132–53.

Farrell, J. and G. Saloner (1985). Standardization, Compatibility, and Innovation. *Rand Journal of Economics*, 16, 70–83.

Feick, L. F., and L. L. Price (1987). The Market Maven: a Diffuser of Market Information. *Journal of Marketing*, 51, 83–97.

Feld, S. L. (1981). The Focused Organisation of Social Ties. *The American Journal of Sociology*, 86(5), 1015–35.

Feldman, M. S. (2000). Organizational Routines as a Source of Continuous Change. *Organisation Science*, 11(6), 611–29.

Feldman, M., and J. March (1981). Information as Signal and Symbol. *Administrative Science Quarterly*, 26, 171–86.

Feldman, M. S., and B. T. Pentland (2003). Reconceptualizing Organisational Routines as a Source of Flexibility and Change. *Administrative Science Quarterly*, 48(1), 94–118.

Fernandez, R. M., and R. V. Gould (1994). A Dilemma of State Power: Brokerage and Influence in the National Health Policy Domain. *American Journal of Sociology*, 99, 1455–91.

Festinger, L. (1950). Informal Social Communication. *Psychological Review*, 57(5), 271–82.

(1954). A Theory of Social Comparison Processes. *Human Relations*, 7, 117–40.

Fleming, L. (2001). Recombinant Uncertainty in Technological Search Management. *Science*, 47(1), 117.

(2002). Finding the Organisational Sources of Technological Breakthroughs: the Story of Hewlett-Packard's Thermal Ink-jet. *Industrial and Corporate Change*, 11(5), 1059–84.

Fleming, L., and K. Frenken (2007). The Evolution of Inventor Networks in the Silicon Valley and Boston Regions, *Advances in Complex Systems*, 10(1), 53–71.

Fleming, L., and M. Marx (2006). Managing Creativity in Small Worlds. *California Management Review*, 48(4), 6–27.

Fleming, L., and O. Sorenson (2003). Navigating the Technology Landscape of Innovation. *MIT Sloan Management Review*, 44(2), 15–23.

Fleming, L., and D. M. Waguespack (2007). Brokerage, Boundary Spanning, and Leadership in Open Innovation Communities. *Organisation Science*, 18(2), 165–80.

Fleming, L., C. King and A. Juda (2007). Small Worlds and Regional Innovation. *Organisation Science*, 18(2), 938–54.

Fleming, L., S. Mingo and D. Chen (2007). Collaborative Brokerage, Generative Creativity, and Creative Success. *Administrative Science Quarterly*, 52(3), 443–75.

Flynn, F., and S. Wiltermuth (2010). Who's with Me? False Consensus, Brokerage, and Ethical Decision Making Organisations. *Academy of Management Journal*, 53(5), 1074–89.

Flynn, F. J., R. E. Reagans, E. T. Amanatullah and D. R. Ames (2006). Helping One's Way to the Top: Self-monitors Achieve Status by Helping Others and Knowing Who Helps Whom. *Journal of Personality and Social Psychology*, 91, 1123–37.

Flynn, F. J., R. E. Reagans and L. Guillory (2010). Do You Two Know Each Other? Transitivity, Homophily, and the Need for (Network) Closure. *Journal of Personality and Social Psychology*, 99(5), 855–69.

Fontana, R., A. Nuvolari and B. Verspagen (2009). Mapping Technological Trajectories as Patent Citation Networks: an Application to Data Communication Standards. *Economics of Innovation and New Technology*, 18(4), 311–36.

Frank, O. (2005). Network Sampling and Model Fitting. In P. J. Carrington, J. Scott and S. Wasserman (eds), *Models and Methods in Social Network Analysis*. Cambridge University Press.

Freeman, C. (1990). Schumpeter's Business Cycles Revisited. In A. Heertje and M. Perlman (eds), *Evolving Technology and Market Structure*. Ann Arbor, MI: The University of Michigan Press.

(1991). Networks of Innovators: a Synthesis of Research Issues. *Research Policy*, 20(5), 499–514.

Freeman, C., and C. Perez (1988). Structural Crisis of Adjustment, Business Cycles and Investment Behaviour. In G. Dosi, C. Freeman, R. Nelson, G. Silverberg and L. Soete (eds), *Technical Change and Economic Theory*. London: Pinter, 38–66.

Freeman, L. (1979). Centrality in Social Networks: Conceptual Clarification. *Social Networks*, 1, 215–39.

(2004). *The Development of Social Network Analysis*. Canada: Empirical Press.

French, J. R. P., Jr., and B. H. Raven (1959). The Bases of Social Power. In D. Cartwright (ed.), *Studies in Social Power*. Ann Arbor, MI: Institute for Social Research, 150–67.

Friedkin, N. E. (1993). Structural Bases of Interpersonal Influence in Groups: a Longitudinal Case Study. *American Sociological Review*, 58, 861–72.

(1998). *A Structural Theory of Social Influence*. Cambridge University Press.

(1999). Choice Shift and Group Polarization. *American Sociological Review*, 64, 856–75.

(2004). Social Cohesion. *Annual Review of Sociology*, 30, 409–25.

Frost, P. J., and C. P. Egri (1991). The Political Process of Innovation. *Research in Organisational Behavior*, 13, 229–95.

Gallegati, M., S. Keen, T. Lux and P. Ormerod (2006). Worrying Trends in Econophysics. *Physica A: Statistical Mechanics and its Applications*, 370(1), 1–6.

Gambardella, A., D. Harhoff and B. Verspagen (2008). The Value of European Patents. *European Management Review*, 5, 69–84.

Gandal, N., M. Kende and R. Rob (2000). The Dynamics of Technological Adoption in Hardware/Software Systems: the Case of Compact Disc Players. *Rand Journal of Economics*, 31(1), 43–61.

Garcia Pont, C., and N. Nohria (2002). Local Versus Global Mimetism: the Dynamics of Alliance Formation in the Automobile Industry. *Strategic Management Journal*, 23, 307–21.

Gargiulo, M., G. Ertug and C. Galunic (2009). The Two Faces of Control: Network Closure and Individual Performance among Knowledge Workers. *Administrative Science Quarterly*, 54(2), 299–333.

Garud, R., and P. Karnoe (2001). *Path Dependence and Creation*. Mahwah, NJ: Lawrence Erlbaum Associates.

Garud, R., and A. Kumaraswamy (1993). Changing Competitive Dynamics in Network Industries: an Exploration of Sun Microsystems' Open Systems Strategy. *Strategic Management Journal*, 14, 351–69.

(1995). Technological and Organisational Designs to Achieve Economies of Substitution, *Strategic Management Journal*, 16, 93–110.

Gassman, O., and M. Zeschky (2008). Opening up the Solution Space: the Role of Analogical Thinking for Breakthrough Product Innovation. *Creativity and Innovation Management*, 17(2), 97–106.

Gassman, O., M. Zeschky, T. Wolff and M. Stahl (2010). Crossing the Industry-line: Breakthrough Innovation through Cross-industry Alliances with 'Non-suppliers'. *Long Range Planning*, 43(5–6), 639–54.

Gavetti, G., and D. A. Levinthal (2000). Looking Forward and Looking Backward: Cognitive and Experiential Search. *Administrative Science Quarterly*, 45, 113–37.

Gavetti, G., and J. Rivkin (2005). How Strategists Really Think: Tapping the Power of Analogy. *Harvard Business Review*, 83(4), 54–63.

Gawer, A. (2011). *Platforms, Markets and Innovation*. Cheltenham, UK: Edward Elgar.

(2014). Bridging Differing Perspectives on Technological Platforms: Toward an Integrative Framework. *Research Policy*, 43(7), 1239–49.

Gawer, A., and M. A. Cusumano (2002). *Platform Leadership: How Intel, Microsoft, and Cisco Drive Industry Innovation*. Boston, MA: Harvard Business School Press.

Gibbons, D. E. (2004). Friendship and Advice Networks in the Context of Changing Professional Values. *Administrative Science Quarterly*, 49, 238–62.

Gick, M. L., and K. J. Holyoak (1980). Analogical Problem Solving. *Cognitive Psychology*, 12, 306–55.

Girvan, M., and M. E. J. Newman (2002). Community Structure in Social and Biological Networks. *Proceedings of the National Academy of Sciences USA*, 99, 7821–6.

Gladwell, M. (2000). *The Tipping Point: How Little Things Can Make a Big Difference*. Boston, MA: Little, Brown.

Glasmeier, A. K. (1991). Technological Discontinuities and Flexible Production Networks: the Case of Switzerland and the World Watch Industry. *Research Policy*, 21, 469–85.

Gnyawali, D. R., and B-J. Park (2011). Co-opetition between Giants: Collaboration with Competitors for Technological Innovation. *Research Policy*, 40(5), 650–63.

Godes, D., and D. Mayzlin (2004). Using Online Conversations to Study Word of Mouth Communication. *Marketing Science*, 23(4), 545–60.

(2009). Firm-created Word of Mouth Communication: Evidence from a Field Test. *Marketing Science*, 28(4), 721–39.

Goel, S., M. Mason and Duncan J. Watts (2010). Real and Perceived Attitude Agreement in Social Networks, *Journal of Personality and Social Psychology*, 99, 611–21.

Goel, S, D. J. Watts and D. G. Goldstein (2012). The Structure of Online Diffusion Networks. Proceedings of the 13th ACM Conference on Electronic Commerce (EC '12), Valencia, Spain, 4–8 June, 623–38.

Goerzen, A. (2007). Alliance Networks and Firm Performance: the Impact of Repeated Partnerships. *Strategic Management Journal*, 28, 487–509.

Goerzen, A., and P. W. Beamish (2005). The Effect of Alliance Network Diversity on Multinational Enterprise Performance. *Strategic Management Journal*, 26(4), 333–54.

Goldberger, P. (2013). Exclusive Preview: Google's New Built-from-scratch Googleplex. *Vanity Fair*, 22 February (www.vanityfair.com/news/tech/2013/02/exclusive-preview-googleplex, accessed 26 July 2016).

Gomes-Casseres, B. (1996). *The Alliance Revolution: the New Shape of Business Rivalry*. Cambridge, MA: Harvard University Press.

Govindarajan, V., and S. Srinivas (2013). The Innovation Mindset in Action: 3M Corporation. *Harvard Business Review* (see https://hbr.org/2013/08/the-innovation-mindset-in-acti-3, accessed 18 December 2015).

Granovetter, M. S. (1973). The Strength of Weak Ties. *American Journal of Sociology*, 78(6), 1360–80.

(1978). Threshold Models of Collective Behavior. *American Journal of Sociology*, 83(6), 1420–43.

(1985). Economic Action and Social Structure: the Problem of Embeddedness. *American Journal of Sociology*, 91(3), 481–510.

Granovetter, M., and R. Soong (1983). Threshold Models of Diffusion and Collective Behavior. *The Journal of Mathematical Sociology*, 9(3), 165–79.

(1986). Threshold Models of Interpersonal Effects in Consumer Demand. *Journal of Economic Behavior and Organisation*, 7(1), 83–99.

(1988). Threshold Models of Diversity: Chinese Restaurants, Residential Segregation, and the Spiral of Silence. *Sociological Methodology*, 18(6), 69–104.

Grant, R. (1996a). Toward a Knowledge-based Theory of the Firm. *Strategic Management Journal*, 17, 109–22.

Grant, R. M. (1996b). Toward a Knowledge-based Theory of the Firm. *Strategic Management Journal*, 17(Winter), 109–22.

Graziano, M., and K. Gillingham (2015). Spatial Patterns of Solar Photovoltaic System Adoption: the Influence of Neighbors and the Built Environment. *Journal of Economic Geography*, 15(4), 815–39.

Greenwood, R., and C. R. Hinnings (2006) Radical Organisational Change. In S. R. Clegg, C. Hardy, T. Lawrence and W. R. Nord (eds), *Sage Handbook of Organisation Studies*. Wiltshire, UK: Sage Publications.

Greve, Henrich R., Joel A. C. Baum, Hitoshi Mitsuhashi and Tim Rowley (2010). Built to Last but Falling Apart: Cohesion, Friction and Withdrawal from Interfirm Alliances. *Academy of Management Journal*, 53, 302–22.

Greve, Henrich R., Hitoshi Mitsuhashi and Joel A. C. Baum (2013). Greener Pastures: Outside Options and Strategic Alliance Withdrawal. *Organisation Science*, 24(1), 79–98.

Griliches, Z. (1957). Hybrid Corn: an Exploration in the Economics of Technological Change. *Econometrica*, 25(4), 501–22.

(1990). Patent Statistics as Economic Indicators: a Survey. *Journal of Economic Literature*, 28(4), 1661–707.

Gudykunst, W. B., S. Yang and T. Nishida (1987). Cultural Differences in Self-consciousness and Self-monitoring. *Communications Research*, 14(1), 7–34.

Guinan, Patricia J., Salvatore Parise and Keith Rollag (2014). Jumpstarting the Use of Social Technologies in Your Organization. *Business Horizons*, 57(3), 337–47.

Gulati, R. (1995). Social Structure and Alliance Formation Patterns. *Administrative Science Quarterly*, 40, 619–52.

(1998). Alliances and Networks. *Strategic Management Journal*, 19, 293–317.

(1999). Network Location and Learning: the Influence of Network Resources and Firm Capabilities on Alliance Formation. *Strategic Management Journal*, 20, 397–420.

Gulati, R., and M. Gargiulo (1998). Where Do Inter-organisational Networks Come From? *American Journal of Sociology*, 104(5), 1439–93.

Gulati, R., and M. C. Higgins (2003). Which Ties Matter When? The Contingent Effects of Interorganisational Partnerships on IPO Success. *Strategic Management Journal*, 24(2), 127–44.

Gulati, R., and P. Puranam (2009). Renewal through Reorganisation: the Value of Inconsistencies between Formal and Informal Organisation. *Organisation Science*, 20(2), 422–40.

Gulati, R., and H. Singh (1998). The Architecture of Cooperation: Managing Coordination Costs and Appropriation Concerns in Strategic Alliances. *Administrative Science Quarterly*, 43(4), 781–814.

Gulati, R., and M. Sytch (2008). Does Familiarity Breed Trust? Revisiting the Antecedents of Trust. *Managerial and Decision Economics*, 29, 165–90.

Gulati, R., and J. Westphal (1999). Cooperative or Controlling? The Effects of CEO–Board Relations and the Content of Interlocks on the Formation of Joint Ventures. *Administrative Science Quarterly*, 44, 473–506.

Gulati, R., M. Sytch and A. Tatarynowicz (2012). The Rise and Fall of Small Worlds: Exploring the Dynamics of Social Structure. *Organisation Science*, 23, 449–71.

Guler, I., and M. F. Guillen (2010). Home-country Networks and Foreign Expansion. *Academy of Management Journal*, 53(2), 390–410.

Gupta, A. K., K. Smith and C. E. Shalley (2006). The Interplay between Exploration and Exploitation. *Academy of Management Journal*, 49(4), 693–706.

Gurciullo, S. (2014). Organised Crime Infiltration in the Legitimate Private Economy – an Empirical Network Analysis Approach. arxiv:1403.5071.

Hackman, J. R., and G. R. Oldham (1980). *Work Redesign*. Reading, MA: Addison-Wesley.

Hagedoorn, J. (1993). Understanding the Rationale of Strategic Technology Partnering: Interorganisational Modes of Cooperation and Sectoral Differences. *Strategic Management Journal*, 14, 371–85.

(1995). A Note on International Market Leaders and Networks of Strategic Technology Partnering. *Strategic Management Journal*, 16, 241–5.

Hagedoorn, J., and G. Duysters (2002). The Effect of Mergers and Acquisitions on the Technological Performance of Companies in a High-tech Environment. *Technology Analysis and Strategic Management*, 14(1), 67–85.

Hagedoorn, J., and H. Frankfort (2008). The Gloomy Side of Embeddedness: the Effects of Overembeddedness on Inter-firm Partnership Formation. In Joel A. C. Baum and Timothy J. Rowley (eds), *Network Strategy*. Bingley: UK: Emerald Publishing, 503–30.

Hagedoorn, J., and R. Narula (1996). Choosing Modes of Governance for Strategic Technology Partnering: International and Sectoral Differences. *Journal of International Business Studies*, 27, 265–84.

Hagiu, A., and J. Wright (2011). Multi-sided Platforms, HBS Working Paper No. 12–024, Harvard Business School.

Hakansson, H., D. I. Ford, L. E. Gadde, I. Snehota and A. Waluszewski (2009). *Business in Networks*. Wiley Press.

Hall, B. H., A. Jaffe and M. Trajtenberg (2005). Market Value and Patent Citations. *Rand Journal of Economics*, 36, 16–38.

Hallen, B. L., and K. M. Eisenhardt (2012). Catalyzing Strategies and Efficient Tie Formation: How Entrepreneurial Firms Obtain Investment Ties. *Academy of Management Journal*, 55(1), 35–70.

Hanaki, N., R. Nakajima and Y. Ogura (2010). The Dynamics of R&D Collaboration in the IT Industry. *Research Policy*, 39(3), 386–99.

Hansen, M. T. (1999). The Search-transfer Problem: the Role of Weak Ties in Sharing Knowledge across Organisation Subunits. *Administrative Science Quarterly*, 44(1), 82–111.

(2009). *Collaboration: How Leaders Avoid Traps, Build Common Ground and Reap Big Results*. Boston, MA: Harvard Business School Press.

Hansen, M. T., and N. Nohria (2004). How to Build Collaborative Advantage. *MIT Sloan Management Review*, 26(1), 22–30.

Hargadon, A. (1998). Firms as Knowledge Brokers: Lessons in Pursuing Continuous Innovation. *California Management Review*, Spring, 40(3), 209–27.

(2003). *How Breakthroughs Happen*. Boston, MA: Harvard Business School Press.

Hargadon, A., and R. Sutton (1997). Technology Brokering and Innovation in a Product Development Firm. *Administrative Science Quarterly*, 42(4), 716–49.

Harrison, D. A., and K. J. Klein (2007). What's the Difference? Diversity Constructs as Separation, Variety or Disparity in Organisations. *The Academy of Management Review*, 32(4), 1199–228.

Harrison, D., and A. Waluszewski (2008). The Development of a User Network as a Way to Re-launch an Unwanted Product. *Research Policy*, 37(1), 115–30.

He, Z. L., and P. K. Wong (2004). Exploration vs. Exploitation: an Empirical Test of the Ambidexterity Hypothesis. *Organisation Science*, 15(4), 481–94.

Heider, F. (1946). Attitudes and Cognitive Organisation. *Journal of Psychology*, 21, 107–12.

(1958). *The Psychology of Interpersonal Relations*. New York, NY: Wiley.

Heimeriks, K. H., G. M., Duysters and W. Vanhaverbeke (2007). An Exploratory Study of Learning Mechanisms and Differential Performance Effects in Alliance Portfolios. *Strategic Organisation*, 5(4), 373–408.

Heimeriks, K. H., E. Klijn and J. J. Reuer (2009). Building Capabilities for Alliance Portfolios. *Long Range Planning*, 42(1), 96–114.

Henderson, R. M., and K. B. Clark (1990). Architectural Innovation: the Reconfiguration of Existing Product Technologies and the Failure of Established Firms. *Administrative Science Quarterly*, 35(1), 9–20.

Henderson, Rebecca, and Iain Cockburn (1996). Scale, Scope, and Spillovers: Determinants of Research Productivity in the Pharmaceutical Industry. *Rand Journal of Economics*, Spring, 27(1), 32–59.

Henkel, J. (2006). Selective Revealing in Open Innovation Processes: the Case of Embedded Linux. *Research Policy*, 35, 953–69.

Hill, C. (1997). Establishing a Standard: Competitive Strategy and Technological Standards in Winner-take-all Industries. *Academy of Management Executive*, 11(2), 7–25.

Hite, J., and W. Hesterly (2001). The Evolution of Firm Networks: From Emergence to Early Growth of the Firm. *Strategic Management Journal*, 22, 275–86.

Hoang, F., and D. L. Rothaermel (2005). The Effect of General and Partner-specific Alliance Experience on Joint R&D Project Performance. *Academy of Management Journal*, 48, 332–45.

Hochberg, Y. V., A. Ljungqvist and Y. Lu (2007). Whom You Know Matters: Venture Capital Networks and Investment Performance. *Journal of Finance*, 62(1), 251–301.

(2010). Networking as a Barrier to Entry and the Competitive Supply of Venture Capital. *Journal of Finance*, 65(3), 829–59.

Hoetker, G. (2005). How Much You Know Versus How Well I Know You: Selecting a Supplier for a Technically Innovative Component. *Strategic Management Journal*, 26(1) 75–97.

(2006). Do Modular Products Lead to Modular Organisations? *Strategic Management Journal*, 27(6), 501–18.

Hoffman, W. H. (2005). How to Manage a Portfolio of Alliances. *Long Range Planning*, 38, 121–43.

(2007). Strategies for Managing a Portfolio of Alliances. *Strategic Management Journal*, 28, 827–56.

Holland, P. and S. Leinhardt (1979). *Perspectives on Social Network Research*. Academic Press.

Hummon, N. P., and P. Doreian (1989). Connectivity in a Citation Network: the Development of DNA Theory. *Social Networks*, 11, 39–63.

(2003). Some Dynamics of Social Balance Processes: Bringing Heider Back into Balance Theory. *Social Networks*, 25, 17–49.

Hurst, N. (2013). To Make a More Efficient LED Scientists Look to Fireflies. *Wired* (www .wired.com/2013/01/firefly-leds/, accessed 7 July 2016).

Huston, L., and N. Sakkab (2006). Connect and Develop: Inside Procter & Gamble's New Model for Innovation. *Harvard Business Review*, 84(3), 58–66.

Ibarra, H. (1992). Homophily and Differential Returns: Sex Differences in Network Structure and Access in an Advertising Firm. *Administrative Science Quarterly*, 37, 422–47.

Ibarra, H., and S. B. Andrews (1993). Power, Social Influence, and Sense Making: Effects of Network Centrality and Proximity on Employee Perceptions. *Administrative Science Quarterly*, 38, 277–303.

Ibarra, H., M. Kilduff and W. Tsai (2005). Zooming In and Out: Connecting Individuals and Collectivities at the Frontiers of Organisational Network Research. *Organisation Science*, 16, 359–71.

Inkpen, A. (2008). Knowledge Transfer and International Joint Ventures: the Case of NUMMI and General Motors. *Strategic Management Journal*, 29(4), 447–53.

Inkpen, A., and N. Choudhury (1995). The Seeking of a Strategy Where It Is Not: Towards a Theory of Strategy Absence. *Strategic Management Journal*, 16, 313–23.

Inkpen, A. C. and E. W. K. Tsang (2005). Social Capital, Networks, and Knowledge Transfer. *Academy of Management Review*, 30(1), 146–65.

Ising, E. (1925). Beitrag zur Theorie des Ferromagnetismus. *Z. Phys.* 31, 253–8.

Iyengar, R., Christophe Van den Bulte and Thomas W. Valente (2011). Opinion Leadership and Social Contagion in New Product Diffusion. *Marketing Science*, 30(2), 195–212.

Jaffe, A. B., M. Trajtenberg and R. Henderson (1993). Geographic Localization of Knowledge Spillovers as Evidenced by Patent Citations. *Quarterly Journal of Economics*, 108, 577–98.

Jaffe, A. B., M. Trajtenberg and P. Romer (2005). *Patents, Citations, and Innovations: a Window on the Knowledge Economy*. US: MIT Press.

Janis, I. L. (1972). *Victims of Groupthink*. Boston, MA: Houghton Mifflin.

Jansen, J. J. P., F. A. J. Van Den Bosch and H. W. Volberda (2006). Exploratory Innovation, Exploitative Innovation, and Performance: Effects of Organizational Antecedents and Environmental Moderators, *Management Science*, 52(11), 1661–74.

Jiang, L., J. Tan and M. Thursby (2010). Incumbent Firm Invention in Emerging Fields: Evidence from the Semiconductor Industry. *Strategic Management Journal*, 32 (1), 55–75.

Johnson, D. (2009). *Managing Knowledge Networks*. Cambridge University Press.

Johnson, S. (2010). *Where Good Ideas Come From*. New York, NY: Riverhead Books.

Jones, C., W. S. Hesterly and S. P. Borgatti (1997). A General Theory of Network Governance: Exchange Conditions and Social Mechanisms. *Academy of Management Journal*, 22(4), 911–45.

Jurvetson. S. (2000). What Exactly is Viral Marketing? *Red Herring*, 78, 110–12.

Kadushin, C. (2012). *Understanding Social Networks*. Oxford University Press.

Kahneman, D., D. Lovallo and O. Sibony (2011). Before You Make that Big Decision. *Harvard Business Review*, 89(6), 50–60.

Kale, P., and H. Singh (2009). Managing Strategic Alliances: What Do We Know Now, and Where Do We Go from Here? *Academy of Management Perspectives*, August, 45–62.

Kalish, Yuval and Garry Robins (2006). Psychological Predispositions and Network Structure: the Relationship between Individual Predispositions, Structural Holes and Network Closure. *Social Networks*, 28(1), 56–84.

Kalogerakis, K., C. Lüthje, and C. Herstatt (2010). Developing Innovations Based on Analogies: Experience from Design and Engineering Consultants. *Journal of Product Innovation Management*, 27(3), 418–36.

Kane, G., M. Alavi, G. Labianca and S. Borgatti (2014). What's Different About Social Media Networks? A Framework and Research Agenda. *MIS Quarterly*, 38(1), 274–304.

Kanter, R. M. (1983). *The Change Masters: Innovation for Productivity in the American Corporation*. New York, NY: Simon & Schuster.

Katila, R., J. Rosenberger and K. M. Eisenhardt (2008). Swimming with Sharks: Technology Ventures, Defense Mechanisms, and Corporate Relationships. *Administrative Science Quarterly*, 53, 295–332.

Katz, M. L., and P. E. Lazarsfeld (1955). *Personal Influence*. New York, NY: Free Press.

Keller, E., and J. Berry (2003). *The Influentials*. New York, NY: Free Press.

Kelley, T. (2001). *The Art of Innovation*. New York, NY: Random House.

Kenis, Patrick, and David Knoke (2002). How Organisational Field Networks Shape Interorganisational Tie-formation Rates. *Academy of Management Review*, 27(2), 275–93.

Kilduff, M. (1992). The Friendship Network as a Decision-making Resource: Dispositional Moderators of Social Influences on Organisational Choice. *Journal of Personality and Social Psychology*, 62, 168–80.

Kilduff, M., and D. Krackhardt (1994). Bringing the Individual Back In: a Structural Analysis of the Internal Market for Reputation in Organisations. *Academy of Management Journal*, 37, 87–108.

Kilduff, M., and W. Tsai (2003). *Social Networks and Organisations*. Gateshead, UK: Sage Publications.

Kilduff, M., C. Crossland, W. Tsai and D. Krackhardt (2008). Organisational Network Perceptions Versus Reality: a Small World After All? *Organisational Behavior and Human Decision Processes*, 107, 15–28.

Kilduff, M., W. Tsai and R. Hanke (2006). A Paradigm Too Far? A Dynamic Stability Reconsideration of the Social Network Research Program. *Academy of Management Review*, 31, 1031–48.

Kim, T. Y., Y. T. Choi and K. Dooley (2011). Structural Investigation of Supply Networks: a Social Network Analysis Approach. *Journal of Operations Management*, 29(3), 194–211.

Kim, T., H. Oh and A. Swaminathan (2006). Framing Interorganisational Network Change. *Academy of Management Review*, 31(3), 704–20.

Kirkels, Y., and G. Duysters (2010). Brokerage in SME Networks, *Research Policy*, 39(3), 375–85.

Kitsak, M., L. K. Gallos, S. Havlin, F. Liljeros, L. Muchnik and H. E. Stanley (2010). Identification of Influential Spreaders in Complex Networks. *Nature Physics*, 6(11), 888–93.

Klein, K., B. C. Lim, J. L. Saltz and D. M. Mayer (2004). How Do They Get There? An Examination of the Antecedents of Network Centrality in Team Networks. *Academy of Management Journal*, 47, 925–63.

Kleinbaum, A. M., and T. Stuart (2014). Network Responsiveness: the Social Structural Microfoundations of Dynamic Capabilities. *Academy of Management Perspectives*, 28(4), 353–67.

Kleinbaum, A. M., A. H. Jordan and P. G. Audia (2015). An Altercentric Perspective on the Origins of Brokerage in Social Networks: How Perceived Empathy Moderates the Self-monitoring Effect. *Organisation Science*, 26(4), 1226–42.

Knoke, D., and S. Yang (2008). *Social Network Analysis*. 2nd Edition. UK: Sage Publications

Kogut, B. (1988). Joint Ventures: Theoretical and Empirical Perspectives. *Strategic Management Journal*, 9, 319–32.

Koka, B., and John Prescott (2002). Strategic Alliances as Social Capital: a Multidimensional View. *Strategic Management Journal*, 23, 795–816.

Koka, B. R., R. Madhavan and J. E. Prescott (2006). The Evolution of Interfirm Networks: Environmental Effects on Patterns of Network Change. *Academy of Management Review*, 31(3), 721–37.

Kossinets, G. (2006). Effects of Missing Data in Social Networks. *Social Networks*, 28(3), 247–68.

Kotter, J. P. (2007). Leading Change: Why Transformation Efforts Fail. *Harvard Business Review*, 85(1) 96–103.

Kotter, J. P., and L. A. Schlesinger (1979). Choosing Strategies for Change. *Harvard Business Review*, 57(2), 106–14.

Koza, M. P. and A. Y. Lewin (1998). The Co-Evolution of Strategic Alliances. *Organisation Science*, 9(3), 255–63.

Krackhardt, D. (1987). Cognitive Social Structures, *Social Networks*, 9, 109–34.

(1988). QAP as a Non-parametric Test of Multiple Regression Models of Dyadic Inter-actions. *Social Networks Conference*, San Diego.

(1990). Assessing the Political Landscape: Structure, Cognition and Power in Organisations. *Administrative Science Quarterly*, 35, 342–69.

(1992). The Strength of Strong Ties: the Importance of Philos in Organizations. In N. Nohria and R. G. Eccles (eds), *Networks and Organisations*. Boston, MA: Harvard Business School Press, 216–39.

(1999). The Ties that Torture: Simmelian Tie Analysis in Organisations. *Research in the Sociology of Organisations*, 16, 183–210.

Krackhardt, D., and R. N. Stern (1988). Structuring of Information Organisations and the Management of Crises. *Social Psychology Quarterly*, 51, 123–40.

Kratzer, J., H. G. Gemuenden and C. Lettl (2008). Revealing Dynamics and Consequences of Fit and Misfit between Formal and Informal Networks in Multi-institutional Product Development Collaborations. *Research Policy*, 37, 1356–370.

Labianca, G. (2014). Negative Ties in Organisations. In D. J. Brass, G. Labianca, A. Mehra, D. Halgin and S. P. Borgatti (eds), *Research in the Sociology of Organisations*, Volume 40. Bingley, UK: Emerald Publishing, 239–59.

Landis, B. (2015). Personality and Social Networks in Organisations: a Review and Future Directions. *Journal of Organisational Behavior*, Supplement, 37, S107–21.

Lane, P. J., and M. Lubatkin (1998). Relative Absorptive Capacity and Interorganizational Learning, *Strategic Management Journal*, 19(5), 461–77.

Langlois, R. N., and P. L. Robertson (1992). Networks and Innovation in a Modular System: Lessons from the Microcomputer and Stereo Component Industries. *Research Policy*, 21, 297–313.

Larson, A. (1992). Network Dyads in Entrepreneurial Settings: a Study of the Governance of Exchange Relations. *Administrative Science Quarterly*, 37, 76–104.

Latour, A. (2001). Trial by Fire: a Blaze in Albuquerque Sets Off Major Crisis for Cell-phone Giants. *The Wall Street Journal* (January).

(2005). *Reassembling the Social: an Introduction to Actor-network-theory*, New York, NY: Oxford University Press.

Laumann, Edward O., Peter V. Marsden and David Prensky (1989). The Boundary Specification Problem in Social Network Analysis. in R. S. Burt and M. J. Minor (eds), *Applied Network Analysis: a Methodological Introduction*. Beverly Hills, CA: Sage, 18–34.

Laursen, K., and A. Salter (2006). Open for Innovation: the Role of Openness in Explaining Innovative Performance among UK Manufacturing Firms. *Strategic Management Journal*, 27(2), 131–50.

(2014). The Paradox of Openness: Appropriability, External Search and Collaboration. *Research Policy*, 43(5), 867–78.

Lavie, D., and S. R. Miller (2008). Alliance Portfolio Internationalization and Firm Performance. *Organisation Science*, 19(4), 623–46.

Lavie, D., and L. Rosenkopf (2006). Balancing Exploration and Exploitation in Alliance Formation. *Academy of Management Journal*, 49, 797–818.

Lavie, D., J. Kang and L. Rosenkopf (2011). Balancing Exploration and Exploitation Within and Across Domains: Evaluation of Performance Implications in Alliance Portfolios. *Organisation Science*, 22, 1517–38.

Lavie, D., U. Stettner and M. Tushman (2010). Exploration and Exploitation Within and Across Organisations. *Academy of Management Annals*, 4(1), 109–55.

Lawrence, P. R. (1969). How to Deal with Resistance to Change. *Harvard Business Review*, 47(1), 4–6.

Lazarsfeld, P. F., and R. K. Merton (1954). Friendship as Social Process: a Substantive and Methodological Analysis. In Morroe Berger, Theodore Abel and Charles Page (eds), *Freedom and Control in Modern Society*. New York, NY: Van Nostrand, 18–66.

Lazarsfeld, P. F., B. Berelson and H. Gaudet (1944). *The People's Choice: How the Voter Makes up His Mind in a Presidential Campaign*. New York, NY: Columbia University Press.

Lee, G. K. (2007). The Significance of Network Resources in the Race to Enter Emerging Product Markets: the Convergence of Telephony Communications and Computer Networking, 1989–2001. *Strategic Management Journal*, 28, 17–37.

Lee, J. (2010). Heterogeneity, Brokerage, and Innovative Performance: Endogenous Formation of Collaborative Inventor Networks. *Organisation Science*, 21(4), 804–22.

Lehnerd, A. P. (1987). Revitalizing the Manufacture and Design of Mature Global Products. In B. R. Guile and H. Brooks (eds), *Technology and Global Industry: Companies and Nations in the World Economy*. Washington, DC: National Academy Press, 49–64.

Leinhardt, S. (1977). *Social Networks: a Developing Paradigm.*, Academic Press.

Leten, B., R. Belderbos and B. Van Looy (2007). Technology Diversification, Coherence and Performance of Firms. *Journal of Product Innovation Management*, 24(6), 567–79.

Levin, D. Z., and R. Cross (2004), The Strength of Weak Ties You Can Trust: the Mediating Role of Trust in Effective Knowledge Transfer. *Management Science*, 50(11), 1477–90.

Levinthal, D. A., and J. G. March (1993). The Myopia of Learning. *Strategic Management Journal*, 14(S2), 95–112.

Levitt, B., and J. G. March (1988). Organisational Learning. *Annual Review of Sociology*, 14, 319–40.

Lewis, J. M., and L. M. Ricard (2014). Innovation Capacity in the Public Sector: Structures, Networks and Leadership. LIPSE Working Papers No. 3.

Lewis, J. M., L. M. Ricard, E. H. Klijn, S. Grotenbreg, T. Ysa, A. Albareda and T. Kinder (2014). Innovation Environments and Innovation Capacity in the Public Sector. Final Report of LIPSE Work Package 1.

Li, Y., and W. Vanhaverbeke (2009). The Effects of Inter-industry and Country Difference in Supplier Relationships on Pioneering Innovations. *Technovation*, 29(12), 843–58.

Li, Y., W. Vanhaverbeke and W. Schoenmakers (2008). Exploration and Exploitation in Innovation: Reframing the Interpretation. *Creativity and Innovation Management*, 17(2), 107–26.

Liker, J. K., and T. Y. Choi (2004). Building Deep Supplier Relationships. *Harvard Business Review*, 82(12), 104–13.

Lin, N. (1999). Building a Network Theory of Social Capital. *Connections*, 22(1), 28–51.

Lincoln, J. R., and J. Miller (1979). Work and Friendship Ties in Organisations: a Comparitive Analysis of Relationship Networks. *Administrative Science Quarterly*, 24(2), 181–99.

Lindsay, G. (2013). Engineering Serendipity. *New York Times*, 5 April.

Lindsley, D. H., D. J. Brass and J. B. Thomas (1995). Efficacy-performance Spirals: a Multilevel Perspective. *Academy of Management Review*, 20, 645–78.

Lippitt, R. (1958). *The Dynamics of Planned Change:* New York, NY: Harcourt Brace.

Lissoni, F. (2010). Academic Inventors as Brokers. *Research Policy*, 39(7), 843–57.

Lissoni, F., P. Llerena and P. Sanditov (2013). Small Worlds in Networks of Inventors and the Role of Academics: an Analysis of France. *Industry and Innovation*, 20(3), 195–220.

Llerena, P, and M. Özman (2013). Networks, Irreversibility and Knowledge Creation. *Journal of Evolutionary Economics*, 23(2), 431–53.

Lorrain, F., and H. C. White (1971). Structural Equivalence of Individuals in Social Networks. *Journal of Mathematical Sociology*, 1, 49–80.

Lovallo, D., and O. Sibony (2010). The Case for Behavioural Strategy. *Mckinsey Quarterly*, March(2), 30–43.

Luce, R. D., and A. D. Perry (1949). A Method of Matrix Analysis of Group Structure. *Psychometrika*, 14, 95–116.

Lundvall, B-Å. (ed.) (1992). *National Systems of Innovation: Towards a Theory of Innovation and Interactive Learning*. London: Pinter Publishers.

Luo, X., and L. Deng (2009). Do Birds of a Feather Flock Higher? The Effects of Partner Similarity on Innovation in Strategic Alliances in Knowledge-intensive Industries. *Journal of Management Studies*, 46(6), 1005–30.

Luo, X. R., K. Koput and W. W. Powell (2009). Intellectual Capital or Signal? The Effects of Scientists on Alliance Formation in Knowledge-intensive Industries. *Research Policy*, 38(8), 1313–25.

Luo, Y., Y. Huang and S. Y. Wang (2012). Guanxi and Organisational Performance: a Meta Analysis. *Management and Organisation Review*, 8(1), 139–72.

Madhavan, R., D. R. Gnyawali, and J. He (2004). Two's Company, Three's a Crowd? Triads in Cooperative-competitive Networks. *Academy of Management Journal*, 47(6), 918–27.

Madhavan, R., B. R. Koka and J. E. Prescott (1998). Networks in Transition: How Industry Events (Re)Shape Interfirm Relationships. *Strategic Management Journal*, 19(5), 439–59.

Magee, Gary (2005). Rethinking Invention: Cognition and the Economics of Technological Creativity. *Journal of Economic Behavior and Organisation*, 57(1), 29–48.

Mahmood, I. P., H. Zhu and E. J. Zajac (2011). Where Can Capabilities Come from? Network Ties and Capability Acquisition in Business Groups. *Strategic Management Journal*, 32, 820–48.

Malerba, F. (2002). Sectoral Systems of Innovation and Production. *Research Policy*, 31, 247–64.

March, J. (1991). Exploration and Exploitation in Organisational Learning. *Organisation Science*, 2, 71–87.

Marinova, D., and J. Phillimore (2003). Models of Innovation. In L. V. Shavinina (ed.), *The International Handbook on Innovation*. London, UK: Pergamon, 44–53.

Marquis, C., M. A. Glynn and G. F. Davis (2007). Community Isomorphism and Corporate Social Action. *Academy of Management Review*, 32, 925–45.

Marsden, P. V. (2005). Recent Developments in Network Measurement. In P. J. Carrington, J. Scott and S. Wasserman (eds), *Models and Methods in Social Network Analysis*. Cambridge University Press.

Marsden. P. V., and K. E. Campbell (1984). Measuring Tie Strength. *Social Forces,*. 63(2), 482–501.

MacCormack, A., J. Rusnak and C. Y. Baldwin (2006). Exploring the Structure of Complex Software Designs: an Empirical Study of Open Source and Proprietary Code. *Management Science*, 52(7), 1015–30.

McDonald, M. L., and J. D. Westphal (2003). Getting by with the Advice of Their Friends: CEOs' Advice Networks and Firms Strategic Responses to Poor Performance. *Administrative Science Quarterly*, 48, 1–32.

McEvily, B., and A. Marcus (2005). Embedded Ties and the Acquisition of Competitive Capabilities. *Strategic Management Journal*, 26(11), 1033–55.

McEvily, B, and M. Tortoriello (2011). Measuring Trust in Organisational Research: Review and Recommendations, *Journal of Trust Research*, 1(1), 23–63.

McEvily, B., and A. Zaheer (1999). Bridging Ties: a Source of Firm Heterogeneity in Competitive Capabilities. *Strategic Management Journal*, 20, 1133–56.

McLeod, P., S. Lobel and T. Cox (1996). Ethnic Diversity and Creativity in Small Groups. *Small Group Research*, 27(2), 248–64.

McPherson, M., L. Smith-Lovin and J. M. Cook (2001). Birds of a Feather: Homophily in Social Networks. *Annual Review of Sociology*, 27, 415–44.

Mehra, A., M. Kilduff and D. J. Brass (1998). At the Margins: a Distinctiveness Approach to the Social Identity and Social Networks of Under-represented Groups. *Academy of Management Journal*, 41, 441–52.

(2001). The Social Networks of High and Low Self-monitors: Implications for Workplace Performance. *Administrative Science Quarterly*, 35, 121–46.

Meyer, M., and A. P. Lehnerd (1997). *The Power of Product Platforms*. New York, NY: Free Press.

Mikkola, J. H. (2003). Modularity, Component Outsourcing, and Inter-firm Learning. *R&D Management*, 33(4), 439–54.

Milgram, S. (1967). The Small World Problem. *Psychology Today*, (1), 61–7.

Miller, D. J., M. J. Fern and L. B. Cardinal (2007). The Use of Knowledge for Technological Innovation within Diversified Firms. *Academy of Management Journal*, 50(2), 308–26.

Milliken, F., B. Bartel and J. Kurtzberg (2003). Diversity and Creativity in Work Groups: a Dynamic Perspective on the Affective and Cognitive Processes that Link Diversity and Performance. In P. Paulus and B. Nijstad (eds), *Group Creativity: Innovation Through Collaboration*. Oxford University Press.

Mintzberg, H. (1987). The Strategy Concept II: Another Look at Why Organisations Need Strategies. *California Management Review*, 30(1), 25–32.

Mintzberg, H., and J. Waters (1985). Of Strategies, Deliberate and Emergent. *Strategic Management Journal*, 6, 257–72.

Miranda, M. S., S. E. Baptista and S. Pinto (2013). Analysis of Communities in a Mythological Social Network. arxiv:1306.2537.

Mitsuhashi, H., and H. Greve (2009). A Matching Theory of Alliance Formation and Organisational Success: Complementarity and Compatibility. *Academy of Management Journal*, 52(5), 975–95.

Mizruchi, M. (1996). What Do Interlocks Do? An Analysis, Critique, and Assessment of Research on Interlocking Directorates. *Annual Review of Sociology*, 22, 271–98.

Mizruchi, M., and L. S. Stearns (2001). Getting Deals Done: the Use of Social Networks in Bank Decision-making. *American Sociological Review*, 66, 647–71.

Moggridge, B. (2007). *Designing Interactions*. Cambridge, MA: MIT Press.

Moody, James (2004). The Structure of a Social Science Collaboration Network. *American Sociological Review*, 69, 213–38.

Moon, F. (2014). *Social Networks in the History of Innovation and Invention, History of Mechanism and Machine Science 22.* Dordrecht: Springer.

Moran, P. (2005). Structural vs. Relational Embeddedness: Social Capital and Managerial Performance. *Strategic Management Journal*, 26, 1129–51.

Moreno, Jacob L. (1934). *Who Shall Survive?* Washington, DC: Nervous and Mental Diseases Publishing.

Morrison, E. (2002). Newcomers' Relationships: the Role of Social Network Ties During Socialization. *Academy of Management Journal*, 45(6), 1149–60.

Morrison, R. (2004). Informal Relationships in the Workplace: Associations with Job Satisfaction, Organisational Commitment and Turnover Intentions. *New Zealand Journal of Psychology*, 33(3), 114–28.

Mowery, D. C., and N. Rosenberg (1979). The Influence of Market Demand Upon Innovation: a Critical Review of Some Recent Empirical Studies. *Research Policy*, 8(2), 102–53.

Mowery, D. C., J. E. Oxley and B. S. Silverman (1998). Technological Overlap and Interfirm Cooperation: Implications for the Resource Based View of the Firm. *Research Policy*, 27, 507–23.

Nadler, D. A., and M. L. Tushman (1997). Implementing New Designs: Managing Organisational Change. In M. L. Tushman and P. Anderson (eds), *Managing Strategic Innovation and Change: a Collection of Readings.* Oxford University Press.

Nakamura, T., and H. Ohashi (2008). Effects of Technology Adoption on Productivity and Industry Growth: a Study of Steel Refining Furnaces. *Journal of Industrial Economics*, 56(3), 470–99.

Nebus, J. (2006). Building Collegial Information Networks: a Theory of Advice Network Generation. *Academy of Management Review*, 31(3), 615–37.

Nelson, R. (1989). The Strength of Strong Ties: Social Networks and Intergroup Conflict in Organisations. *Academy of Management Journal*, 32(2), 377–401.

Nelson, R., and S. Winter (1982). *An Evolutionary Theory of Economic Change.* Cambridge, MA: Harvard University Press.

Nemeth, C. J., and B. Nemeth-Brown (2003). Better than Individuals? The Potential Benefits of Dissent and Diversity for Group Creativity. In P. Paulus and B. Nijstad (eds), *Group Creativity.* Oxford University Press.

Nerkar, A., and S. Paruchuri (2005). Evolution of R&D Capabilities: the Role of Knowledge Networks within a Firm. *Management Science*, 51(5), 771–85.

Newcomb, Doug (2012). Why Connected Car Revolution Could Come from Outside the Auto Industry. *Wired*, 19 September.

Newcomb, T. M. (1961). *The Acquaintance Process.* New York, NY: Holt, Rinehart & Winston.

Newman, M. E. J. (2001). The Structure of Scientific Collaboration Networks. *Proceedings of the National Academy of Science USA*, 98, 404–9.

(2006). Modularity and Community Structure in Networks. *Proceedings of the National Academy of Sciences of the USA*, 103(23), 8577–82.

(2012). *Networks.* Oxford University Press.

Newman, M. E. J., Steve Strogatz and Duncan Watts (2001). Random Graphs with Arbitrary Degree Distributions and Their Applications. *Physical Review* E 64: 0126118.

Nohria, N., and C. Garcia Pont (1991). Global Strategic Linkages and Industry Structure. *Strategic Management Journal*, 12, 105–24.

Nomaler, Ö., K. Frenken, and G. Heimeriks (2013). Do More Distant Collaborations Have More Citation Impact? *Journal of Informetrics*, 7(4), 966–71.

Nooteboom, B., W. Haverbeke, G. Duysters, W. Gilsing and A. Oord (2007). Optimal Cognitive Distance and Absorptive Capacity. *Research Policy*, 36, 1016–34.

Obstfeld, D. (2005). Social Networks, the Tertius Iungens Orientation, and Involvement in Innovation. *Administrative Science Quarterly*, 50(1), 100–30.

Obstfeld, D., S. Borgatti and J. Davis (2014). Brokerage as a Process: Decoupling Third Party Action from Social Network Structure. In D. J. Brass, G. Labianca, A. Mehra, D. S. Halgin and S. P. Borgatti (eds), *Research in the Sociology of Organisations. Volume 40*. Bingley, UK: Emerald Publishing.

Oerlemans, L. A. G., J. Knoben and T. Pretorius (2013). Alliance Portfolio Diversity, Radical and Incremental Innovation: the Moderating Role of Technology Management. *Technovation*, 33, 234–46.

Oh, H., and M. Kilduff (2008). The Ripple Effect of Personality on Social Structure: Self-monitoring Origins of Network Brokerage. *Journal of Applied Psychology*, 93, 1155–64.

Ohly, S., R. Kase and M. Skerlavaj (2010). Networks for Generating and for Validating Ideas: the Social Side of Creativity. *Innovation: Management, Policy and Practice*, 12(1), 41–52.

Oldham, G. R., and A. Cummings (1996). Employee Creativity: Personal and Contextual Factors at Work. *Academy of Management Journal*, 39(3), 607–34.

Oliver, C. (1990). Determinants of Interorganisational Relationships: Integration and Future Directions. *Academy of Management Review*, 15(2), 241–65.

Oreg, Shaul, Alexandra Michel and Rune Todnem (eds) (2013).*The Psychology of Organisational Change*. Cambridge University Press.

O'Reilly, C. A. (1980). Individuals and Information Overload in Organisations: Is More Necessarily Better? *Academy of Management Journal*, 23, 684–96.

Orsenigo, L., and V. Sterzi (2010). Comparative Study of the Use of Patents in Different Industries. Kites Working Paper No. 033.

Orsenigo, L., F. Pammolli, M. Riccaboni, A. Bonaccorsi and G. Turchetti (1998). The Evolution of Knowledge and the Dynamics of an Industry Network. *Journal of Management and Governance*, 1, 147–75.

Owen-Smith, J., and W. W. Powell (2004). Knowledge Networks as Channels and Conduits: the Effects of Spillovers in the Boston Biotechonology Community. *Organisation Science*, 15, 5–21.

Oxley, J. E., and R. C. Sampson (2004). The Scope and Governance of International R&D Alliances. *Strategic Management Journal*, 25, 723–49.

Özman, M. (2005). Interactions in Economic Models: Statistical Mechanics and Networks, *Mind and Society*, 4(2), 223–8.

(2008). Network Formation and Strategic Firm Behaviour to Explore and Exploit. *Journal of Artificial Societies and Social Simulation*, 11(17).

(2010). The Knowledge Base of Products: Implications for Organisational Structure. *Organisation Studies*, 31(8), 1129–54.

(2011). Modularity, Industry Life Cycle and Open Innovation. *Journal of Technology Management and Innovation*, 6(1), 26–37.

Ozmel, U., J. Reuer and R. Gulati (2013). Network Interdependencies: Signals from Venture Capital and Alliance Networks in Determining Future Alliance Formation. *Academy of Management Journal*, 56(3), 852–66.

Panzar, John C., and Robert D. Willig (1981). Economies of Scope. *American Economic Review*, 71(2), 268–72.

Parkhe, A. (1998). Building Trust in International Alliances. *Journal of World Business*, 33, 417–37.

Paruchuri, S., and M. Eisenman (2012). Microfoundations of Firm R&D Capabilities: a Study of Inventor Networks in a Merger. *Journal of Management Studies*, 49(8), 1509–35.

Paulus, P. B., and B. A. Nijstad (2003). *Group Creativity: Innovation through Collaboration*. Oxford University Press.

Pavitt, K. (2005). Innovation Processes. In J. Fagerberg, D. C. Mowery and R. R. Nelson (eds), *The Oxford Handbook of Innovation*. Oxford University Press, 86–114.

Pentland, B. T., M. S. Feldman, M. C. Becker and P. Liu (2012). Dynamics of Organisational Routines: a Generative Model. *Journal of Management Studies*, 49(8), 1484–508.

Perrow, C. (1961). Organisational Prestige: Some Functions and Dysfunctions. *American Journal of Sociology*, 66, 335–41.

Perry-Smith, J. E. (2006). Social Yet Creative: the Role of Social Relationships in Facilitating Individual Creativity. *Academy of Management Journal*, 49, 85–101.

Perry-Smith, J. E., and C. E. Shalley (2003). The Social Side of Creativity: a Static and Dynamic Social Network Perspective. *Academy of Management Review*, 28, 89–106.

Petroski, H. (1996). *Invention by Design*, Cambridge, MA: Harvard University Press.

Pfeffer, J. (2010). *Power: Why Some People Have It and Others Don't*. New York, NY: Harper Business Press.

Phelps, C. (2010). A Longitudinal Study of the Influence of Alliance Network Structure and Composition on Firm Exploratory Innovation. *Academy of Management Journal*, 53, 890–913.

Phlippen, S., and M. Riccaboni (2008). Radical Innovation and Network Evolution. *Annales d'Economie et de Statistique*, 87–8, 325–50.

Podolny, J. M. (1993). A Status-based Model of Market Competition. *American Journal of Sociology*, 98, 829–72.

    (1994). Market Uncertainty and the Social Character of Economic Exchange. *Administrative Science Quarterly*, 39, 458–83.

    (2005). *Status Signals: a Sociological Study of Market Competition*. Princeton, NJ: Princeton University Press.

Podolny, J. M., and J. N. Baron (1997). Resources and Relationships: Social Networks and Mobility in the Workplace. *American Sociological Review*, 62, 673–93.

Polidoro, F., G. Ahuja and W. Mitchell (2011). When the Social Structure Overshadows Competitive Incentives: the Effects of Network Embeddedness on Joint Venture Dissolution. *Academy of Management Journal*, 54(1), 203–23.

Pollet, T. V., S. G. B. Roberts and R. I. M. Dunbar (2011). Extraverts Have Larger Social Network Layers: But Do Not Feel Emotionally Closer to Individuals at any Layer. *Journal of Individual Differences*, 32, 161–9.

Porac, J. F., H. Thomas, F. Wilson, D. Paton and A. Kanfer (1995). Rivalry and the Industry. *Administrative Science Quarterly*, 40(2), 203–27.

Powell, W. (1990). Neither Market Nor Hierarchy: Network Forms of Organisation, *Research in Organisational Behaviour*, 12, 295–336.

Powell, W. W., K. W. Koput and L. Smith-Doerr (1996). Inter-organisational Collaboration and the Locus of Innovation: Networks of Learning in Biotechnology. *Administrative Science Quarterly*, 41, 116–45.

Powell, W. W., D. R. White, K. W. Koput and J. Owen-Smith (2005). Network Dynamics and Field Evolution: the Growth of Interorganisational Collaboration in the Life Sciences. *American Journal of Sociology*, 110(4), 1132–205.

Quinn, J. B. (1985). Managing Innovation: Controlled Chaos. *Harvard Business Review*, 63(3), 78–84.

Reagans, R., and B. McEvily (2003). Network Structure and Knowledge Transfer: the Effects of Cohesion and Range. *Administrative Science Quarterly*, 48, 240–67.

(2008). Contradictory or Compatible? Reconsidering the Trade-off in Network Effects on Knowledge Sharing. *Advances in Strategic Management*, (25), 275–313.

Reagans, R., L. Argote and D. Brooks (2005). Individual Experience and Experience Working Together: Predicting Learning Rates from Knowing What to Do and Knowing Who Knows What. *Management Science*, 51, 869–81.

Reingen, Peter H., and Jerome B. Kernan (1986). Analysis of Referral Networks in Marketing: Methods and Illustration. *Journal of Marketing Research*, 23, 370–8.

Reuer, J. J., M. Zollo and H. Singh (2002). Post-formation Dynamics in Strategic Alliances. *Strategic Management Journal*, 23, 135–51.

Rice, Ronald E., and Carolyn Aydin (1991). Attitudes toward New Organisational Technology: Network Proximity as a Mechanism for Social Information Processing. *Administrative Science Quarterly*, 36, 219–44.

Rivera, Mark, Sara Soderstrom and Brian Uzzi (2010). Dynamics of Dyads in Social Networks: Assortative, Relational, and Proximity Mechanisms. *Annual Review of Sociology*, 91–115.

Rochet, J. C., and J. Tirole (2010). Platform Competition in Two-sided Markets. *Journal of the European Economic Association*, 1(4), 990–1029.

Rodan, S., and C. Galunic (2004). More than Network Structure: How Knowledge Heterogeneity Influences Managerial Performance and Innovativeness. *Strategic Management Journal*, 25, 541–62.

Rogers, E. (2003). *Diffusion of Innovations*, 5th Edition. New York, NY: Free Press.

Rogers, E. M., and D. G. Cartano (1962). Method for Measuring Opinion Leadership. *The Public Opinion Quarterly*, 26(3), 435–41.

Roijakkers, N., and J. Hagedoorn (2006). Inter-Firm R&D Partnering in Pharmaceutical Biotechnology since 1975: Trends, Patterns, and Networks. *Research Policy*, 35, 431–46.

Romero, D., Wojciech Galuba, Sitaram Asur and Bernardo A. Huberman (2011). Influence and Passivity in Social Media. *Lecture Notes in Computer Science*, 6913, 18–33.

Rosen, E. (2009). *The Anatomy of Buzz Revisited*. New York, NY: Doubleday.

Rosenberg, N. (1983). *Inside the Black Box: Technology and Economics*. Cambridge University Press.

(1996). Uncertainty and Technological Change. *Federal Reserve Bank of Boston in its Journal Conference Series*, 40, 91–125.

Rosenkopf, L., and G. Padula (2008). Investigating the Microstructure of Network Evolution: Alliance Formation in the Mobile Communications Industry. *Organisation Science*, 19, 669–87.

Rosenkopf, Lori, and M. L. Tushman (1998). The Coevolution of Community Networks and Technology: Lessons from the Flight Simulation Industry. *Industrial and Corporate Change*, 7, 311–46.

Rosenkopf, Lori, Anca Metiu and George Varghese (2001). From the Bottom Up? Technical Committee Activity and Formation. *Administrative Quarterly*, 46(4), 748–72.

Ross, L., D. Greene and P. House (1977). The 'False Consensus Effect': an Egocentric Bias in Social Perception and Attribution Processes. *Journal of Experimental Social Psychology*, 13, 279–301.

Rothaermel, F., and W. Boeker (2008). Old Technology Meets New Technology: Complementarities, Similarities and Alliance Formation. *Strategic Management Journal*, 29, 47–77.

Rothwell, Roy,(1994). Towards the Fifth-generation Innovation Process. *International Marketing Review*, 11(1), 7–31.

Rowley, T., D. Behrens and D. Krackhardt (2000). Redundant Governance Structures: an Analysis of Structural and Relational Embeddedness in the Steel and Semiconductor Industries. *Strategic Management Journal*, 21, 369–86.

Rowley, T. J., H. R. Greve, H. Rao, J. A. C. Baum and A. V. Shipilov (2005). Time to Break Up: Social and Instrumental Antecedents of Firm Exits from Exchange Cliques. *Academy of Management Journal*, 48(3), 499–520.

Ruef, M., H. E. Aldrich and N. M. Carter (2003). The Structure of Organisational Founding Teams: Homophily, Strong Ties, and Isolation Among U.S. Entrepreneurs. *American Sociological Review*, 68(2), 195–222.

Ryan, B., and N. C. Gross (1943). The Diffusion of Hybrid Seed Corn in Two Iowa Communities. *Rural Sociology*, 8, 15–24.

Sabidussi, G. (1966). The Centrality Index of a Graph. *Psychometrika*, 31, 581–603.

Salancik, G. R., and J. Pfeffer (1978). A Social Information Processing Approach to Job Attitudes and Task Design. *Administrative Science Quarterly*, 23, 224–53.

Salganik, Matthew J., Peter S. Dodds and Duncan J. Watts (2006). Experimental Study of Inequality and Unpredictability in an Artificial Cultural Market. *Science*, 311, 854–6.

Sanchez, R., and J. T. Mahoney (1996). Modularity, Flexibility, and Knowledge Management in Product and Organisational Design. *Strategic Management Journal*, 17(Winter Special Issue), 63–76.

Sanditov, B. (2006). *Essays on Social Learning and Imitation*. Maastricht University unpublished PhD Thesis.

Sasovova, Z., A. Mehra, S. P. Borgatti and M. C. Schippers (2010). Network Churn: the Effects of Self-monitoring Personality on Brokerage Dynamics. *Administrative Science Quarterly*, 55, 639–70.

Saxenian, A. (1994). *Regional Advantage: Culture and Competition in Silicon Valley and Route 128*. Cambridge, MA: Harvard University Press.

Scanlon, J. (2009). How 3M Encourages Collaboration. *Bloomberg Business* (see www.bloomberg.com/news/articles/2009-09-02/how-3m-encourages-collaboration, accessed 7 July 2016).

Schelling, T. C. (1978). *Micromotives and Macrobehavior*. New York, NY: Norton and Company.

Schilling, M. A. (2000). Toward a General Modular Systems Theory and Its Application to Inter-firm Product Modularity. *Academy of Management Review*, 25(2), 312–34.

(2008). Understanding the Alliance Data. *Strategic Management Journal*, 30(3), 233–60.

(2012). *Strategic Management of Technological Innovation*, McGraw-Hill.

Schoenmakers, W. and G. Duysters (2006). Learning in Strategic Technology Alliances. *Technology Analysis and Strategic Management*, 18(2), 245–64.

(2010). The Technological Origins of Radical Inventions. *Research Policy*, 39, 1051–9.

Schumpeter, J. A. (1934). *Theorie Der Wirtschaftlichen Entwicklung.* Leipzig: Duncker & Humblot. English translation published in 1934 as *The Theory of Economic Development.* Cambridge, MA: Harvard University Press.

Scott, W. R. (1981). *Organizations: Rational, Natural, and Open Systems.* Englewood Cliffs, NJ: Prentice Hall.

Scott, W. R., and G. Davis (2007). *Organizations and Organizing: Rational, Natural and Open System Perspectives.* Upper Saddle River, NJ: Pearson Prentice Hall.

Seibert, S. E., M. L. Kraimer and R. C. Liden (2001). A Social Capital Theory of Career Success. *Academy of Management Journal*, 44, 219–37.

Seidman, S. B. (1983). Network Structure and Minimum Degree, *Social Networks*, 5, 269–87.

Seo, P., L. L. Putnam and J. M. Bartunek (2004). Dualities and Tensions of Planned Organisational Change. In M. S. Poole and A. S. Van De Ven (eds), *Handbook of Organisational Change and Innovation.* Oxford University Press.

Shane, S., and Toby Stuart (2002). Organizational Endowments and the Performance of University Start-ups. *Management Science*, 48(1), 154–70.

Shapiro, C. (1983). Premiums for High Quality Products as Returns to Reputations. *The Quarterly Journal of Economics*, 98(4), 659–80.

Shen, C., and P. Monge (2011). Who Connects with Whom? A Social Network Analysis of an Online Open Source Software Community. *First Monday*, June 2011. Available at: http://firstmonday.org/ojs/index.php/fm/article/view/3551/2991, accessed 7 May 2015.

Shipilov, A. (2005). Should You Bank on Your Network? Relational and Positional Embeddedness in the Making of Financial Capital. *Strategic Organisation*, 3(3), 279–309.

(2009). Firm Scope Experience, Historic Multimarket Contact with Partners, Centrality, and the Relationship between Structural Holes and Performance. *Organisation Science*, 20(1), 85–106.

Shipilov, A., and S. Li (2008). To Have a Cake and Eat it Too? Structural Holes' Influence on Market and Network Performance in Collaborative Networks. *Administrative Science Quarterly*, 51(3), 73–108.

(2012). The Missing Link: the Effect of Customers on the Formation of Relationships among Producers in the Multiplex Triads. *Organisation Science*, , 23(2), 472–91.

(2014). Towards a Strategic Multiplexity Perspective on Inter-Firm Networks. In D.Brass, J. Labianca, A. Mehra, D. Halgin and S. Borgatti (eds), *Research in the Sociology of Organisations*, Volume 40. Bingley, UK: Emerald Publishing.

Shipilov, A., H. Greve and T. J. Rowley (2010). When Do Interlocks Matter? Institutional Logics and the Diffusion of Multiple Corporate Governance Practices. *Academy of Management Journal*, 53(4), 846–64.

Shipilov, Andrew, Ranjay Gulati, Martin Kilduff, Stan Li and Wenpin Tsai (2014). Relational Pluralism within and between Organisations. *Academy of Management Journal*, 57(2), 449–59.

Simmel, G. (1950). *The Sociology of George Simmel.* Glencoe, IL: Free Press.

Simon, H. (1962). The Architecture of Complexity. *Proceedings of the American Philosophical Society*, 106(6), 467–82.

Singh, J. (2005). Collaboration Networks as Determinants of Knowledge Diffusion Patterns, *Management Science*, 51(5), 756–70.

Singh, J., and L. Fleming (2010). Lone Inventors as Sources of Breakthroughs: Myth or Reality? *Management Science*, 56(1), 41–56.

Singh, J., M. T. Hansen and J. M. Podolny (2010). The World is Not Small for Everyone: Inequity in Searching for Knowledge in Organisations. *Management Science*, 56(9), 1415–38.

Smelser, N., and R. Swedberg (2005). *The Handbook of Economic Sociology*. Princeton, NJ and Oxford, UK: Princeton University Press.

Smith, K. G., C. J. Collins and K. D. Clark (2005). Existing Knowledge, Knowledge Creation Capability and the Rate of New Product Introduction in High Technology Firms. *Academy of Management Journal*, 48, 346–57.

Smith, M., L. Rainie, B. Shneiderman and I. Himelboim (2014). Mapping Twitter Topic Networks: From Polarised Crowds to Community Clusters (see www.pewinternet.org/2014/02/20/mapping-twitter-topic-networks-from-polarized-crowds-to-community-clusters/, accessed 26 July 2016).

Smith-Doerr, L., and W. Powell (2005). Networks and Economic Life. In N. Smelser and R. Swedberg (eds), *The Handbook of Economic Sociology*. Princeton, NJ and Oxford, UK: Princeton University Press, 379–402.

Snijders, T. A. B. (1996). Stochastic Actor-oriented Models for Network Change. *Journal of Mathematical Sociology*, 21, 149–72.

Snijders, T. A. B., G. G. Van de Bunt and C. E. G. Steglich (2010). Introduction to Actor-based Models for Network Dynamics. *Social Networks*, 32, 44–60.

Snyder, M. (1974). Self-monitoring of Expressive Behavior. *Journal of Personality and Social Psychology*, 30, 526–37.

Sobrero, M., and E. B. Roberts (2002). Strategic Management of Supplier–manufacturer Relations in New Product Development. *Research Policy*, 31(1), 159–82.

Soda, G. A., and A. Zaheer (2012). A Network Perspective on Organisational Architecture: Performance Effects of the Interplay of Formal and Informal Organisation. *Strategic Management Journal*, 33(6), 751–71.

Soda, G., A. Usai and A. Zaheer (2004). Network Memory: the Influence of Past and Current Networks on Performance. *Academy of Management Journal*, 47, 893–906.

Soh, P. H. (2010). Network Patterns and Competitive Advantage Before the Emergence of a Dominant Design. *Strategic Management Journal*, 31(4), 438–61.

Soh, P. H., I. Mahmood and W. Mitchell (2004). Dynamic Inducements in R&D Investment: Market Signals and Network Locations. *Academy of Management Journal*, 47(6), 727–44.

Solla De Price, D. (1965). Networks of Scientific Papers. *Science*, 149, 510–5.

(1976). A General Theory of Bibliometric and other Cumulative Advantage Processes. *Journal of the American Society for Information Science*, 27(5–6), 292–306.

Solow, Robert (1957). Technical Change and the Aggregate Production Function. *The Review of Economics and Statistics*, 39(3), 312–20.

Sosa, M. E. (2011). Where Do Creative Interactions Come From? The Role of Tie Content and Social Network. *Organisation Science*, 22, 1–21.

Sosa, Manuel, Steven Eppinger and Craig Rowles (2004). The Misalignment of Product Architecture and Organisational Structure in Complex Product Development. *Management Science*, 50(12), 1674–89.

Sorenson, O. and D. M. Waguespack (2006). Social Structure and Exchange: Self Confirming Dynamics in the Hollywood Film Industry. *Administrative Science Quarterly*, 51, 560–89.

Sorenson, O., J. Rivkin and L. Fleming (2006). Complexity, Networks and Knowledge Flow. *Research Policy*, 35, 994–1017.

Sparrowe, R. T., R. C. Liden, S. J. Wayne and M. L. Kraimer (2001). Social Networks and the Performance of Individuals and Groups. *Academy of Management Journal*, 44, 316–25.

Spence, M. (1973). Job Market Signaling. *Quarterly Journal of Economics*, 88, 355–74.

Stam, W. (2010). Industry Event Participation and Network Brokerage among Entrepreneurial Ventures. *Journal of Management Studies*, 47, 625–53.

Starbuck, W. H., and F. J. Milliken (1988). Executives' Perceptual Filters: What They Notice and How They Make Sense. In D. C. Hambrick (ed.), *The Executive Effect: Concepts and Methods for Studying Top Managers*. Greenwich, CT: JAI, 35–65.

Stettner, U., and D. Lavie (2014). Ambidexterity under Scrutiny: Exploration and Exploitation via Internal Organization, Alliances and Acquisitions. *Strategic Management Journal*, 35(13), 1903–29.

Stuart, T. E. (1998). Network Positions and Propensities to Collaborate: an Investigation of Strategic Alliance Formation in a High Technology Industry. *Administrative Science Quarterly*, 43, 668–98.

Stuart, Toby, and Joel Podolny (1996). Local Search and the Evolution of Technological Capabilities. *Strategic Management Journal*, 17(Summer Special Issue), 21–38.

Stuart, T., and O. Sorenson (2005). Social Networks and Entrepreneurship. In S. A. Alvarez, R. Agarwal and O. Sorenson (eds), *Handbook of Entrepreneurship Research: Disciplinary Perspectives*. New York, NY: Springer, 233–51.

Subcommittee for the Study of Diffusion in Farm Practices (1955). *How Farm People Accept New Ideas. North Central Regional Extension Publication No. 1*. Ames, Iowa: Agricultural Extension Service.

Sutton, R. I. (2001). Weird Rules of Creativity. *Harvard Business Review* , 79(8), 94–103.

Swisher, K. (2013). 'Physically Together': Here's the Internal Yahoo No-work-from-home Memo for Remote Workers and Maybe More. 22 February (http://allthingsd.com, accessed 15 February 2015).

Sytch, Maxim, and Adam Tatarynowicz (2014). Friends and Foes: the Dynamics of Dual Social Structures. *Academy of Management Journal*, 57(2), 585–613.

Sytch, Maxim, Adam Tatarynowicz and Ranjay Gulati (2012). Toward a Theory of Extended Contact: the Incentives and Opportunities for Bridging Across Network Communities. *Organisation Science*, 23, 1658–81.

Szulanski, G. (1996). Exploring Internal Stickiness: Impediments to the Transfer of Best Practice within the Firm. *Strategic Management Journal*, 17(Special Issue), 27–43.

Taylor, A., and C. E. Helfat (2009). Organisational Linkages for Surviving Technological Change: Complementary Assets, Middle Management, and Ambidexterity. *Organisation Science*, 20(4), 718–39.

Teece, D. J., and G. Pisano (1994). The Dynamic Capabilities of Firms: an Introduction. *Industrial and Corporate Change*, 3(3), 537–56.

Ter Wal, A. L. J. (2013). Cluster Emergence and Network Evolution: a Longitudinal Analysis of the Inventor Network in Sophia-Antipolis. *Regional Studies*, 47, 651–68.

(2014). The Dynamics of the Inventor Network in German Biotechnology: Geographical Proximity versus Triadic Closure. *Journal of Economic Geography*, 14(3), 589–620.

Ter Wal, A., and R. Boschma (2009). Applying Social Network Analysis in Economic Geography: Framing Some Key Analytic Issues. *Ann. Reg. Sci.* 43, 739–56.

Tesfatsion, L. (2001). Introduction to the Computational Economics. Special Issue on ACE. *Computational Economics*, 18(1), 1–8.

Tidd, J., and J. Bessant (2013). *Managing Innovation: Integrating Technological, Market and Organisational Change*, 5th Edition. Chichester, UK: John Wiley & Sons.

Tiwana, A. (2008). Do Bridging Ties Complement Strong Ties? An Empirical Examination of Alliance Ambidexterity. *Strategic Management Journal*, 29, 251–72.

Tortoriello, M., and D. Krackhardt (2010). Activating Cross-boundary Knowledge: the Role of Simmelian Ties in the Generation of Innovations. *The Academy of Management Journal*, 531(1), 167–81.

Tortoriello, M., R. Reagans and B. McEvily (2012). Bridging the Knowledge Gap: the Influence of Strong Ties, Network Cohesion, and Network Range on the Transfer of Knowledge between Organizational Units. *Organisation Science*, 23(4), 1024–39.

Triandis, H. C. (1989). The Self and Social Behavior in Different Cultural Contexts. *Psychological Review*, 96, 269–89.

Tripsas, M., and G. Gavetti (2000). Capabilities, Cognition, and Inertia: Evidence from Digital Imaging. *Strategic Management Journal*, 21, 1147–61.

Tsai, W. (2001). Knowledge Transfer in Intraorganisational Networks: Effects of Network Position and Absorptive Capacity on Business Unit Innovation and Performance. *Academy of Management Journal*, 44(5), 996.

Tucker, Catherine (2008). Identifying Formal and Informal Influence in Technology Adoption with Network Externalities. *Management Science*, 54(12), 2024–38.

Tushman, M. L. (1977). Special Boundary Roles in the Innovation Process. *Administrative Science Quarterly*, 22, 587–605.

Tushman, M., and P. Anderson (1986). Technological Discontinuities and Organisational Environments. *Administrative Sciences Quarterly*, 31, 439–65.

Tushman, M., and C. A. O'Reilly (1996). Ambidextrous Organisations Managing Revolutionary and Evolutionary Change. *California Management Review*, 38(4), 8–30.

Tushman, M. L., and T. J. Scanlan (1981). Boundary Spanning Individuals: their Role in Information Transfer and their Antecedents. *The Academy of Management Journal*, 24(2), 289–305.

Tushman, M. L., M. J. Roberts and D. Kiron (2005). USA Today: Pursuing the Network Strategy. Harvard Business School Case, Case No. 9-402-010.

Tversky, A., and D. Kahneman (1974). Judgment under Uncertainty: Heuristics and Biases. *Science*, 185(4157), 1124–31.

Ulrich, K. (1995). The Role of Product Architecture in the Manufacturing Firm. *Research Policy*, 24(3), 419–40.

Uotila, J., M. Maula, T. Keil and S. A. Zahra (2009). Exploration, Exploitation, and Financial Performance: Analysis of S&P 500 Corporations. *Strategic Management Journal*, 30(2), 221–3.

Utterback, J. (1994). *Mastering the Dynamics of Innovation*. Boston, MA: Harvard Business School Press.

Utterback, J., B. Vendin, E. Alvarez, S. Ekman, S. Sanderson, B. Tether and R. Verganti (2006). *Design-inspired Innovation*. New York, NY: World Scientific.

Uzzi, B. (1996). The Sources and Consequences of Embeddedness for the Economic Performance of Organisations: the Network Effect. *American Sociological Review*, 61, 674–98.

(1997). Social Structure and Competition in Interfirm Networks: the Paradox of Embedd-edness. *Administrative Science Quarterly*, 42(1), 35–67.

(1999). Embeddedness in the Making of Financial Capital: How Social Relations and Networks Benefit Firms Seeking Finance. *American Sociological Review*, 64, 481–505.

Uzzi, Brian, and Jarrett Spiro (2005). Collaboration and Creativity: the Small World Problem. *American Journal of Sociology*, 111(2), 447–504.

Uzzi, B., L. A. N. Amaral and F. Reed-Tsochas (2007). Small-world Networks and Manage-ment Science Research: a Review. *European Management Review*, 4, 77–91.

Uzzi, B., S. Mukherjee, M. Stringer and B. Jones (2013). Atypical Combinations and Scientific Impact. *Science*, 342(4), 468–72.

Valente, T. W. (1993). Diffusion of Innovations and Policy Decision-making. *Journal of Communication*, 43(1), 30–45.

(2005). Models and Methods for Innovation Diffusion. In P. J. Carrington, J. Scott and S. Wasserman (eds), *Models and Methods in Social Network Analysis*. Cambridge University Press.

(2012). Network Interventions. *Science*, 337(6090), 49–53.

Valente, T. W., and R. L. Davis (1999). Accelerating the Diffusion of Innovations Using Opinion Leaders. *The Annals of the American Academy of the Political and Social Sciences*, 566, 55–67.

Valente, T. W., and K. Fujimoto (2010). Bridges: Locating Critical Connectors in a Network. *Social Networks*, 32(3), 212–20.

Valente, T. W., and P. Pumpuang (2007). Identifying Opinion Leaders to Promote Behavior Change. *Health Education and Bahaviour*, 34(6), 881–96.

Valente, T. W., K. Coronges, C. Lakon and E. Costenbader (2008). How Correlated are Network Centrality Measures? *Connections (Toronto, Ont.)*, 28(1), 16.

Van De Ven, A. H., and M. S. Poole (1995). Explaining Development and Change in Organizations. *Academy of Management Review*, 20, 510–40.

Van den Bulte, C., and G. L. Lilien (2001). Medical Innovation Revisited: Social Contagion Versus Marketing Effort. *American Journal of Sociology*, 106, 1409–35.

Van Liere, D. W., O. R. Koppius and P. H. M. Vervest (2008). Network Horizon: an Information-based View on the Dynamics of Bridging Positions. *Advances in Strategic Management*, 25, 595–639.

Vanhaverbeke, W., V. Gilsing, B. Beerkens and G. Duysters (2009). The Role of Alliance Network Redundancy in the Creation of Core and Non-core Technologies. *Journal of Management Studies*, 46, 215–44.

Vasudeva, G., A. Zaheer and E. Hernandez (2012). The Embeddedness of Networks: Insti-tutions, Structural Holes, and Innovativeness in the Fuel Cell Industry, *Organisation Science*, 24(3), 643–63.

Venkatraman, N., and C-H. Lee (2004). Preferential Linkage and Network Evolution: a Conceptual Model and Empirical Test in the U.S. Video Game Sector. *Academy of Management Journal*, 47(6), 876–92.

Vernet, A., M. Kilduff and A. Salter (2014). The Two-pipe Problem: Analysing and Theorizing about 2-mode Networks. *Research in the Sociology of Organisations*, 40, 337–54.

Verspagen, B. (2007). Mapping Technological Trajectories as Patent Citation Networks: a Study on the History of Fuel Cell Research. *Advances in Complex Systems*, 10(1), 93–115.

Vissa, B. (2011). A Matching Theory of Entrepreneurs' Tie Formation Intentions and Initiation of Economic Exchange. *Academy of Management Journal*, 54(1), 137–58.

Vissa, B., and A. S. Chacar (2009). Leveraging Ties: the Contingent Value of Entrepreneurial Teams' External Advice Networks on Indian Software Venture Performance. *Strategic Management Journal*, 30(11), 1179–91.

Von Hippel, Eric (1976). The Dominant Role of Users in the Scientific Instrument Innovation Process. *Research Policy*, 5(3), 212–39.

(1978). Successful Industrial Products from Customer Ideas. *Journal of Marketing*, 42(1), 39–49.

Wagner, C. S., and L. Leydesdorff (2005). Mapping the Network of Global Science: Comparing International Co-authorships from 1990 to 2000. *International Journal of Technology and Globalisation*, 1(2), 185–208.

Wang, C., Simon Rodan, Mark Fruin and Xiaoyan Xu (2014). Knowledge Networks, Collaboration Networks, and Exploratory Innovation. *Academy of Management Journal*, 57(2), 454–514.

Wasserman, S., and K. Faust (1994). *Social Network Analysis: Methods and Application*. New York, NY: Cambridge University Press.

Watts, D. J. and P. S. Dodds (2007). Influentials, Networks, and Public Opinion Formation. *Journal of Consumer Research*, 34(4), 441–58.

Watts, D. J., and S. H. Strogatz (1998). Collective Dynamics of 'Small-world' Networks. *Nature*, 393, 440–2.

Weick, K. E., and R. E. Quinn (1999). Organisational Change and Development. *Annual Review of Psychology*, 50, 361–86.

Weitzman, M. L. (1998). Recombinant Growth. *Quarterly Journal of Economics*, 113, 331–60.

Wernerfelt, B. (1984). A Resource-based View of the Firm. *Strategic Management Journal*, 5(2), 171–80.

White, H. C. (1981). Where Do Markets Come from? *American Journal of Sociology*, 87(3), 517–47.

Whyte, W. H. (1952). Groupthink. *Fortune*, March 1952.

Williamson, O. (1975). *Markets and Hierarchies*. New York, NY: The Free Press.

(1991). Comparative Economic Organization: the Analysis of Discrete Structural Alternatives. *Administrative Science Quarterly*, 36, 269–96.

Winter, S. G., and G. Szulanski (2001). Replication as Strategy. *Organisation Science*, 12(6), 730–43.

Womack, J. P., D. T. Jones and D. Roos (1990). *The Machine that Changed the World: the Story of Lean Production*. New York, NY: Free Press.

Woodman, R. W., J. E. Sawyer and R. W. Griffin (1993). Toward a Theory of Organisational Creativity. *Academy of Management Review*, 18(2), 293–321.

Wu, Lynn (2014). Network-biased Technical Change: Evidence from Enterprise Social Media Adoption, SSRN No. 2433113.

Xiao, Z., and A. S. Tsui (2007). When Brokers May Not Work: the Cultural Contingency of Social Capital in Chinese High-tech Firms. *Administrative Science Quarterly*, 52, 1–31.

Yang, H., Z. Lin and M. Peng (2011). Behind Acquisitions of Alliance Partners: Exploratory Learning and Network Embeddedness. *Academy of Management Journal*, 54(5), 1069–80.

Yayavaram, S., and G. Ahuja (2008). Decomposability in Knowledge Structures and its Impact on the Usefulness of Inventions and Knowledge-base Malleability. *Administrative Science Quarterly*, 53, 333–62.

Yoffie, David B., and Mary Kwak (2006). With Friends Like These: the Art of Managing Complementors. *Harvard Business Review*, 84(9), 88–98.

Yoganarasimhan, H. (2012). Impact of Social Network Structure on Content Propagation: a Study Using YouTube Data. *Quantitative Marketing and Economics*, 10(1), 111–50.

Young, H. P. (2009). Innovation Diffusion in Heterogeneous Populations: Contagion, Social Influence, and Social Learning. *American Economic Review*, 99(5), 1899–924.

Zaheer, A., and G. Soda (2009). Network Evolution: the Origins of Structural Holes. *Administrative Science Quarterly*, 54(1), 1–31.

Zaheer, A., B. McEvily and V. Perrone (1998). Does Trust Matter? Exploring the Effects of Interorganisational and Interpersonal Trust on Performance. *Organisation Science*, 9(2), 141–59.

Zahra, S. A., and R. Das (1993). Innovation Strategy and Financial Performance in Manufacturing Companies: an Empirical Study. *Production and Operations Management*, 2(1), 15–37.

Zahra, S. A. and R. Eltantawy (2009). Fatal Attraction: the Dangers of Leaders Flocking Together. *Leadership in Action*, 29(1), 8–12.

Zeppini, P., K. Frenken, and R. Kupers (2014). Thresholds Models of Technological Transitions. *Environmental Innovation and Societal Transitions*, 11, 54–70.

Zheng, K., R. Padman, D. Krackhardt, M. P. Johnson and H. S. Diamond (2010). Social Networks and Physician Adoption of Electronic Health Records: Insights from an Empirical Study. *Journal of the American Medical Informatics Association*, 17(3), 328–36.

Zhu, D. H. (2013). Group Polarization on Corporate Boards: Theory and Evidence on Board Decisions about Acquisition Premiums. *Strategic Management Journal*, 34, 800–22.

Zollo, Maurizio, and Sidney G. Winter (2002). Deliberate Learning and the Evolution of Dynamic Capabilities. *Organisation Science*, 13(3), 339–51.

Zollo, M., J. J. Reuer and H. Singh (2002). Interorganisational Routines and Performance in Strategic Alliances. *Organisation Science*, 13(6), 701–13.

Zott, C., and Q. N. Huy (2007). How Entrepreneurs Use Symbolic Management to Acquire Resources. *Administrative Science Quarterly*, 52, 70–105.

Index

Entries in bold typeface denote tables or figures.